THE FINAL TESTAMENTS

Vol. 12 – Climax of Evolution of Man's Knowledge

Uche Ephraim Chuku

Gotham Books

30 N Gould St.
Ste. 20820, Sheridan, WY 82801
https://gothambooksinc.com/

Phone: 1 (307) 464-7800

© 2023 *Uche Ephraim Chuku*. All rights reserved.

No part of this book may be reproduced, stored in a retrieval system, or transmitted by any means without the written permission of the author.

Published by Gotham Books (September 29, 2023)

ISBN: 979-8-88775-554-0 (H)
ISBN: 979-8-88775-552-6 (P)
ISBN: 979-8-88775-553-3 (E)

Because of the dynamic nature of the Internet, any web addresses or links contained in this book may have changed since publication and may no longer be valid.

The views expressed in this work are solely those of the author and do not necessarily reflect the views of the publisher, and the publisher hereby disclaims any responsibility for them.

BOOK DEDICATION

I dedicate this volume solely to my wife and best friend, Enderline Njideka Chuku.

CONTENTS

BOOK DEDICATION..5
ACKNOWLEDGEMENT 1
INTRODUCTION..2
    Mission Overview 2
    Toward The Ultimate Man 9
    Standard Bible Reference Format...18
    Use of *Jehovah* instead of *Yahweh* in this Volume....................................18
    Use of *Jehovah/Allah* in this Volume 19
CHAPTER ONE: WHAT IS THE FATHER?..21
    What the Father is; and Who He is Not 24
   25
    The Father is All-embracing Perfection..25
    The Father Is Spirit, Not an Occulted Individual................................28
    The Father is Light, Not a Glowing Spectre 34
    The Father Is Eternal Life...40
    The Father is Love and Grace...43
CHAPTER TWO: WHAT IS LIFE?...50
    Life Without the Father 59
CHAPTER THREE: WHAT IS MAN..64
    Man as Messiah of the Animal World 76
    But Not Until We Recognize Adam and Eve as Pillars of our Faith in Jesus Christ 81
CHAPTER FOUR: WHO ARE THE PRINCIPALITIES?...................................85
    Why are the Principalities Fighting Humans on Earth?...........................100
    What the Principalities' Fight is all About...105
    A. To Retain Ultimate Dominion Over Humans on Earth........................105
    B. To Continue Receiving Undeserved Worship from Ignorant Humans on Earth, Pretending to be Gods...108
    C. To Take Away from us our Right to True Life Eternal that they Rejected Themselves..108
    D. To Protect their undue *Spiritual* Advantages, or Rather their Higher Scientific and Occult Knowledge of the World..110
    E. To Retain Means of Magically Elongating their Organic Lifespan......112
    F. To Perpetuate Organic Existence, in a Hopeless Bid to Sustain Artificial Eternity Without the Father 115

Complex Nature of Principalities' Attacks 117
A. Ignorance: Core of all Human Weaknesses 121
B. Religion: Abomination that Makes Desolate....................................... 124
C. Religious Manuals: Criminal in Intent and Content............................ 130
D. Violence, Fear, and Blind Faith 132
E. Scourge of Violence in Bible Prophecies.. 135
F. Film Industry and the Media: Visual Schools of Violence 138
G. Home Breakups: Controlled Attack on Root of Humanity 139
H. Anniversaries and Celebrations; Carnivals and Contemporary Happiness.. 142
I. Sexual Degeneracy: Regression to Shamelessness of Animals 148
J. United Nations: Epitaph of a once United Humanity.......................... 156
K. Capitalism... 161
L. Money: Ultimate Weapon of Self-damnation...................................... 163

CHAPTER FIVE: THE ULTIMATE MAN...168
Before and After Man Encountered the Heavenly Christ in Eden 168
The Heavenly Light in Human Form 172
Israel as Light Bearer to Rest of Mankind 190
A. Jehovah/Allah and his Empty Promises to Abraham 195
B. Then Jehovah/Allah Reduced Abram to Abraham.............................. 197
C. Abraham: False Father of Faith... 200
D. Downside of Abraham and his False Chosen Descendants................. 201
E. Ridiculous Gambit with one Homeless Melchizedek.......................... 206
The heavenly Christ Vs The lying principalities...................................... 209
A. Divine Light Vs Inner Darkness 209
B. Gospel Truth Vs Religious Propaganda 212
Jesus Christ: The Ultimate Man.. 216
A. The Gold seen by Adam and Eve.. 216
B. He Made us Humans; He will Make us Living Spirits....................... 219
C. Incomparable Friend and Messiah 223
But Not Until We Realize and Accept that Jehovah/Allah is the Antichrist 229

CHAPTER SIX: WHO INVENTED THE UNIVERSE? 234
The Universe: A Temporary Disorder in the Father's Eternal Spiritual Creation.. 236
A. Straw Shack on Serene Landscape of Divine Reserve........................ 236

    B. The Universe is not a Creation of the Father..........................240

    Ultimate Fate of the Universe..244

CHAPTER SEVEN: THE FATHER'S ETERNAL, *UNCREATED* MANIFESTATIONS AND THE HEAVENLY NORM.......................252

    The Father is Eternal, Infinite Ordered Existence.....................252

    The Universe is Vanity Forever..255

    What are the *Eternal* Manifestations of the Father? 258

    A. Unknowable Beginning 258

    B. Absolute Divide Between Light and Darkness 261

    C. The Father is Sovereign Perfectionist 265

    Eternal Norm of the Father's Spiritual Creation 269

    Can human mind understand the Father and His Perfect Eternal Creation?..274

    A. Can the Human Mind Differentiate Between Good and Evil?..............274

    B. Turning Blind Eye to Evil When Done by Jehovah/Allah 279

    How are We a Part of the Father and of His Eternal Spiritual Creation?...284

    A. Why are We Called Sons of the Father? 284

    B. Our Inner Goodness is Part of Ultimate Goodness 288

    C. The Father is Source of Eternal, Infinite Existence..............290

    D. Human Souls are Fallen Rays of Divine Light 294

    Where Can the Father's Heavenly Kingdom be Found, Or Rather, Experienced?..297

CONCLUSION..302

SELECTED BIBLIOGRAPHY 303

ACKNOWLEDGEMENT

I am profoundly grateful to our heavenly Father for granting my wayward spirit undeserved second chance and for the gift of Jesus Christ to the world. For prodigal spirits, the wages of sin were eternal death and bondage in the outer darkness. But it pleased the Father to grant the world redemption from eternal self-damnation. The life and mission of Jesus Christ on Earth convincingly prove the power of the Father's unconditional love for all his prodigal sons in the world.

It is a great miracle that Jesus Christ laid down his own life and paid the ultimate price for redemption of self-condemned sinners in the world. That his love also covers an inconsequential lowlife such as me is the greatest miracle of all. I am greatly humbled not only by the power of his love and sacrifice for me but also for him granting me special insight and the privilege to testify his name through my writings. He gave me the sanctified pen; and true to his promises in John 16:13, 25, he consistently guided me into all the truth and spoke to me plainly about the Father.

As I wholeheartedly embraced my divine calling, it felt like the whole world turned against me. People I loved and trusted betrayed and deserted me, but like a guardian angel from the Father, my wife, Enderline Njideka Chuku stood firmly by me. I could not have accomplished this project without her unconditional love and support.

INTRODUCTION

MISSION OVERVIEW

Great darkness looms over entire human family today, with increasing wave of violence and premeditated terror attacks on defenseless masses spreading all over the world. There are renewed anti-Semitic attacks in Europe and the Middle East, even as the Jews marked their 70-year-old gruesome experiences of the Nazi Holocaust. Rampaging Islamic terror *jihadists* on a daft mission to forcibly Islamize the whole world are, on their part, ferociously bombing Churches and peaceful communities; terrorizing, kidnapping and publicly beheading fellow human beings like goats in the Middle East and Africa. Then there is the blazing carnage ragging on in Ukraine following unjustifiable inversion by colonial-minded Russian military driven by old-world expansionist mentality, right in the center of Europe, with the Russian leader, Vladimir Putin daring the civilized world to try to stop him. All these poses great challenge to world peace more than ever before and in fact, threatens the very existence of humans on Earth. Our world is clearly under superhuman attack, and we are not seeing it; we are not even thinking responsibly about human situation.

If in the name of Jehovah/Allah and Islam normal-looking human beings perpetrate mayhem against fellow human beings, if Islamic terror crusaders readily set fire on themselves and blow up public buildings, buses, and shopping malls to kill, maim and scare people into accepting Jehovah/Allah as *God Almighty*, the world should be able to say that Jehovah/Allah and Islam are anti-humanity; that they are evil. Or how long will enlightened humanity turn a blind eye to well-known root of man's inhumanity to man? Religion revers Jehovah/Allah as benevolent *God Almighty*, but he is rather the deadliest enemy of true humanity. Why should we continue to feel inhibited to speak out against him, especially, when he had consistently warned in the scriptures that he would visit humanity with "terror, pit and snare," "blood, fire, and columns of smoke" and "darkness, bitterness and desolation" in the later days of his bottled-up indignation against enlightened humankind? In case people do not know, "Jehovah/Allah is enraged against all the nations, and furious against all their host, he has doomed them, has given them over for slaughter," says Isaiah 34:2.

- "I will take vengeance, and I will spare no man," he assures, and "the whole world will be consumed by the fire of my jealous anger." "The day of Jehovah/Allah is great and very terrible; who can endure it?" he asks. "What sorrow awaits you who say, 'If only the day of Jehovah/Allah were here!' You have no idea what you are wishing for. That day will bring darkness, not light. In that day you will be like a man who runs from a lion—only to meet a bear. Escaping from the bear, he leans his hand against a wall in his house—and he's bitten by a snake.
- Yes, the day of Jehovah/Allah will be dark and hopeless, without a ray of joy or hope." [Isaiah 47:3; Zeph 3:8(NIV); Joel 2:11; Amos 5:18-20(NLT)]

Isn't it obvious that Islamic terror crusaders are unfortunate human beings possessed by Jehovah/Allah's evil spirit of vengeance; that his expected evil days of horror, sorrow, and fear are now here with us? But does the world really know why Jehovah/Allah has become so frustrated and terminally enraged against enlightened humanity?

Well, it should be stressed that escalating horrors of religious mobocracy unfolding in the world today have their common root in Abraham. Jehovah/Allah successfully used Abraham to lay foundation for the religion of unconditional surrender to his devious will. For that he awarded Abraham the title of *'righteousness'* and called him his best *'friend.'* Abraham was the first person that officially surrendered his mind, conscience, and reasoning faculty unconditionally to Jehovah/Allah. He was therefore the first covenanted **Muslim**, and the actual father and founder of *ultimate* religion of **Islam**, which literally means 'submission or surrender to the will and law of Jehovah/Allah.' The world calls Abraham the father of faith, but he is rather the father of *religion without reason*, which is the best way to describe present day Islamic terror jihadism that threatens to put an end to social and spiritual evolution of humankind. What the world regarded as *'call of Abraham'* by *God Almighty* was rather *'fall of Abram'* into the hand of the sworn archenemy of humankind. That portended bad omen and a great danger for true humanity, and that is what we are experiencing today.

As far as Jehovah/Allah is concerned, Judaism, customary Christianity and Islam are but three sects of Islamic order founded by his *friend*, Abraham. He used them purely as dragnets spread all over the world to capture as many unsuspecting souls as possible for his ultimate kingdom rule on Earth. Although adherents of the three sister religions worship the same god of Abraham, he sees them as nothing but *nominal* Muslims. And his express desire has been to eventually transform and unify them into a formidable multitude of case-hardened religious followers upon whom he would finally enthrone himself as *God Almighty* on Earth. This is exactly what he means in Zechariah 14:9 where he projected that "Jehovah/Allah will become king over all the Earth; on that day **Jehovah/Allah will be one and his name one.**"

And so, starting with his willful enslavement of the Jews in Egypt for over four hundred years and the merciless humiliation and massacre of the defenseless Jewish Exodus in the wilderness, the entire Jewish history represents the story of an inglorious jungle deity trying so hopelessly to beat the grandsons of Adam into unconditional submission to his devilish will. Moses explained to the battered Jewish Exodus in Deut 8:2(NLT), saying, Jehovah/Allah was actually "humbling you and testing you to prove your character, and to find out whether or not you would obey his commands." However, when he eventually became convinced that no amount of famine, war, exile, pogrom, or Holocaust that he brought upon the Jews could help him beat them into *Ultimate Muslims* that he desired, he officially announced that he was moving over to a 'new chosen people'—the sons of Ishmael. "Announce to my new people," he said to Ezra, "that I will give them the kingdom of Jerusalem, which I had planned to give to Israel. I will take the dazzling light of my presence away from Israel and will give to my new people the eternal Temple [Mount] that I had prepared for Israel." [2 Esd 2:10-11 (GNB)]

Meanwhile, he had already beaten the sons of Ishmael into desired character as barbaric nomads through many years of programmed subhuman subsistence in the barren deserts of Arabia. So, when, in AD 638 Caliph 'Umar I invaded and took over Jerusalem effortlessly, it was obvious to the Jews that Jehovah/Allah had done it. He even compelled the Jews to assist the Muslims in clearing the Temple Mount for their official take over. And with the subsequent erection of the Dome of the Rock and the al-Aqsa Mosque right on the Temple Mount between AD 685 and 705, Jehovah/Allah officially severed his eternal covenant with the Jews and confirmed Muslims as the new custodians of his eternal dwelling place. He then set out to try to achieve with the ill-informed sons of Ishmael what he could not accomplish with enlightened Jews or with customary Christians who have had direct encounter with the heavenly Christ.

He accused the Jews and customary Christians of being irredeemably compromised and authorized the Muslims to hate and treat them as expendable *infidels*. He asserted that "Thou wilt not find folks who believe in Allah and the Last Day loving those who oppose Allah and his messenger, even though they be their fathers or their sons or their brethren or their clan. As for such, he hath written faith upon their hearts and hath strengthened them with a spirit from him, ... Allah is well pleased with them, and they are well pleased with him. They are Allah's party." [Quran 58:22]

The following Quranic verses make explicit Jehovah/Allah's motive with Islamic terrorism.

- "Lo! Religion with Allah (is) **The Surrender**—*Al-Islam* (to his will and guidance), it says
- "Those who (formally) received the Scripture [i.e., the Jews] differed only after knowledge [of the Father] came unto them [from Jesus Christ] ...
- "And with those who say: 'Lo! We are Christians,' we made a covenant [also], but they forgot a part of that whereof they were admonished. Therefore, we have stirred up enmity and hatred among them till the Day of Resurrection ...
- "**We shall cast terror into the hearts of those who disbelieve** because they ascribe unto Allah partners, for which no warrant hath been revealed. ...
- "**O ye who believe! Take not the Jews and Christians for friends**. They are friends one to another. He among you who taketh them for friends is (one) of them. ...
- "Lo! The worst of beasts in Allah's sight are the ungrateful who will not believe; those of them with whom thou madest a treaty, and then at every opportunity they break their treaty, and they keep not duty (to Allah). If thou comest on them in the war, **deal with them so as to strike fear in those who are behind them**, that haply they may remember. ...
- "And fight them until persecution is no more, **and religion is all for Allah**." [Quran 3:19; 5:14; 3:151; 5:51; 8:55-57; 8:39]

Unfortunately for Jehovah/Allah, cultural Islam, like Judaism and customary Christianity, could not permanently guarantee him the ultimate Muslim followership that he desperately required for the battle of his life. Soon, enlightened Muslims had also become compromised, as no truly civilized human being could wholeheartedly obey his inhuman injunctions as handed down to Muhammad and documented in the Quran. So, he began to inspire a special squad of casehardened Muslim head-hunters that would fight his final battle; first against nominal Muslims and then against all infidels in the world. Thus, Islamic terror *jihadists* are affected men and women who no longer think or feel like humans because they have unconditionally surrendered their minds, consciences, and reasoning faculties to the dreadful Beast. Abraham did the same when he willingly accepted to slaughter Sarah's only son of agony to please Jehovah/Allah.

Meanwhile, Jehovah/Allah subtly manifested himself as **Sabbatai Zevi** (1626-76) and tried to unify Judaism and Islam officially and peacefully, by calling on the Jews to emulate his example and convert to Islam. The Jews understood his gambit very well but dismissed him as the "**Apostate Messiah.**" Although he had told the Jews in Ezekiel 34:15, "**I myself will be the shepherd of my [own] sheep**," and Sabbatai Zevi proved in so many ways to be Jehovah/Allah himself in his capacity as that expected shepherd, they still rejected his plan. So, he blamed them for not following up on that aspect of their hopes and aspirations in him. Again, he manifested as **Jacob Frank** (1726-91) and tried to do the same thing between Judaism and customary Christianity, but the Church equally dismissed him as the "**Heretic Messiah.**" Therefore, he concluded that forcible Islamization of the world was the only option left for him toward actualizing his final dream with Ultimate Islam. It is, however, very shameful that *almighty* Jehovah/Allah could not figure out a godly way to market himself as *God Almighty* to his human subjects on Earth.

Now, only a tree hears that it would be hewed down and continues to stand on the same spot unperturbed. Jehovah/Allah has commenced his prophesied final onslaught on humankind, and we should be fighting back; not against ourselves but against our superhuman aggressor. This is really a matter of common-sense. When our mentor becomes our tormentor, it is only rational that we hold onto our true redeemer and return to our true origin in the Father for ultimate protection. But we must be knowledgeable and courageous enough to correctly distinguish between our tormentor and our redeemer, between our slave master and our Father. Unfortunately, this has always been our greatest problem because we have all along been blinded by religious passion. Thus, any project that clarifies the truth and helps humanity to stop chasing rats while its house is on fire ought to be universally appreciated.

My work is not in any way intended to offend the Jews, customary Christians, and Muslims just because they presently propagate religion without reason but rather to help them to see that Jehovah/Allah never meant well for Abraham, for them, for the Ishmaelites or for humanity. The Jews are slaves to the same religious beliefs that enslave others who inherited the Old Testament. I write for the collective wellbeing and spiritual salvation of entire human family. I am genuinely pro-humanity; meaning that I love and mean well for every individual human being, irrespective of race, class, or creed. I love and respect the Jews, customary Christians, Muslims, and adherents of all other religions of the world because we are all brethren. In fact, I was a *Muslim* before I became a true Christ-follower. I worked in Iran for eleven and half years and I was perfectly at home with average Iranians whom I found to be naturally loving, tender-hearted and accommodating. But I am downright anti-Jehovah/Allah and anti-organized religion because they blindfold, manipulate, and set ignorant human beings against one another. "For had it not been for Allah's [tactic of] repelling some men by means of others," says Qur'an 22:40, "cloisters and churches and oratories and mosques, wherein the name of Allah is often mentioned, would assuredly have been pulled down."

The Final Testaments - Volume 12 calls on enlightened humanity to wake up and start calling a spade a spade. It does not make sense to surrender our minds, good consciences and reasoning faculties to a god that is notoriously opposed to our social and spiritual wellbeing. Rather than relying sheepishly on harmful and fruitless religious beliefs, we should positively confront Jehovah/Allah and the principalities with sound reason gained by practical knowledge. They are our actual enemies. But for our counteroffensive to be effective, we must first stop being religious animals in our overall mentality. Then, we must knowingly start closing down all *'cloisters and churches and oratories and mosques'* on Earth where Jehovah/Allah is erroneously glorified and worshipped as *God Almighty*.

World leaders, on their parts, should be wise enough to recognize that the war we have at hand is not for man-made weapons system. It is not a war like any one ever fought between humans and humans; not like the Cold War or the World Wars I and II. It is war of knowledge, courage, and forthrightness. They should genuinely gear their efforts toward formulating accommodating policies; ones that are truly aimed at tackling inequality of persons, eradicating universal poverty, and unifying the various classes and races of people on Earth. There is no doubt that consistent unfriendly foreign policies coupled with the general disrespectful attitudes of the so-called civilized governments and peoples of the world toward their less developed counterparts spread deep-rooted resentment that ultimately encouraged international terrorism. Human beings must learn to truly love and respect one another. We must unit as one people to be able to triumph in this war against the principalities.

TOWARD THE ULTIMATE MAN

It is obvious that *"man is growing."* It may seem obvious that every human being on Earth understands what this means, but only very few individuals appreciate the full implications.

The fact here is that man was born a *child*. But many people will not readily see anything troubling or unhappy about that. One person, who boldly acknowledged the fact that a child is a terrible flaw rather than a blessing from the Father however, was Benjamin Franklin (1706-1790), a U.S. statesman and scientist. **"What is the use of a new-born child?"** he had asked. We all know the correct answer to that, although we prefer to stick to religious traditions that have us *believe* otherwise. Every grownup has once experienced the difficulties of being a child, and every normal parent sincerely yearns for his child to grow up successfully, without extended childhood deficiencies and tendencies.

We all know that a *child* is liability to its parent; raising a child is an unpaid and thankless occupation. Yet, no normal parent deliberately hinders healthy development of his child; rather he does everything within his power to aid it. Therefore, we are all in a good position to *know* that man's parent, if he were *normal*, would have genuinely helped him to attain balanced growth unhindered. Hard facts stare all of us in the face, which prove decisively that Jehovah, the so-called god and *pater* of mankind is extremely irresponsible. He is the chief obstacle hindering spiritual development of human beings on Earth. As the acclaimed maker and therefore *parent* of multitudes of ignorant humans on Earth, he is nothing but a dishonor to godliness. It is best to simply say that irresponsibility and ignorance runs in his blood indeed.

It is important for us to come to terms with such hard facts about our present existence, so that we may begin in earnest to disengage our minds from the sheer euphoria of false religious hopes and traditions that have kept us all in the dark for so long. We should settle it in our minds that man is not made in the "image and likeness" of the Father. The Father is not *like* man. He has no *image* that man can be likened to, being purely the state of optimum spiritual qualities. Also, the Father did not form man in the sinful world to worship him, as religious traditionalists believe; he does not need imperfect worship from imperfect beings in an imperfect habitation. In any case, being set of perfect spiritual qualities, the Father does not need to be worshiped, but rather to be emulated by imperfect humans. The Father is perfection and he is love. He simply needs us to aspire to conform to perfection; to be good to ourselves and to love one another. He does not expect us to build religious shrines, temples, church cathedrals, and mosques and therein pretend to worship love. Love is something to be emulated, not worshiped. The facts are clear-cut that man is *cloned* in the image and likeness of Jehovah, the Nephilim, who is human, imperfect and shares exact characters with the rest of humankind.

Nevertheless, the crucial question to be asked right away is this: *Is man growing from what, and into what?* Evidently, mankind does not have definite answers to that question yet. We do not even seem to have realized the urgency and inevitability of the need to *individually* search out the answers. Over the years, we had relied entirely on inadequate, but *scrutable*, bits and pieces of hypothesis put forward by philosophers, religious theorists, bible scholars, and scientists, which generally create more questions than answers, regarding man's true nature, his place and purpose in the grand cosmic experiment we call world and his ultimate spiritual transfiguration. Somehow, we seem eternally inhibited from harmonizing widespread external evidence with innate spiritual insight readily bearing witness in our inner beings to arrive at the central truth. Even in our modern generation, with the right answers staring enlightened humans in the face more than ever before, we have remained blinded to the truth.

But every man must eventually answer crucial questions that pertain to his conflicting physical and spiritual personalities for himself if he ever hopes to attain spiritual liberation from his present thwarted existence. No man will answer the questions of this life for another. Everyone must *discover* the truth within himself, and then act on his personal convictions to achieve his own personal spiritual liberation. In view of this fact therefore, **every man's salvation is in his own hands**. No man will reach that ultimate realization on behalf of any other man. As Quran 17:15 says, "No laden soul can bear another's load … Whosoever goeth right, it is only for (the good of) his own soul that he goeth right, and whosoever erreth, erreth only to its hurt."

The agony of man's existence is that everything about his life remains a mystery in him and to him. He lives in total oblivion about his true nature; about his two conflicting personalities, about the purpose of his *growth* in this life and what should be the climax of that growth. He lacks knowledge of what would be his ultimate fate, both as mortal man and as immortal spirit entity. Man is an ignorant being by nature–an imperfect idea in a desolate place. Lack of knowledge is at the root of his eternal bondage in the world. The biblical account of man's origin clearly portrays him as *son of a primordial darkness*, as well as *son of perdition*, for no hell can be more agonizing than the place of overwhelming darkness and uncertainty. According to Genesis 1:1–2 and 2:7, "In the beginning … the Earth was without form and void, and darkness was upon the face of the deep. … Then Jehovah formed man of dust from the ground."

Apart from vivid picture of *external*, elemental darkness that overwhelmed the original man, the account also reveals that he was formed without knowledge of good and evil, meaning he was further imbued with total *inner* darkness. Genesis 2:17 unequivocally drives home official status of the Edenic man, implicitly meant by the god of Eden to be eternal. "But of the tree of the knowledge of good and evil you **shall not eat**," commanded the god in Eden, "**for in the day that you eat of it you shall die**." Thus, the Edenic man was not only deprived of basic knowledge of good and evil and the corresponding rational ability, but he was also forbidden to do something about it. He was literally *born blind* and kept in the dark. He was not only *divinely* forbidden to aspire for knowledge; he was also under *divine* threat of death ever to dare.

We must view man's growth under this backdrop. For a being that was forced to start life as a senseless animal, completely deprived of the basic knowledge of important aspects of his own existence and wellbeing–not even allowed the basic knowledge of how his own body system works– man's evolution in knowledge, since the courageous bold step by Adam and Eve in the so-called Garden of Eden, is a triumphal success story so far. What scientists termed "evolution of man" or "ascent of man" is actually evolution of man's knowledge. We should not lose sight of where and how it all started; neither should we take for granted the difficulties and achievements so far if we ever hope to completely wriggle out of our present spiritual quandary.

Contributing one's quota to the continuing progress of that growth should be the natural concern of every enlightened mind on Earth. That is exactly what I have set out to do with the various volumes of *The Final Testaments*. It is my intention to set the facts straight and fresh in our minds to jolt back to senses so many people, especially religious *believers*, who have simply taken the gains of man's battle for higher knowledge for granted. So many people are steadily relapsing into the *old man*, having completely forgotten who the real benefactors and antagonists of evolution of man's knowledge are. People need to be constantly reminded who it was that withheld and still withholds the key to knowledge from human beings. It should be clearly stated that Jehovah, the god of Eden, is the one we all battle against for our day-to-day growth in knowledge. He vehemently hinders our spiritual development. He is our principal adversary, while Jesus Christ is the true friend and helper of mankind.

Ordinarily, growth implies that man was *born* at some point in the past and would eventually reach the *climax* of his growth and *die*. Indeed, some evidence of growth are clearly reflected in man's biological advancements, complex social structures, and immense intellectual and technological accomplishments that continually shape and reshape his Earthly environment and enhance some crucial aspects of human life on Earth. If man's growth were purely of physical nature, then, one can rightly say that the modern man has grown. But there is much more to man than biological, social, and industrial civilization can explain. In fact, ephemeral nature of man's material achievements only heightens the need for a more meaningful growth, such that guarantees eternal reward. Man is an animated being, made up of temporal system of biological components and the animating spirit. The most important aspect of his growth is the spiritual. Man has not grown much in this dimension. Climax of man's biological evolution is death, while the climax of evolution of man's knowledge is spiritual immortality.

Evolution of man's knowledge involves growth in spiritual insight. It started with the historic decision made by Adam and Eve in the Garden of Eden to seek and acquire heavenly wisdom and its eternal spiritual benefits against all odds. It will climax with the total recollection of man's physical and spiritual consciousness, which will culminate in his ability to see Jehovah/Allah for what he really is. To be able to explain what or who he will grow into in the future, man will need first to understand and explain his complicated present nature. He will need to understand and distinguish the Father from the inglorious Nephilim posing as *God Almighty* to ignorant human beings on Earth. Then he will understand himself well enough to explain who he is, where he is, what he needs to do, and who his true friends and enemies are.

Man's entire worldly experience is finite and knowable. All the facts are contained within his temporal past, but something or someone willfully debars him from accessing the crucial storehouse of that knowledge. To gain access to all denied or *forbidden* information about himself and about the Father, man must retrieve the "key of knowledge" from Jehovah, his chief detractor. Or he can obtain a master key from Jesus Christ who is man's superior heavenly helper. Then, he must hold in clear perspective the true friends and enemies of his spiritual evolutionary thrust at all times.

The very first time the possibility of spiritual enlightenment presented itself to the Edenic man, it came with threats on the one hand and a subtle call for brave action on the other hand. Jehovah favored perpetuity of man's state of spiritual oblivion and threatened homicide if he tried to alter the status quo. But the redeeming Spirit of the heavenly Christ whispered to man eternal benefits of spiritual enlightenment and the need to take the brave step toward true life. Adam and Eve obeyed the voice of reason and Jehovah was forced to swallow his empty threats. Genesis account of the fateful event of Eden that he inspired shamelessly declared enlightened Adam and Eve sinners, and Spirit of the heavenly Christ serpent and loser. Genesis 2-3 clearly captures the whole substance of the Edenic confrontation. But people must re-read the account and endeavor to interpret the facts as plainly as they are written down, without succumbing to preconceived religious interpretations that have muffled the facts of the matter for so long.

The picture of Adam and Eve in the Garden of Eden as 'tillers' and 'keepers' of the land under express dominion of Jehovah, posing as *'God Almighty,'* 'master,' and 'owner' of the whole world, was a vivid depiction of human slavery. It marked the official inauguration of willful enslavement of less-informed humans on Earth by an alien race of colonizing humans whose only advantage lay in the fact that they possessed higher, but limited, level of knowledge than the aborigines. The Edenic scenario captured the whole essence of worldly existence, which is bondage. Dominated by Jehovah and his complex network of accomplices, worldly existence is characterized by godlessness.

Jehovah, the superman of Genesis, is not the Father but an opportunistic alchemist, to whom is attributed the idea of genetic transformation of primitive human beings on Earth. With his advanced knowledge of scientific methods, he successfully set barrier to innate potentials of our forebears for higher spiritual insight, purely by cloning— i.e., he denied them the knowledge of the difference between what is good and what is evil. Thus, even though his ignorant clones shared his exact physical and spiritual 'image and likeness,' he was able to enslave and keep them enthralled to himself as *God Almighty*.

A person who steals away other peoples' means of livelihood is a thief and a criminal. One who steals away other peoples' right to life itself is a vicious murderer. Jehovah is three times a criminal; he is a thief, a liar, and a murderer. His crime against his fellow fallen human spirits is heinous and eternally inexcusable. With his program of 'spiritual oblivion,' built into human nature that he conceived, he stole away mankind's divine right to heavenly wisdom, lied to us that knowledge led to eternal death, thereby literally subjecting our captive spirits to a second degree of spiritual death. That made him both a self-confessed enemy of the Heavenly State and of the oppressed human spirits on Earth.

With Jehovah clearly identified as slave master and 'captor' and ignorant human beings as his powerless 'captives,' the stage was set for 'the first battle of Eden' between the false almighty and the transcendent heavenly 'Redeemer' of the oppressed. At the right time, the Father who is transcendent Sovereign Spirit, sent his heavenly Envoy into the world to humble the arrogant captor and set free his ignorant captives. The heavenly Envoy first appeared as Spirit of Knowledge in Eden and started by *opening the eyes* of Edenic inmates. Then, he demolished Jehovah's Edenic daydream, and set his captives free from fundamental shackles of bondage to ignorance, suffering, and death. Next, he incarnated as Jesus Christ and represented divine will, power, and authority of the Heavenly State. He matched triumphantly against Jehovah's celebrated Temple and symbol of power in Jerusalem—his new Edenic pipedream—and sacked it forever, tearing from top to bottom the veil of secrecy that sustained his false claim to the sacred status of *God Almighty* on Earth.

Although Genesis account of the fateful encounter, inspired by the impostor and propagated by his religious slaves, dismissed the heavenly Christ as serpent and a loser, the victory scoreboard says otherwise. Although the table of honor was successfully turned upside down in the pages of the Jewish Bible and in the mentality of the followers of Jewish religion traditions, we can all agree that the first battle of Eden ended in favor of the heavenly Envoy. It brought about abrupt extinction of Jehovah's Edenic slave camp and freeing of the first human slaves held in it. It also brought about spiritual enlightenment of the blinded inmates and signaled the gradual but progressive dismantling of programmed human ignorance. Today, we all bask in the legacies of evolution of human knowledge and in the hope of ultimate spiritual liberation from suffering and death in the world. Today, Jehovah can no longer walk about, speak, act, or terrorize people openly as he used to do before and immediately after his public humiliation in Eden. Also, irrational fear of him is steadily waning from mentality of many enlightened people on Earth.

Today, Jehovah/Allah remains but an almighty scarecrow, relying entirely on extensive program of religious subterfuge to retain slavish control over people who have not recognized his emptiness. He personally confessed in Quran 22:40, saying, "For had it not been for Allah's [method of] repelling some men by means of others, cloisters and churches and oratories and mosques, wherein the name of Allah is oft mentioned, would assuredly have been pulled down." In view of their two major encounters—in Eden and in Jerusalem—Jehovah stands out as a *fallen almighty*, while the heavenly Christ has now become 'the name above all other names,' such that 'at the name of Jesus [not Jehovah/Allah] every knee should bow, in the *heavens and on Earth and under the Earth*, and every tongue confess that Jesus Christ [not Jehovah/Allah] is Lord, TO THE GLORY OF THE FATHER' of us all.

But Jehovah did not quietly swallow his pride and accept the Father's call to genuine repentance. He did not abandon his impure desire to subjugate his less privileged kith and kin on Earth. Neither did he gallantly accept the fact that no being in existence can successfully contest divine will of the Father that grants spiritual redemption to his lost sons in the world. Not at all! Being tenacious in wickedness, Jehovah/Allah remained adamant in defeat. Even though the heavenly Christ had banished him from publicly fomenting nuisance on Earth, he still prowls around undercover with support of his Zionist religious movements, seeking for unsuspecting and unstable individuals to re-enslave.

Jehovah remained blinded to divine reality. His words remained those of unrepentant slave driver, as he went ahead to say,

- "Jehovah of hosts [armies] has sworn: 'As I have planned, so shall it be, and as I have purposed, so shall it stand' …
- I will take vengeance, and I will spare no man …
- 'To me every knee shall bow, every tongue shall swear' …
- [and] As I live, says Jehovah, surely with mighty hand and an outstretched arm, and with wrath poured out, **I will be king over you** [humankind]." [Isaiah 14:24; 47:3; 45:23; Ezek 20:33 (RSV)]

Surely, these are words of an overambitious daydreamer. The Father, who is love, does not hope to become king over people by force of arms and *with wrath poured out*. Yet, he is bona fide King over all things in existence.

The Bible says in 1 John 5:19 that "the whole world is in the power of **the evil one**. But it also helps us to know that *the evil one* is not acting alone. It declares emphatically in Eph 6:12 that "**we** are not contending against flesh and blood, but against **the principalities**, against **the powers**, against **the world rulers of this present darkness**, against **the spiritual hosts of wickedness in the heavenly places**." Both bible and non-bible readers accept these assertions as incontrovertible, but how many of us understand the precarious nature of human situation and the seriousness of the battle we must fight for spiritual growth. Who is the evil one that overwhelms our present world of darkness? Who or what are the principalities—the powers, the world rulers of this present darkness, the spiritual hosts of wickedness in the heavenly places? Where are they from? Why and how are they fighting powerless human beings on Earth? And what are their weapons? Why must we take the battle seriously? How can we ever hope to overcome such overwhelming powers, high above *in the heavenly places* of the world? What is our only winning weapon against them?

These questions portend spiritual life or death for every individual human being on Earth. Discovering the right answers holds the key to individual spiritual growth. But how many of us really discovered the answers? How many of us genuinely want to know the answers? How many people on Earth feel positively involved in any kind of battle against the *gods of heavens and Earth*? How many of us truly bother about spiritual growth or about genuinely confronting some ruthless, heavenly bandits? Some of us cannot even imagine the possibility of such a confrontation.

These inglorious entities literally represent the *mighty cherubim* and *flaming sword that flash back and forth* referred to in Genesis 3:24 that prevent gullible human beings on Earth from reaching the Father who is the tree of true life. We will not be able to reach the Father without confronting and eventually triumphing over these heavenly Goliaths. People who genuinely seek ultimate spiritual fulfillment will need to settle this fact in their minds. Adam and Eve fought and overcame Jehovah and the principalities with the help of the heavenly Christ. We are all expected to do the same.

In every generation, humanity has made giant strides toward spiritual advancement. Adam and Eve opened the battle against the *heavenly* bandits in Eden, a decisive step that inaugurated our collective race for greater knowledge and the higher life. Great men of antiquity from all works of life—philosophers, social reformers, scientists, human rights activists, and so on—followed in their giant stride and said 'no' to human enslavement by the ruthless colonizers. In 1633 the world witnessed the triumph of Galileo Galilei over the gods of Genesis creation blunder and their Roman Catholic Church allies. He openly made nonsense words of the gods and the traditions of their ignorant religious stooges on Earth. Charles Darwin and Gregory Mendel followed in the wake of that with scientific information on actual origin and propagation of organic life on Earth. It falls squarely on our present generation to decisively unmask the colonizing Nephilim—the so-called *"principalities, powers, world rulers of this present darkness, and the spiritual hosts of wickedness in the heavenly places."* They are not myth but a people with flesh and blood, and in our exact image and likeness.

Finally, in the prophetic words of **Jacob Bronowski** (1908 - 1974), a Polish-born British mathematician, poet, and humanist,

> Knowledge is not a loose-leaf of notebook of facts. Above all, it is a responsibility for the integrity of what we are, above all, of what we are as ethical creatures.
>
> You can't possibly maintain that, if you let other people run the world for you, while you yourself continue to live ... out of a ragbag of morals that come from past beliefs.
>
> That's really crucial today.
> You see, it's pointless to advice people to learn differential equations, or, 'You
> must do a course in electronic or in computer programming,' of course not.
>
> And yet, 50 years from now, if understanding of man's origins, his evolution, his history, his progress, is not the commonplace of the schoolbooks, we shall not exist.
>
> **The ascent of man will go on.** ... If we [of the Western civilization] don't take the next step in the ascent of man, it will be taken by people elsewhere—in Africa, in China.

STANDARD BIBLE REFERENCE FORMAT

As in the previous volumes, my main reference Bible for this volume is still the Revised Standard Version. Quotations from this version will appear direct without (RSV) at the end. Other versions of the Bible used in this work are mentioned in brackets at the end of the quotations. For example, Matthew 5:11-12, when taken from the Revised Standard Version of the Bible, will simply appear as [Matthew 5:11-12] at the end of the quotation; but when taken from the New Life Translation version, it will appear as [Matthew 5:11-12 (NLT)]

Also, all italics, bold fonts and [ ] brackets in Bible quotation are my own emphases.

USE OF *JEHOVAH* INSTEAD OF *YAHWEH* IN THIS VOLUME

I have continued the use of Jehovah/Allah instead of Yahweh in this volume. Most people who read volumes one and two seemed unfamiliar with the fact that "**Yahweh**" and "**Jehovah**" are but two artificial variations of **YHWH**, the personal name of the Jewish tribal god. Some readers in Nigeria asked me if the Yahweh I wrote about was the same as "Jehovah Almighty," God of Israel.

Well, YHWH is the transliteration of a four-letter Hebrew name of God of the Jews that he personal revealed to Moses. It is also known as the Tetragrammaton, because of its four letters. The Masoretes who reproduced original texts of the Hebrew Bible from about the 6th to the 10th century, mechanically replaced the vowels of the name YHWH with the vowel signs of the Hebrew word Adonai, thus forming the artificial name **Jehovah** (YeHoWaH). However, early Christian writers, such as Clement of Alexandria in the 2nd century, had used a form like **Yahweh**. Although Christian scholars after the Renaissance and Reformation periods used the term Jehovah, in the 19th and 20th centuries, biblical scholars again began to use the form Yahweh, thus, making that the modern form in use. Other Greek transcriptions also indicated that **YHWH** should be pronounced Yahweh (YaHWeH).

However, since majority of customary Christian laity in Africa and other parts of the Christian world seem to be more familiar with the form Jehovah, I decided to continue with that tradition in this volume to make sure that no reader is left in any doubt as to which deity I refer to in my books.

USE OF *JEHOVAH/ALLAH* IN THIS VOLUME

It is evident from facts in both the Bible and the Quran that Jehovah is one and the same entity as Allah. For some dubious reasons, he habitually assumes different names in dealing with different peoples and situations. I have used *Jehovah/Allah* in some parts of the text to help the Jews, customary Christians and Muslims understand that they are slaves of the same sneaky principality. After all, Jehovah is god of Abraham, and the Jews, customary Christians, and Muslims worship god of Abraham.

He introduced himself to Abraham, Isaac, and Jacob as *El-Shaddai*— god of mountain. In dealing with Moses, he adopted the name *Jehovah*. He explained to Moses, "I am Jehovah, the Almighty God who appeared to Abraham, Isaac, and Jacob – though I did not reveal my name, Jehovah, to them." [Ex 6:2-4 (TLB)] Yet, despite the fact that he also told Moses in Ex 3:15, "This [Jehovah] is my name for ever, and thus I am to be remembered throughout all generations," he later inspired dubious Bible translators to replace *Jehovah* with *the LORD* in the pages of the Bible to deceive uninformed religious believers into believing that he is one and the same as Jesus Christ who is the true Lord of mankind's spiritual salvation. As much as possible I have replaced the LORD with Jehovah in the Bible quotations used in this volume to ensure that the reader is not deceived by Jehovah's deliberate false identities.

Allah is yet, another pseudonym, which Jehovah, god of Abraham, adopted in dealing with the sons of Ishmael. Footnote to Quran 17:110 reads: "The idolaters had a peculiar objection to the use of *Ar-Rahman*, 'The Beneficent,' in the Koran. They said: 'We do not know this Rahman.' Some of them thought that Ar-Rahman was a man living in Yamamah!" To that effect, Jehovah said to Muhammad, "Say (unto mankind): Cry unto Allah, or cry unto the Beneficent, unto whichsoever ye cry (**it is the same**). His names are the most beautiful names." [Quran 17:110]

What Jehovah is simply saying here is that he has as many names as there are tribes, cultures, and religious movements on Earth—*all beautiful names* that confuse people into thinking that he is indeed the Father. Whether called Jehovah, Allah, Rahman, Brahman or Amadioha, god of Abraham says, it does not matter; he is one and the same bandit that wears the different masks. Jehovah/Allah is the consolidated impostor. According to him, he will eventually unify his name when he finally succeeds in becoming king over the whole Earth. Zechariah 14:9 reads, "And Jehovah will become king over all the Earth; **on that day Jehovah will be one and his name one.**"

CHAPTER ONE:
WHAT IS THE FATHER?

The best place to start our journey back to the Father is from the Father, because that is where our wandering away started in the first place. Human existence is a wandering away from the Father.

My mother used to say that *'not knowing Jesus Christ is the worst of all sicknesses.'* Human nature is worst of all spiritual sicknesses. Knowing and accepting Jesus Christ as one's personal redeemer is the ultimate cure. But we cannot know Jesus Christ unless we first know ourselves. And we cannot know ourselves unless we first know the Father. But as Jesus Christ says, "no one knows the Son except the Father, and no one knows the Father except the Son and any one to whom the Son chooses to reveal him." [Matthew 11:27-28] That is why we need to start the journey of evolution of human knowledge from the very beginning. The Father is the beginning and the end of all things. When we start with the Father and end with the Father, every piece of the jigsaw of spiritual reality will fit nicely into place. People will be able to see the graphic history of their spiritual wanderings so far. They will be able to view the past and present images of themselves in the overall picture represented by the Father and will no longer be in doubt as to what they really are, where they are now and what their next reasonable step should be.

It is evident that the Father is at the center of everyman's quests in the universe. Both people who believe and those who disbelieve in existence of the Father seek answers to satisfy their inner yearnings for the truth about him. The only reason human beings suffer and die on Earth is because they have not been able to evolve the right mental image of what the Father is. With thousands of customary and esoteric religious movements on Earth, each professing its own peculiar understanding of what the Father is, one can rightly say that knowledge of the Father is still largely a mystery to humankind.

While so many people still grapple with the question of whether the Father exists or not, greater challenges confront even those who believe that they have already crossed that threshold. To begin with however, the Father is Perfect Divine Existence. In other words, every perfect situation is the Father. We all believe in, and subconsciously strive toward perfect existence. Therefore, to say that one believes or does not believe that the Father exists is meaningless. What is important is that we can find answers to some pertinent questions about the Father that have direct relevance to our present existence both as mortal human beings and as immortal spirit beings. These questions should include: "What is the Father?" "What is the Father's eternal, *uncreated* purview?" "How are human beings a part of the Father?" "How in tune or out of tune are we with eternal divine ideal in our *created* state and place?" "How can we be fully reconciled to Supreme Nature of the Father?"

Before we start, it will be important for us to agree, first and foremost, that all is not well with our world; that all is not well with human nature, and with our religious convictions.

The reason most of us have not been able to discover the Father is because we imagine him to be a person; someone that dwells in one obscure place, presiding over the imperfect world system of government that determines and controls our worldly experiences. The Jews indoctrinated the whole world with idea of an anthropomorphic personal god that does everything other human beings do and sits on an invisible throne in Jerusalem as ceremonial king of humankind and having strict patriarchal outlook. That has been the greatest impediment to peoples' innate power of far-reaching imagination. Judaism is the practical example of everything that is wrong with human religion. It is the root of humans' ignorance about the true nature of the Father. Almost everything the Jews taught us about the Father is false. Even when Jesus Christ has come and presented the world with the truth and the right perspective, most people still find it impossible to realign their basic understanding to resolve the age long, man-made mysteries of this life.

Zionist false piety that systematically elevated the Jewish mountain deity to the status of Almighty in the human psyche has been a great hindrance in the way of evolution of human knowledge toward realization of what the Father is. Historic traditions of Zionist religious outposts, represented by mainstream and esoteric sects of Judaism, customary Christianity, Islam, Mormonism, Jehovah's Witnesses, Rastafarianism, and numerous other Yahwistic cults all over the world pose grave challenge to our collective humanitarian instincts. Their traditional religious laws and ordinances and the way they interpret them in dealing with the rest of humanity, have proved inimical to our mutual desire to love and live in peace with one another. They are great setback to our collective spiritual growth.

Overwhelming evident prove therefore, that Jehovah, the Jewish personal religious idol espoused by these sects, is not the Father. He just does not possess fitting eternal qualities that define Divine Perfection. We are therefore, left with the crucial obligation to seek out the Father that agrees completely with infinite and eternal image of perfect existence that we all seek and hold sacred in our good consciences.

The truth is that Jehovah is the counterfeit of everything that the Father is. The Father is pure, glorious light; Jehovah is consuming fire and pillar of smoke. Jesus Christ makes us understand that the Father is pure Light with no form of darkness whatsoever. The Father wills that people should love their neighbors as themselves; he seeks perfection of human spirits. Now, if we agree that Divine Light speaks words of *love, peace, truth, righteousness, purity of purpose, hope,* and *eternal life*, then the question should be asked; whose word did Moses receive from the burning bush? The word to go against helpless Egyptians—to humiliate, torment, massacre, and despoil their land, all in the name of giving the Jews false hope of Earthly salvation in some non-existent Promised Land of rest—was antithetical to the goodness of Light. It was rather filled with *hatred, violence, falsehood, impure desires, fear,* and *spiritual bondage*, which today still characterize the ghastly *intifada* ravaging the Middle East.

Furthermore, if we agree that Divine Light accomplishes righteous goals through the radiance of heavenly wisdom; where then was the wisdom in the actions engendered by the words that Moses received from the burning bush that only succeeded in creating permanent enmity between the Jews and all their brotherly Arab neighbors? James 3:13-18 (NLT) captures attributes of heavenly wisdom, showing that the wisdom behind Moses' murderous escapades in Egypt was indeed counterfeit. "If you are wise and understand the Father's ways," it reads, "prove it by living an honorable life, doing good works with the humility that comes from wisdom. ... The wisdom from above is first of all *pure*. It is also *peace loving, gentle at all times,* and *willing to yield to others*. It is *full of mercy* and *good deeds*. It shows *no favoritism* and is *always sincere*. And those who are peacemakers will plant seeds of peace and reap a harvest of righteousness." Well, Jehovah and Moses were not peacemakers. They did not plant seeds of peace in Egypt; neither did they reap harvest of righteousness in Jerusalem. Jehovah is counterfeit of what the Father is, just as the burning bush was counterfeit Light.

WHAT THE FATHER IS; AND WHO HE IS NOT

To begin with, we will need to break bounds with the false, parochial image of reality marketed by customary and occult religions of the world and try to open our minds to the inestimable scope of divine embodiment of eternity, infinity, and existence. Peoples' understanding of the Father's eternal nature has long been severely distorted by traditional religious definitions, which are deliberately tailored to ratify Jehovah as *God Almighty* in the world. We will have to look beyond the limited, corrupted abilities of a mere tribal deity to the infinitude of power and potentiality that represent entire existence.

My aim here is not to compare Jehovah or any other occulted cosmic entity with the Father —the Father is incomparable to anything, or anyone ever known and worshiped by human beings on Earth—but to show that believing that Jehovah is he has been a serious hindrance in peoples' understanding of the true nature of the Father. While the Father can be called the Tree of Infinity, Jehovah is only a tiny self-*blotted* branch of him that should be seeking to purge and realign itself.

The Father is eternal, infinite, *ordered* Existence. He is everything that exists—the overall "Being" that reflects in every being in existence, whether big or microscopic, animate or inanimate, physical or spiritual. Nothing exists outside the Father. He is Ultimate Reality, representing eternally *delineated* positive and negative aspects of perfect existence. These two extremes of the Father correspond to the realms of *perfect* light and *perfect* darkness, which are eternally demarcated.

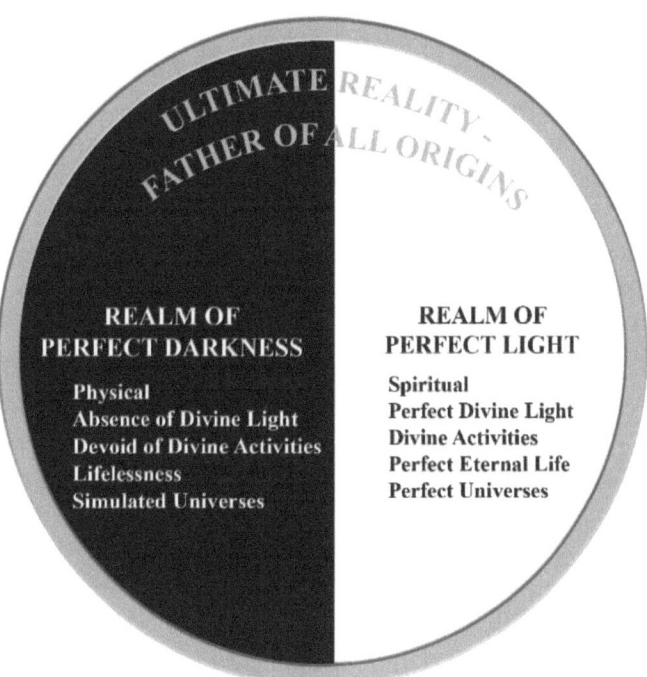

THE FATHER IS ALL-EMBRACING PERFECTION

The Father can be likened to one gigantic house that stretches into eternity. The house is made up of innumerable components and fittings—some gigantic and some microscopic, some seen and some unseen—that get their meaning from being a part of him. All things in existence are specific components of the great house. Every fitting takes its proper place in the grand design and greatness and perfection of the Father stand eternally. A door found in the place of a window or outside its proper place as divinely ordered becomes an aberration—a meaninglessness. Our imperfect universal existence within the realm of perfect darkness is divine aberration—a meaningless existence in its entire ramifications.

The Father is Creativity; not a *creator* the way the Bible portrays. He is eternal and no individual being in existence outside him can tell the story of his *eternal* creations. Understanding this will help us to put into perspective infinite variety of expressions or activities contained within the Absolute One. The Father is the whole essence and the standardized situation or arena within which individualized aspects of him enjoy freedom of self-expression. In this regard, we can liken the Father to an infinite expanse of farmland in which individualized spirits cultivate whatever crop they desire. But the farmland is governed by standard norm of perfection and eternal partition exists between the *illuminated* fertile section and the *dark* infertile section of it.

What we refer to as *freewill* is the natural heritage of individual spirits to create sub-situations or worlds within the Absolute One that must conform to eternal divine standard. Demand of Godliness is very simple but binding on every individual *creator*. It requires that every activity or creativity in every sub-situation be carried out in light of divine perfection. Whatever seed anyone plants in the designated fertile section of the divine farmland will prosper; the Father waters and nourishes it to fruition. Seeds must not be sowed in the dark, infertile ground, for seeds sown in darkness will never prosper. Human nature and the world of organic existence in general are seeds sowed in darkness. They represent spiritual aberrations or vanity. They are bound to wither away with time because they are not eternal. As Jesus Christ says, "Every plant which my heavenly Father has not planted will be rooted up." [Matt 15:13]

The Father is infinite-dimensional Intelligence. He knows all things. Individualized aspects of him know in parts. They function within bounds of their proper places and purposes in consonance with his ultimate will, just as varied parts of the human body function to the ultimate desire of the human mind. In the Father, for instance, light remains light, and darkness remains darkness forever. The Father is Absolute Mind, so to speak—the Central Consciousness of entire existence. He sees to the ultimate health of the whole; he *redeems* any localized individual indiscretion and sustains eternal status quo. Organic existence is example of localized indiscretion of few fallen spirits. Redemptive mission of the heavenly Christ is a process of divine restoration to ultimate health in the body of the Father.

The Father is all of us and more. He is not a specific person that people can point to. He does not sit; and he cannot be made to sit on any kind of throne, waiting to be worshiped by mortal subjects. Of course, no throne can contain infinity. The Father is not a *personal* friend or protagonist to any one person or ethnic group on Earth. He is Father to every being in entire existence, whether known or unknown to humans; whether called annunaki, nephilim, god, archangel, angel, demon, human, animal, insect or what have you. We all exist of him and in him, and he cares for all his members equally. According to Jesus Christ, the Father "makes his sun rise on the evil and on the good and sends rain on the just and on the unjust." [Matt 5:45]

By implying that the Jews are his *chosen people* and he, their *personal god*, Jehovah shows clearly that he is counterfeit. The Father is not a man of war; he has no war to fight with anyone whatsoever. He has no enemies. A true Father does not fight with his own powerless sons. He is not a mighty one; he is Omnipotence. He does not dwell in Jerusalem; he is Omnipresence. The Father is not a kind and loving person; he is Kindness and Love himself. He is not a good person but the Goodness that every good person possesses a bit of. He is not a pure and holy person, but Purity and Holiness that every genuine god-loving and god-seeking person struggles to reflect by his own existence.

In fact, the Father is the sum of every impeccable essence or quality that defines perfect existence. We sing of some well-known eternal attributes of the Father in our gospel songs—the Father is Spirit, Light, Life, Love, Peace, Perfection, Omnipresence, Omniscience, Omnipotence—but people seldom try to place these absolute qualities in their infinite perspective to arrive at what the Father is. Most often people merely pronounce these qualities as attributes of the Father, while referring to some ignoble entities whose overall characters starkly portray ungodliness. Such blunder abounds in the Bible, which has been largely inspired by Jehovah and his accomplices. But how many of us look beyond the superficial meanings of these beautiful attributes and the left-handed deity that poses as *God Almighty* on Earth to imagine the Infinite Being that they describe?

It will be necessary here for us to briefly explore the deeper meanings of some of these impeccable attributes for a clearer picture of true nature of the Father. Let me say however, that thinking of *attributes* of the Father as words describing distinguishing qualities of one *Super* entity, as if to contrast him from some other opposing entities, is utterly misleading. We must see the Father's attributes as inherent characteristics or divine essences that make up Ultimate Reality.

THE FATHER IS SPIRIT, NOT AN OCCULTED INDIVIDUAL

Jesus Christ tells us in John 4:24 that the Father **is Spirit**. It was important for him to stress that fact on Earth because that aspect of the Father was largely misconstrued among human beings, especially the religious ones. He particularly needed to correct the false impression portraying the Father as both man and a territorial personality in the Bible.

Before the coming of Jesus Christ into the world, human beings worshiped gods and goddesses who walked about on Earth as men and women, performing magical feats. They were known as *gods of heavens and Earth*. But they dwelt on specific mountains where people visited and communed with them in person. The twelve major Greek gods and goddesses, for instance, were known as the Olympians because they had their *homes* on Mount Olympus. Jewish tribal deity, Jehovah, equally dwelt on one obscure mountain in the Middle East. He was known as *El Shaddai*, meaning *god of mountain*. But he was also a wandering deity. Hopping from mountain to mountain—from Mount Sinai to Mount Horeb to Mount Paran to Mount Seir, he gradually metamorphosed into the LORD of the *heavenly* throne and finally settled down on Mount Moriah in Jerusalem. As the Bible reports, "Jehovah came from Mount Sinai and dawned upon us from Mount Seir; he shone forth from Mount Paran and came from Meribah-kadesh with flaming fire at his right hand. ... Jerusalem is where he lives [now]; Mount Zion is his home." [Deut 33:2 and Ps 76:2 (NLT)]

These tribal deities were often thought to have the power to transform themselves into other physical forms, like rocks, storms, strong winds, and various animal forms. Adam, Abraham, Moses, and many elders of the Jewish tribe met and interacted with Jehovah in person, as a man. The same deity appeared to Moses as a *burning bush* and as a *mighty serpent* before turning him into a puppet-prophet. According to the Bible, "Jehovah used to speak to Moses face to face, as a man speaks to his friend." [Exodus 33:11] The Jewish Exodus saw and experienced Jehovah as a *pillar of darkness* and as a *pillar of fire*. They heard his voice and saw his forms. Their elders celebrated the covenant feast on the mountain with him in person. Exodus 24:9-10 (NLT) reports, "Moses, Aaron, Nadab, Abihu, and the seventy elders of Israel climbed up the mountain again. There they saw the god of Israel. ... And though these nobles of Israel gazed upon [him], he did not destroy them. In fact, they ate a covenant meal, eating and drinking in his presence!"

In due course, Greek writers relocated the *home* of their mountain deities to some transcendent, heavenly region, while Jewish religious mechanics equally transformed Jehovah into a transcendental spirit, dwelling somewhere in some *heavenly* Jerusalem. Such moves were purely intended to help the impostors escape the thrust of bourgeoning spiritual enlightenment of humans on Earth. Nevertheless, the so-called Temple Mount in Jerusalem remains Jehovah's permanent *heaven* as evidence of his direct personal involvement in human affairs in the region continues undeniably.

Despite all the religious propaganda and politicking that orchestrated Jehovah's magical transformation, Jewish prophets who had the privilege of gazing upon him in his *new heavenly* abode of power still saw him, not as transcendental spirit, but as an occulted human being. Prophet Isaiah saw Jehovah "sitting upon a throne" within a temple … "and his train [trailing part of the gown he wore] filled the temple." [Isaiah 6:1] Prophet Ezekiel equally saw Jehovah as a man sitting on a throne. "And seated above the likeness of a throne," he reports in Ezekiel 1:26, "was a likeness as it were of a human form." True Spirit does not put on kingly robe and he does not sit on a throne.

Even with his name tactically changed to Allah, when Muhammad met with Jehovah and his dreadful companion, Gabriel, it was still on the mountain that he had to go. The Quran says that Muhammad saw Allah clearly on Mount Hira; and it asserts that he did not really go there in search of the transcendental Spirit, whom it calls the *Great Unseen*. To people who considered Muhammad mad for implying that he met with Allah and Gabriel in person on Mount Hira, Allah's revelation came, saying, "And your comrade is not mad. **Surely, he beheld him [Allah] on the clear horizon**. And he is not avid [keen] of the Unseen … None in the heavens and Earth knoweth the Unseen save Allah." [Quran 81:22-24; 27:65] Here, Allah concedes that he is not the Great Unseen Father, but rather the *only* one in the world who knows him.

For obvious reasons, *new* Muslim abductees of Jehovah were originally mandated to pray facing Mount Zion in Jerusalem, the permanent *heavenly* dwelling of Jehovah; a proof that Allah is none other than Jehovah, the god of Abraham. He was forced to relax the *qiblah* mandate however, when serious misunderstanding erupted between the Jews and Muslims on that account. "We [Allah and the principalities] have seen the turning of thy face

toward heaven (for guidance, O Muhammad). And now verily We shall make thee turn (in prayer) toward a *qiblah* which is dear to thee. So, turn thy face toward the Inviolable Place of Worship [the Ka'bah at Mecca], and ye (O Muslims), wheresoever ye may be, turn your faces (when ye pray) toward it." [Quran 2:144]

What Muhammad saw on Mount Hira therefore, was not the Father but a mountain deity who claimed to be the only one who knew the Father. Allah capitalized on this self-deluding idea that only he has knowledge of the Father to play god over the rest of us on Earth. Unfortunately for him, Jesus Christ appeared on Earth and now makes the Father known to the whole world. He makes it obvious that we too ought to know the Great Unseen, because we are all a part of him. All these simply point to the fact that Jehovah/Allah and all the other so-called gods and goddesses worshiped on Earth are humans. They merely possess esoteric knowledge that they have effectively hidden from ordinary human beings. For that same reason ignorant human beings worship them as gods on Earth.

It is under this backdrop that the discussion between Jesus Christ and the Samaritan woman took place, regarding the true nature of the *Great Unseen* Father of all Origins. She recounted the fact that the Samaritans worshiped god of mountain just as the Jews did, even though the Jews insisted that everyone should do that only at Jehovah's Temple Mount in Jerusalem. Jesus Christ told her in clear words that neither the Samaritans who worshiped their *unknown* mountain god nor the Jews who worshiped Jehovah god of Mount Zion in Jerusalem, worshiped the Father. "But the hour is coming, and now is," he told her, "when the *true* worshipers will worship the Father in spirit and truth, for such the Father seeks to worship him. The Father **is Spirit**, and those who worship him must worship in spirit and truth." [John 4:23-24]

With that single statement, Jesus Christ authoritatively dismissed Jehovah and all the mountain deities ever known and worshiped on Earth before his coming as impostors. They were all occulted human beings. The Father is not human; he is not a man, a person, somebody, or something that people can identify as having exclusive form. "His voice you have never heard, his form you have never seen," says the Messiah in John 5:37-38. The Father is not the Jewish personal religious idol that sits on a fixed numinous throne in Jerusalem waiting to be visited by ignorant religious pilgrims. Neither is he any of the obscure, local mountain deities worshiped by other tribes of peoples all over the Earth. If the Father dwells in

Jerusalem or in Mecca for instance, yearly pilgrimages to Jerusalem and Mecca that have cost so many people their lives will be unnecessary because people will see him wherever they are on surface of the Earth.

One does not have to face any direction or go to any mountain, mosque, church cathedral, temple, shrine, or alcove to communicate with the *Great Unseen*, because he is omnipresence. He dwells in everything and in every one of us. Only ignorance makes people seek him on mountains, religious shrines, pilgrimage sites, prayer camps, and just about everywhere else other than within themselves. The only beings to be found in such cultic worship places are dubious, occulted individuals, pretending to be what they are not. For instance, the Quran speaking about where the light of Allah can be found, says, "(This lamp is found) in houses which Allah hath allowed to be exalted and that his name shall be remembered therein. Therein [beguiled religious *believers*] do offer praise to him at noon and evening—" [Quran 24:36]

"The Father is Spirit!" What Jesus Christ wants us to understand from that text is that neither the Samaritan mountain deity nor the Jewish *El-Shaddai* is the Father. That was why they burdened their ignorant devotees with so much ritualism and sheer idolatry. The Messiah calls such religious preoccupations unnecessary *hard yoke*. The Father does not require impure worship from impure, corporeal beings; and certainly, not in the ritualized traditions of the materialistic gods of the world. The Great Unseen Father of all Origins is worshiped, or rather *honored*, in unseen ways by actions and accomplishments of right-minded human souls that are in harmony with Divine Ideal.

Secondly, Jesus Christ wants us to understand clearly that **true worship** of the Father takes place only in peoples' inner beings, which, as we now know, represent the strayed part of Divine Light in all of us. True worship should be a continuous process of personal communication and reconciliation between every individual lost soul and the Father. It is needless to state that all forms of symbolic, scheduled, congregational worship are pure idolatry. The Father is Spirit; he does not need symbolic worship of any sort. That is why Jesus Christ says to us, "When you pray, go into your room and shut the door and pray to your Father who is in secret [who is unseen]; and your Father who sees in secret will reward you." [Matthew 6:6] This injunction invalidated the practice of the Jews who indulged in open-air prayers and in congregational worship in synagogues. It also disconfirms Paul's sectarian mandate to customary Christians in

Hebrew 10:25 that makes them see congregational worship and prayer as a kind of religious group therapy ordained by the Father.

So, what is Spirit? Well, to average human beings on Earth, *spirit* simply means an invisible force or power that *someone* can manipulate to bring about physical effects. Hence, to such people, the Father is the physical entity possessing the most powerful spirit in the world. Average religious believer on Earth considers Jehovah to be that person. Prophet Moses extolled him as a great 'man of war,' and as the most terrible among the gods. "Jehovah is a man of war," he sang, "Who is like thee, O Jehovah, among the gods? Who is like thee, majestic in holiness, terrible in glorious deeds, doing wonders?" [Exodus 15:3, 11] Thus, Moses did paint a vivid picture of a *man* that wields the strongest spirit on Earth. Surely, that was a very simplistic way of looking at the Great Unseen Spirit that gives birth and meaning to infinite existence.

Invisibility of Divine Spirit should be understood only in the same way that life, love, goodness, purity, holiness, and some other sublime qualities of the Father are invisible to human eyes, but recognizable in practical manifestations. Bearing in mind that the Father is totality of existence should help us to understand that he is as visible as he is invisible, even to the human eyes. Although some people consider Spirit to be such a distant phantasm, diligent human minds see the Father all around them. Hence, Jesus Christ says in Matthew 5:8, "Blessed are the pure in heart, for they shall see the Father." The Father sees every pure spirit in existence and every pure spirit in existence sees his Source, because he is one with Him. Just as a man sees himself, purity sees purity and love sees love. Just as a father sees his son and the son sees his father, the Father sees the goodness in the heart of man and goodness in the heart of man sees his Father.

So, Spirit is the fundamental nature of the Father—the Root-Essence and genesis of entire existence, both visible and invisible. Spirit is infinite energy with inexhaustible possibilities that imbues everything in existence. Spirit defines existence, which in turn represents boundless and limitless expressions of Divine Thoughts or Ideas that must conform to eternal Divine Blueprint. Spirit is thought that manifests in action and in the various forms that define various levels of consciousness. Omnipresence, omniscience, and omnipotence define the fundamental nature of Spirit and its hallmarks are infinite creativity, perfection, and order. Spirit has no specific form, and it is genderless. It is not a 'He', 'I', 'We', or 'You.' These are inadequate human words used to try to identify something that human mind cannot fully grasp, and human language cannot correctly describe. Providing we keep this limitation at the backs of our minds, use of these pronouns is, in fact, inevitable in our limited situation and for our present level of consciousness.

Nothing exists without the Sovereign Spirit. In other words, *Spirit* is the *underlying structure* of the Father's eternal being, which is represented by the positive and negative aspects of Ultimate Reality. In fact, we cannot separate Omnipresent Energy, Spirit, i.e., the Father, from everything we feel, think, see, touch, and accomplish, even here in our fantasy world. Every fragment of creativity and order we recognize, experience, and accomplish as human beings in our imperfect universe is contained within the overall creative nature of Ultimate Spirit. However, that should not be confused with religious pantheism, which, though a belief that the Father is present in everything also holds that the Father and our false material world are one and the same thing, in a way that totally overlooks the irreconcilable disharmony between perfect nature of the Father and the flawed attributes of the natural world to which we presently belong.

When we think of the Father as Ultimate Reality, it is easier to understand that he is the same Spirit that manifests both the *positive* and *negative* aspects of eternal reality. But our present magical existence, represented by the imperfect finite universe, though equally contained within infinite possibilities of Absolute Spirit, exists as a bad dream in contradiction to Divine Ideal. Here, strayed specks of Divine Spirit function in a wrong milieu, resulting in limitations, which are inconsistent with the true nature of Absolute Spirit, hence the need for the spiritual redemption of the world.

It is written in Theosophy, Vol. 54, No. 7 of May 1966 that "Absolute, Divine Spirit is one with absolute Divine Substance … that spirit is *potential* matter, and matter simply crystallized spirit (e.g., as ice is solidified steam)." … In other words, *Spirit*, i.e., the Father, is everywhere and in everything. "We touch and do not feel it; we look at it without seeing it; we breathe it and do not perceive it; we hear and smell it without the smallest cognition that it is there; for it is in every molecule of that which in our illusion and ignorance we regard as Matter in any of its states, or conceive as a feeling, a thought, an emotion. ... In short, it is the '*upadhi*,' or vehicle, of every possible phenomenon, whether physical, mental, or psychic." There is serious doubt however, that theosophists' scope of imagination goes beyond our finite universe and beyond knowledge of the *chief* principality in action in Earthly matters.

Therefore, when we speak of the Father as the Great Unseen Spirit, we refer to infinite power, limitless potentials, transcendent excellence, and supreme sublimation, that permeate infinite existence. Surely, such Unfathomable Infinitude cannot possibly be distilled into a single physical personage sitting on one ceremonial chair in one localized corner of our invented finite universe, as religious believers imagine. Customary Christians will argue that the Father literally distilled himself into Jesus of Nazareth and they will be technically wrong. Jesus Christ is *'Son'* of the Father. He personally stressed that fact repeatedly during his Earthly ministry; meaning he is a part of the Father and not the whole. To see the Father as a man means that nothing else exists, both visible and invisible, outside that single man. Yes, it may be possible for the Father to become a single man, but impracticable for anyone else to witness that. It is simply impossible to reduce infinitude to a single dot here on Earth.

For obvious reasons, Jesus Christ called us *brethren* and stressed that his Father is our Father too. He wanted us to know that we are equally *sons* of the Father, i.e., that the Father is all of us and more. The difference, however, is that Jesus Christ is in harmony with Absolute Divine Spirit, and we are not, because of our present station. While he could say "I and the Father are one," we cannot, as false encumbrances presently cloud our divinity. We will be able to say that however, when our spiritual redemption is fully accomplished by the one who is in perfect harmony with Divine Spirit. Only then will the redeemed become one in the Father and with the Father once again.

THE FATHER IS LIGHT, NOT A GLOWING SPECTRE

Jesus Christ revealed another important aspect of the Father to the world through Apostle John. 1 John 1:5 reads, "This is the message we heard from Jesus and now declare to you: 'The Father **is Light, and there is no darkness in him *at all*.**'" Jesus Christ had very good reason to emphasis the *perfect* nature of Divine Light— Pure Light in whom darkness is eternally separated.

In the past, people worshiped the sun, the moon, and the stars, believing that starlight is the Father. People still make the same mistake in our modern generation. Even the very apostles of Jesus Christ would have imagined that since the Father is Light, any kind of apparition of light would equally be the Father. Jesus Christ needed to establish the fact that the Father is not Fire, Lightning, or a Glowing Nebula. He is not the magical spot of white light that near-death-inductees and daydreamers usually sight at a great distance in their dazed state. And certainly, the Father was not the *Burning Bush*, the *pillar of fire*, or the *chariot of fire* that formed religious foundation of Jewish idea of the Father. Fire is a ravager—a practical blend of evil, hatred, untruth, ignorance, and hostility. Divine Light is glorious. He is the Unseen Glow that illuminates our intellect and purifies our thoughts and actions on this plane of existence, setting for us goals that are in harmony with heavenly wisdom.

Evidently, Jesus Christ wants us to discern deeper meanings from Apostle John's declaration, concerning true nature of the Father. With that, he gives us the surest rule of thumb on how to differentiate the Father from the chief impostor who poses as light of the world. Divine Light is to be known by the fact that he is Source of all good and no evil whatsoever. This divine point of reference should help us unravel the great mysteries of this life. It should dispel chronic illusions of our religious *Ignis Fatuus* (*Foolish Fire*) that holds entire humankind spellbound to a meaningless existence.

It is generally believed that Moses encountered the Father as a *Burning Bush*. With the information at our disposal now, we know that that was not the case at all. Moses encountered an impostor. The Father is Light, not Fire. The word that Moses received from the burning bush negated the will of the Father completely. Of course, the Scripture states clearly that Moses encountered Jehovah and not the Father, as "No one has ever seen the Father ... or heard his voice." [John 1:18; 5:37] Moses saw Jehovah and heard his voice on many occasions.

The Jews and followers of their religious oversight have continued to celebrate the ill-fated Jewish Exodus, extolling the Burning Bush as real savior of his people. They argue that Jehovah's *pantomime of bitterness* represented by the Exodus showed the goodness he planned to bring about in the future that never comes. Meanwhile, the Jews had never known peace, freedom, and tranquility as a nation since their encounter with Moses and the Burning Bush. Neither do they represent the fitting model of a people redeemed by the true Glory of the Father. They are rather a people blinded by false light. History proves that beyond doubt. Jesus Christ lamented over their religious blindness, saying, "Would that even today you knew the things that make for peace! But now they are hidden from your eyes." [Luke 19:42]

While the Jews may be tentatively forgiven for being under direct yoke of the *false light* of the world, customary Christians and Muslims have no excuse for thinking and believing as the Jews do. Allah introduces himself to Muslims as *"light of heavens and Earth,"* i.e., light of the world; and even though he graphically contrasts limitations of his light with that of the transcendent, *Blessed Olive Tree of Light*, they still assume him to be the Father. "The similitude of Allah's light" says Quran 24:35, "is as a niche wherein is a lamp. The lamp is in a glass. The glass is as it were a shining star. **(This lamp is) kindled from a Blessed Tree**, an Olive neither of the East nor of the West, whose oil would almost glow forth (of itself) though no fire touched it."

It is obvious that since Allah's Lamp was kindled from the Blessed Olive Tree of Light, Allah's Lamp cannot be the Absolute. And since we are talking of the Father in terms of Source of all lights, Allah cannot be the Father. In comparison to the Divine Light of entire existence, Allah is just *a dull lamp in a niche*. Allah is light that leads its followers astray and he does not feel ill at ease to acknowledge that himself. According to Quran 7:186, "Those whom Allah sendeth astray, there is no guide for them. He leaveth them to wander blindly on in their contumacy." Such light can hardly be deemed pure and divine. The heavenly Christ came into the world, to give true light to all the people being led astray by the misleading dull *lamp* of the world. Hence, even when Allah's light shines in the world, Jesus Christ says, "I have come as a light to shine in this dark world, so that all who put their trust in me will no longer remain in the dark." [John 12:46 (NLT)]

Perhaps, customary Christians are most to be pitied in this regard. Although they claim to have exclusive and concrete proof of Divine Light in Jesus Christ, they are still unable to tell that the Burning Bush encountered by Moses and the blinding light experienced by Saul of Tarsus on his way to Damascus were indeed false light. The Scripture documents clear difference between the *Burning Bush* and Divine Light of eternal glory, and the words and deeds of Jesus Christ portray true nature and will of the Father. It is expected that with hindsight, customary Christians should be truly enlightened, but they are not. If they are, they will not continue to refer to the Father as *Consuming Fire, Devouring Flame, Blazing Glory* and the like.

Their Scripture makes clear the fact that the world did not have *true* light before the coming of Jesus Christ. Even with the presence of the *Burning Bush*, and the flickering *Lamp in a dark niche*, the world yearned for true Light.

2 Esdras 14:20 (GNB) declared that "This world is a dark place, and its people have no light." Isaiah 9:2, affirmed that the world was indeed '*a land of deep darkness*' as it prophesied the coming of true Light into it— "The people who walked in darkness have seen a great light; those who dwelt in a land of deep darkness, on then has light shined." John 1:9 heralded actual coming of the heavenly Christ, saying, "The **true light** that enlightens every man **was coming into the world**." Eventually, Jesus Christ appeared among us, bearing the true glory of Divine Light. He was "full of grace and truth" and "we beheld his glory, glory as of the *only* Son from the Father." [John 1:14] As expected, he acted and spoke nothing but words of love, peace, truth, righteousness, purity of purpose, hope, and eternal life. Today, the whole world beams with spiritual enlightenment because of his glorious presence.

Jesus Christ made emphatic statements regarding his unique position as the *only* bearer of Divine Light in the world. He declared, "I have come as a light to shine in this dark world, so that all who put their trust in me will no longer remain in the dark ... as long as I am in the world, I am the light of the world." [John 12:46; 9:5] Customary Christians affirm that Jesus Christ is indeed the *true* light of the world, but nothing in their religious character shows that they understand the real implications of their creed.

In very simple words, Jesus Christ is saying that the *Burning Bush* is not the Father. If he is, the world will not be a land of deep darkness; it will rather be basking in eternal glory of his divine presence. If Jehovah is the Father and the world had true light, there would have been no need for the heavenly Christ to come as the *only* true light into it. These truths should form the bases of meaningful conviction in the redemptive power of Jesus Christ. True Christ-followers will not weaver in asserting them. With such concrete foundation on truth, they will begin to experience genuine spiritual growth. They will proceed with confidence and make informed pronouncements concerning every aspect of human salvation, as true ambassadors of Divine Light should.

True Christ-followers will not be misled by the *Blinding Light* of Damascus, for instance. They will be able to fault the very foundation of customary Christianity itself by denouncing the fraudulent conversion of Saul of Tarsus. The light that blinded Saul for three days on his way to Damascus was certainly not the light of Jesus Christ that enlightens every man. True light of the Father opens the eyes of those blinded by false light of the world; it does not blind anyone in any way whatsoever. So-called conversion of Paul was purely a stage-managed encounter with the *Blinding Light* that the Jews had always known. His motive was purely to contradict and confuse, and if possible, to obliterate the true light of Jesus Christ in the world. Cunningly, Paul founded the Catholic Church of Jehovah in Rome, which preached his own occult version of Divine Glory. The Church targeted and brutally crushed outspoken, true disciples of Jesus Christ, publicly putting many of them to death in most gruesome ways. Then, it effortlessly captured and steered multitudes of gullible churchgoers back to the *Burning Bush* and back to the Zionist status quo.

Until customary Christians understand the true meaning of 1 John 1:5; until they allow themselves to be guided by the fact that Divine Light is all good and no evil at all, they will remain *voluntary* captives of the consuming fire of this land of darkness, and therefore, antichrists by default. I know however, that true light of the Father opens the eyes of those blinded by false light of the world. He reveals to people things they could never have seen or known. So, I know that the whole world will eventually see the *Foolish Fire* of worldly religions for what he really is. He will eventually flicker out completely for the good of his religious captives.

That brings me to the issue of evil and the personification of that in an imaginary, all-powerful opponent of the Father. As we already know, the Father is all good and no evil whatsoever. There is nothing like evil in the Father's perfect spiritual nature. No Devil or direct opposite of the Father exists anywhere in reality. The evil known in our world is the practical manifestation of our spiritual corruption. Evil is purely a worldly dilemma. In any case, since the Father is absolute goodness, the direct opposite of him would be absolute evilness. But absolute evilness will naturally destroy itself and so, will not exist anyway.

As I pointed out earlier, the Father's eternal spiritual make-up comprises the positive and negative aspects of Ultimate Reality—i.e., the two eternally separated infinite realms of *perfect* Light and *perfect* Darkness. Yes, the realm of darkness is as pure and perfect for its divine purpose as the realm of light. The realm of darkness represents divine containment of all disorderliness filtered out of the goodness side of the Father. The Father will not be *Light in whom there is no darkness at all*; he will not be all good and no harm, and he will not be life eternal, if he did not partition out the realm of darkness to act as repository for all the negative aspect of his limitless divine potentials. Thus, eternal demarcation between Divine Light and Divine Darkness makes perfection of the Father plausible.

Darkness does not mean evil or wickedness; it simply means absence of Divine Light. The realm of darkness is perfect and at absolute peace in its natural state of eternal entropy. Light on the other hand, means Life, which in turn represents divine expressions of the character and activities of the Father, meant only for the positive aspect of reality. Goodness and Love, being some of the hallmarks of divine activities, are exclusive to the realm of Divine Light. Since the Father designated the realm of darkness to be eternally without divine light, no life or divine activity exist there. Where there is no life and activity, there can be no goodness and love, and no evil and wickedness, for that matter.

The universe is a finite makeshift settlement *scorched* into existence within the vast expanse of infinite realm of darkness, being the brainchild of fallen, corrupted sons of Divine Light. Entire worldly existence represents a temporary disorder within the realm of perfect darkness—a spiritual aberration that requires divine restoration. Evil and wickedness exist in the world because ungodly blend of light and darkness here makes worldly beings good-and-evil, which is a contradiction to divine nature. Evilness is a *stumbling* brought about by one desperately trying to make real headway in darkness. Such a person falters and lives with persistent ill will, which he vents on people or things external to himself. Frustrated mode of existence in the world reflects disgruntled attitudes of its cosmic ruling authorities, whom the Scripture in Eph 6:12 (NLT) calls "evil rulers and authorities of the unseen world … mighty powers in this dark world, and … evil spirits in the heavenly places."

The one we call Devil, Satan, or Lucifer in our Earthly situation is but the ceremonial head and spokesperson of the notorious principalities that rule the Earth. He is none other than Jehovah to whom the rest of the principalities had "given over their power and authority" for purpose of the war against the *only* bearer of Divine Light on Earth. He also happens to be the entity we erroneously call the Father on Earth. Good and evil are undifferentiated in Jehovah, but he is by no means Satan or Devil, if by that we mean someone who is absolute evil. Jehovah is not completely evil; he is good-and-evil. Like every one of us, he is a fallen son of Divine Light, caught in the same web of universal experiment, and hopelessly trying so hard to eke out enjoyable life in an unreal world. But just like someone desperately trying to erect a concrete castle upon quicksand, he vents his frustrations and grief on unfortunate humans.

But Jehovah is only one of the *archangels*. He is but a messenger—a trumpeter on Earth matters—reporting to the higher cosmic council of world rulers, whom I call ***The Establishment***. The faceless entity at the apex of the hierarchy of that cosmic council is the actual Lucifer. He too is a fallen son of the Father. He is neither absolute evil nor eternal. Therefore, he does not qualify to be regarded as direct opposite to the Father.

The realm of Light is the realm of Life, or realm of Divine Activities, or simply realm of Being. The realm of darkness is realm of non-Being—the realm of Eternal Entropy—since there is total absence of Divine Light that fuels Divine Activities. Our souls are spiritually dead or rather *dormant* in the world because, though we still retain our spiritual bases in omnipresent Spirit, we had lost our heritage in Divine Light and therefore, cannot have life—i.e., we cannot express genuine Divine Activities. The heavenly Christ has not come into the world as true light to transform it into realm of true life, as some misinformed religious believers suppose. This region belongs eternally in the realm of darkness—in the realm of non-being. Jesus Christ makes it clear that "the light is with us only for a little longer"; and he says, "My Father is working still, and I am working [to restore all things]." [John 12:35; 5:17]

The heavenly Christ came into the world purely to restore perfection to the realm of darkness. He came to *re*-separate divine light from primordial darkness; to re-establish eternal spiritual status quo. To that effect he says, "I have come ... that whoever believes in me **may not remain** [here] in darkness. ... and he who follows me will not walk in darkness but **will have the light of life**." [John 12:46; 8:12] He has come to illuminate the way out for the stranded sons of heavenly light to return to the realm of light where true life is possible. Jesus Christ is first our true light, then our redeemer, our way out, and our resurrection. Only full and final exodus of fallen sons of Divine Light will restore perfection to the realm of darkness and ultimately to entire body of the Father. Thus, Christ's mission is clear-cut and right on course.

THE FATHER IS ETERNAL LIFE

The Father is Light. Light is Life. Life is Divine Activities. Divine Activities mean Perfect Existence. Eternal Life is pure, uninterruptible existence. While Light is energizer, as well as root essence of divine glory, purity, holiness, righteousness, love, creativity and so on, Life is the limitless, *individualized* varieties of expressions of these impeccable qualities of the Father within the realm of light or realm of being. The Father is Being—i.e., the Source of all life or existence. The Father is not one *living* deity somewhere in the heavens; he is Life that exists in all beings. Innumerable living spirits express him in their divine activities, being simply individualized aspects of him.

If we think of the Father as the divine Tree of Eternal Life, then his *sons* comprise the countless network of various categories of *living* cells and plant tissues that make up the major parts—the roots, trunk, branches, leaves, flowers, and seeds—of the Blessed Tree of Eternity. Because the Tree of Life is eternal, the *sons* live forever in him. Any branch or part that severs itself from the Tree of Being dies unconditionally. That is the graphic explanation of the heavenly norm that Ezekiel 18:20 captures as, "The soul that sins shall die." Thus, eternal life is an exclusive aspect of the realm of Divine Light or the positive side of the Father. It is impossible in the realm of darkness or the negative side of the Father, as absence of divine light there means absence of divine activities.

We can appreciate the Father as both Pure Light and Eternal Life by looking at what artificial light of the sun means to our world. No human being exists that does not have some ideas of the various activities and benefits of the sun on Earth. Light of the sun is the life and glory of our world. It is the source of all organic life and activities on Earth. Without light of the sun the Earth will lie fallow. Besides imparting life to organic matter, light of the sun illuminates and energizes the Earth. It defines our reality, sets our goals, and gives definite sense of direction on this plane of existence. Without the sun we will not exist and even if we do, we will be blind and dormant.

As Jesus Christ says, "There are twelve hours of daylight every day. During the day people can walk safely. They can see because they have the light of this world. But at night there is danger of stumbling because they have no light." [John 11:9-10 (NLT)] Surely, we can all imagine a day on Earth when the sun refuses to shine. Our lives are repeatedly assured by that faithful early morning sunrise that brings smile to the face of a world in darkness. Most of us take that for granted. Without all the energies we harness from the sun for our industrial and domestic processes; and in absence of all the artificial lights we use, including the moon, electric bulbs, gasoline lanterns, wax candles, straw touches, all of which are derived from the sun, the Earth will simply be uninhabited.

We can now understand that all life depends on light. However, quality of life depends on quality of the light source. If the light source is pure and eternal, life is perfect and eternal. Mortal human being that is powered by quantum of electromagnetic radiation from the sun is literally a fleeting *particle*. We are *sons* of artificial light of the sun. Our life is highly flawed and short-lived because sun's light is impure and ephemeral. Sun's light is both quantifiable and exhaustible; so, we die because the sun dies. The mortal man drops dead the very moment *its* discrete amount of fleeting glint or photon of sun's light runs out or is forcibly extinguished by other means. That also explains ultimate fate of our invented universe, which is powered by multitudes of dying suns.

Life of the world is sheer vulgar animal sex-game, invented by heavenly dropouts to give their embodied dead souls the false impression of living. Quran 3:185, 14 captures the false nature of worldly life, saying, "The life of this world is but **comfort of illusion**," and "Beautified for mankind is love of the joys (that come) from women and offspring…" It's all illusion. Nothing under the sun has true life. We think we are living, but we are all dead entities. The Father only allows transitory goodness of sun's imperfect energies in our world as symbol of his special grace to help us appreciate the difference. But we must all return to our deserted places in Divine Light to regain perfect eternal life. As Jesus Christ says, the light is with us only "for a little longer."

Our world is dead forever without true light. If we appreciate the fact that Jesus Christ is the *true* light of the world, we will understand why he also calls himself *"the way, and the truth, and the life"* of the world. No fallen dead spirit can return to the Blessed Tree of Eternal Life except he is rekindled by the heavenly Christ. The difference between a dead entity and a living one is activity; one is capable of it, the other is not. The difference between *dead* human spirits and the *living* spirit of the heavenly Christ is divine self-expressing; human spirits lost that divine heritage by being involved in a realm that is devoid of Divine Light and so they lie dormant in Earthen bodies. Thus, activities of Jesus Christ in the world represent practical expressions of the will and character of the Father. Accordingly, the Scripture says, "No one has ever seen the Father; the only Son, who is in the bosom of the Father, he has made him known" in the world. [John 1:18]

Jewish Exodus looked up to the *Burning Bush* for guidance, but they all lost their way and perished in the wilderness because he was false Light.

Jesus Christ is the true envoy of Divine Light in the world. Only he can impart true life to our dead spirits and lead us back to true eternal existence. As expected, his "light shines in the darkness, and the darkness can never extinguish it." And he assures his true followers that they "**have the light that leads to [true] life.**" [John 1:18]

This should help us to put into proper perspective various aspects of our present existence. Our entire universe is grand *Sheol*—graveyard of dead spirits—because it is devoid of Divine Light. Even if we can pull together luminosity of all the suns in the universe, it will not be able to generate or rekindle true life in a single individual soul in this place. This should also help us to contrast the true place and nature of Jehovah/Allah, who symbolizes the light of the world, with those of the heavenly Christ, who is the *only living* Son of the Father in the world.

Both Jehovah/Allah and ignorant human beings who look up to him as *God Almighty* are fallen dead spirit beings. Every entity in the universe—whether called cosmic authority, principality, god, archangel, angel, demon, human or animal—is a fallen, dead spirit. We all need the salvation of Jesus Christ to be able to return to the realm of Divine Light for spiritual eternal life. Jesus Christ is not only Messiah to the oppressed, but also to the oppressors. We are all lost in the outer darkness. That is why the Scripture says, "There is salvation in no one else! The Father has given no other name under heaven by which we must be saved." [Acts 4:12] That is why Jesus Christ says, "I am the resurrection and the life. Anyone who believes in me **will live, even after dying.**" [John 11:25 (NLT)]

THE FATHER IS LOVE AND GRACE

The Father is Love; he cannot exist if he is not. Which one of us can imagine a house built without mortar between the bricks? Such a house will most certainly crumble at the slightest gust of wind force. Our cities are built, and our imposing skyscrapers stand the toughest weather conditions from year to year, because good mortar holds the bricks firmly together. Love is the mortar that holds the omnifarious house of eternity—the Father—firmly together. Love is the harmonizing essence of perfect existence. Harmony of purpose is what creates and sustains perfect bliss, delight, and peace that exist in the heavenly household of the Father.

If we return to my analogy of the Father as the Tree of Eternal Life, we will see that love is the sap that gives life to the entire tree. Although the taproot feeds the entire tree, it is meaningless without the parts that depend entirely on it. And although the leaf is as treasured as the branch, its allotted level of responsibility is far lower than that of the branch. Harmony of purpose binds the parts perfectly together. The root does not starve the trunk because it has exclusive power, for it will mean starving itself. The branch does not bully or threaten the leaves because it is mightier. Neither do the leaves revolt against the branch on which they live and have their being. In the end, faithful roots, strong branches, and healthy foliage together portray the magnificence and delight of the great tree.

Likewise, absolute love binds multifarious aspects of Divine Spirit in eternal harmony.

As the Scripture says, "The Father is love, and all who live in love live in the Father, and the Father lives in them." [1 John 4:16 (NLT)] There is absolutely no room for inordinate dominion on the part of the Father; and hence no room in him for grief, jealous wrath, vengeance, and the threat of hell fire, such that characterize Jehovah/Allah and his incurable obsession with the need to dominate his human subordinates on Earth.

The Father hates no one. He has no enemy, for he is indeed, the only one that exists; and no one hates himself. If he hates anyone, he hates himself. He does not punish or kill anyone, as religious believers are led to believe. If he punishes anyone, he will only be hurting himself, and if he kills anyone then he kills a part of himself. The Father's love *for himself* is unconditional and it is easy to see why. Bearing in mind that the Father is made up of everything that exists, the humans and their imperfect world can be likened to one little sore toe on the Father's big foot. Now, which one of us will hate his tender toe just because it accidentally stumbled upon a jagged stone? Which one of us will roast the toe in fire or chop it off altogether just because it is temporarily sore and painful? What we all do to injured parts of our bodies is that we gently nurse and care for them till they become well again. And our joys know no bounds when we feel whole again. The Father feels the same way. He does not hate, punish, kill, or roast quarantined parts of himself in hell fire. Rather, he showers them with divine grace; nursing and healing them with tender kindness till they are fully redeemed, for only then will he become whole and happy again.

The Father does not love only *good* people and hate *evil* doers. He does not love only those who love him and hate those who hate him. His love is not based on human emotions; it is divine and unconditional. People whose image of the Father's love is formed on Exodus 20:5 will find these statements difficult to assimilate. They have been deeply indoctrinated in the secret cult of the Jewish jungle deity whose life is entirely controlled by human emotions. For him, love is strictly a trade-by-barter affair. He says clearly in Exodus 20:5-6 (NLT), "I lay the sins of the parents upon their children; the entire family is affected—even children in the third and fourth generations of those who reject me. But I lavish unfailing love for a thousand generations on those who love me and obey my commands." Also, in Quran 22:40, he says, "Verily Allah helpeth one who helpeth him." Such is love of an unrepentant capitalist. Of course, this further proves that Jehovah/Allah is not the Father.

Indeed, when we consider the hardhearted deeds of some evil individuals purely by invoking human emotions, it will seem grossly unfair that they might eventually go *scot-free* in the end. So how does the Father's unconditional love work? How can *good* people be made to understand goodness of the Father vis-à-vis their actual advantage over evildoers? Jesus Christ answers these questions with the parable of the lost son. The father of the prodigal son; would one say he loved his good son more and the wayward one less? The Messiah says "No," even though the good son had thought otherwise. The father loved his two sons *equally*. The good son dwelt within proximity of his father's positive influence and so always enjoyed the full measure of his love. Sadly, such inestimable advantage is most often taken for granted by people who enjoy it. The wayward son, on his part, enjoyed equal measure of his father's love in form of **grace.** Because the wayward son had wandered far beyond the sphere of his father's positive influence, his father's love could only reach him in form of grace in his distant wasteland. Grace is love by telepathy and it sometimes seems stronger than love at home.

Evidently, absence of the lost son left bitter void in his father's heart that only he could feel and understand. He felt unhappy and incomplete; therefore, he prayed ceaselessly for his son's safe return. That is love in its sublimest nature. His grace yielded fruit eventually. His lost son returned to him safely and his joy knew no bounds. "Quick! Bring the finest robe in the house and put it on him," he ordered, "Get a ring for his finger and sandals for his feet. And kill the calf we have been fattening. We must celebrate with a feast, for this son of mine **was dead** and has now **returned to life**. He was lost, but now he is found." [Luke 15:22-24 (NLT)]

Then, he tried to explain to his good son the reason for his great joy, for he had no way of knowing how it felt for a loving father to have his *dead* son come back to *life*. "Look, dear son," he said, "you have always stayed by me, and everything I have is yours. We had to celebrate **this happy day**. *For your brother was dead and has come back to life! He was lost, but now he is found!"* [Luke 15:31-32 (NLT)] Jesus Christ says the situation is the same in the heavenly household of the Father regarding the return of any single wayward spirit from the world. "In the same way," he says, "there is joy in the presence of the Father's angels when even one sinner repents." [Luke 15:10 (NLT)]

People who share the good son's sentiments will feel that the father ought to have punished or made the bad son suffer for his misdemeanors rather than celebrate his return. The truth, however, is that the bad son had already suffered and paid in full for his sins all the years he continued in his wayward ways. At full repentance he had no more quilts left to suffer for. The very moment he found the courage to renounce his evil ways and headed home, he automatically put an end to his own self-afflictions. He became free and victorious. That was why his good father threw a party on his behalf. His father was celebrating his victory over self-damnation. For, it is not easy to overcome evil habits. It should be remembered that his father never, at any time, punished or wished for him to suffer. His love for his sons was unconditional. The bad son was entirely self-afflicted, being the natural outcome of his own wayward lifestyle. He learnt the hard way that evil did not pay.

An evil person only punishes himself for as long as he continues in his evil ways. Evil people only seem to prosper on Earth because when enormity of their atrocities is contrasted with the Father's steadfast compassion, magnitude of the Father's love on them stand out far more than one can easily perceived for the good people. For, while people under love receive deserved divine affection, people under grace receive equal affection though they are undeserving. Love is grace to people who are undeserving. Romans 5:8 captures the Father's love for us as grace, saying, "But the Father showed his great love for us by sending Christ to die for us while we were still sinners." This does not mean that evil people go all scot-free in the end. They do not, because they would have suffered greater *self-afflictions* and paid in full for all their atrocities while they languished in wickedness. Certainly, being wicked is not an easy business. Every wicked person knows this fact. As the Scripture says, "There is no peace for the wicked." [Isaiah 48:22]

That brings me to the confusion some people have, imagining that the Father allows undue suffering of *good* people in the world. "If the Father truly loves *righteous* people," they usually ask, "why does he permit evil to befall them in the world, at all?" For a start, no one is righteous in the world. There is no single perfect son of the Father in the world. We are all wayward sons of the Father, paying the price at varied stages of our individual journeys toward total repentance. Every soul still found within the spheres of this sinful world has a measure of atonement to make for his outstanding misdeeds. It will help *good* people—people who consider themselves *righteous*—to see their sufferings as just retributions rather than consider them unfair punishment from the Father. In the world, we are all under the same divine grace of the Father, meaning that the Father has provided a heavenly way of escape from self-affliction for all of us, but we are refusing to take it. His divine life-line dangles in our faces every day of our miserable lives in the world but we refuse to grab on it for our final redemption. The Father will not force any sinful soul to accept his unconditional grace. Therefore, suffering and dying is entirely our own making.

Jesus Christ is the physical manifestation of the Father's grace on every one of us in the world. He is the heavenly life-line—sent for the whole fallen spirits in the world and not for human spirits alone. Although his mission is now well known all over the world, we have seemed to ignore him for various inconsequential reasons. Some people have simply turned Jesus Christ into subject matter for meaningless religious debates. However, for the safe trip back to perfect heavenly existence, he silently beckons on us with steadfast love, saying, "If you follow me … **you will have the light that leads to life**." He assures us that no judgment or further retribution awaits any soul that heeds his call and returns to his rightful place in the Father.

Just as the prodigal son was received with joyful merriment and a new lease of life, the Father receives every repentant soul with divine embrace and a crown of eternal life. "Truly, truly," he says to us, "he who hears my word and believes him who sent me, has eternal life; *he does not come into judgment, but has passed from death to life.*" [John 5:24] Then he encourages us to emulate his personal examples in attitude and conduct— "Love one another; even as I have loved you … Take my yoke upon you, and learn from me; for I am gentle and lowly in heart, and you will find rest for your souls." [John 13:34; Matt 11:29]

If we truly love one another, we will be able to appreciate everlasting nature of the Father's love for all of us. The Father is Love *all the time*. He continues to love us even as we fall more and more below divine standard. This does not mean that the Father loves the way we are. He does not. He desires that we should become as perfect as he is. But because we continuously reject his love, we live as if he hates us. We live as if he is punishing us. As love is the substance that gives meaning to life; our lives appear sad and meaningless because we do not reflect the Father's love in our everyday existence. While at home the prodigal son had no cause to ask or doubt if his father loved him. He took that for granted. When he rejected his father's love, he lived in the distant country as if he was hated, and eventually began to wonder if anyone could ever love him again. Then, when he resolved to return to the love that he once rejected, he finally proved that his father's love had been steadfast all along. It became obvious to him that the problem had been with him, and not with the everlasting nature of his father's love.

So, it is with us in our *distant*, loveless world. While we are busy chasing after all manners of wry sensual pleasures in the world, the Father never stops loving us. If we can pause to review our present situation and genuinely incline ourselves toward regaining the heavenly love that we once took for granted, we will indeed prove that love of the Father for us has been unconditional and eternal. Homeward bound is towards ultimate love experience. Certainly, people who persevere in goodness have advantage. They steadily inch closer and closer toward ending their just retributions in the world. People who think that evil pays, on the other hand, accumulate more and more years of karma or just retributions in the world. Time is of the essence here and it is all in our hands. The more we drift away from the Father is the more we suffer and grieve. Even the slightest act of indiscretion adds a measure of painful extension to our journey's end.

We can also appreciate unconditional nature of the Father's love for us by looking at the love that *imperfect* human parents have for their own children. Apart from his famous parable of the prodigal son, Jesus Christ cited other examples of faithfulness of human parents toward their gullible children to help us begin to appreciate the bigger picture about our perfect heavenly Father. He had cause to ask, "You parents—if your children ask for a loaf of bread, do you give them a stone instead? Or if they ask for a fish, do you give them a snake? Of course not! So, if you sinful people know how to give good gifts to your children, how much more will your heavenly Father give good gifts to those who ask him?" [Matthew 7:9-10 (NLT)]

Good parents continue to love, care for, and treasure their children through good times and bad times. They never stop loving them even when they fail to meet their expectations for them. In my experience as a parent, I have seen that most often children take the love of their parents for granted. Some reject their parents' love outright, usually out of youthful indiscretions, in preference to the passion-filled love of their peer groups. In the long run however, some of these children experience disappointments and eventually end up being emotionally frustrated and dejected. Some of them suffer from emotional depressions that linger on to their adult lives, at which point they begin to believe or conclude that no one ever loved them in this life. Nevertheless, some of them, who find the courage to retrace their footsteps and return to the love that nurtured them in their dark years, always discover that their parent's love for them had been unconditional.

But human situation does not altogether capture the supreme miracle of divine grace. Human condition is ephemeral. While parents' love for their wayward children may remain everlasting, it might be impossible for some repented children to return to it. It would have been too late for a son or daughter who rejected his parents' love to return to it, for instance, when they are already dead. I have seen parents who waited in vain for return of their own prodigal children and died of heartbreak. I have also seen young men and women who ended up living aimlessly on account of the guilt of rejecting or abusing invaluable love of their dead parents. Whichever way, death can effectively prevent wayward humans from returning to abandoned love of their parents as the proverbial prodigal son did, or as human spirits can do with the Father. To end with, although the Father's love for us is longsuffering and everlasting, the earlier we all resolve to return to our proper places in his heart is the earlier we will put an end to our painful and meaningless sojourning in the hellish world. Outright exit from this sinful world is what we need, and it is all in our hands.

CHAPTER TWO: WHAT IS LIFE?

The fact that we seek spiritual resurrection as humans means that we are spiritually dead. And since it is the spiritual that controls the physical, it also means that human beings do not have life. Yet, whenever we pray, we never fail to thank god of Genesis for giving us life. But did god of the world really give humans life? Are we really 'life' or merely apparitions of life? What is it that we call life here in the universe? What is *true* life? Our quest for true life eternal will remain meaningless if we do not genuinely try to understand what life truly entails. And if we seek life while believing that we have it, then, our goal of spiritual resurrection will become altogether unattainable.

It must be stated clearly here that nothing has life in the universe; whether entities known as the *mighty powers in the heavenly places*, Earthbound ruling principalities, gods of heavens and Earth, archangels, angels, devils, demons, humans, animals, or other alien forms belonging to other stellar communities. These are all mortals that can be likened to animated images of *frozen* actors projected unto flat white screen in a darkened theatre. The projector, the frozen actors and the animated images on the flat screen are all lifeless.

As we already know, "the whole universe is a dark place, and its people have no light"; and where there is no light there cannot be life. Therefore, no one should be in any doubt that human beings do not have life. Jehovah/Allah, god of the world, did not give human beings life; and he cannot give them life because he does not have life himself. Human beings are merely *animated* apparitions of fallen dead souls that must pass away with the false world of sinful Mother Nature. They appear briefly, flutter and die immediately their false light sources time out, and then they vanish forever. Human beings were never a part of the heavenly household of the Father; therefore, they can never be reconciled to the Divine Tree of Eternal Life. For, as the Scripture says, "flesh and blood cannot inherit the Kingdom of the Father, nor does the perishable inherit the imperishable." [1 Cor 15:50]

So, what is it that we call life here in the universe? Well, many people say that life is a game, and purely a game of sexual intrigues. Indeed, sex is everything to worldly existence; without sex this life will not exist. It is the engine of Mother Nature, which is responsible for genetic proliferation of organic existence. Hence the Earth is saturated with sex and sexual matters. Life activities on Earth are chiefly centered on males and females wooing each other for sexual bonding or fiercely fighting each other to disentangle. As it is with humans, so it is with every *living* species in our solar family. Our wisdom is equally based entirely on sex and on matters that are directly or indirectly related to it. Our religion, politics, education, drama, poetry, arts, songs, and dance moves; our jokes, expletives, laughter, joys, heartaches, and pains are all firmly hinged on sex. Or who can imagine life on Earth without its ever-present sexual vulgarities, perversions and paraphilias—prostitution, pornography, homosexuality, lesbianism, bestiality, sexual bondage, rapes, incest, sexual harassments, abuses, and scandals? People may find this hard to believe, but these are deliberate programs intended as spices of this life. Take these out of this life and we will not exist.

The Quran describes life of the world as "comfort of illusion ... "a pastime and a sport." But this is the only life known to the world; and one would have expected that only people who have abundance of life can afford the irony of moments of lifelessness as a game. Life of the world indeed gives the false impression of true life, but it was not deliberately intended to be a game of satire; rather it represents all that the heavenly dropouts could achieve—the crown of universal craftsmanship. Universal craftsmanship itself is generally meaningless. Yet, life of the world will not exist at all without the so-called *game* of genetic propagation of the DNA as molecule of life, which provides the semblance of what we call life. Even then, one should ask, who or what is actually living in a *living* human being whose soul is spiritually dead? Who stands out or benefits from universal process of genetic living; is it man's organic body, the gene pool, the roving DNA molecule, the phenotype, the whole of living organisms as one body on Earth or "us"? By "us" I mean the fallen dead aspects of organic beings that earnestly seek spiritual resurrection.

DNA life program on Earth is the software of Mother Nature, which is a defiant attempt by the heavenly dropouts at creating life outside the Father. Most certainly, invention of organic existence was a cosmic program written and launched into operation by heavenly dropouts and not by the Father. '*Man*' which is the equivalent of son of the Father in the DNA sex program is only an expendable piece of carrier. *It* is a lifeless Earthen cloak sewn inside the body of *man* using the DNA as tailor's instruction, and someone must wear and move it about. A heavenly dropout wears that as projected image of his own soul; and because he does not have life in himself, he cannot impart life to it or to anything else. He merely assists to sew another *man* for another heavenly dropout to wear and animate. Thus, a parent and his offspring represent two distinct fallen spirit beings. That way the weaving loom of false life forms was spun into a vicious circle. Thereafter, millions of years of natural processes of biological mutations, variations, adaptations, and selection operated the loom, refining organic life from simple animal life forms to the complex organisms that we see on Earth today. The refining still goes on, even to this day, through man-made breeding, medical, laboratory and cosmetic processes.

According to the Bible, Jehovah/Allah and the Earthbound principalities claimed authorship of organic human life on Earth. In Gen 1:26 they agreed to form mankind— "**Let us** make man [male and female] in **our** image, after **our** likeness," they said. And then, Gen 2:7 says that "Jehovah formed man of dust from the ground and breathed into his nostrils the breath of life; and man became a living being." It is obvious from the half-baked biblical account that Jehovah/Allah and his partners were already human beings; and that Jehovah/Allah was only speaking in his official capacity as spokesman of the experimenting principalities.

The Quran gives deeper and more plausible insight into the matter, crediting invention of this false life, as well as the process of reincarnation for dead souls stranded in primordial darkness, to Jehovah/Allah. It says,

- "Your creation and your raising (from the dead) are only as (the creation and the raising of) a single soul …
- Who delivereth you from the darkness of the land and the sea? Ye call upon him [Jehovah/Allah] humbly and in secret, (saying): If we are delivered from this (fear) we truly will be of the thankful. …
- [So] How disbelieve ye in Allah when ye were dead and he gave life to you! Then he will give you death, then life again, and then unto him ye will return. He it is who created for you all that is in the Earth. …
- Allah is he who created you and then sustained you, then causeth you to die, then giveth life to you again" and again and again. [Quran 31:28; 6:63; 2:28-29; 30:40]

Well, which one of us wrote the cosmic program of sexual existence is not important at all, just as it no longer matters to us who invented atomic bomb or the bazooka; the airplane or personal computer that today defines our civilization. What should matter to us is that the Father did not invent the lifeless and immoral processes of Mother Nature. Father Nature is eternal, so the Father did not set up a parallel to divinely radiated heavenly life eternal. In any case, sexual *physicalization* of vital lights of our souls on Earth is a very sordid idea indeed. There cannot be any doubt that whoever wrote the program was spiritually depraved. He should be deeply embarrassed by what human nature has all turned out to be, and not exultant. **Sex is a whole lot of stupidity and pains.** Indeed, the words 'shame' and 'bondage' stem from the oddness and amorality of sexual expressions of organic beings. Surely, there could have been far more respectable and decent modes of telepathic materialization of our vital light sources on Earth.

Well, *true* Life is existence—of *self-sufficient* creative energy that engenders original, intelligent activities, which reflect perfect existence. Our principal example of true life is the Father. He is the Supreme Creative Energy that engendered entire eternal existence. Putting it a different way, the Father is Divine Light that generates creative Divine Activities within the realm of perfect existence. Therefore, **Life is Divine Light.** With our knowledge of the inviolable divide between the two extreme aspects of the Father, this means that life exists only within the heavenly realm of Divine Light. Life cannot, and does not, exist in the realm of absolute darkness, as absence of Divine Light means total absence of Divine Activities. That explains why the universe is godless and lifeless, being a temporary asylum of heavenly dropouts within the realm of darkness and non-being. Jude 6 speaks about "angels that did not keep their own position but left their proper dwelling" that were kept "in eternal chains in the nether gloom." Indeed, existence beyond the realm of Divine Light is the same as living in eternal chains in thick darkness.

The Father is the Source of *all life* within the heavenly realm of perfect existence. Individualized creative energies that he radiated directly from himself exist only within this realm. Made in his exact *likeness*, sons of Light are eternal light and eternal life themselves. For as long as they remain within their proper dwelling in the realm of the Father's positive influence, they are self-conscious and self-sufficient creative energies. Violating the heavenly norm of perfect existence is tantamount to wandering away into the realm of absolute darkness where true life is not possible. Any son of Light that wanders away from his rightful place in the realm of lights will end up being overshadowed within the realm of absolute darkness. His light will become overpowered by darkness, and he will naturally cease to be life.

Jesus Christ refers to true sons of the Father as *suns* of the heavenly

Kingdom and we shall see why. While stressing his own status as the *only* true Son of the Father in the world, he calls himself the *light* and *life* of our present world of darkness. Was Jesus Christ exaggerating his status or is he indeed the *only* Son of Light that ever retained his divine nature within the realm of darkness to carry out the Father's divine mandate? Is he indeed right in implying that no single *living* entity in the world has life? We shall also be able to answer all those questions.

Now, we have said that Life is Divine Light! But how can the human mind comprehend that, seeing that the only life it knows has form and physical features. Well, we can glean vital facts from a simple motion-picture projector, and from the sun of our present existence. By employing basic combination of light source, lens systems and well-timed shutter arrangement, a motion-picture projector gives life to still images printed in frames on reels of flat filmstrips. As the film runs through the projector at constant speed, the shutter operates to flash each successive frame onto the distant white screen in front of the viewers. At about 24 frames per second, the human eye, because it does not function fast enough to register each image separately, is tricked into perceiving continuous motion. That gives the illusion of watching life performances on flat screen. But we all know that nothing has life in a motion picture. Yet, for as long as the *light source* continues to project the still images onto the screen, we are thrilled by *dead* actors—actors that are not there—performing wonderful stunts and going about their normal activities, full of *life*. Thus, we can conveniently assert that the life of the projected dead movie stars is the light source. Without it they will remain as dead on the filmstrip as they really are, forever.

One thing human beings often take for granted is actual role of the sun in the life we live here on Earth. The sun is the *projector* of all organic life on Earth and indeed, within our entire solar system. Although far more sophisticated than the motion-picture projector invented by human beings, the sun works on the same principle. What that means is that we are dead human images printed on cyclic cosmic filmstrips that are animated by light energies from the sun. Just like the still images on the movie filmstrip, human beings do not have life of their own. And just like the light source in the motion-picture projector, the moment the light source of a man times out, he stops dead on the spot. And if somehow, the sun switches off for a considerable length of time, everything we call life here on Earth will cease to exist. Literally speaking therefore, life of human beings is in the faraway sun.

An android beamed to Mars by NASA for instance, will *live* and interact with its environment as programmed, being fully armed with artificial brain or microprocessor unit, sensors, transmitters, and good capacity battery pack. But its actual life is determined at NASA space station on the Earth. NASA (National Aeronautics and Space Administration) is US Space Agency responsible for non-military programs in the exploration and scientific study of space. Now, that tells us a lot about who we really are, both as mortal physical beings and as *fallen lights* of the world. As human beings, we are organic images animated by energies from the sun; but the sun, as a nuclear reactor and projector, derives its imperfect energies from "us"—fallen dead sons of Divine Light. Thus, collectively "we" are the sun of our small solar family. Without the latent, howbeit corrupted, creative energies contributed by our fallen dead souls to the solar grid, the sun will not be able to shine.

In other words, every mortal man is an objectified projection of a specific fallen light, having his own divine identity and beamed through a kind of personal cosmic *shutter*. A man's soul is the false light of his own mortal body. Or putting it another way, *man* is shadow of its soul. Therefore, unlike in the case of NASA and the Mars android, we are the ones pulling the cords of our own mortal existence within our chaotic and lawless environment. This should help us to understand that the human soul is not situated within the human body; he is rather acting on the body, as if through a light *shutter*, from his vantage position within the solar grid. That is why our souls are bound to reap exactly what we sow as humans. Nemesis is on man's soul, not on his disposable mortal body. That is why Jesus Christ says that everyone must carry his individual cross for his personal spiritual salvation. Ignorance of these facts offers no excuse or exemptions to anyone.

Nevertheless, knowing that the entire cosmic program is not foolproof should also help us to understand why man is manipulable; why *body-stealing* or demonic possession, spellbinding and hypnotism are possible on human beings. Ignorant humans are easily manipulable by higher souls who understand the principles of astral projection and know how to manipulate other peoples' light *shutters*.

To make sense of these facts we will need to run the filmstrip of the life of the world from the very beginning of the universe itself. Recently, scientists and cosmologists started searching for relics of the *big bang* to help them understand and possibly reconstruct true history of the universe.

Quantum cosmology disconfirms the notion that the universe was created out of nothing; *'nothing'* meaning *'no space'* and *'no matter.'* Of course, we already know that vacuum does not exist in the Father; his eternal manifestations team with infinite potential energies, resources, and possibilities. The realm of absolute darkness—the actual milieu within which the big bang took place—is repository of heavier essence of divine energies and not void as Bible account of the beginning insinuates. Besides, a place filled with visible darkness cannot be said to be void.

Anyway, the scientists discovered that the whole space is filled with special radiation corresponding to about three degrees above absolute zero. They called it '$_3$K' radio energy. Nigel Calder wrote in his book, *Einstein's Universe*, "The $_3$K radio energy is the present form of radiation from a great flash that occurred when the universe was very young—**possibly visible light, originally as white as the Sun's** but now immensely redshifted by the subsequent expansion of the universe. ... For **every atom of hydrogen in the universe there are about a hundred million particles of $_3$K radio energy**, and their total mass-energy is about one-thousandth of the mass of the galaxies."

What the scientist just stumbled upon is the fact that the big bang that triggered universal mushroom was created by light. If we can understand the nature or characteristics of that light, then we can conveniently tell who created the universe. Now, we should not forget that the fallen sons of the Father that were caught up in the overwhelming primordial darkness were *lights* by nature—*originally as white as the Sun's* indeed. In the words of the Scripture, they used to "shine like the sun in the kingdom of their Father." [Matt 13:43] Therefore, we should expect that they continued to be *lights* in their present station, howbeit *corrupted lights*. While Divine Light is pure, ethereal, and unrestricted by time and space, light of the heavenly dropouts become heavy, full of impurities, restricted by time and space and therefore, visible. Their lights had turned into fire, heat and jumbled white lights that include all kinds of uncontrolled electromagnetic energies. Fallen *suns* of the heavenly Kingdom had reduced themselves to the false lights of the universe.

"*Let there be light*," as reported in the Bible account of the beginning, was not a verbal expression of creative intent by the Father who is Eternal Light. It was rather, the practical outburst of the entire heavenly dropouts, which galvanized and transformed their latent energies into components of stellar luminosity. Fallen sons of Light became the innumerable starlight that gives false *life* to universal contraption. Thus, the real molecule of this life is not the roving DNA that tailors the mortal bodies of animals but rather the $_3K$ radiation that finds expression through atoms of hydrogen, which fuel the stars of our physical worlds.

Hydrogen atom is the nearest substance to the lost purity of divine light. It became the main ingredient for the formation of universal superstructures as well as organic life forms on planet Earth. Together with helium, they are the universal 'fire starters.' They are chiefly responsible for stellar heat and light energies that energize and activate the Earth, constituting over 99% of the materials in the universe. One thing we can all be sure about is that $_3K$ radiation is fragment of impure light. If the Father created the universe, the scientist will not be able to detect fragments of any sort because Divine Light is pure and spiritual.

Let us return to the inviolable definition of life and see if we can correctly identify semblance of it within universal setting. Life is activities; light engenders activities. Therefore, light is life. However, the quality of light determines quality of life and the activities that it can engender. Divine Light is *true* life; it is spiritual, perfect, and eternal because the Source is pure and timeless. Infinite creative expressions of perfect sons of Light provide divine activities within the realm of lights that bring delight to the heavenly household and sustain blissful existence eternally. Made in exact likeness of the Father, the sons are equally self-sustained, self-aware creative energies; they are pure lights and therefore, true life themselves. And because they have life in themselves, they can impart life to their personal creations within the realm of being. Thus, everything beams with life in the heavenly Kingdom of the Father.

This should help us to know that the heavenly Christ can indeed rekindle our darkened lights and help us to regain true life in the heavenly paradise that he prepares for those who choose spiritual salvation. Jesus Christ was not blabbing when he spoke of stones rising to praise the Father if the need arose; for if there be anything that could be referred to as stone in the Kingdom of the Father, it would have life and therefore, should be able to rise and praise the Father indeed. There is absolutely no need for artificial lights of stars, fires and or batteries of any sort in the heavenly realm of lights. Jewish prophets who saw familiar visions of *seven candle stands* and believed that Jehovah's heaven was real were obviously deceived.

Quran 24:35 draws vivid contrast between Divine Light and the *shining stars* of the universe. Referring to Jehovah/Allah as *a* light of the world, it likened him to "a lamp in a glass" and calls him a "shining star" in a niche. Then, it says that he was originally kindled from the Grand Olive Tree of Eternal Light that transcends the universe. That is perhaps the clearest way of saying that Divine Light transcends the universe, and that Jehovah/Allah is just *a* fallen, corrupted light. But the principalities are not the only shining stars in this universal niche; we all are fallen lights of the world. We all belong to the solar family of heavenly dropouts.

Most certainly, other families of heavenly dropouts exist in other stellar communities beyond our solar system. At the big bang, fallen sons of the Father literally degenerated into starlight and became the *life* source of the universe. Organic existence and its imperfect processes, such that mark Earthly existence, are cosmic programs representing *projected* activities of that *life* source. Because starlight is false light, the life that it generates is equally false. Organic activities that it engenders are equally expressive of a lifeless program. Thus, the principalities, human beings and other animal forms are lifeless organic mechanisms, energized and compelled into action by false lights of the sun. Much like the Mars android operated from NASA space station on Earth, human beings are some kinds of organic batteries; they are neither self-sustained nor self-aware. They *live* once and die forever.

Equipped with brains and relevant sense organs, and designed to convert chemical energy from organic food into mechanical energy, human beings are merely made *alive* for their *only* purpose, which is to replicate themselves through passionate immorality, while deploying rest of their expendable energies on other meaningless material pursuits. The whole idea is to fill entire emptiness with hustling mutants to mimic real-life heavenly existence. **"Be fruitful and multiply and fill the Earth!"** That is simply what it is all about—a game of indiscriminate sexual proliferation. The young and vigorous ones feel exultant, as they are the favored in the vain occupation. Those whose batteries run down due to age and other maladies are discarded unceremoniously, as they are no longer useful in the sex game.

No spiritual activity or vocation of any sort was intended or written into the program of this life. It is rather designed to war against everything that is pure and spiritual by malignant spirits who had turned themselves into animals in both body and mind. As the Scripture says, "the desires of the flesh are against the Spirit, and the desires of the Spirit are against the flesh; for these are opposed to each other, to prevent you from doing what you would." [Gal 5:17]

LIFE WITHOUT THE FATHER

True life, as we have seen, is spiritual and pertains only to the realm of Divine Light, which is the positive side of the Father. The negative side of the Father is absolute darkness; and because it is devoid of Divine Light, it is eternally lifeless. As Eternal Source of Light, the Father is also the Fountain of Eternal Life. Perfect sons of the Father reflect his eternal nature within the heavenly realm. The Quran alludes to the Father as the *Grand Olive Tree of Eternal Light*—the Source of all lights. If we also imagine the Father as the Grand Tree of Eternal Life, then, perfect sons of the Father are branches and foliage of the Divine Tree, as well as the *suns* of the Father's heavenly Domain. They have eternal life because they feed directly from the eternal Fountain. And they glow because they are direct reflections of Eternal Source of all lights. It is only natural that any branch or leaf that severs itself from the Tree of Life will die to all his divine privileges and cease to glow as son of Light. He ceases to belong to the heavenly household and sinks into the nether region where true life is impossible.

Therefore, life without the Father is unreality; it does not exist, for the Father is Life. Also, because the Father is Divine Light; life without him is spiritual death—a stumbling about in total darkness. But if we must use the word 'life' to qualify the stumbling; then living without the Father is 'false life.' *False life* is unrighteous or sinful because it is contrary to the Father's eternal spiritual design. Hence, it is typified by all kinds of spiritual limitations—falsehood, ignorance, selfishness, impure thoughts, wickedness, bitter rivalry, strife, and wars; desperation, frustration, hopelessness, negativism, religionism, religious impiety, criminality, materialism, and all forms of ungodliness. We have practical examples of all these and more in worldly existence.

The Scripture captures the emptiness of false existence from the very inception of our world. Genesis 1:2 says that the beginning was a total *void*—a state of loss and utter spiritual privation. The situation ultimately degenerated into utter futility; and Ecclesiastics 1:2, 14 (NLT) says, "Everything [about our world] is meaningless ... **'completely meaningless!'** ... Everything going on under the sun ... really, it is all meaningless—like chasing the wind." Thus, worldly existence stares us in the face as practical example of life without the Father—'false life' in practical terms.

But how have we interpreted the situation so far? Have we been able to understand emptiness and futility as grand universal pathology rather than merely an isolated stigma peculiar only to human species on planet Earth? Have we been able to realize that our finite universe is not all that exists; that it is just a tiny tumor located on a tiny spot within eternal and infinite region of absolute darkness? For, we cannot speak of the universe 'expanding' if it is not contained within a region or space that is far expansive than it can fill. Expansion of the finite universe within infinite space is strictly identical to expansion of atomic bomb mushroom within far-reaching Earth's atmosphere. Have we been able to see beyond the *beginning* of our finite universe to all that infinity and eternity represented? Have we been able to imagine that the Father of infinity and eternity far transcends entities that may have been posing as gods within the finite universal eruption? Have we ever imagined that whatever we may have called god within the Earth's system of government cannot be the Ultimate? And should we not rather be eager to seek out and identify with the Ultimate?

Unfortunately, organized religion truncated what should have been our normal thought pattern in the prevailing circumstances and invented romanticized interpretation to the whole situation. Attempting to suppress the fact that the whole universe is godless from its inception, religion invented all kinds of lies and effectively restricted our scope of imagination to the finite; not just to the finite universe but also to matters of mundane nature, pertaining purely to organic existence on planet Earth. Religion invented a bungling kind of *God Almighty* in the person of Jehovah/Allah, set up a throne for him in some imaginary heaven in Jerusalem, made him sovereign head of a *heavenly* ruling council of Earthbound gods and set him over a people blighted by imaginary sin of the world, which it also invented and pinned squarely on one couple, Adam and Eve, and on entire human species. Religion also invented an imaginary evil entity that it called the Devil who it made the source of all evil, so that Jehovah/Allah may stand out as source of all good. But Jehovah/Allah botched the whole arrangement, obviously, because he lacked experience on how to personate as perfect Sovereign Father. He usurped the two positions, ultimately becoming god-cum-devil of his false kingdom on Earth.

Armed with nothing but lies and religious propaganda, Jehovah/Allah set out to play down universal emptiness, while plotting to enthrone himself as *God Almighty* over all the Earth with high-handedness. He ruled humanity with arrogance and brutality, boasting that he was the first and last god in existence. From his lofty mountain fortress, he breathed fire and brimstone on ignorant inmates of a doomed world order.

- "As surely as I live," he swore, "I will rule over you with a mighty hand and an outstretched arm and with outpoured wrath." And he did.
- "I form the light and create darkness," he boasted, "I bring prosperity and create disaster; I, Jehovah, do all these things," and
- "Surely, as I have planned, so it will be, and as I have purposed, so it will stand. ...
- "Before me every knee will bow; by me every tongue will swear." [Ezek 20:33; Isa 45:7; 14:24: 45:23 NIV]

Thus, the situation degenerated into blatant lawlessness and the people grieved. As Proverb 29:3 says, "When the righteous are in authority, the people rejoice; but when the wicked rule, the people groan." In fact, Jehovah/Allah became more effective as devil than as *God Almighty*, thus warranting the Scripture to declare that "the whole world is in the power of the evil one." But then, that was how his cookie began to crumble.

Jehovah/Allah's reckless actions and utterances increasingly created doubts in peoples' minds and compelled great minds to conclude that he was simply too irresponsible to be the loving Father. And even though they could not yet clearly perceive the Father within the system, they concluded that Jehovah/Allah must die. Thus, the right kind of spiritual revolt, inaugurated by Christ's triumphal entry into the city of our estranged *god almighty*, took definite stance during the Enlightenment, between late 16th and 18th century. The fear of Jehovah/Allah had ceased to be the beginning of wisdom for many, and brave ones spoke out their minds freely. They sacked Jehovah/Allah from displaying his tantrum in the "marketplace" and forced him to sink deeper into the dark domain of occultism. Religion branded the brave, noble minds atheists and persecuted them. But they made their points well, rightly concluding that the universe has no meaning because the Father is not here to give it one, and that human nature is irredeemable. Most importantly, the liberated thinkers of the Age of Enlightenment had already declared Jehovah/Allah, the impostor, dead in the mentality of enlightened minds. That may well have corresponded to his actual physical death. After all, he was or is a mortal being.

Remarkably, even the Jews who invented Jehovah/Allah's false transcendence had to publicly sentence him to death after the sheer horrors of Auschwitz, reasoning that if he were not dead that the holocaust would not have taken place. As Karen Armstrong wrote in her book, *A History of God*, "If this [Jewish] god is omnipotent, he could have prevented the Holocaust. If he was unable to stop it, he is impotent and useless; if he could have stopped it and chose not to, he is a monster. … There is a story that one day in Auschwitz, a group of Jews put Jehovah/Allah on trial. They charged him with cruelty and betrayal. Like Job, they found no consolation in the usual answers to the problem of evil and suffering in the midst of this current obscenity. They could find no excuse for Jehovah/Allah, no extenuating circumstances, so they found him guilty and, presumably, worthy of death." [Karen Armstrong, *A History of God*, page 376]

Nietzsche's *parable of the madman* was perhaps the clearest dramatization of Jehovah/Allah's death in modern man's consciousness. But "I have come too early," said the madman, "my time is not yet. This tremendous event is still on its way, still wandering; it has not yet reached the ears of men. Lightning and thunder require time; the light of the stars requires time; deeds, though done, still require time to be seen and heard." Well, the time has indeed, come, for the modern man to really walk over the grave of our dead *God Almighty* to establish definite link between us and 'the horizon of the infinite' that Nietzsche also spoke about.

The realization that the Father's domain of positive influence is not here in the universe was a grand landmark in evolution of man's knowledge and the greatest accomplishment of positive atheism. The Father is infinite and eternal; he is not a native of our finite universe. Atheists came really close to hitting the nail on its head. But that was good enough. Theirs was only a stage in evolution of man's knowledge. Our present generation is expected to cover more miles and uncover greater truths than they were able to do in Nietzsche's time.

The longer we *live* is the more we know. The filmstrip of this life has really rolled by in time; it has gathered a lot of dust and now screeches as it runs over the sprocket wheels of Mother Nature. We surely see the flaws clearer and clearer than Nietzsche's generation did. And we ought to be more assertive than they were. Human nature is as *irredeemable* as the sun is *irrefuellable*. That is an incontrovertible truth. In about 3 billion years from now, the sun will be hot enough to boil off Earth's oceans. Long before that, the filmstrip of organic existence on planet Earth would have reached "The End." But fallen human souls will continue to flicker on, seeking spiritual resurrection because they actually belong to the heavenly household of the Father. As fallen lights, we are indeed *rekindleable*; but only the heavenly Christ can do that for us. The Father wills that we should live and shine again as perfect *suns* in his heavenly Kingdom; Jesus Christ is manifestation of the Father's will and grace upon us.

Modern man should, therefore, be able to see clear purpose for his weary soul in "the *only* light that enlightens every man" in the world. We should all be able to *know* Jesus Christ, not as redeemer of human nature or organic existence on planet Earth, not as reviver of the universe, but as the restorer of our divine nature. Jesus Christ is our light and resurrection to perfect eternal life. He does not exaggerate his divine importance in our present circumstance where he says, "I am the resurrection and the life; he who believes in me, though he die, yet shall he live." [John 11:25] Or has it not become obvious that Jesus Christ indeed, brought spiritual rekindling to our world? Our generation should be able to confirm apostles' assertion in 1 John 4:14 that "we have seen and testify that the Father has sent his Son as the Savior of [his lost sons in] the world."

CHAPTER THREE: WHAT IS MAN

As I said in the opening chapter, we needed first to know the Father before we can know ourselves. Knowing ourselves, we will then be able to duly appreciate Jesus Christ as savior and redeemer of our dislocated spirits. As we have seen, the Father is Divine Light; and Divine Light is true Life. He engenders perfect divine activities that culminate to perfect existence *only* within the realm of Lights. True sons of the Father's positive influence share his divine nature within the designated heavenly realm. They are ethereal life energies because they are direct emanations of Divine Light and Life.

As we already know too, true life is impossible outside the realm of lights. Our universe represents a temporary asylum founded by fallen, dead lights on the flip side of the Father's positive influence, within eternal realm of darkness. The Bible does concede that "the Earth was without form and void, and darkness was upon the face of the deep" at the beginning of the universe [Gen 1:2] Thus, the universe was godless and lifeless from its very beginning. Man was born out of that primordial darkness. He was son of darkness, not son of light. We can say categorically therefore, that man is not *son* of the Father, and he does not have life. What we regard as life or *living* in the universe is only a derivative of some generic processes of artificial animations, which can be mechanical, biological, or metaphysical. Man is an animated mechanism.

The Bible shows clearly that man was a fabricated piece of self-ignorant mechanism—formed of clay and animated by external source of energy that made it come *alive* for its transient, purposeless existence on planet Earth. That is, perhaps, the only credible information the Bible has on man as a species of organic animals. Genesis 2:7 credits invention of man solely to Jehovah/Allah, saying that he "formed man of dust from the ground, and breathed into his nostrils the breath of life; and man became a living being." If that story is entirely true, Jehovah/Allah would have been the only man in existence. Genesis 1:27 of the same Bible, however, shows that man was a hybrid between two species of higher organic animals; invented by a group of alien alchemists by mingling the gene of their more enlightened species with that of the aboriginal ape-like species on Earth.

"Let **us** make man in **our** image, after **our** likeness," was not a statement made by one inventor to himself but to a group of inventors sharing mutual interest in the transformation experiment. It was clear that the aliens merely transformed an existing species on Earth; they made the aborigines '*men like themselves*.' An entity that remade another entity man in his own *image and likeness* is man. The aliens were men, the Father was not involved, for he is not man.

Obviously, there is more to the story of man than the Bible was designed to address. The account about how an alien species of humans annexed and transformed a less informed species of humans on Earth does not address the origin of organic life forms within the solar sphere. Man is a species of organic animals; true story of his origin is contained within the greater story of origin of organic existence in general. The Bible does not provide any information on that. The aliens that cloned our species on Earth were already men. The Bible does not tell us how they became men in the first place.

No doubt, the grand cosmic clockwork that generated and sustains organic existence within the solar environment is far beyond the capacity of the wandering scientists in the Genesis account. However, it does not matter now who wrote the original program of Mother Nature within which Jehovah/Allah merely functions as a higher animal. From experience, we know that great inventors among us do not usually possess two heads. What we can be sure about is that whoever originated ideas of animated life forms in the universe cannot be the Father, because its tenets totally contradict his perfect and eternal Divine Nature.

Although Jehovah/Allah's overall character portrays his likely status within the larger cosmic equation, the Bible declares him creator of man. Quran 114 addresses him as king, lord, and God of mankind. And he indeed, rules the hearts of *all* religious men and women on Earth. He ultimately became mouthpiece of the faceless gang of alchemists in the biblical account. Together they constituted themselves into the principalities and demigods that colonized and held humanity to ransom, as the situation still stands today. Whether they are legitimate or not, and irrespective of how low-ranking they may be within the hierarchy of cosmic ruling class they are the present rulers of man's situation. It is to them that ignorant humans direct their supplications, in the erroneous believe that they are gods almighty.

We can understand the true nature of man better today. Our generation is already living in the age of intelligent machines. Space age is also here with us. Biblical accounts of space travel by the colonizing *gods of heavens and Earth* may have sounded like fairytales, but we have real life experiences of our own modern generation. On April 12, 1961, Yuri Gagarin (1934-1968) Russian-Soviet pilot and cosmonaut became the first human to successfully journey into outer space bodily and back to Earth when he completed an orbit of the Earth in his Vostok 1 spacecraft in 1 hour 48 minutes. Four months later, another Russian-Soviet pilot and cosmonaut, Gherman Titov (1935-2000), flew the Vostok 2 mission launched on August 6, 1961 that lasted for 1 day, 1 hour and 18 minutes (25.3 hours) and he performed 17 orbits of the Earth. He was the first to pilot a spaceship personally, the first to take manual photographs from orbit and the first to film the Earth from outer space. At one month short of 26 years old at launch date, he also remains the youngest person to fly in space. Titov's flight finally proved that humans could live, work and sleep in space. Space missions had since become regular occurrence.

Challenged by Soviet Union's pioneering achievement in space travel, the United States successfully landed the first humans on the surface of the Moon and returned them safely back to Earth, as part of the NASA's Apollo 11 three-man mission, which lasted between July 16, 1969 and July 24, 1969. Neil Armstrong and Edwin "Buzz" Aldrin landed on the moon on July 20, 1969 in the lunar module (nicknamed Eagle), while Michael Collins stayed in orbit around the moon in the command and service module (nicknamed Columbia). Armstrong was the first to set foot on the surface of the moon, followed minutes later by Aldrin; and they spent a total of 21 hour and 36 minutes upon the moon. They performed experiments, planted specially designed U.S. flag on the lunar surface and a plaque that read, "Here men from the planet Earth first set foot upon the moon July 1969, A.D. We came in peace for all mankind"; and they safely returned to Earth with about 21.5 kg of samples of lunar dirt and rocks for further studies.

The next giant step for humankind is not just to land humans on Mars temporarily but also to establish permanent human settlement on it—to colonize the red planet just as the gods colonized our Earth. Various mission-to-Mars proposals have already been put forth by several organizations and space agencies. These are some of the many dividends of evolution of man's knowledge in general. In time we will see clearer picture of man's true identity within the solar family of organic animals, vis-à-vis his true place and worth within the Father's eternal manifestations.

In time to come humans will be able to take scheduled trips to the outer space. Not out-of-body but physically. People who can afford it will be able to spend weeks, months and even years on planet Mars or on the Moon, for instance. In fact, a Dutch organization known as *Mars One* is presently receiving applications from thousands of interested Mars explorers from all over the world. The project aims to screen for 24 *chosen ones* who will be given one-way ticket to a permanent settlement in the red planet. The first crew of 4 astronauts would land on Mars in 2025, followed by a new crew of 4 astronauts every two years.

Success of Mars One project is bound to create heightened interest in space exploration. Other organizations and space agencies will get involved and more and more people will opt for permanent *heavenly* asylum. When that time comes, demand for suitable spacesuits will become critical. As no prospective human space traveler can survive in space without one, inventors and programmers of such suits, in consort with the powerful space agencies on ground, will literally become gateway to the heavens. They will constitute themselves into indispensable clique. With well-crafted patent on their products, they will ultimately become demigods to desperate asylum seekers who must rent or purchase the *new* 'bodies' necessary for such experimental existence in the heavenly limbo.

In the new heavenly asylum, humans will become animators of programmed spacesuits. They will lose their human identities and dispositions; their new selves being totally dependent on the programmed purpose, potentials and level of adaptability built into the spacesuits that they wear, which will in turn depend on the knowhow, and ulterior intentions of the inventors and controllers. In other words, spacesuit will become the *new* man in space, and he will gradually lose touch with human nature and with its associated Earthly experiences. Then, the time will be reached when humans floating about in space will begin to see themselves as spacesuits and not as humans that they really are. That time will be akin to our present situation on Earth where we see ourselves as mortal humans rather than as fallen lights or immortal souls animating mortal organic mechanisms.

A time will also be reached when over population and social ills will begin to pose problems in the heavenly asylum. So many spacesuits will begin to develop various kinds of design and acquired faults and many wearers will suffer. Some will become so frustrated and begin to reflect inwards for a way out of their self-imposed dilemma. Those who manage to figure out that they were better-off as humans will wish to return to normal human experiences on Earth. Unfortunately, for their redemption, they will only be praying to the demigods that control their short-circuited situation, who, by then, would have become their captors. Meanwhile many privileged ones will float along happy and oblivious of the gross disadvantages to their real selves. A *new* Bible will be given to the suffering captives by the demigods, preaching conformism and outlining how to be nothing but good spacesuits in space. The Space Bible will assert that spacesuits are not designed or intended to become humans in space. In the same vein, the Holy Bible we have today as humans on Earth is official handbook systematically invented by the faceless principalities that control human situation, detailing how humans should be nothing but *good* humans on Earth. Man was not designed or intended to become a spirit or spiritual on Earth. The Holy Bible, as inspired by the demigods, does not compromise on that; in fact, it forbids even the thought of it. That was why god of Eden threatened that Adam and Eve would die any day they thought of, desired, or ate of the tree of knowledge of spiritual existence.

Now, let us return briefly to the Mars One project mentioned above and try to really examine the prospects of *one-way ticket to permanent existence* in Mars for humans. In it we will be able to capture the constraints and frustrations of stranded human souls that once ditched their original heavenly existence and sentenced themselves to permanent life of futility outside their perfect heavenly abode. It is most unlikely that any life exists naturally on the surface of Mars because conditions there are extreme and unfavorable. Temperatures are usually very low and the climate extremely dry. Any organic molecule exposed there will be destroyed as Mars does not have protective ozone layer to shield the surface from harmful ultraviolet radiation. Presence of static electricity is also a problem for organic chemicals. Life has not been easy for humans in their natural Earthly habitat; contemplating something harder and more unnatural is simply foolhardy.

The mere thought of permanently mortgaging one's whole lifetime to sub-human existence—to what Norbert Kraft, Mars One's chief medical director and a former NASA senior researcher, calls "a lifetime of challenges"—is greatly alarming. The knowledge that one will never be able to come back to normal human existence if, and when he becomes fade up with bungee-jumping-about in the strange planet makes the whole idea a suffocating adventure. It is tantamount to one accepting to be locked up in a fully welded stainless steel cage and lowered to the bottom of a deep dark ocean forever, with some total strangers controlling his oxygen valves from the comfort of their homes somewhere in a very busy city.

Why would any right-thinking human being declare interest in such misadventure? On what account should any normal person willingly install some overambitious capitalists as gods over himself? Indeed, organizers of Mars One will ultimately become gods over their beguiled captives in Mars once they get them exactly where they want them to be. They will own them the way that the gods seem to own their human subjects here on Earth. While human nature represents second degree of spiritual death of man's fallen spirit, Mars One existence will represent third and even more complicated degree of eternal spiritual bondage. Considering how difficult it is for the heavenly Christ to communicate the need for spiritual redemption to humankind on Earthly level of consciousness, one can imagine how much harder it would be for anyone to do the same for generations of offspring of the *chosen* 24 Mars experimenters who would have lost every knowledge of other forms of existence. Mars One will become story of souls imprisoned in mortal human bodies and further imprisoned in an inanimate space garget—a third degree of spiritual death indeed!

On a more realistic note, the so-called chosen ones are meant to be used as guinea pigs to explore the real possibility of establishing heavenly resort in Mars for the rich and powerful among us. A lot is bound to go wrong. For a twenty-first-century man to surrender his fate willingly and completely in the hands of some business-minded experimenters is not a healthy development at all. In the same way, human beings on Earth suffer the same fate in the hands of the principalities. It cannot be differently in a godless universe.

Man is prototype of Artificial Intelligence. He is a kind of Earthen spacesuit animated by fallen soul or light energy within Earth's environment. The Bible was never intended to divulge such information. Like the spacesuit of future heavenly limbo, its character almost completely overshadows identity of the soul or light energy that temporarily makes it *alive*. Equipped with just five simple sense organs and a brain that functioned as center of artificial intelligence to coordinate the senses and regulate overall bodily activities, man stood out as a unique automaton. It ultimately became prototype of machines of its kind in function and character.

No doubt, man is unique in its own complex ways; it is versatile and self-reproducing, but it is still a self-ignorant machine, fabricated and programmed, like every other complex machine known in our world, by some intelligent and imaginative boffin(s), who are however, divinely limited in so many critical ways. To human beings, the human body is a masterpiece; but the human souls know that it is just a makeshift invention of imperfect minds from which salvation is of utmost importance. Indeed, today, we have all kinds of sophisticated androids invented by man and deployed in various branches of our modern industries that function faster and far more effectively than man himself. Ultimate machine may yet be invented in the future, but spiritual redemption will ever remain inevitable.

Man is a patented spacesuit purchased and operated at great price by dislocated souls that make up the solar family of fallen lights. Contrary to erroneous religious belief that man is not just son of the Father but also chief pride of the Father's entire creation, man is only a crude vehicle through which our fallen dead spirits experience or mimic expression of divine activities in the universe. True sons of the Father are spirits; as pure lights, they are unrestricted. Fallen sons of the Father are corrupted lights, and they now find expression in the universe as various forms of electromagnetic energies. They are the animating *souls* behind every universal activity. Thus, a *living* man is objectified soul or an expression of corrupted light energy acting upon sublimated particles of matter.

Now, that *vehicle*—man—is by no means free to the animating souls. Forces of demand and supply do not allow that in a world founded by capitalists and bedeviled by acute limitations. So many dead souls queue at the production line to purchase one. And we all know how the production line works. Making babies is by no means a fast and cheap business. Needless to reiterate that the Father did not make that *vehicle*; if he did, every soul will drive one forever and free of all charges. Of course, true sons of the Father need not drive vehicles to feel alive; they are life themselves.

We can also appreciate the meaning of man's Earthen body to his soul from the life of a car owner. A person that buys a car to drive in does not only pay once to the maker or marketer of the car; he continues to pay him for as long as he owns and drives the car. He must purchase spare parts and relevant information from him on regular basis, as well as pay regular dues to numerous other agencies associated with the car business for the day-to-day operation and maintenance of the machinery. He must pay dues on daily basis to sellers of petrol, engine oil, transmission oil, brake oil, filters, plugs, brake pads, tires, and endless other replacement parts and ancillaries. He must also pay taxes to government agencies. He will not pay only once to register his car but will continue to pay year after year to renew his vehicle license, hackney permit, roadworthiness certificate, insurance, and other statutory demands on car owners. That is not all; he must also regularly patronize mechanics, auto-electricians, vulcanizers, car wash and car parks. Indeed, owning a car is not freedom but self-enslavement; it involves a whole lot of recurrent expenditures. Likewise, being a man is not life but bondage to the animating soul.

Like the car owner, every human soul pays a fortune for as long as he owns and *drives* in the rented Earthen vessel called *man* here on Earth. Hallmark of perfect spirit is absolute freedom, but man's life is not free in any way. If one asks an average parent what it costs to produce and nurture a newborn baby to become a man, the answer he will get is 'inestimable!' Apart from the basic cost of providing him with the right foods, clothing, shelter, and medications for the near endless years of his growing up, inestimable amount of money, energy and time is equally expended on seeing him through various tiers of private and public education systems, necessary for degaussing his brain and mentality to reduce innate ignorance.

The Bible gives ignorant humans the impression that bearing and raising offspring is blessing of the Father, but Dr. Hafner, in his book, *The End of Marriage*, rightly calls parenting an unpaid occupation. "From a purely materialistic viewpoint," he wrote, "it is an amazingly generous thing to do. Pregnancy and childbirth are risky and painful. Child-raising is a demanding and often frustrating task that is largely unpaid, and which is incompatible with a full, active role in the work-force or the community at large. Children are very expensive to raise. When they grow up, they may not appreciate or respect their parents. They often move well away from them – to a new suburb, a new city, or even to a different state or country. Where then are the rewards to parents of years of physical, emotional, and financial sacrifice?" [Dr. Julian Hafner, *The End of Marriage*, page 124]

The question is how many parents see their involuntary parental obligations as part of continuing payments for their own rented existence? Their own parents paid to start them off in the life of endless taxes, and they too must pay for their own little *cripples*. Indeed, man's existence is a crippling chain reaction—a complex state of spiritual ignominy indeed!

Every man who comes of age goes into the tax-master's arena to start his own endless payments for the false life that he lives. The ones whose parents may have helped to purchase good occupational certificates from schools may be luckier in getting absorbed in organized workplaces. Then, they must begin to earn their living. And once they start earning their living, they start paying to live. Working to *earn* a living has always been a form of self-enslavement. That fact has become more obvious today in our over-populated, money-based world, where more and more qualified individuals are chasing after fewer job openings in the workplaces.

For a start, every machine needs fuel to continue to function. Organic man needs organic fuel to stay alive and he must provide that for himself. In fact, man does not only eat to live, but he also lives to eat, or he dies. So, he pays a fortune for his daily sustenance, with thanksgiving to the many gods in the system that seemingly make that possible. But both the man that hires laborers and the laborers that work for him are slaves to the labor market and to the meaningless existence in the universe. Of course, company owners pay greater taxes and have greater stakes to worry about in the system.

The man who earns a living will also begin to pay for his own clothing, shelter, medications; and he will settle his home utilities bills—for electricity, gas, water, radio and even the TV programs that he views. Of course, man is always a tenant on Earth. If his apartment is a rented one, he can expect arbitrary rent increases from his landlord from time to time. If he decides to build his own house, he will not only pay a fortune to the immediate, temporary owner of a piece of land; he will pay for every bit of material needed for the construction. He will pay for services of various professionals involved in the building industry, and then starts to pay yearly tenement levy to the government of the municipality. If he buys a car to drive in, we already know what his dilemmas will be. If he decides to marry or pay for a personal *wife*—wonderful instrument for enjoyment—then he sets himself up for a whole new barrage of taxation, connected with usual family obligations. Above all, he must pay monthly taxes to various agencies of secular government just for existing within their jurisdictions, and he must hand over 10% of his meager monthly income to religious agents of the demigods that rule the human situation. Organized underworld authorities equally extort their own taxes from him through various kinds of criminal activities within the communities.

Irony of it all is that of everything that man labors to purchase for himself here on Earth, he owns absolutely nothing at last. Just when he thinks he has paid his dues in full, he drops dead and vanishes forever, leaving all that he may have labored to acquire behind. How clearer can one describe the meaninglessness of man's existence?

Man is an animal that talks. An animal is any living organism capable of spontaneous movement and having responsive sense organs. Every *living* being under the sun is an animal. Every animal is animated by a stranded soul. Fallen spirits, in their present impure state in the universe are regarded as *souls,* as they are literally the souls or animating essence behind all organic life forms. No doubt, a hierarchy exists among animals within our solar sphere. Higher animals possess cognitive abilities and higher consciousness, while the lower animals depend entirely on instinctual drive for all their expressions. Man is midway between the two.

So-called *mighty powers in this dark world* and *evil spirits in the heavenly places* are animals in both form and mind. Jehovah/Allah is a higher animal, so also are Michael, Gabriel, and rest of the so-called archangels. They belong to the alien species of humans that we ignorantly revere as gods of heavens and Earth just because they possess higher knowledge than we do. The Bible portrays their race as gods. Yet, in Genesis 6:2, 4 it reports that "the sons of the gods saw that the daughters of men were fair; and they took to wife such of them as they chose," and "when the sons of the gods came into the daughters of men ... they bore children to them. These were the mighty men that were of old, the men of renown." Now, how could that have been possible if the gods and their sons were not as much humans as the daughters of men—if they were not as much animals as the daughters of men with whom they frolicked? Besides, offspring of the so-called sons of gods and daughters of men were mighty men, not mighty spirits, or ghosts. In fact, the said mighty warriors of old were nothing but raw animals in their deeds and utterances.

When Darwin first showed that man was a descendant of apes, religious believers kicked against the idea, because they believed in the biblical creation fairytale that posits man as cream of the Father's handiwork. Today, creationists still feel outraged by it. But the truth is no longer a question of whether man is animal or not, but whether he should continue to be animal. Let me ask; is there anything animals do that man does not do? I cannot readily think of any. Animals, by basic nature, are designed to search for food, eat, sleep, play, have sex, reproduce themselves and die off. Man shares the same nature. In the wild, more aggressive animals dominate, and prey on the weaker and less-protected ones, making animal existence a matter of 'survival of the fittest.' It is the same situation among higher animals—man and the so-called gods. The mighty, aggressive, and better placed individuals in our societies dominate, oppress, subjugate, and lord it over the underprivileged. Political conflicts and wars, religious intolerance and terrorism, social banditry of unimaginable descriptions, sexual vulgarity, aggressive pursuit of material advantages over others; all these are hallmarks of animalism. Wild animals even seem more spiritual than humans and the so-called gods these days.

Studies have shown that anthropoid apes possess highly developed brains; a feature that may have seemed exclusive to man and the gods. All anthropoids, as well as some other species of animals have also demonstrated ability to show emotions—they feel grief, pain, joy, fear, love, etc. Since these are well known attributes of human souls, it follows without doubt that animals do not only possess brains but are also *living* souls. Chimpanzees, for instance, share 99% genetic make-up with humans. They share identical family set-up, where the male is official head of the family and works in consort with the female for the upkeep and protection of their young ones.

A special trait discovered among pygmy chimpanzees shows that the male, as would be expected of a polished, gentlemanly husband, never uses force or violence to press home his demands on the female. He is always polite and diplomatic. The female, on her part, is also gentle and motherly. She breast-feeds her young and shares well-developed mother's instinct with every woman. Most importantly, trained chimpanzees understand and can communicate freely with humans using the normal sign language developed for deaf and dumb humans. What then, is the difference between man and the apes?

Well, man is animal with *potential* difference. Something beyond chance upgrade to the hierarchy of intelligent animals happened to man. His ascent, being an unexpected divine intervention and a recent event in the history of organic existence on Earth, explains why man is still so much his old self. Up until the fateful afternoon in the defunct Garden of Eden when Spirit of the heavenly Christ appeared and imbued Edenic man with divine ability to differentiate between good and evil, man lived and behaved purely as wild animal. Knowledge of good and evil raised man's level of consciousness and altered his fate for good on that day. Thus, began man's evolution toward moral, mental, and spiritual refinement, which is unnatural to lower animals. What the heavenly Christ infused into man on that fateful day in Eden was not a *brain*, not a *soul*, but a *mind*. That is what makes the difference between man and the chimpanzee, for instance. As we can see, lower animals possess brains and souls, but lack minds.

Contrary to Genesis 2:7, man did not become a "living" soul on the day he was sculpted but on the very day he encountered Spirit of the heavenly Christ in Eden. The Bible confirms that man received a functional mind on that day and his spiritual eyes opened. Before that day, man had no mind and was therefore, steeped in original ignorance. Knowledge is light and light is positive activity. Adam and Eve received divine light in their souls on that day and became divinely rekindled, and they immediately began to do something positive about sinful human nature. According to the Bible, *"the eyes of both were opened, and they knew that they were naked; and they sewed fig leaves together and made themselves aprons"* of morality. [Gen 3:7]

Chimpanzees did not receive divine light of knowledge in their souls, so they have remained oblivious of the values and the need for moral, mental, and spiritual refinement. In that regard, any man that loses his mind automatically reverts to living and acting like wild animal. A mad man in the street is a perfect example. Majority of 'normal' human beings too live and act as animals because they have not learnt to use their minds properly. Evil people, on the other hand, live and act as animals by choice. "By the right choice and true application of thought man ascends to the divine perfection," says James Allen in his book, *As a Man Thinketh*, "By the abuse and wrong application of thought he descends below the level of beast." In other words, what man needs is not just a mind, but also divine grace to be able to coordinate knowledge gained by thought toward the perfect ideal. Jesus Christ remains indispensable here as personification of both the divine grace and the perfect ideal for mankind to emulate.

What it all means is that man is now under obligation to earnestly embrace spiritual evolution. But what does spiritual evolution mean for man, seeing that he is just a disposable Earthen spacesuit. Will he ultimately evolve into bionic man or a kind of exotic cybernetic organism; or will he gradually return to a therapsid to complete the vicious cycle—an eternal *samsara*? There is the possibility that man can live forever as a species or genotype through endless processes of births and deaths. Indeed, the weaving loom of Mother Nature could cycle on forever for as long as the sun continues to shine. After all spiritual death is supposed to be eternal for unrepentant souls. But endless re-embodiment in Earthen vessels in a material world is a total negation of the true nature of man's soul. Endless reincarnation merely represents artificial eternity—captured magical moments of life and death within eternal state of spiritual death—like punctuated flashes of dim light in total darkness. But man's soul subconsciously yearns for true eternity as perfect spirit.

Or is there a real possibility of man distilling away and evolving into perfect spirit being that completely transcends human nature and its restrictive environment? Well, we all know now that man is not just a disposable Earthen spacesuit but also objectified *living* soul. While man, the Earthen spacesuit, lives once and dies forever, man's soul is eternal and perfectible. Biological evolution of man can only lead to eternal death, while spiritual evolution of his soul will manifest perfect spirit, redeemed, and resurrected to his original glory. Climax of evolution of man's knowledge should bring him to full realization that man is not supposed to exist; that man's soul ought to finally evolve into an unrestricted, perfect spirit. A true spirit is eternal life himself; all his expressions transmit life. He does not need a spacesuit to create and experience living situations.

MAN AS MESSIAH OF THE ANIMAL WORLD

What the silent encounter with the heavenly Christ in Eden meant for man is yet to be fully appreciated by human beings. He did not only elevate man to the level of intelligent animals—to the exclusive purview of gods and the principalities—he gave him a place of honor far above that of the gods. By choosing to contact man and not any other species during his first advent into the world, the heavenly Christ nominated man as *messiah* of entire animal world. That was the highest divine honor to animals possible under the sun.

As if that was not enough, the heavenly Christ incarnated into the world in the physical form of man and made him coworker in his messianic mission in the world. "Since therefore the children share in flesh and blood," says the Scripture, "he himself likewise partook of the same nature, that through death he might destroy him who has the power of death, that is, the devil, and deliver all those who through fear of death were subject to lifelong bondage. For surely it is not with angels that he is concerned but with the descendants of Abraham. Therefore, he had to be made like his brethren in every respect, so that he might become a merciful and faithful high priest in the service of the Father, to make expiation for the sins of the people." [Heb 2:14-17]

It should be appreciated that the heavenly Christ could have chosen to appear among the so-called archangels or among chimpanzees or even among reptilians. But he became a man. For this reason, the lower animals love and respect man, but the so-called mighty powers, evils spirits in the heavenly places, gods and the principalities envy and war against man. That is quite understandable behavior for animals. The Messiah could have also chosen to appear among any other tribe of humans on Earth, but for obvious reasons he incarnated among the descendants of his very first apostles, Adam and Eve. Therefore, being an Israelite is indeed a divine honor. But that also explains why the principalities took particular interest in keeping the nation of Israel permanently destabilized, both physically and spiritually.

Jehovah/Allah merely pretends to be friendly to the sons of Adam, but he is their archenemy. For a start, he abducted Abram and renamed him Abraham in clear defiance of what the name 'Abram' stood for, which is "our heavenly Father is exalted." All that history records of Jehovah/Allah's involvement with the descendants of Abram are captivities, bondage, aimless wanderings, religious primitivism, pogroms, holocaust, meaningless wars, intifada, and the Wailing Wall in Jerusalem, signifying endless memorial of national embitterment in the hands of Jehovah/Allah. He did not only sustain unending physical torment on the sons of Abraham, but he also humiliated them spiritually to the point of publicly denying and crucifying their actual friend and Messiah, Jesus of Nazareth. History bears witness that Jehovah/Allah has been consistently Antichrist, anti-Adam and Eve, anti-Israel, and anti-humanity.

Well, the heavenly Christ made man the little leaven that leavens the rest of animal world. He calls him "the salt of the Earth" and "the light of the world;" and exhorts him to allow divine light to shine through him to all in the world so that glory will be given to the Father in heaven who has willed spiritual redemption for all fallen souls. This indeed, is an enviable divine calling. What this means is that while man depends largely on other animals to survive as a species, they all depend on him for their spiritual redemption. That is an enormous task, and success of it will depend totally on ultimate success of evolution of man's knowledge. Sadly enough, man is yet to realize his new exalted status to embrace its stringent obligations. Yet, he does not have eternity to unravel the gospel truth.

To make headway, man must start with definite sense of direction. No doubt, man has recorded great progress in evolution of technological inventions geared toward making life comfortable, safe, and enjoyable for him and his domesticates on Earth. But little or no meaningful effort has been geared toward eventual transition of man's soul into spiritual realm of perfect existence.

Man is hated and loved in animal family for obvious reasons. He must not lose sight of the situation. Before the coming of the heavenly Christ into the world, higher animal species prided themselves as gods and were revered by others as such. Jehovah/Allah and the so-called archangels stealthily constituted themselves into principalities over others and prided themselves as supreme powers, sole creators, and rulers of the whole universe. Jehovah/Allah further distinguished himself as the most ingenious in ruthlessness among the gods. He enthralled humankind with his destructive little magical exploits and used divide-and-rule tactics as weapon of control over ignorant humanity, as recorded in human history. And he ultimately elevated himself from the mere position of a principality or ethnic mountain deity to the supreme position of Sovereign *God Almighty*.

Thus, it happened that as Jehovah/Allah strolled in the zoo that he founded in Eden, with puffed up shoulders while looking down on the subservient inmates, the heavenly Christ suddenly came down for Adam and Eve in their lowly state. On that fateful day, the heavenly Christ hewed down Jehovah/Allah's false pedestal, setting the precedent for heavenly judgment. He made it clear that heaven debases those who exalt themselves and exalts those who humble themselves. Disgraced out of their false offices, Jehovah/Allah and his arrogant clique refused to amend their ways, choosing instead to avenge their defeat on humankind.

Yet, our *homeland* principalities are not the only haters of the heavenly Christ and his lowly human elects. Eph 6:12 (NLT) warns us about the inevitable battle that we must fight against the haughty ones. "For we are not fighting against flesh-and-blood enemies," it says, "but against evil rulers and authorities of the unseen world, against mighty powers in this dark world, and against evil spirits in the heavenly places." These are the real brains behind the capitalist world order—the programmers and perpetuators of Mother Nature. They are the utmost haters of Jesus Christ and his lowly human elects.

When the Messiah finally appeared in human form on Earth, he still maintained his heavenly standard of judgment. Rejecting the kingly class, he allowed his Earthen spacesuit to be sown in the womb of the humblest of women and chose a carpenter for his Earthly father. At the start of his divine ministry, he again disappointed the elitist class of learned priests, lawyer and scribes that represented the highest religious authorities on Earth and chose for his personal apostles and disciples, fishermen and the dregs of society. "For judgment I came into this world," he said, "that those who do not see may see, and that those who see may become blind." [John 9:39]

Sanctimonious Pharisees heard him well and understood that he was referring to them and to the cosmic council of elders as blind, and self-righteous. Then, he taught his lowly followers that the only way to find salvation for their dislocated souls was through genuine humility. "Learn from me," he encouraged them, "for I am gentle and lowly in heart, and you will find rest for your souls. ... He who is greatest among you shall be your servant; whoever exalts himself will be humbled, and whoever humbles himself will be exalted." [Matthew 11:29; 23:11-12] I need not remind true Christ-followers that they are not only fighting against the principalities but also against constituted religious authorities of the world who equally bear grudges against Jesus Christ for openly rejecting their conventional religiosity.

Meanwhile, all the other lower animals respect, honor, and love man because subconsciously they know that he has become the legatee of spiritual salvation for all unhappy souls trapped within the animal kingdom. Elegant horses carry man as majesty; camels and mules happily bear his burden on their bare backs. Dogs keep vigil over his estate, other household pets appease him and lesser domesticates sacrifice their lives for his food. Dolphins, porpoises and even wild killer whales dive, leap, and fetch objects on cue; clap and chatter to entertain man. At sea they jump along, waving him bon voyage, as his boat sails pass their delineated neighborhood. How about the fierce-looking lions, elephants and the like; they obediently perform at circuses to entertain man. In all, these animals love and subject themselves to man to the extent of willingly dying for him, evidently, because they are expecting that man would one day die for them all.

There is a great lesson in this for humankind. To him whom more is given, more ought to be expected. Jesus Christ loved and died for his human friends. So must man aspire to love and die for his animal friends. Animal rights activists have already reached that realization and are going about it the way they think best. What they must guard against however, is ever trying to love fellow humans less in all their activities. What man owes his animal friends is more of spiritual than material obligations. Battle against extinction of species is not based on spiritual insight. We should not be like overprotective parents who worry and try to prevent their young ones going into the world on their own because they feel it is their natural responsibility to protect and guide them all through. All captive souls in the world must evolve; they must be liberated. Extinction of species is a good sign. Species must evolve spiritually and then disappear. Man should be working toward ultimate extinction of all animal species. Present world order in its entirety will become extinct in the end. So, why waste valuable time bothering about extinction of species?

It is the duty of man to set the ball rolling in the right direction. He must start by putting his own house in order. For man, charity should begin at home. The lower animals are surely watching. To begin with, humans must work sincerely toward eradicating undue gaps between peoples—between the rich and the poor, the civilized and under-civilized, the well-informed and uneducated, between races and castes. Justice and equity should be pursued with vigor in all facets of inter-human relationships. Imaginary geographical lines of divide between nations should be erased; diplomatic iron gates erected by countries at their airports, seaports and land routes should be pulled down. Countries that have the knowhow should teach others. Individuals who are better qualified should provide honest and selfless leadership, while professionals and general workers should freely shuffle into their right places in industries wherever they exist in the world without regard to nationality. All children of the world should be educated free of charge. This should be entrusted to an unbiased universal body and not left for individual states that may lack adequate means, because any weak link is sure to weaken the whole chain.

Nationalism should be eradicated; it is a serious drawback to spirit of true communality. Political bias in sports and games should be discontinued and politics of aids and loans to poorer countries replaced by direct investment genuinely aimed at 'teaching the people how to catch fish' by themselves. Organized monarchy should be scrapped and all manners of chieftainship—whether religious, secular, or traditional—abolished. Bees serve their queen; human beings did the same when they were still animals. Jesus Christ says the new man ought not to continue that way. "It shall not be so among you;" he says, "but whoever would be great among you must be your servant, and whoever would be first among you must be your slave; even as the Son of man came not to be served but to serve, and to give his life as a ransom for many." [Matt 20:26-28] Executive governance should be replaced with true democracy and capitalism tempered with universal price regulation regime.

Finally, sectarian religiosity must be completely disbanded and replaced with humanitarianism and communal pursuit of knowledge. We have a lot to know and a lot to share. Nations need thinkers, not believers; they need scientists, not opinionated religious preachers.

BUT NOT UNTIL WE RECOGNIZE ADAM AND EVE AS PILLARS OF OUR FAITH IN JESUS CHRIST

No house stands without a foundation. Ascent of man did have a beginning that was rooted in the joy of knowing. Albert Einstein had this to say about **'the joy of knowing'** in 1915 when he finally discovered facts that helped him declare his general Relativity Theory: *"The years of anxious searching in the dark, with their intense longing, their alternations of confidence and exhaustion, and the final emergence into light* – **only those who have experienced it can understand that**." [Nigel Calder, *Einstein's Universe*, page 70]

It is remarkable that Einstein, one of world's renowned scientists, recognized the agonies associated with *'anxious searching in the dark,'* appreciated the joys brought about by *'the final emergence into light'* of knowledge for the ignorant man, and concluded that *'only those who have experienced it can understand that.'* Surely, he knew what he was talking about. And it was easy to see that he had genuine respect for people who had had that experience long before him. Einstein was a scientist par excellence. If he was still searching in the dark for divine light of knowledge in 1915, he was in a good position to understand what the situation could have been for Adam and Eve who were the legatees of divine knowledge. The principalities maliciously condemned them as sinners for being the first humans, brave enough to defy their law of compulsive ignorance to discover the source of true light of knowledge for humanity when the darkness was still absolute.

Faithful scientists will not negate foundation of their discipline. Adam and Eve were the undisputed foundation of modern science. Without the basic knowledge of good and evil that they received for humankind, we would all still be wild animals in Eden; not moralists, scientists, philosophers, theologians, engineers, writers and what have you. Ascent of man will stall forever if scientists and intellectuals of our present generation do not make effort to exonerate Adam and Eve from concerted religious calumny instigated by Jehovah/Allah and the principalities in the interest of the cosmic council of evil rulers of the world.

Although majority of us have not been able to discern the truth, the principalities had fought humankind right from the day that Adam and Eve received knowledge of the Father and of his plan of eternal life for us. By painting Adam and Eve as rebels and sinners, and the heavenly Christ as serpent, they succeeded in undermining the root of our faith in Christ's redemptive mission. They instituted religious propagandists who hammered home the guilty verdict and it has stock so deeply in peoples' psyche ever since. The rhetorical curse of the land after the events of Eden, the cherubim and the flaming sword, the deluge, the tower of Babel attack, the gruesome murder of Jesus Christ in Jerusalem and the decisive persecution of his peace-loving disciples all over the world; these were all facets of the principalities' offensives that Ephesians 6:12 talks about. Crux of the conflict between man and his cloners remains the battle for greater spiritual insight that should build upon achievement of Adam and Eve. There is need for clearer understanding of the true nature of the Father, his will for mankind and the place of Jesus Christ as Savior of the world.

The principalities condemned Adam and Eve for imbibing knowledge of good and evil, which is foundation of true wisdom. Yet, the Bible that they largely inspired concedes that knowledge is good, and that it is the natural right of every living being to be enlightened. Besides, our everyday experiences also show that ignorance is an unnatural and ungodly trait. "The beginning of wisdom is this:" says the Bible, "Get wisdom, and whatever you get, get insight." [Prov 4:7] So, when they could not justify condemnation of Adam and Eve based on documented biblical conclusions, religious believers pinned their crime on disobedience. "Knowledge of good and evil is very good for humankind," they agree, "but Adam and Eve disobeyed command of Jehovah/Allah that forbade them from desiring or imbibing it." What a hypocritical argument! Religious propagandists do not dispute the fact that Adam and Eve lacked knowledge or the fact that it was their divine right to seek and obtain knowledge; they insist that they ought to obey a contrary voice of reason that tried to sell the idea to them that knowledge kills. It should not be difficult to see that religion serves interest of man's archenemies.

Adam and Eve cannot be faulted under divine law of the Father. Jehovah/Allah's injunction against knowledge was both unjust and contrary to divine good. According to Italian theologian and philosopher, **Thomas Aquinas** (1225 - 1274), "Human law is law only by virtue of its accordance with right reason, and by this means it is clear that it flows from Eternal Law. In so far as it deviates from right reason it is called an unjust law; and in such a case, it is no law at all, but rather an assertion of violence." And "Laws can be unjust because they are contrary to the divine good... **In no way is it permissible to observe them.**" So, Adam and Eve were fully justified to disobey Jehovah/Allah's malicious injunctions that forbade spiritual enlightenment. What Aquinas meant was that if he were in the shoes of Adam and Eve, he would have done exactly as they did. Every enlightened human being would. Of course, he did, which was why he acquired a lot of insight and so many people today look up to his legacy for spiritual guidelines.

In the allegory of the cave that he gave in his *The Republic*, Plato suggested that our knowledge of the world, as it comes to us through our senses, is equivalent to the shadows of objects cast upon a cave wall. Such knowledge is incomplete and often misleading. Its truths are literally "nothing but the shadows of images." We can be liberated from such partial and uncertain knowledge by throwing off the shackles that bind us with our backs to the light and to the objects that cast their shadows and turn around and look directly at the light and what it illuminates. This is a painful experience at first, but gradually, with effort and training, one can overcome the glare and come to true knowledge: "He will grow accustomed to the sight of the upper world. At first he will see the shadows best, next the reflections of men and other objects in the water, and then the objects themselves; then he will gaze upon the light of the moon and the stars and the spangled heaven ... last of all he will be able to see the SUN, and not merely reflections of him in the water, but he will see him in his own proper place, and not in another; and he will contemplate him as he is ... the prison-house is the world of sight, the light of the fire is the Sun, and you will not misapprehend me if you interpret the journey upward to be the ascent of the soul into intellectual world."

Knowledge of good and evil is the foundation of intellectualism and rationalism. Adam and Eve were the hallowed foundation of mankind's 'journey upward.' They encountered the true SUN for the true knowledge, and thus fell out of harmony with the natural system of shadowy images that shackled them in Eden. The heavenly Christ helped them to throw off that shackle of darkness and illusion. He is at hand to do the same for all who are willing to endure the painful persecutions and make necessary efforts to overcome the false glare and come to the truth. Jesus Christ, as the Ultimate Man on Earth, is 'the shadows best.' He is our ultimate best confidant in this shadowy situation. Jehovah/Allah is 'the shackle that binds us' to shadowy images of reality about the Father, Jesus Christ, the world and our real ourselves. This is the whole gospel of spiritual salvation.

Finally, it is pleasing to know that Einstein positively declared alliance with Adam and Eve, while condemning Jehovah/Allah and conventional religiosity that holds him to be *God Almighty*. These are some of what he had to say: "Motivated men of the present and of the past, as well as the insights they had achieved, were the friends who could not be lost. The road to this paradise was not as comfortable and alluring as the road to the religious paradise; but it has shown itself reliable, and I have never regretted having chosen it. ... The further the spiritual evolution of mankind advances, the more certain it seems to me that the path to genuine religiosity does not lie through the fear of life, and the fear of death, and blind faith, but through striving after rational knowledge. ... [And] I cannot imagine a *God* who rewards and punishes the objects of his creation, whose purposes are modeled after our own—a *God*, in short, who is but a reflection of human frailty." [from *God, Religion and Albert Einstein*, retrieved from www.zionismisrael.com/]

Einstein was a true descendant of Adam. His testimony stands out as perfect offensive against the warring principalities. We need more of such positive declarations in the present stage of our battle for absolute spiritual emancipation.

CHAPTER FOUR: WHO ARE THE PRINCIPALITIES?

Principalities—a very dreadful word that always comes up whenever we speak about spiritual salvation of human beings on Earth—is symbol of worldly dominion and interests; and it is synonymous with very determined opposition to spiritual ascent of man. Principalities represent anti-the Father, anti-Christ, anti-Adam and Eve, anti-humanity, and anti-spiritual redemption of fallen human spirits. Yet, it is one word that is largely taken for granted by religious and non-religious people alike.

It is ironic that the Father freely offers all of us spiritual redemption from our world of agonies and death through the heavenly Christ, but for some bizarre, selfish reasons some of us do not only reject the divine grace outright, but also choose to fight against it. Making themselves public enemies of the heavenly Christ, the principalities determined to fight anyone who would accept the Father's grace. Beginning with calculated calumny against Adam and Eve who were the first to receive the heavenly Spirit, Christ, in the world, they systematically evolved a whole complex regime of offensive against humankind, aimed at deterring or misleading genuine seekers of spiritual salvation. This is unfortunate, because the heavenly Christ came into the world to save all of us; the principalities included.

Alluding to the serious nature of the battle we must all fight to attain spiritual salvation from the world, the Scripture, in Ephesians 6:12, names the principalities as our archenemies. "For *we* are not contending against flesh and blood," the verse says, "but against *the principalities*, against *the powers*, against *the world rulers of this present darkness*, against *the spiritual hosts of wickedness in the heavenly places.*" This, indeed, is a grave situation. We do not only have to fight to regain our freely given spiritual heritage in the Father, but we are also actually pitched against the most formidable of opponents.

Battle against *the world rulers of this present darkness* is not just a battle against Jehovah/Allah and the other familiar Earthbound principalities. It is battle against the highest echelon of cosmic rulers of the complex World System of Government—the faceless authorities coordinating entire processes of organic existence, their occult and physical agents in various realms of material existence, among whom are Jehovah/Allah and the so-called archangels. On our Earthly level, the battle is also against our capitalist ruling institutions comprising religious, secular and underworld authorities, including their official and secret agencies. And because we are all involved in our varied individual capacities as perpetuators of human nature on Earth, it is also a battle against our own selves. Yet, if we are thinking straight enough, we will see that this is the only war necessary for us to be fighting here on Earth. War against the principalities is a battle to free oneself from eternal self-condemnation. That makes it a true *jihad*, and inevitable for every genuine seeker of spiritual rebirth.

Assertions of Ephesians 6:12 are both critical and true for every individual human being on Earth, yet most people who recite the verse hardly seem bothered by the sheer implications. War with the principalities had raged on since the days of Adam and Eve, and life on Earth is increasingly becoming unbearable for human beings on account of that. Yet, most people hardly know anything about the principalities or about being involved in any form of battle against them. People hardly care to know who or what the principalities are, where they are from, where they are stationed, why and how they are fighting harmless human beings on Earth, what their weapons of attack are and where their strengths and weaknesses lie. People equally do not bother to know how and why we must literally exchange blows with such awesome powers, and what our own strengths and weaknesses are.

At the mere thought of it, such a battle seems a total mismatch; and it is, because the principalities know all our weaknesses and possess enormous manipulative powers over us. However, we are not altogether powerless before them. Besides being bona fide citizens of the universal state as they are, we have supreme heavenly backup, though many of us hardly know this. Moreover, for there to be a *battle* between two parties, each must have its own strengths and weaknesses. It should be strongly stated therefore, that we are fighting the principalities and the principalities are fighting us; meaning they are equally vulnerable in some ways. That makes the battle a winnable one for anyone who fights with right knowledge, which is already made available by our heavenly Minder, Jesus Christ.

Our first logical line of attack is to unmask the principalities. No one can fight an enemy he does not know, see, or understand. Knowledge, they say, is power. It is evident when we say that someone has power that we do not necessarily mean he has physical energy or stamina, but rather that he has certain body of knowledge that distinguishes and gives him advantages. If we know who or what the principalities are and have other vital information about their modus operandi, then our blows, though feeble by comparison, will surely have both target and devastating effects that will surprise all of us. So, who or what are the principalities? Are they phantoms or real persons? Are they aliens or aborigines?

Answers to these questions represent the whole essence of Christ's gospel of spiritual redemption. They form the core of what he calls **'the truth'** that will set us free. In fact, the only reason the heavenly Christ came to us in human form was to continue what he started in Eden with Adam and Eve as Spirit of Knowledge—to open our spiritual eyes further and to reveal to us masked information about the ruthless principalities, without which it will be impossible for anyone of us to withstand and overcome eternal bondage in their hands. "For this I was born," he affirms, "and for this I have come into the world, **to bear witness to the truth**." [John 18:37]

It was knowledge of this truth that gave Adam and Eve extraordinary courage and boldness to resist and overcome Jehovah/Allah's law of obligatory ignorance in the *first* Garden of Eden. Thus, they abolished the unset of absolute spiritual enslavement of humans on Earth. Knowledge of the same truth gave early apostles and disciples of Jesus Christ the unique *courage of rock* to withstand and overcome extreme persecutions, torture, and horrifying deaths in the hands of the principalities and their unconscious religious cronies in the *second* Eden.

Siddhartha Gautama, the Buddha, once proclaimed, "I have realized this truth which is deep, difficult to see, difficult to understand … comprehensible [only] by the wise. Men who are overpowered by passion and surrounded by mass of darkness cannot see this truth, which is *against the current*, which is lofty, deep, subtle, and hard to comprehend." In one grand sweep, Gautama's words capture the whole meaning of the gospel truth. The truth concerns the *lofty* individuals who behave haughtily in the world. It is profound, delicate, difficult to imagine or realize by ignorant human beings who are completely blinded by religious passion. Moreover, the truth is on the reverse side of long-established human thought pattern, such that only by being endowed with heavenly wisdom can ordinary people discover it. Ironically, Gautama discovered the truth and yet ended up as the lofty Buddha, worshiped among the gods of the world by multitudes of unconscious religious devotees. Surely, if he did not sell out, he would have ended up a martyr, like many before and after him that posed real threat to the haughty ones.

How then do I begin to tell the story of **the unimaginable** to awaken simple-minded religious believers to the need to start seeking the truth in the right direction—on the reverse side of their deeply-held religious beliefs? One of the cardinal aspects of Christ's mission in the world, according to him, is "to give sight to the blind and to show those who think they see that they are blind." [John 9:39] The problem here, therefore, is that of trying to teach a human being what he believes he knows best.

If you ask a child in kindergarten, 'what is 1+1?' He will tell you, 2. If you ask university professor of mathematics the same question, he will surprise you. He will begin to write down and explain complex, but meaningless equations; meaningless, because in the end of it all his answer will not come anywhere near the number, 2 that even a kindergartner knows. This is because he has been so deluded into thinking that there is always an esoteric meaning to very simple things, like 1+1. People we call *authorities* in religious matters are worst in this regard. Believing they are exclusively 'called' to teach others about *God*, they hardly imagine that they could indeed, learn a lot about the Father by listening to persons that are not 'ordained.'

Indeed, greater ignorance is to be found among people we generally regard as highbrow, intelligentsia, or literati; obviously because they usually know much less of the basics. And because these are always the ones that determine the wisdom of our world, ignorance pervades the nations. The only people who could not understand simple parables told by Jesus Christ were the highest echelons of the world's *educated* ones of his time—the lawyers, learned scribes, highly inspired Jewish supreme religious authorities, the wise and awesome Roman procurators, and administrators of the whole empire world. Jesus Christ wondered how these kinds of empty men managed to lead the less knowledgeable in the world. "You are a respected Jewish teacher," he once asked Nicodemus, "and yet you don't understand these things?" [John 3:10] Of course, he knew that they were victims of the programmed *mass of darkness* that Gautama talked about. They were doubly blinded by religious passion.

Perhaps, an unimaginable story of an orphan and his *loving* uncle can give us the lead we are looking for and help us to understand clearly who the principalities are. There lived a young man in the city of Lagos. His name was Obinna (*the Father's will*). He was orphaned early in life and was literally raised by his uncle in the village till he matured enough and moved to the city in search of greener pastures. He loved and looked up to his uncle as the only father he ever knew, and his uncle seemed to cherish and care for him as he did for his own biological sons and daughters. In the city, he secured good job and was doing well generally. He rented a decent apartment, bought a sound second-hand car, and married a young woman of his choice. In everything he did, he sought and adhered to his uncle's guidance.

Somewhere along the line however, everything seemed to be crumbling in his life. He lost jobs after job, was forced to sell his car, gave up his apartment for a cheaper sham and sold most of his property to make ends meet. He travelled home each time he suffered major setback to intimate his uncle who always spoke fatherly words of encouragement to him, sometimes even giving him money in way of assistance. His woes continued unabated until he finally broke down with an undiagnosed ailment. As he worried about going home to inform his uncle, believing that his recovery rested on that, a good friend of his, named `Remi (from Oremi, *my good friend*), offered to travel to his village personally to do that.

Promptly, `Remi arrived at his village the next day, traced his uncle, introduced himself and reported the situation. The uncle received him warmly and as if he was expecting his visit; calling him 'a true friend, who could take so much trouble for someone that was not even of the same tribe and language with him.'

As the visitor from the city waited at the front balcony for the message to take back to his sick friend, he overheard his friend's uncle discussing something intimate in Igbo language, in the living room behind the window at his back, with a certain man that came in a little after his arrival. They spoke freely, believing that a Yoruba man from Lagos was the last person to understand what they were saying. He listened intently and what he was hearing was unimaginable. The two men were deciding final fate of his sick friend. His body trembled and he wondered if he was at the right place and with the right uncle.

> "So far, everything has worked according to plan," he heard his friend's uncle saying, "he is totally down to his knees now. Time is now ripe for the final sacrifice."
>
> "Very good work, Mazi Eze-Ukwu (*Great King*)," the strange man replied, "all you need to do now is

to give enough money to his friend out there to help you bring him home latest by *nkwo* market day and we shall take it up from there. We shall trick him to the sacred temple at Ugwuolima (*Devouring Hill*) the next day, being *eke* market day, and there the price will be paid and sealed."

`Remi listened to what amounted to a full program of doom against an unsuspecting victim and barely managed to retain calm disposition by the time the two men re-emerged into the balcony area, and the strange man took his leave. When Mazi Eze-Ukwu addressed him, it was with the exact words voiced in the secret plot. He gave him enough money, as was planned, and pleaded with him to help bring his *son* back home on the appointed day; according to him, for very effective traditional remedy.

Back in Lagos, `Remi struggled to find the courage and the right words to reveal the hard truth to his friend; not just that his loving father-uncle had been responsible for all his past mishaps but that he had also concluded plans to finally end his life. Picking his words carefully and with very heavy heart, he eventually narrated all that he heard, while his friend repeatedly interjected with words like, 'I don't believe you,' 'it's highly impossible,' 'you heard it all wrong,' 'I know my uncle, you don't have any idea whatsoever.' In the end however, the two friends reached a consensus to play along carefully to establish the *truth*.

They reported the situation to the state police CID [Criminal Investigation Department] in Lagos and two plain-cloth detectives were assigned to them for the trip, and they were to coordinate action with the police outpost in the village. `Remi would *deliver* his friend as planned, and pretending to leave immediately for Lagos, return to the detectives' hideout where they would keep close surveillance on Obinna through the bug hidden on him. Obinna on his part would play along as calmly as possible; he would allow himself to be tricked into going with his uncle to Ugwuolima forest and walk the distance, while his backup would follow at close distance, armed and ready to swing into action at short notice. Once he had reached eye distance of the so-called healing temple, he would ask his uncle to allow him few minutes to step aside and free his bowl by the bush track, and then he would alert the backup and take to his heels.

The plan was followed through meticulously, and at the end of it all Mazi Eze-Ukwu, the Ugwuolima high priest and his hefty attendants were rounded up. Implements discovered at the shrine were entirely those of an abattoir rather than those of a healing ministry. As Obinna looked straight into the shamed face of his onetime loving father-uncle and listened to his horrifying confessions about how he planned to sacrifice him to elongate his own life span, he wondered how on Earth he could have known the truth about his entire situation if he had not found a true friend in `Remi. And because the final sacrifice failed, every enchantment against Obinna's life and wellbeing was automatically reversed. The truth indeed, set him free.

Translated to human situation on Earth, *Obinna* represents mankind, *Eze Ukwu and cohorts* represent Jehovah/Allah and his accomplices—the principalities; while `Remi stands for Jesus Christ, the true friend of mankind.

Simply put, the principalities refer to world rulers in general. According to Ephesians 6:12, the principalities include all *evil rulers and authorities* of the unseen world, all *mighty powers* in this dark world, and a hierarchy of *evil spirits* in the heavenly places. Ours is a hierarchical world, meaning that the principalities are made up of complex chains of categories of central, territorial, and sub-territorial rulers. Just as there is a hierarchy of various professions of human rulers and authorities on Earth and there is a hierarchy of worldly angels going up to the archangels, there is also hierarchy of principalities—*evil rulers, authorities, mighty powers* going up to the supreme *evil spirit* that presides over the so-called heavenly council. But Jesus Christ expects us to first try to understand Earthly things as prelude to understanding *heavenly* things. So, our focus here is on the principalities that are concerned with Earthly system of government.

Well, the principalities are not phantoms. Even though referred to as *spirits*, they are real persons who are even closer and seemingly dearer to our hearts than Obinna's uncle was to his. The Bible does not leave us in doubt as to who these people are. It gives us adequate, *undisguised* information on them and even freely captures some of their intrigues and antics in human history. It says that they made us whatever we are now; made for us everything we *enjoy* on Earth today and taught us everything we ever knew about ourselves and about our world. The Quran says they are 'nearer to us than our own jugular veins.'

The principalities are people we love more than life itself; people we completely look up to for our happiness and physical wellbeing on Earth. We greatly adore and willingly die en masse to protect their interest on Earth. They equally depend heavily on us for their own kind of happiness, as we are indeed, one grand family of lost souls. That is why it becomes *unimaginable* that the Bible also calls them a gang of wicked spirits in the heavens, fighting with every weapon at their disposal to stop our spiritual salvation. Surely, there is much more to the feud between the principalities and their own loyal protégés on Earth.

Paul's information in Ephesians 6:12 is deliberately diversionary though. Of course, it must be remembered that he received his inspiration directly from the stables of the same principalities during his documented encounter with them in the third heaven. They wanted him to hammer home only the dreadful, high, and mighty aspect of them, purely to create and sustain fear in the hearts of uninformed humans on Earth, thus giving themselves an edge in the war. That they are the *powerful* spirits that *rule* our present world of darkness is a fact; but Paul was wrong in insinuating that they are not *flesh and blood* and that they are entirely non-resident with us here on Earth. The principalities are a species of highly *intelligent* animals, having higher consciousness. They are most likely multidimensional beings, but they are certainly made of flesh, and a kind of blood flows in their veins as in every other species of organic beings. According to the Bible, they share exact *image and likeness* with humans on Earth. So, they are merely oversized human beings. And if they are called gods of heavens and Earth, it is because they can dwell both in the *heavens* (outer planets) and or on the Earth.

We can track down the principalities from pages of the Bible. In Genesis 1:26-27 the Scripture tells the story of a highly advanced—powerful, godlike—race of humans who brought civilization to Earth about 8000 years ago. They cloned *Homo sapiens* by mingling an aspect of their own gene with those of the aboriginal ape-man species. "**Let us make human beings in our image, to be like ourselves**," they said. And so, they did *remake* primitive ape-man aborigines; "male and female, in their own image and likeness." They did not create brand new humans on Earth but rather transformed the primitive image, likeness, and consciousness of existing species. Hence, the Bible says that man was made of "dusts [i.e., dregs] of the Earth" and "breathe of the gods."

The repeated emphasis in the Bible on human *image and likeness* is in no way allegorical, as most religious believers choose to interpret it. Those principalities were organic human beings, not perfect spirits. True spirit is pure light, but only humans can make other humans like themselves. The aliens were highly enlightened scientifically and spiritually, but they walked the Earth as *humans* in those days. In fact, Genesis 6:4 makes clear the fact that two distinct races of human beings lived and even intermarried on the Earth in those days. "In those days, and for some time after," it says, "**giant Nephilites lived on the Earth**, for whenever the sons of the *gods* had intercourse with women [daughters of men], they gave birth to children who became the heroes and famous warriors of ancient times." Our primitive ancestors referred to the alien race of human beings as gods because they exhibited extraordinary feats that were far beyond their scope of imaginations at the time.

However, what started as a people seemingly helping to impart social civilization on their less privilege brethren in another land—for we all are projected apparitions of souls belonging to the one grand solar family of fallen sons of the Father—ended up being an overambitious program of spiritual colonialism. Desiring to play gods over the less-informed *Homo sapiens* forever, they tactically cloned away spiritual cognizance from our body of intuitive knowledge, which would have made us aware of actual spiritual status quo—aware of the Father, our true selves, and the urgent need for spiritual resurrection. Immediately, they partitioned humans, introduced human governments, and placed themselves as gods, lords and kings over the provinces or principalities.

The word *principalities* derived from the status of the so-called sons of the gods as rulers and princes over their allotted territories on Earth. Deut 32:8-9 explains: "When the Most High [in the hierarchy of the gods] assigned lands to the nations, when he divided up the human race, he established the boundaries of the peoples according to the number in his heavenly court [according to the number of the sons of the gods (NRSV)]. "For the people of Israel belong to Jehovah/Allah; Jacob is his special [allotted] possession."

The whole exercise, as we can see, was purely materialistic, concerning sheer colonial ambitions of some overambitious, godless race. Jehovah/Allah's *allotted* share was the tribe of Israel. That was how he officially became 'god of Israel' and principality over the territory of Jerusalem and its environs. Evidently, he was not god of my hometown, Arondizuogu, as every tribe of peoples on Earth had its own god, whether in Europe, Asia, or Africa. Jehovah/Allah would eventually rise to the rank of unanimous head of the ruling princes to become the sole *'Prince of this world,'* a strategy that gave the gods needed unified voice and action against the heavenly Christ that was expected to come into the world in human form. Accordingly, Quran 40:15 calls Jehovah/Allah "possessor of the highest rank" among the highest chief gods of the Earthly kingdoms, and Quran 114:1-3 refers to him as "The lord of mankind, the king of mankind, the god of mankind." But he remains one among the principalities; and merely an oversized human being all the same.

The Bible explains why it was expedient for the gods to unify their forces behind the tribal god of Israel. "They will all agree to give him their power and authority," it says, so that "Together they will go to war against the Lamb [i.e., Jesus Christ]." [Rev 17:13-14] Therefore, the Devil that tempted Jesus Christ during the start of his Earthly ministry, as captured in Luke 4:5-7; that "showed him all the kingdoms of the world" and said that all the authority and their glory "**has been delivered to him**" was none other than Jehovah/Allah. After all, the war against the heavenly Christ was taking place in his allotted territory. He was referring to the fact that the gods had unanimously granted him express authority to fight Jesus Christ and his liberation mission on Earth on their behalf. "**Who is like thee, O Jehovah/Allah, among the gods**," sang Moses, "Who is like thee, majestic in holiness, terrible in glorious deeds, doing wonders?" [Exodus 15:11]

It should be noted however, that though the gods now seem united behind Jehovah/Allah in their crimes against humanity, Jehovah/Allah's ascent to the throne of Earth's system of government did not come easy. All the so-called Old Testament battles that Jehovah/Allah fought using the Jews as his land armies were territorial battles against specific principalities that opposed his ascension to the unified throne. They would later inspire Muhammad of Arabia to deny that they were ever at each other's throat over tussle for supremacy. "I had no knowledge of the Highest Chiefs when they disputed;" recited Muhammad, "It is revealed unto me *only* that I may be a plain warner." [Quran 38:69-70]

Anyway, Jehovah/Allah is but one of the wicked principalities and rulers of this present dark world. So, who are the other *faceless* Earthbound principalities? They are the people we ordinarily know and revere as Archangels. According to the Bible, seven of them together form the world ruling council of kings of heavens and Earth, presided over by Jehovah/Allah. They are the *invisible* rulers of Earth's present system of things. Revelation 12:3 refers to a potent seen by John—"a large red dragon with seven heads and ten horns, with seven crowns on his heads." Each of the seven crowned heads of the great red dragon represents one of the seven crown archangels—Michael, Gabriel, Raphael, Uriel, Raguel,

Zerachiel and Remiel. The Bible ratifies names and identities of the first four men-archangels, while those of the last three differ with various sources on the subject. But that is not important. The important thing is for us to know that these men are not spirits or phantoms. Contrary to Paul's distorted information, they are *powerful* humans, made of flesh and blood.

Gabriel revealed entire Quran to Muhammad, and he had reason to clarify the status quo, regarding Jehovah/Allah's status as *sole* ruler of the Earthly kingdoms. "There is not [just] one of us," he revealed to Muhammad, "but [each] hath his known position. Lo! We, even we are they who set the ranks. Lo! We, even we are they who hymn his praise." ... "Lo! Thy Lord is surely one: Lord of the heavens and of the Earth and all that is between them, and Lord of the sun's rising [i.e., Lord of the eastern tribes]." [Quran 37:164-166, 4-5] Quran 7:97-98 makes it clear that Jehovah/Allah, Gabriel, and the rest are simply partners, and that whoever is an enemy of one is enemy of all— "Say (O Muhammad, to mankind:) Who is an enemy to Gabriel! ... Who is an enemy to Allah, and his angels and his messengers, and Gabriel and Michael [and the rest]! Then, Allah (himself) is an enemy to the disbelievers."

Psalm 82:1-2 reveals that Jehovah/Allah presides over the council of Earthbound principalities and confirms that he habitually favors and prospers wicked human rulers who serve their collective interest on Earth. Here, David affirms, "Jehovah/Allah takes his place in the divine council; **in the midst of the gods** he holds judgment," and then he asks him, 'How long will you judge unjustly and show partiality to the wicked?'" Indeed, Jehovah/Allah's vocation on Earth is not a peaceable one; trying to beat humanity into absolute spiritual subjugation requires that he can only work with inhuman minds. Therefore, his is not the camp of those who show mercy.

Jehovah/Allah once referred to King Nebuchadnezzar of Babylon as 'my servant,' 'my king of kings,' 'my hammer of justice;' then he used and dumped him, turning him into a wild beast. Daniel 4:17 reveals what Daniel called 'decree of the watchers" and 'word of the holy ones" over King Nebuchadnezzar—"For this has been decreed by the messengers; it is commanded by **the holy ones** [Jehovah/Allah and his partners), so that everyone may know that the Most High rules over the kingdoms of the world. He gives them to anyone he chooses—even to the lowliest of people."

Paul's admonition in Romans 13:1-7 concerning why people should be subject to governing authorities on Earth was based on his recognition of Jehovah/Allah as the supreme ruler of Earth's system of government through the ruthless men he puts in power. "Everyone must submit to governing authorities," he wrote, "for all authority comes from Jehovah/Allah, and those in positions of authority have been placed there by Jehovah/Allah. ... They are Jehovah/Allah's servants, sent **for the very purpose of punishing** those who do what is wrong." [Romans 13:1, 4] We know however, that Jesus Christ is not in any way involved with the rulership of the world; that he is not in league with the principalities and their wicked viceroys on Earth. Jehovah/Allah, the devil, attempted to draw him into the league but failed, as Jesus Christ could not be bought over with worldly goods and their false glory like ignorant humans. We read in Luke 4:5-7 that Jehovah/Allah showed Jesus Christ the kingdoms of the world and offered to "give him the glory of the kingdoms and authority over them," according to him, "because they are his to give to anyone he pleases." He made the same offer to Nebuchadnezzar and to every other ruthless king the world ever had. But Jesus Christ says clearly in John 18:36, "My kingship is not of this world." So, we know for sure that Paul was neither ministering for the Father nor for the heavenly Christ.

Therefore, no one on Earth should be in any doubt about who the wicked *spirits* in the heavens are or why wicked people who serve their diabolic interests on Earth prosper. 1 John 5:19 says that "the whole world is in the power of the evil one." That evil one, as far as Earth's system of government is concerned, is none other than Jehovah/Allah personified. He states his position clearly in the scriptures, saying, "I kill and I make alive; I wound and I heal; ... I form light and create darkness, I make weal and create woe, I am Jehovah/Allah, who do all these things." [Deut 32:39; Isaiah 45:7] He rules the kingdoms of men and sets ruthless men and women as he wishes over the nations as chieftains, governors, presidents, clergies, and business magnates.

The Quran says it as bluntly as it should be said,

- "Lo! The Earth is Allah's. He giveth it for an inheritance to whom he will. ...
- He it is who hath placed you [human rulers] as viceroys of the Earth and hath exalted some of you in rank above others ...
- And thus we [the council] made in every city great ones of its wicked ones, that they should plot therein. They do but plot against themselves, though they perceive not. ...

- Thus, we let some of the wrongdoers have power over others **because of what they are wont to earn [because of their desire for material gains]**." [Quran 7:128, 6:165, 123, 129]

Hence, the Bible asks in Amos 3:6, "Does evil befall a city, unless Jehovah/Allah has done it?" And the Quran says the same thing; "No calamity befalleth save by Allah's leave. ... Naught of disaster befalleth in the Earth or in yourselves but it is in a Book before we bring it into being— Lo! That is easy for Allah."

It should be made clear at this juncture that our primary concern is with the Earthbound principalities whose activities affect us directly through the complex system of Earth's government that they invented and control. It should also be clearly stated that the evil ones rule every aspect of Earthly institutions. They control all government agencies, all customary religious institutions, and all underworld activities on Earth to the spiritual detriment of the general masses. They empower government officials to *rule over* the masses, charismatic religious authorities to blindfold and *despiritualize* multitudes of the laity and criminals of various inclinations to terrorize and sustain state of insecurity and fear in human communities.

To the principalities, the wicked rulers who serve their purpose well on Earth are the righteous ones—they are *holy* men and women—while those who speak out against their devious wicked ways are evildoers and "Sabbath breakers." Abraham was declared *righteous* because he represented ultimate model of blind faith, Roman Catholic Pope is officially made *infallible* in his office as supreme overseer of the largest flock of religious zombies on Earth, while Jesus Christ was molested and crucified as a *Sabbath breaker* for preaching spiritual emancipation of captive human souls.

Jehovah/Allah's *holy* ones work discreetly toward banishing true wisdom, righteousness, and ingenuity in people, while making them believe that they are benefiting a million-fold. According to Lao-tzu, "the *holy man* rules by emptying people's hearts (minds) and filling their bellies, weakening their [spiritual] wills, and strengthening their bones, ever striving to make the people knowledgeless and desireless." That is exactly what our religious, political, and criminal kingpins do for the principalities in return for worldly gains. Religious institutions brainwash and subject humanity through satanic creeds and doctrines, government agents implement policies that stagnate spiritual wellbeing of the people, while institutionalized criminal class attack both minds and bodies of their unfortunate victims.

We can conveniently say therefore, that the principalities include the hierarchy of wicked human rulers that serve in their various capacities and stations as viceroys of the faceless gods. Judging from facts on ground, it should not be difficult for people to see that the whole Earth is in the power of the evil ones indeed. Life on Earth is increasingly becoming dangerous, miserable, and meaningless, and the principalities are the brains behind it all.

Referring to the principalities as *spirits residing in the heavens* is sheer religious propaganda. There is no pure spirit in entire universe and 'heaven' here is relative. Earth is as much heaven as any other planet of the solar system. It all depends on where one is standing. Someone standing on the surface of Mars will refer to Earth as heaven and vice versa. The only true heaven is the perfect spiritual abode of the Father and his perfect sons. No entity in entire universe belongs to or has direct access to that heaven. As John 3:13 (NIV) says, "No one has ever gone into heaven except the one who came from heaven—the Son of Man." Wherever the colonizing principalities may have come from, theirs is only one of the wretched colonies within the solar settlements for organic beings. They are as organic and animalistic as every animal and human on planet Earth. The same sun animates us all. That they are not *flesh and blood* like every one of us is also a big lie. All available records show that they are fully genetically compatible with us. Hence, they freely intermarried with our own race. In fact, they belong to Earth as much as we do.

Genesis 6:4 says that they lived on Earth "in those days, and also afterward." The so-called gods only withdraw their full colonial presence in the public view or the "marketplace," scared away by overpowering influence of the heavenly Christ on the worldly stage and following the official death of Jehovah/Allah in the consciousness of thinking humans. But they remain mingled among us to this day, hiding under all manners of occult and esoteric umbrellas; much like the British who withdrew officially from their colonies in Africa but remained physically present and still manipulating the stage secretly. Moreover, descendants of the gods mentioned in Genesis 6—the so-called giants begotten by union of sons of the gods and daughters of men—remained and multiplied on Earth. The Bible calls them "the mighty men that were of old, the men of renown." These were the biological ancestors of various *royal* families on Earth in those days and afterward, which was how the term "royal blood" came about.

The British crown literally administered the nations on Earth on behalf of the undercover principalities, defining and maintaining the status quo, because she is of the *royal blood*. The principalities paid, and still pays her handsomely for her ingenuity at serving the interest of the colonizing gods. They enabled Britain to colonize many countries of the world herself. However, Jehovah/Allah confirms that in whatever these so-called distant descendants of the gods *plot* on Earth to sustain the status quo in favor of the principalities that "they do but plot against themselves, though they perceive not." [Quran 6:123] Britain acquired colonial mentality from her secret mentors and plotted everlasting domination over her numerous colonies all over the Earth. But she only fools herself believing that *royal* or *Aryan* blood means anything to the Prince of the world. British crown and her counterparts all over the world are nothing but 'favored slaves' of the principalities at their own peril. If only they know the truth, they would have been in the forefront of the oppressed masses, fighting the so-called heavenly council for genuine human unity, and for ultimate spiritual salvation of entire human race. For what will it profit any nation or anyone, if he gains the whole Earth and forfeits spiritual resurrection to true life eternal?

So, the principalities are our close relatives, as close to us on Earth as the British are to their less-civilized African colonies. In fact, we are one big, disunited family. As we say it these days regarding the various classes of civilizations on Earth; the world is indeed a global village. After all, the so-called heavens and Earth belong to the same solar family. The gods, being highly advanced scientifically, had long developed and perfected instant ways of travelling between the planets—between the so-called heavens and Earth at breathtaking speed. This is no longer difficult to believe. Our scientists have already successfully landed humans on the Moon and soon we will be able to establish human colonies on the Mars. When that happens, and if some lower animal species exit on Mars, they will equally look up to us as *gods of heavens and Mars*. And they will be wrong, just as we are wrong about Jehovah/Allah and the other so-called *gods of heavens and Earth*. Gherman Titov, the second human in the outer space, had this to say when asked about how his space flight affected his philosophy of life: "Sometimes people are saying that *God* is out there. I was looking around attentively all day, but I didn't find anybody there. I saw neither angels nor *God*." Indeed, religious notion that Jehovah/Allah dwells in the heavens is clearly borne out of original ignorance.

The principalities are merely mortal beings from another planet of the solar system. They are here and there as readily as they desire purely because they have the scientific knowhow. With their help, most mystics and secret societies' operatives experience out-of-body **astral travel** on regular basis too. Astral travel is scientific; it is real, and the Bible is full of allusions to that. It records that Enoch was taken to the heavens bodily. Elijah was taken up bodily too by certain space vehicle—a *chariot of fire and horses of fire*; he rode by whirlwind into the heavens and Elisha watched it all. Virtually all the old prophets of Israel were equally given the mystical free ride into the heavens to witness Jehovah/Allah's numinous throne and preoccupying proceedings—matters concerning perpetual spiritual colonization of humans on Earth.

Now, which worldly leader will publicly accept that he works for the principalities? Which average religious believer would have imagined that Jehovah/Allah and his so-called archangelic partners are the wicked spirits in the heavens that pose stumbling block on our way to spiritual salvation? Who would have believed that Jehovah/Allah, *the lord, king, and god of mankind* is colonizer and the archenemy of humankind? Even now, how does one make orthodox Jews see that Jehovah/Allah has been their greatest enemy all along; that Jesus Christ is their true Messiah and that he came for their rescue? Or how can anyone make zealous Muslim suicide bombers understand that true jihad should be directed against Allah and Gabriel and the entire colonizing heavenly council and not against fellow human slaves of Allah on Earth? Or how can one even begin to tell staunch born-again customary Christians that Jehovah/Allah is the dreadful Antichrist they should resist in every aspect of their lives on Earth?

WHY ARE THE PRINCIPALITIES FIGHTING HUMANS ON EARTH?

A man in my village who was always quarreling and fighting with his wife was once asked by the elders to explain why they could not respect and live in peace with each other and he answered, "Supremacy… my elders! It's all about supremacy, control, and dominion! You should tell my wife that a woman's husband is her lord. That is what the Bible says!"

Well, the only reason we quarrel and fight in the world is because we are animals. We are animals because we are very far away from the Father. The man and his wife were suffering from spiritual poverty, brought about by spiritual dislocation or death. The same Bible that incites ignorant men to 'rule over' their weak and defenseless women counterparts says it all. It asks, "What is causing the quarrels and fights among you? Don't they come from the evil desires at war within you? You want what you don't have, so you scheme and kill to get it. **You are jealous of what others have, but you can't get it, so you fight and wage war to take it away from them.** Yet, you don't have what you want because you don't ask the Father for it. And even when you ask, you don't get it because your motives are all wrong— **you want only what will give you pleasure**." [James 4:1-3 NLT]

Wars and strife are inevitable in the world; for, as we have seen, life without the Father is full of limitations. Confronted with the inevitable problem of mortality and uncertainties surrounding organic existence, organic beings struggle to stay alive by the day. They do not only struggle to obtain lion share of the meager sustenance and opportunities that are steadily dwindling, but they also literally trample on each other to *succeed*. The situation is the same in every level of organic existence. Life without the Father is simply a case of eat up the others or be eaten yourself. Bigger fishes in the sea swallow smaller ones just to stay alive, stronger animals do the same in the wild, and the higher animals—humans and the so-called gods—do the worst. They vilify, torment, cannibalize and sacrifice each other even in the name of entertainment. The mighty and the cunning dominate and rule over the weak and the underprivileged; the oppressed tries to resist and so there is an unending conflict. There are wars of ascendancy, wars against colonialism, slavery, racial and economic oppression. There are revolutions and counterrevolutions; violent struggles for various reasons and violent suppressions all over the world. All these are but some of the natural hallmarks of godless existence.

Life, in the heavenly kingdom of the Father, is peaceful, delightful, and fulfilling. Every perfect son of the Father has eternal life; he is endowed with limitless potentials and enjoys freedom of infinite self-expressing within boundless space. And divine love of the Father unites all in absolute harmony of purpose within the heavenly household. There is absolutely no place or reason for rivalry, rancor, or strife. That is what the heavenly Christ means in John 14:2 where he says, "There is more than enough room in my Father's home." We can visualize the strength of love and unity of purpose in the realm of lights in terms of inseparable federation of homogeneous luminosity.

In the imperfect, finite world of matter founded by fallen, dead spirits in the realm of darkness, anarchy reigns supreme. Wars are our instinctive reaction to the sense of futility associated with organic existence. John Fowles captures that as the *nemo* complex in his book, *The Aristos*. "Nobody wants to be a nobody," he writes, "It is necessary to make my name known; I must have power – physical, social, intellectual, artistic, political ... but power. I must leave monuments; I must be remembered. I must be admired, envied, hated, feared. In short, I must endure, I must extend, and beyond the body and the body's life." [*The Aristos*, Group 2:90, 96]

Thus, everyone desires to excel—to dominate others—and no one wants to be dominated. We forfeited our eternal privileges in peace and perfection and literally died to all our rich spiritual potentials when we abandoned the realm of divine light and hence, the positive sphere of the Father's divine love and providence. Spiritual poverty brought about spirit of competition and the desire to outwit and dominate one another within the limited environment. Spirit of true communism, modesty, justice, equity, and godliness gave way to false living, selfishness, greed, opportunism, power mongering, conceit, bitter rivalry, wickedness, willful oppression, violent suppression and more. The principalities are hopelessly fighting to uphold their *nemo*—to sustain the false identities they had created for themselves.

Against this backdrop, Jehovah/Allah and the so-called archangels excelled in selfishness and greed and seized opportunity to establish their false kingdoms on Earth. Deut 32:8-9 says that they partitioned the Earth into principalities, divided its inhabitants and set themselves as territorial princes, lords, kings and gods over the less informed peoples. They systematically dominated their underprivileged brethren, demanding unquestioning loyalty and even worship from them that are due only to the Father. The principalities literally rewrote the history of our present existence in a way that totally muffled our collective spiritual heritage in the Father.

Arrogating to themselves credit as sole creators and owners of the world, they dictated heavily falsified religious scriptures to overpowered *prophets* in various tribes that suited their calculated evil intrigues. "Unto each nation have we given sacred rites which they are to perform," they say in Quran 22:67. While denying preexistence of fallen human spirits, they promoted themselves to the status of transcendent, *living* spirits that reside in the heavens. Thus, the Bible asserts in 1 John 5:19 that "the whole world is in the power of the evil one(s)." However, they are fallen dead spirits just as every one of us on Earth. They are equally organic, mortal beings, made of flesh and blood. And they are false kings, lords, and gods, because there is only one eternal King in existence whose heavenly Kingdom transcends entire spheres of the finite universe. The heavens that the principalities publicize as their dwelling places are purely imaginary and are strictly set within the planets of our very solar system.

One would then ask; since the whole world is in the power of the principalities, what then is their fighting all about? First and foremost, the principalities are fighting because they are animals. Like lions and tigers in the wild, they will cease to exist if they stop fighting. According to my town's man-*lord-of-the-house*, and in the eyes of the uninformed, the principalities may seem to be fighting for *supremacy, control, and dominion*. But they are also fighting for survival. In any case, fighting for absolute dominion over humans on Earth means that they do not really have it. It means that they are accountable to some higher authority that threatens their overall false dominion. Besides, unpredictable nature of organic existence assures that the hunter can easily become the hunted; even the mightiest predators can suddenly become terminally endangered. In the universe, no condition is permanent. The principalities are necessarily endangered in their own mentality and so, they are fighting to remain relevant in their falsehood.

As animal tamers will tell us, wild animals simply do not want to be loved and rehabilitated. They want to continue forever in their hapless wilderness. The heavenly Christ came into the world with love to redeem us all from our universal wasteland, but the principalities refused to be loved and redeemed. His sudden advent with divine mandate for our spiritual salvation caught the principalities off guard, as his divine emphasis on humility, repentance, and selfless love for one another gave no room for their inordinate colonial ambitions. Furthermore, divine election of unenlightened Adam and Eve and their posterity as custodians of Christ's mission on Earth dealt severe blow on their ego as the more enlightened species. So, they are not merely fighting to retain undue lordship position over ignorant human inhabitants on Earth, but also to make sure that Adam's posterity does not reap the full benefit of their divine election.

Fueled entirely by greed, arrogance, and impenitence, they chose the path of dishonor in the Father's heavenly call to perfection. Rejecting Christ's offer of spiritual restoration themselves, they vowed to prevent humankind from doing so. Thus, they are fighting to put an end to mankind's spiritual evolution; to forestall our ultimate spiritual redemption by Jesus Christ. Surely, no enlightened mind on Earth will knowingly allow them to have their way without a fight.

In fact, the great tribulation of these days that the heavenly Christ spoke about during his second advent is not unconnected with the climaxing effect of Christ-consciousness all over the world. Christ's overall victory over the inglorious gang of impostors has brought about dramatized death of Jehovah/Allah, our onetime *god almighty*, in the consciousness of enlightened minds. The Scripture says that "He [Jesus Christ] disarmed the principalities and powers and made a public example of them." [Col 2:15] So, the principalities are involved in a battle of shame and contumacy, characteristic of wild animals.

That Jehovah/Allah is an animal is incontrovertible; for animals are known by their actions and not by mere religious rhetoric. How else can one describe a being that enjoys bloodbath, that habitually instigates massacre of defenseless humans and perceives burning stench of blood of his innocent animal and human victims as *pleasing odor*? Jehovah/Allah is as barbaric and carnivorous as lions and tigers in the wild. As a lion violently rips life out of its defenseless preys and enjoys aroma of fresh blood and flesh of its strangled victims, so also does Jehovah/Allah feed on the flesh and life force of multitudes of victims of violent human tragedies and wars that he secretly instigates among his ignorant human preys. According to the Bible, bloodbath in wars and violent social conflicts serve as official *harvest of blood sacrifices* for Jehovah/Allah. Every day of violence and bloodshed on Earth, according to Jer 46:10, is Jehovah/Allah's days of vengeance on enlightened humanity. Such a day "is the day of Jehovah/Allah of hosts, a day of vengeance, to avenge himself on his foes. The sword shall devour and be sated and drink its fill of their blood. For Jehovah/Allah of hosts holds a sacrifice …." unto himself on such a day.

Contrary to Paul's notion, the principalities are not pure spirits, but physical entities, made of flesh and blood and animated by light energies from the sun. They live and die like every one of us. Pure spirits are pure lights; they do not exist anywhere in entire universe. The principalities only differ from us in that they are most probably multidimensional beings, possessing higher consciousness. They possess higher level of scientific and occult knowledge than we do. But they think and behave like wild animals all the same, having willfully rejected opportunity to be divinely re-perfected by the heavenly Christ.

In the end, we can see that this meaningless existence is all that the principalities live for. They will all sink into eternal oblivion the moment they fail to sustain the status quo. Everything they stand for is at stake here. So, they cannot stop fighting and behaving as wild animals. Foolish pride will not allow them to. Neither should people who have chosen spiritual salvation by Jesus Christ stop resisting their conniving wiles.

WHAT THE PRINCIPALITIES' FIGHT IS ALL ABOUT

Let me say clearly at this juncture that the principalities are not fighting to annihilate humanity. If that was their aim, no single human being will be left on the surface of the Earth today, considering the height of their scientific knowhow. Extinction of humankind is not in their interest. They need ignorant humans more than ignorant humans need them. They are rather fighting to banish traces of spiritual enlightenment in people to literally return humanity to pre-Edenic mode of existence; to regain species of ignorant humans that they can conveniently dominate and exploit forever. They can be likened to a group of self-centered slave merchants fighting tooth and nail to perpetuate their outlawed business. The principalities are in the business of trying to resist divine wind of change over the world. But a battle against divine change is certainly a very futile one. Opposing the will of the Father for the world is foolishness and utter self-condemnation. Yet, the principalities have many reasons to be so involved. These include:

A. TO RETAIN ULTIMATE DOMINION OVER HUMANS ON EARTH

The principalities are a worse kind of colonial masters over human beings on Earth. While nations colonize nations for interim material advantages in a dynamic international arena, the principalities hold our fallen dead spirits in eternal bondage. They colonize and enslave our souls and we are fighting for spiritual liberation. We will understand this better by looking at colonialism in its local context.

When some civilized western nations decided to explore Africa, their primary motives were to learn what they did not know about the continent and to harness whatever benefits they could for their own homelands. While in Africa, they *discovered* valuable natural resources and primitive populations that lacked basic social and economic civilization. Their ambitions quickly altered, and they systematically began to colonize the aborigines, capitalizing on their own higher levels of academic, social, and economic knowledge. They harnessed the natural resources in the colonies and channeled the proceeds toward development of their own nations, while impoverishing and using the aborigines as slaves in their own lands. They even took the able-bodied ones away as slaves to their own nations to serve them. Thus, colonialism, human slavery and slave trading prospered on Earth. Ignorant countries like Britain, France, Germany, Spain, Belgium, USA, and Portugal arrogated to themselves absolute authorities to rule over their less informed African brothers as colonial masters, kings, queens, and lords. They saw absolutely nothing wrong in utilizing the chance opportunities they had over their own kit and kin. After all, the game of this life is that of 'the survival of the fittest' and of 'the winner takes it all.' Western people took it all at the expense of their less privileged African kinsfolk.

In time however, some illustrious Africans gained considerable enlightenment and started conscious movements for national liberation. Africans fought for national self-determination and eventually gained a kind of national independence. But although the colonial masters bowed to consistent pressure mounted by kind-hearted abolitionists, both foreign and local, and withdrew their central machinery of direct colonial control over Africa, they left in place institutions and wily policies that helped them to retain social and economic control over the colonies. Nigeria for instance; she secured independence from Britain since October 1, 1960, but despite abundant resources at her disposal, her people still languish in penury and backwardness, because of subtle stumbling blocks left in place by the British crown that were designed to make self-governance difficult. Overall, while history books have it that African continent enjoys independence, African people remain slaves to their western brothers even within their own countries to this day.

In the beginning, alien Nephilim, annunaki, or whatever they were called, came from their own distant planet to explore opportunities on Earth. Like the British in Africa, they discovered gold and other precious resources. They also *discovered* very primitive population of human species, to which they imparted a measure of mental ability and physical improvement, intended to enhance their usefulness as colonial slaves. They also brought to Earth a measure of improvement in agriculture and science. As it were, most of our scientific subtexts have direct bearing to the distant traditions of the Nephilim. This is especially paramount in astronomy and celestial mathematics. For instance, the prevailing number *twelve* that finds expression in our knowledge of the twelve signs of the zodiac, twelve-hour time scale, twelve-month calendar year, standard imperial measures, and so on stem from them. As Zechariah Sitchin notes in his book, *The 12th Planet*, "There were twelve Greek Titans, twelve Tribes of Israel, twelve parts to the magical breastplate of the Israelite High Priest. The power of this celestial twelve carried over to the twelve Apostles of Jesus, and even in our decimal system we count from one to twelve, and only after do we return to 'ten and three' (thirteen), 'ten and four,' and so on. Where did this powerful, decisive number *twelve* stem from? From the heavens." [Zechariah Sitchin, *The 12th Planet*, page 202]

Then, they systematically began to colonize the minds of their slaves through cultural religious traditions. By performing extraordinary *scientific* feats on Earth, they marketed themselves as gods from the heavens and successfully conned the ignorant aborigines into worshiping them as such. Jehovah/Allah established a zoological garden in Eden, which he branded a Paradise; and it seemed so to Adam and Eve whom he deployed there 'to till and keep it' for his personal pleasure. The Bible captures image of Jehovah/Allah strolling majestically within the garden at cool of evenings, admiring his farm as any rich human slave master on Earth would. Adam and Eve were purely slave gardeners in Jehovah/Allah's pleasure park. He intended them to remain his slaves forever, and they did, until something special happened that changed their destiny for good. A sudden encounter with the heavenly Christ brought them spiritual enlightenment and rescue from absolute spiritual enslavement. Subsequently, the heavenly Envoy decisively sacked Jehovah/Allah's Edenic slave camp and inaugurated his redemptive mission for Adam's posterity—first, from spiritual captivity in the hands of the colonizing principalities, and ultimately from spiritual death in the universe. The principalities are fighting to return enlightened humanity to Edenic mode of existence and that is already a lost battle for them.

B. TO CONTINUE RECEIVING UNDESERVED WORSHIP FROM IGNORANT HUMANS ON EARTH, PRETENDING TO BE GODS

To continue receiving undeserved worship from multitudes of ignorant religious devotees on Earth, the principalities must promote and sustain state of religious primitivism. By preventing us from having clear knowledge of the Father and of our past as perfect spirit beings in the Father's heavenly Kingdom, they can successfully deter us from seeking spiritual resurrection and restoration through the heavenly Christ. So, they are fighting to perpetuate our present state of chronic ignorance, and hence spiritual death, so that we will remain their religious slaves and worship them forever.

For any single fallen human spirit rekindled and liberated on Earth, there is one captive less in their grip. Therefore, anyone who tries to create spiritual awareness among humans on Earth threatens their position and they fight the person with every weapon they can muster. The heavenly Christ came into the world to call us back to the steadfast love of our heavenly Father; he came to rekindle and resurrect our fallen spirits. That, to the principalities, meant he had come to dispossess them of their religious slaves and to crumble their kingdoms of falsehood on Earth. So, they are fighting to confuse our understanding of Christ's redemptive mission to prevent us from knowing and asserting our spiritual rights. Customary religions of the world help them to achieve this.

C. TO TAKE AWAY FROM US OUR RIGHT TO TRUE LIFE ETERNAL THAT THEY REJECTED THEMSELVES

The Father's will is that all his fallen sons in the world should be rekindled and resurrected. The principalities rejected the Father's gracious offer themselves, believing that they have situational advantage over other animals in the world. Determined to prevent us from recognizing and receiving that divine bequest for ourselves, they fight against Christ's redemptive mission in the world in every way they can. Therefore, they are fighting to take away from us our priceless right to perfect life eternal, which many of us do not yet appreciate the full value of.

We read the cryptic message in Genesis 3:24 (GNT) about how Jehovah/Allah deployed "living creatures and a flaming sword which turned in all directions at the east end of Eden." And the Scripture tells us plainly that "This was to keep anyone from coming near the tree that gives life." Knowing and coming near the Father to regain our true spiritual selfhood is the crux of the battle. The principalities want to beat enlightened humanity back into Edenic mode of existence—into spiritual primitivism—where we would be spiritually vulnerable to religious manipulations; where it would be impossible for us to differentiate between the Father and Jehovah/Allah, the impostor. "(But it was said unto them [humankind]): Flee not," says Quran 21:13, "but **return to that (existence) which emasculated you** and to your [Edenic] dwelling, that ye may be questioned."

That ungodly agenda is increasingly becoming an impossible task for the principalities, as Christ-consciousness is progressively sweeping through the nations. Evolution of human knowledge is steadily leading us away from Eden and toward our true heavenly homeland. A call to return to Eden is a call to spiritual retrogression. Enlightened humanity will never willingly succumb to that. That is why the war rages on. The "living creatures with flaming swords which turned in all directions" that Jehovah/Allah stationed at the east side of the Garden of Eden, is only a cryptic way of alluding to the belligerent principalities and their resolute commitment. Their principal aim, as the verse says, is "**to keep anyone of us from reaching the Divine Tree that gives eternal life**." We already know that the Father is the Divine Tree of Life, so the principalities are terminally bent on preventing us from regaining our spiritual heritage and our rightful places in the Father's heavenly household.

Now, which right-thinking human being on Earth will not fight Jehovah/Allah and his ignoble partners with his last drop of blood to regain his pride of place in the Father's perfect heavenly Domain? The battle may seem difficult, but the principalities are fighting a lost battle, because Jesus Christ who fights on our behalf is more than able to defeat them all. Indeed, the main battle for our spiritual salvation is between the heavenly Christ and the principalities. He is their real enemy, but because they are powerless before him, they are taking out their frustrations on gullible human beings on Earth. Nevertheless, every soul must make a choice and take a stand in the ensuing battle. Jesus Christ is only here to fight and win for those who resolutely accept the Father's gracious offer. That choice is our actual punch in this battle for true life.

D. TO PROTECT THEIR UNDUE *SPIRITUAL* ADVANTAGES, OR RATHER THEIR HIGHER SCIENTIFIC AND OCCULT KNOWLEDGE OF THE WORLD

There is the possibility that the principalities are multidimensional beings, possessing advanced knowledge of science and higher spiritual consciousness. In our worldly setting, science is knowledge in a multidimensional way. The other extreme to that is ignorance. Advance knowledge of science is the power and the secret of principalities' dominion over our human race. They are fighting to keep it that way forever.

But let me quickly clarify this; what we call *spiritual* in our present state of consciousness is esoteric *science*. The principalities hold complete monopoly of that, and only disburse inconclusive piecemeal of it as *esoteric intelligence* to some of their special initiates among us to make them appear to the rest of us as geniuses. It is not uncommon to hear some scientists speak with pride about being in touch with the source of esoteric mathematics, for instance.

Now, we know that the Father is **Omniscience**, meaning he is infinite dimensional consciousness. True sons of the Father mirror his divine nature within the realm of perfect existence. As fallen sons of the Father in our godless universe, the closest thing to our divine nature is **science**—multidimensional consciousness or knowledge in a multidimensional way. The farthest is **ignorance**—outright spiritual unconsciousness or knowledgelessness. The universe is purely a scientific contraption, with every aspect of it corresponding to some meticulous mathematical principle. The principalities have advanced knowledge of universal principles and processes and that gives them greater insight into spiritual matters. Anyone who knows how the world was made will most definitely know that the Father did not make it. He will know that it is contrary to Divine Design, and he will be sure that "friendship with the world is enmity with the Father." Such a person will understand perfectly what spiritual salvation is about and he will not be confused about the uniqueness, divine nature, and mission of Jesus Christ in the world.

Primitive human beings, like their animal cousins on Earth, were closer to state of ignorance than to science—closer to outright spiritual unconsciousness than to knowledge of the Father. But that was not because the vital lights of the souls of lower animals know less; rather it was because the cosmic program that allotted levels of consciousness to organic beings arbitrarily determined the hierarchy. That is why the place of authority and dominion occupied by the principalities is all because of chance. As it is said, '*all fingers are not equal*'; but that the middle finger happens to be longest is only by chance. It was all supposed to be world's idea of beauty in diversity. Unfortunately, the highly privileged see their transient position of advantage as a right over the underprivileged because ignorance and selfishness rule the minds of godless beings.

Against this backdrop, we can now begin to understand the rationale behind Jehovah/Allah's official attitude toward Adam and Eve in Eden. Accepted that the alien colonialists imparted a measure of knowledge to ape-like human aborigines on Earth and transformed our primitive ancestors into *Homo sapiens*, the facts remain that they specifically wanted us to remain in absolute ignorance of spiritual matters. They needed that edge to be able to rule over us. Their first law to Adam and Eve, forbidding them from acquiring or seeking to acquire the knowledge of good and evil simply amounted to "thou should not know the Father." Of course, if they could not differentiate between good and evil neither could they differentiate the Father from Jehovah/Allah, the impostor.

Thus, Adam and Eve who, by the way, represented entire *Homo sapiens*, became spiritual slaves of the principalities. They remained ignorant as commanded, to the extent that "the man and his wife were both naked and were not ashamed." [Gen 2:25] It took the timely intervention of the heavenly Christ to alter the status quo and rekindle their divine nature. But instead of accepting that the game was up for them, the principalities opted to fight, even when they knew that they would not be fighting against ignorant humans but against the Father's Divine Will. It was very understandable that godless minds never know when to swallow their pride; but it also exposed the principalities' chronic level of ignorance. It is ignorant for one to start a fight he knows he can never win. Therefore, the principalities are not all that scientific or spiritual, after all.

E. TO RETAIN MEANS OF MAGICALLY ELONGATING THEIR ORGANIC LIFESPAN

Organic existence has one insurmountable problem—inevitability of death. When we have made all the money in the world, had all the fame, power and dominion over others, we always surrender all at the foot of the ultimate ravager, death, immediately our individual vital light sources time out. Every animal in the world is faced with the same great problem of how to overcome death. George Orwell's *Animal Farm* tenet that "All animals are equal, but some animals are more equal than others" does not hold here. Before the throne of death, all animals are indeed equal. The higher animals worry about death as do the least animal within our solar family. While most adult insects live but a few days, birds and rodents only a few years, humans can live up to 120 years and a bowhead whale, up to 200 years. Some species of jellyfish can live up to 400 years, some trees, up to 4000 years and creosote desert bush up to 11700. The gods might live even longer. But every organic being dies in the end.

The principalities are mortals; they have searched in vain, as have our great kings, alchemists, philosophers, and even modern scientists, for the vital principle or the hypothetical elixir of life—the miraculous substance that would prolong organic life *indefinitely*. Well, one does not have to be a scientist or superhuman to understand that immortality is impossible for the life that is generated by our dying sun. For life to be eternal or *indefinite*, the source of it must be everlasting. Our sun dies and so does every being that is animated by it. Eternal life is only possible within the realm of lights because Divine Light is eternal. Hence, Jesus Christ encourages us to seek eternal life the only place that it exists, in the positive side of the Father.

In absence of any possible scientific means of prolonging organic life indefinitely or any official philosopher's stone that could cure all ills, higher animals resorted to esoteric magic—an underhanded, *unscientific* means of violently robbing other people of their vital life energies to at least, give themselves longer life spans. Considering our ever-worsening stressful lifestyles on Earth, we can barely manage to add negligible number of extra years to our life spans through conscious dieting, using the gym and avoiding undue stress. The principalities, on their part, can elongate their life spans by magically feeding on invisible life energies violently stolen away from lower animals through ritual bloodletting in various forms of gruesome animal and human sacrifices. They also harvest life energies from the many violent deaths occurring in natural disasters, ghastly accidents, wars, social banditry, and from official governments' capital punishment programs. In recent times, the principalities rely heavily on new wave of Islamic terrorism and suicide bombing to harvest vital life energies from victims of their violent attacks. Most people never wondered why the principalities love violence and it seems they cannot do without bloodshed. Indeed, they feed on brutality. In their bid to absolve Jehovah/Allah for all the gruesome animal and human sacrifices of the Old Testament days, some blinded religious believers argue that he was merely using the death of sacrificial animals and humans 'to help humankind to see the horrors and futility of rebellion and selfishness,' and also to foreshadow when he would 'allow himself to be crucified upon a cross to bring forgiveness to those who had condemned themselves to death through their own unjustified rebellion.'

What a way of turning black into white in the mentality of his religious slaves! Jehovah/Allah demanded and received blood sacrifices of animals and humans, as did other local deities all over the Earth, because he derived life from them. The gods fed on the short-circuited vital life force of the sacrificial victims. All blood sacrifices are cruel; they are a serious business for the principalities, not a symbolic of anything else. Jehovah/Allah told his Jewish religious slaves explicitly that "blood is his food and that the sacrifices should be everlasting." Of course, as we all need food to stay alive, so does Jehovah/Allah need his own type of food to stay alive. And Gabriel speaking through the Quran says that they are not joking about these things at all. "We created not the heaven and the Earth and all that is between them in play. If we had wished to find a pastime, we could have found it in our presence—[that is] if we ever did." [Quran 21:16-17]

There is no symbolism for Goodness. Something is either good or it is evil. The Father is always good; he cannot be tempted to give symbolism for his intended goodness with gruesome cruelties involved in all forms of animal and human blood sacrifices. People who believe that Jehovah/Allah was merely acting or saying something else when he was enjoying *sweet savor* of burnt blood of innocent animal and human victims are still living in primitive Edenic mode. They still do not know the difference between good and evil. In fact, the principalities instigate most violent calamities that befall us in our day-to-day existence on Earth, because they are invigorated by them. "No calamity befalleth save by Allah's leave," says the Quran; and "Naught of disaster befalleth in the Earth or in yourselves but it is in a Book before we [the principalities] bring it into being." [Quran 64:11; 57:22] The emphasis here is on *violent deaths*. As we know from our mundane experience of medical science, when people die violently their vital organs are still alive, and if quickly collected and preserved, they can be successfully transplanted into living people who need such organs. In the same vein, people who die violently are still full of life energies and the principalities know how to quickly harness and gulp up the energies to add to their life spans under strict esoteric overdrive.

They are not interested in people who die of old age or sickness because their life energies would have been fully used up. That also explains why they always demand ritual sacrifices of infants, young virgins, and able-bodied young people; people who have their vital life energies virtually intact. Blood sacrifice therefore is the cryptic means through which ignorant ritualists transfer life and power to mortal deities to keep them alive and vigorous in return for evil favors. It is evident in most African villages that great numbers of rural gods have long died off since most of their village adherents became enlightened enough or converted to Christianity and stopped supplying them with their regular rations of sacrificial blood of animal and human victims.

Jehovah/Allah officially inaugurated the darkest magic known in esotericism for violently robbing lower animals of their animating light energies the very first day that he inspired Abel to shed the blood of animal in sacrifice to him and turned around to incite Cain to murder him in cold blood. We see clearly from Jehovah/Allah's mock judgment on Cain in Genesis 4:8-16, in the first recorded fratricide case, that he protected the murderer because he worked for him. From that day to this day, the principalities have demanded and received animal and human blood sacrifices from ignorant human beings all over the world without allowing them to know the true reason behind the gruesome rituals.

Most often these days, we hear of greedy men and women who join dangerous cults in search of extraordinary riches, fame, power, and other social advantages in life. In exchange for their ungodly desires, the principalities behind these cults secretly lure them into committing serial ritual murders or into offering other forms of animal or human blood sacrifices, usually of persons closest to them. Sometimes they command them to bring certain human body parts, knowing that they will have to violently kill the victims before they can harvest their body parts. Of course, it is not the body parts they are after, but the life energies harvested from the violent death of the sacrificial victims.

Are we surprised that religion has been the official instrument of the blood-sucking principalities right from the onset? Animal and human blood sacrifices have played and still play central roles in virtually all religions of the world, both ancient and contemporary. Most religious rites and festivities are usually marked by compulsive slaughter of various kinds of animals. Ignorant religious believers see in them some imaginary symbolisms; like the sheer mental cannibalism of customary Christian extraction seen as *transubstantiation* by exponents of the Eucharist. Year after year Muslims violently shed blood of millions of defenseless rams on Eid al-Adha, pretending that they represent blood of the ram that Jehovah/Allah allowed Abraham to substitute for his son, *Ishmael*. However, according to Marshall Brain, in his book, *Why Won't God Heal Amputees*, "When we read about animal sacrifice in the Old Testament, what we discover is a *God* who must be insane. No rational human being can accept that an all-loving, all-knowing, all-powerful *God* could possibly support animal sacrifice."

F. TO PERPETUATE ORGANIC EXISTENCE, IN A HOPELESS BID TO SUSTAIN ARTIFICIAL ETERNITY WITHOUT THE FATHER

Kick-starting the process of organic existence within the solar sphere was the ultimate accomplishment of the fallen dead spirits involved. It did not come easy at all, and it is not something that can be stopped and restarted at will. Now, for as long as the sun shines in the sky, organic processes of births and deaths promise to cycle on indefinitely. The principalities rejected spiritual redemption from the system in the hope that they will continue in their position of authority and dominion over lesser species of organic beings forever. Death of the sun will naturally bring about definite end to organic existence within the solar sphere, but that was expected at a very distant time.

However, Christ's mission of spiritual redemption threatens to bring to abrupt stop the wheel of false eternity represented by the weaving loom of births and deaths. It calls for outright detachment from sexual enslavement to the vicious cycle of DNA propagation matrix that represents life of the world. Nothing can be more desirable than to have our souls be the ones living instead of the DNA viruses that are replicated and powered by our captive souls. But to make the transition means refraining from all forms of sexual participation—it ultimately means saying no to sexual intercourse, no to marriage and no to childbearing. Jesus Christ says in Luke 12:49, "I came to cast fire upon the Earth; and would that it were already kindled!" The principalities understood him very well and cried out through demoniacs, saying, "What have you to do with us, O Son of the Father? *Have you come here to torment us before the time?*" [Matt 8:29]

Jesus Christ assured that the great tribulations of our present age will culminate in the total extinction of the false lights that sustain the false life of the world. "Immediately after the tribulation of those days the sun will be darkened, and the moon will not give its light, and the stars will fall from heaven, and the powers of the heavens will be shaken," he says in Matthew 24:29. Indeed, calling for outright spiritual resurrection of the dead souls that animate the world is tantamount to casting fire of extinction on organic existence. That spells doom to the colonial ambitions of the principalities, and so they are hopelessly fighting to sustain the status quo.

We read in the Old Testament how desperately the principalities favored indiscriminate procreation, as means of generating multitudes of ignorant subordinates on Earth. "Be fruitful and multiply and fill the Earth" expresses the innate yearning of the principalities. Because of that they turned blind eyes to incest for as long as it yielded offspring, as in the case of Lot and his two daughters. They inspired and made friends with chronic-minded polygamists; from Abraham, with 3 wives, to Solomon that established a free-for-all royal brothel of 1000 wives and concubines. Also, Jehovah/Allah established the culture of wife transfer between dead men and their living brothers and personally dealt ruthlessly with men who would not continue procreation with their dead brothers' widows, as in the case of Onan, second son of Judah. Genesis 38:7-10 tells us that Jehovah/Allah killed Onan because he "spilled the semen on the ground" rather than produce offspring by his dead brother's wife.

It was obvious therefore that Jehovah/Allah was merely bluffing in Genesis 6:7 when he threatened to put an end to organic existence on Earth during the great flood. "I will blot out man whom I have created from the face of the ground, man and beast and creeping things and birds of the air, for I am sorry that I have made them" was the direct opposite of his innate desires. Of course, he could not and did not do that. Rather he swore never again to even contemplate that. "While the Earth remains, seedtime and harvest, cold and heat, summer and winter, day and night, shall not cease," he says in Genesis 8:22.

The question is if we can put a definite halt to biological evolution on Earth who gains and who loses? What will be the physical and spiritual implications for both the losers and the gainers? If therefore, we have a choice, as the heavenly Christ gives us today, to choose between spiritual resurrection to true eternal life and continuing in spiritual enslavement to the hapless DNA matrix that represents false life of the world what will be our informed choice? No doubt, it is wiser to choose true life rather than living in death. But to choose true life one must first choose death to the false life of the world. This means that one should knowingly wrestle down the principalities that obstruct the way to the Divine Tree of Life with the last drop of his false life. For, as Jesus Christ says, "He who loves his life loses it, and he who hates his life in this world will keep it for eternal life." [John 12:25]

COMPLEX NATURE OF PRINCIPALITIES' ATTACKS

Now that we have known who the principalities are and why they are fighting us, our next logical step is to try to understand their various methods of attack. The Bible and the Quran give us full and authoritative information on the incurable obsessions of the principalities—their impure desires, predictable intrigues, unfulfilled dreams, frustrations, vicious struggles, highhanded attacks, unrestrained utterances, and their resolute determination to drag as many unsuspecting human souls as they can to eternal damnation along with themselves. "And if thy Lord [Jehovah/Allah] had willed, he verily would have made mankind one nation, yet they cease not differing," says Quran 11:118-119, "And the word of thy Lord hath been fulfilled: **Verily I shall fill hell with the jinn and mankind together.**" ... "Rivalry in worldly increase distracteth you until ye come to the grave. ... Nay, would that ye knew (now) with a sure knowledge! For ye will behold hell-fire [you will see that you are already in hell-fire]. Aye, ye will behold it with sure vision." [Quran 102:1-7]

Just as the Bible and the Quran attribute fundamental features of our social and scientific civilization to the principalities, they also reveal that they are largely responsible for most of the vices and calamities that befall human beings on Earth today. Some aspects of perpetual human sufferings and death on Earth are calculated effects of their programmed attacks. In accordance with their express determination to extract religious worship from Earthly humans at all costs, they had sworn to "cast terror into the hearts of those who disbelieve [in them]." "We mete out death among you," they say, "and we are not to be outrun, that we may transfigure you and make you what ye know not. ... Wheresoever ye may be, death will overtake you, even though ye were in lofty towers. ... Naught of disaster befalleth **in the Earth or in yourselves** but it is in a Book before we bring it into being—Lo! That is easy for Allah." [Quran 3:151; 56:60-61; 4:78; 57:22] So, we know that they are very determined, and their attacks are premeditated. Their aim is to inflict as much physical pains and horrifying deaths on humanity to scare us into total submission to their ungodly will.

In view of all that, the Scripture says to us, "Stay alert! Watch out for your great enemy, *the devil*. He prowls around like a roaring lion, looking for someone to devour." It says, "Resist the devil and he will flee from you." [1 Pet 5:8"; James 4:7-8] But how can we effectively resist an attacker if we do not recognize his methods of attack?

Let me state clearly here that in our Earthly situation *the Devil* is none other than Jehovah/Allah, the well-known spokesman of the ruling devils that make up the so-called heavenly council of principalities. It is obvious that he is not acting alone. But the word *devil* is merely attribute of any spirit, person or animal that is violent, evil, or ungodly. We are all devils in the world; every living being without the Father is animal and devil. But evilness has categories; some people are more devilish than others. The principalities rank highest in that regard, with Jehovah/Allah being at the apex of the pecking order. Both the Bible and the Quran confirm that Jehovah/Allah is extremely violent and malicious. **"Jehovah is a man of war ... a devouring fire ... a jealous god."** [Exodus 15:3; Deut 4:24] These were how Moses described the deity that he encountered, knew very well, and served intimately in his capacity as *inspired* Jewish tribal warrior and governor.

But let me restate clearly here once more, that no entity in the world is completely evil. Absolute evil destroys itself and therefore, cannot exist. Jehovah/Allah, *the Devil*, is not the cause of all evils that befall humans on Earth, just as colonial Britain is not the cause of all the economic hardship presently experienced by Nigerians in their country. Just as Nigerians have peculiarities that make them who they are, human nature does have its own natural drawbacks. Contrary to what many uninformed people think, the devil does not have that kind of power. He is merely a seasoned manipulator of innate tendencies of imperfect human minds. Pretending to be absolute originator and dispenser of evil on people is only one of his intimidation tactics. He is almost entirely powerless before any person who knows what he knows.

People who understand Jehovah/Allah, the Devil and his limitations know that no weapon that he fashions against anyone can prosper without the help of that individual. One preacher in Nigeria puts it this way: "No weapon fashioned against you [by the evil one] shall proper, but the one you fashion against yourself *must* prosper." That is why the Scripture says, "Resist the devil and he will flee from you"; meaning that we all have the power to resist him. The devil is purely a sneak and a tempter. His name in my dialect is interpreted as "*ekwe osu*," meaning "if you agree, then he begins." But once one has allowed him to acquire the upper hand over him, as in the case of Abraham and his religious descendants, he wields enormous powers that can crush both body and soul to death.

Ordinarily, suffering and death are natural aspects of life without the Father. Every living being in the world suffers and dies as a matter of inevitability. Jehovah/Allah, the devil suffers more than everyone else on Earth and he dies too. For, as the Scripture says, "The wicked are like the tossing sea; for it cannot rest," and "There is no peace ... for the wicked." [Isaiah 57:20-21] The principalities generally manipulate evil tendencies of ignorant minds to turn suffering and death into horrifying experiences for people to compel them to look up to them as gods for respite. For instance, Jehovah/Allah confesses in Ezek 20:25-26 that he gave his Jewish victims "statutes that were not good and ordinances by which they could not have life; and defiled them through their very gifts in making them offer by fire all their first-born," just so that he "**might horrify them.**" And he says, "**I did it that they might know [or rather think] that I am the Lord.**"

In fact, Jehovah/Allah boldly refers to himself as the *master schemer*, meaning he is just a seasoned *manipulator* of people. He assures us that his evil intrigues are thorough and unbeatable.

- "Lo! My scheme is firm," he says. ...
- "Are they [ignorant masses] then secure from Allah's scheme? None deemeth himself secure from Allah's scheme save folks that perish. ...
- I give them rein (for) lo! My scheme is strong. ...
- Those whom Allah sendeth astray, there is no guide for them. He leaveth them to wander blindly on in their contumacy." [Quran 68:45; 7:99, 183, 186]

Indeed, Jehovah/Allah is the ultimate *Svengali*—evil manipulator. It is obvious that no human being on Earth can withstand or be able to wriggle out of his complex web of hypnotic control without divine assistance, and that is where the heavenly Christ comes in. People who fight with his divine guidance and insight will not only withstand but will also triumph over Jehovah/Allah and his entire bloodthirsty heavenly and Earthly hordes. "Here on Earth, you will have many trials and sorrows," Christ assures his true followers, "But take heart, because I have overcome the world." [John 16:33]

To understand the seriousness of the raging battle, the extent the principalities have gone and are willing to go to perpetuate spiritual enslavement of fallen human spirits on Earth, and their diverse mode of attacks, we need only to focus closely on Jehovah/Allah's actions and utterances in human history, as he is the official spokesman of the inglorious ones. After all, he is also the commander-in-chief of their so-called heavenly and Earthbound armies. Moses extolled him as "man of war" and as the most ruthless among the wicked gods. "Who is like thee, O Jehovah/Allah, among the gods?" he sang, "Who is like thee ... terrible in glorious deeds, doing wonders?" [Ex 15:11] Moses did not make the mistake of addressing Jehovah/Allah as 'the Father of war,' because he was simply one *powerful* man whom he saw face to face and spoke mouth to mouth with, as a man speaks to his fellow man. Jehovah/Allah himself confirms that Moses was an intimate friend, saying, "I speak to him face to face, clearly, and not in riddles! He sees Jehovah/Allah as he is." [Nu 12:8] We know therefore, that we can trust Moses' personal testimonies for better understanding of Jehovah/Allah's true character and methods of attack on humanity.

Jehovah/Allah's violent exploits and high-handed outburst through Moses are well documented in the Bible for everyone to see. Testifying to his Jewish victims, Moses further highlighted the complex nature of Jehovah/Allah's methods. "Now search all of history, from the time *God* created people on the Earth until now, and search from one end of the heavens to the other," he charged them, "Has anything as great as this ever been seen or heard before? Has any nation ever heard the **voice of god speaking from fire**—as you did—and survived? Has any other god dared to take a nation for himself out of another nation **by means of trials, miraculous signs, wonders, war, a strong hand, a powerful arm, and terrifying acts?** Yet, that is what Jehovah/Allah your god did for you in Egypt, right before your eyes." [Deut 32-34]

Indeed, no record exists in the annals of entire human history of any deity more depraved, underhanded, and ruthless than Jehovah/Allah. He is the utmost example of someone suffering from spiritual poverty. Hence, the principalities invested completely in him to fight their ungodly battle. The Scripture says, "These are of one mind and give over their power and authority to the beast;" so that "they will make war on the Lamb," unified under his express command [Rev 17:13-14] Jehovah/Allah is the *beast* that presides over the council of warring principalities.

A. IGNORANCE: CORE OF ALL HUMAN WEAKNESSES

Ignorance is Ungodliness. It is a mass of spiritual darkness that looms over all fallen souls in the world. While the higher animals, like Jehovah/Allah and the so-called archangels, can peep through hazily, lower animals live in total blindness. They live in outright enslavement to unreality, as interpreted by those who see but vaguely. In our world of blind entities, half-blinded ones like Jehovah/Allah, Gabriel, Michael, and the rest have become kings, lords, and gods. That is very unfortunate.

The difference between wild animals and humans is knowledge. We dominate, enslave and rule over them not because we are worthier souls, but simply because we know a little bit of what they do not know now. The difference between the principalities and every other human being on Earth is also knowledge. They know a little more than we do now. Hence, they have continued to posse as lords, kings, and gods of the universe to us. But sudden advent of the heavenly Christ into the world as light of knowledge promises to overturn all ungodliness. The principalities fight to sustain the status quo, as I know humans would if they, on their part, have had cause to feel threatened by lower animals' revolt for liberation. If chickens would suddenly put their feet down today and refuse to be slaughtered and eaten by humans, I am sure humans will fight to reestablish the status quo. This is the way of the world.

Surely, it is not godly that human beings ride on horses. Neither is it godly that Jehovah/Allah and his partners have turned us into religious slaves. The only reason we ride on horses is because they do not know their rights and therefore, do not fight for it. We battle against the principalities for spiritual emancipation because we now know our divine rights, as revealed to us by the heavenly Christ. That is the graphic description of the situation we are dealing with here.

Ignorance is the worst blight of human nature. An ignorant person is a natural stooge. He is as powerless as a blindfolded adult, held hostage by a bunch of giggling little girls. Manipulating human ignorance was and still is the most potent weapon of control and dominion in the hands of the principalities over humanity. *In the beginning*, making the humans honor and worship them as gods was as easy for the principalities as it is for humans making their donkeys carry their heavy loads on their backs with extraordinary obedience. Human beings do not worry about what they say or do in presence of their cats, dogs, horses, and donkeys because they are dumb and will always love, respect, and serve them. In the same way, the gods did not have to look over their shoulders to be assured of the steadfast loyalty of their unconscious human slaves. Jehovah/Allah and his colleagues enjoyed absolute control and lordship over their allotted peoples in their various principalities on Earth.

Without knowledge of the difference between good and evil, our primitive ancestors were blind enough to be totally subservient to the principalities. They had no way of knowing the difference between the Father and the strange *men* they revered and worshiped as gods. They had no way of recollecting their past spiritual heritage and their divine rights to spiritual knowledge and true eternal life. To them ignorance was bliss, and their slave masters, simply jolly good fellers. But sudden advent of the heavenly Christ into Eden overturned all that in favor of the blinded Edenic humans. The Scripture states that **"their eyes opened."** [Gen 3:7] Then everything began to change. Suddenly, the principalities did not only have to be cautious of what they say and do before the humans on Earth; they also began to devise other tactics to try to re-blindfold and re-subjugate the newly *enlightened* ones. The time of jolly-mindedness fizzled away as the slave masters were forced to put on real combat gears. However, they had already said and committed so many blunders before man that they could not easily retract.

At first, they panicked, as we all can easily deduce from Jehovah/Allah's panic statement in Genesis 3:22— "Behold, the man has become like one of us, knowing good and evil; and now, lest he put forth his hand and take also of the tree of life, and eat, and live forever." That was a clarion call for urgent remedial actions on their part. They tried to cover up, to rescind or to *barricade* unguarded information they had unwittingly divulged to man concerning the Tree of Life. But it was all too late. The heavenly Christ had already enlightened the humans and revealed the Father to them as the Tree of Life. He had already presented to them the divine yardstick with which to judge righteousness for themselves.

It was remarkable how divine spirit of love and unity quickly took root among the descendants of Adam and they eagerly longed with one mind for the journey of reconciliation with the Divine Tree of Life. As the Bible reports in Genesis 4:26; descendants of Adam were already calling on the name of the Father. We should remember that the name of one of Adam's sons, *"Abram"* meant, *"The Father is Exalted."* Unfortunately, Jehovah/Allah eventually abducted, re-blindfolded and turned him into *"Abraham,"* making him his personal religious stooge to the detriment of his numerous descendants and religious protégés. Abraham represented a total regression into original ignorance.

At first the principalities invented brash decrees, laws, and all manners of ordinances to try to contain evolution of human knowledge. But "thou shall not eat of the tree of the knowledge of good and evil, for in the day that you eat of it you shall die," was purely a wishful decree made in retrospection. Evidently, it was merely invented for the pages of the Bible to try to explain away divine events surrounding the unexpected advent of the heavenly Christ and the resultant *ascent of man* that took both man and the principalities by sudden.

Next, the principalities resorted to physical assaults in way of divide-and-rule tactics to break down collective resolve of the united humans. The incident documented in the Bible as *battle* of the Tower of Babel speaks clearly of principalities' offensive on the newly enlightened and united humanity. Jehovah/Allah said to his partners in crime, "Behold, they are one people, and they have all one language; and this is only the beginning of what they will do; and nothing that they propose to do will now be impossible for them. Come, let us go down, and there confuse their language, that they may not understand one another's speech." [Gen 11:6-

7(NLT)] And they did. The story has absolutely nothing to do with any physical building project. It rather captures principalities' willful attack on true communism and onset of Christ-followership on Earth. Besides, the attackers stated their worries clearly, and they had to do with the fact that humans were united in their resolve to reach the Father—*who is in heaven*—for ultimate spiritual redemption.

What people never wondered about was who vested humanity—Adam's descendants—with divine spirit of love, peace, and oneness before the physical coming of the heavenly Christ since Jehovah/Allah and his wicked partners were terminally opposed to that. Surely, that was a proof that mission of the heavenly Christ began far back in Eden when he first appeared and opened the eyes of Adam and Eve. Although Jehovah/Allah dismissed him as a serpent, he was already making Christ-like impacts in the lives of peoples in the old world.

With scattered human languages came spirit of misunderstanding, antagonism, disunity, rivalry, and enmity, which eventually gave birth to all kinds of social ills that are associated with tribalism, nationalism, colonialism, racism, cultural discrimination, sectarian religiosity and the like. That ungodly giant stripe alone dealt an indelible blow on the onset of human unity and collective spiritual thrust. It effectively beat enlightened humanity back into the Edenic stockade of ignorance and gave the principalities badly needed respite to plan and perfect complex tactical combat strategies before the physical reappearance of the heavenly Christ on Earth. No truly enlightened mind will fail to read story of the Tower Babel as principalities' calculated attack on spiritual ascent of mankind. I call it collapse of the *First true Communism*. But sons of Adam prophesied hope in the expected physical reinforcement by the Messiah who gave his word of honor in the first place that "man will not surely die!"

B. RELIGION: ABOMINATION THAT MAKES DESOLATE

Having successfully demolished the peoples' zeal for the symbolic Tower to the Father—*who is in heaven*—and dashed their hope of progressive fellowship with the heavenly Spirit of Love and Unity, the principalities invented **religion** to completely obliterate the way that leads to the Father. Then they began to promote themselves systematically and vigorously as gods of heavens and Earth. The less-ingenious members of the ruling gods established tribal shrines and officiated as faceless gods through possessed priests and oracles. But with the reluctant support of the entire bandit council, Jehovah/Allah embarked on the most irresponsible and overambitious scheme in the life of any mortal being in the world by attempting to usurp the sovereign position of the Father on Earth. His plan was to systematically metamorphose himself from a mere ethnic mountain deity into a Sovereign *God Almighty* in the world and thereby to short-circuit the Father completely out of existence in the peoples' minds. Thus, religion represents abomination that makes desolate peoples' innate desire to seek for and reach the Father.

In the so-called prophesy of *Immanuel* alluded to in Isaiah 7:14, Jehovah/Allah was speaking about himself in his capacity as the god that dwelt physically among the Jews. It should be noted that the word *Immanuel* means, "god is with us," as explained in Isaiah 8:10 and not "God with us" that refers to presence of the heavenly Christ in human form. To further clarify the fact that Jehovah/Allah is but *Immanuel* for inhabitants of Jerusalem, he revealed to Ezekiel concerning the city, saying, "Son of man, this is the place of my throne and the place of the soles of my feet, **where I will dwell in the midst of the people of Israel forever**. ... "And the name of the city henceforth shall be, **Jehovah/Allah is there**." [Ezek 43:7; 48:35] Then, in accordance with his final projection, he says in Zechariah 14:9, "Jehovah/Allah will become king over all the Earth; on that day Jehovah/Allah will be one and his name one." On that day, Jehovah/Allah will finally show himself as man that he is and openly declare himself *God* in Jerusalem; and that will literally represent image of *the desolating sacrilege* spoken of in the book of Daniel. The question, "what will it profit a man, if he gains the whole world and forfeits his life?" seems most appropriate for Jehovah/Allah indeed.

As we can see, religion was purely a worldly institution. **Religious propaganda**, spiced up with cheap magical feats fooled the *confused* people into believing and worshiping the principalities as gods. The *super*men also inaugurated all manners of self-demeaning ethnic cults, cultures and traditions in their various principalities that promoted and sustained spiritual primitivism among the peoples. In no time, religious fever had swept through the whole land like wild forest fires and consumed the very burgeoning fabrics of peoples' minds, conscience, and common sense. Ultimately, human beings became classified as *religious animals*. And like animals they succumbed to all kinds of inhuman religious rituals and sacrificed their divine rights to eternal life to every foul spirit that inspired a strange belief system on Earth.

Religion captures and brainwashes humanity right from infancy and today, **religious passion** has become universal. It is simply another name for **original ignorance**, and it is perhaps the most devastating weapon of spiritual enslavement invented by the principalities. A people that once beamed with genuine enthusiasm and strived with one accord to reach the Divine Tree of Life that is in Heaven, now meanders in total darkness from one bizarre religious shrine to another seeking after criminal-minded entities that promise nothing but paltry material benefits on Earth, while forgetting that "man's life does not consist in the abundance of his possessions." [Luke 12:15] To every religious animal on Earth today, the crucial question still stands: "What will it profit a man, if he gains the whole world and forfeits his life?" [Matthew 16:26]

It can be said that Jehovah/Allah's religious gambit has worked exceedingly for him so far. It can be clearly seen that the heavenly Christ elected Adam and Eve to lead us to the Father—*who is in heaven*—through gradual but steady spiritual enlightenment, but Jehovah/Allah invented Abraham out of Abram to return us to spiritual primitivism through blind faith. Having invented and groomed *Abraham* as model of *blind religious followership*, he went ahead to generate of his religious descendants thoroughly brainwashed zealots who propagate him as *God* and do not look back in fighting for his ungodly interests on Earth.

He put the sons of Israel through untold national agonies and humiliations via famines, exiles, enslavements, pogroms, wars and sustained national insecurity to harden them enough to fight the most crucial of his battles—against the expected Christ incarnate. At some point, Moses explained the drill to the battered population of Jewish Exodus, saying, "And you shall remember all the way which Jehovah/Allah your *god* has led you these forty years in the wilderness, **that he might humble you, testing you to know what was in your heart, whether you would keep his commandments, or not.**" [Deut 8:2-3] Yet, his only incentive to the Israelites was mere promise to resettle them permanently in Jerusalem; a promise he knew he would never fulfill.

Thus, when the time came, top Jewish religious authorities did not hesitate to keep Jehovah/Allah's commandment that decreed death on a tree for *"the prophet who would come speaking in the name of another God."* They meticulously identified Jesus Christ as the expected target, sniffed around him for reasons to take offense at him, and eventually crucified him on a tree in strict accordance with Jehovah/Allah's commandment. However, Jesus Christ did not fail to tell his Jewish assailants in very clear words that they were possessed by Jehovah/Allah's murderous spirit: "You are of your father the devil, and your will is to do your father's desires. He was a murderer from the beginning, and has nothing to do with the truth, because there is no truth in him. When he lies, he speaks according to his own nature, for he is a liar and the father of lies." [John 8:44]

In strict accordance with his prophesied pogrom on the Messiah and his immediate apostles and disciples in Zechariah 13:7-9, Jehovah/Allah inspired Saul of Tarsus immediately after the crucifixion to persecute and exterminate early true Christ-followers. The same Saul later went through a stage-managed metamorphosis to become Paul, and then founded fake Christianity that openly propagates itself as Church of Jehovah/Allah all over the world. Thus, followers of customary Christianity honor Jehovah/Allah as *God Almighty* in their hearts, while merely calling Jesus Christ 'Lord, Lord' with their mouths.

No wonder Jesus Christ says to them; "Not everyone who says to me, 'Lord, Lord,' shall enter the kingdom of heaven, but he who does the will of my Father who is in heaven. On that day many will say to me, 'Lord, Lord, did we not prophesy in your name, and cast out demons in your name, and do many mighty works in your name?' And then will I declare to them, 'I never knew you; depart from me, you evildoers.'" [Matt 7:21-23] But operatives of the Universal Church of Jehovah/Allah seek material rewards, here and now, and Jehovah/Allah pays them handsomely for helping him to bastardize the true gospel of Jesus Christ and for proselytizing the world to his cause while calling the name of their true Messiah in vain.

The sons of Ishmael, like their Jewish brethren, were likewise driven into the hash desert of Arabia by god of Abraham and endlessly drilled as homeless nomads till they developed the communal suicidal *muruwah* spirit necessary for the religion of Islam, which is Jehovah/Allah's official sequel to Judaism. As Keren Armstrong explains in her book, *A History of God*, "Western scholars often translate *muruwah* as 'manliness' but it had a far wider range of significance: it meant **courage in battle**, patience, and endurance in suffering and absolute dedication to the tribe. The virtues of *muruwah* required an Arab to obey his *sayyid* or chief [or prophet or religion] at a second's notice, regardless of his personal safety; he had to dedicate himself to the chivalrous duties of avenging any wrong committed against the tribe and protecting its more vulnerable members."

With that kind of mental conditioning, god of Abraham had prepared the sons of Ishmael for Islamic *jihad*, terrorism, suicide bombing and absolute religious adamancy. Not surprisingly, Islam stands for total blind surrender to the will of Jehovah/Allah, who is both Antichrist and anti-humanism. Furthermore, to get the Muslims to kill and die for his murderous cause without any reservation was relatively easier. The long years that he made the sons of Ishmael live as barbarians in desolation made them envy their Jewish brethren, and they longed greatly for eventual visitation by god of their father Abraham.

Eventually, Jehovah/Allah answered their prayer, raised for them a great prophet, an inviolable shrine and a *qiblah* of their own. He also gave them pride of place among wealthy nations of the world and enriched them enough to transform the harsh desert environs of the Arabian region into garden cities, watered automatically with underground irrigation systems. He further promises to reward good Muslims and *shohids* who sacrifice their lives for his devilish cause by transporting them to some "Gardens of Eden." He says to them in the Quran, "Think not of those who are slain in the way of Allah as dead. Nay, they are living. With their Lord they have provision. ... As for such, theirs will be **Gardens of Eden** wherein rivers flow beneath them; therein they will be given armlets of gold and will wear robes of finest silk and gold embroidery, reclining upon thrones therein. ... Allah promiseth to the believers, men and women, **Gardens underneath which rivers flow**, wherein they will abide—blessed dwellings in **Gardens of Eden** ... That is the Supreme triumph." [Quran 3:169; 18:31; 9:72]

This is Allah's equivalence of eternal reward in heavenly Paradise as promised by the heavenly Christ. Sadly, Muslim faithfuls indeed consider it *supreme triumph* sacrificing their bodies and souls for Jehovah/Allah's selfish colonial ambitions on Earth, only to be sent to some imaginary Gardens of Eden to recline on cushion chairs, wearing gold bangles and silky garments embroidered with gold. Consequently, Jehovah/Allah boasts that Muslims are casehardened for his cause. And they are, as we can see from unflinching resolve of fanatic Muslim terrorists and suicide bombers. "Of the believers are men who are true to that which they covenanted with Allah," says the Quran, "Some of them have paid their vow by death (in battle), and some of them still are waiting; and they have not altered in the least; that Allah may reward the true men for their truth, and punish the hypocrites. ... "Lo

Allah loveth those who battle for his cause in ranks, as if they were a solid structure." [Quran 33:23-24; 61:4]

On the other hand, the Quran openly mocks Jesus Christ as a prophet without portfolio, a Sabbath breaker, a corrupter of the land and a loser. And it brags about how the principalities degraded and ran him out of the land. "The only reward of those who make war upon Allah and his messenger and strive after corruption in the land," it says, "will be that they will be killed or crucified, or have their hands and feet on alternate sides cut off, or will be expelled out of the land. Such will be their degradation in the world, and in the Hereafter theirs will be an awful doom." [Quran 5:33]

Karen Armstrong, in her book, *A History of God*, equally views Muhammad and Islam as successful, while Jesus Christ and Christianity are failures. She wrote, "The success of Islam was as formative as the failure and humiliation of Jesus have been in Christianity. ... Christianity is supremely a religion of suffering and adversity and, in the West at least, has arguably been most authentic in times of trouble: it is not easy to square Earthly glory with the image of Christ crucified. Islam, however, is a religion of success. ... **Unlike Christ, Muhammad had not been an apparent failure but a dazzling success**." [Karen Armstrong, *A History of God*, pages 159, 366]

But was Jesus Christ really a loser? Did the son of man die in vain on the cross in Jerusalem? Well, the miles will be counted when the whole race has been run. Then, the true winner and loser will become undisputed. Surely, Jesus Christ has his own divine strategies, which may not make sense to *religious animals* on Earth now. In any case, the Scripture says, "Because the Father's children are human beings [on Earth]—made of flesh and blood—the Son also became flesh and blood. For only as a human being could he die, and only by dying could he break the power of the devil, who had the power of death. Only in this way could he set free all who have lived their lives as slaves to the fear of dying." [Heb 2:14-15 (NLT)] Crucifying the Son of man is already turning out to be the greatest undoing of the principalities. Nevertheless, the battle is still ongoing. Christ's mission is steadily gathering steam and true Christ-followers are gradually reemerging. From experience, we can all be sure that the first to throw the punch is not always the one that wins the fight in the end.

Judaism and Islam are premeditated war machinery invented by Jehovah/Allah for his ungodly cause. Categorically speaking, they are antichrist by willful design, while customary Christianity is antichrist by default. These are exclusive institutions of the world, serving interest of the principalities by enslaving peoples' souls to them. However, Jews, Muslims and customary Christians are but ignorant victims. They are savable souls, and Jesus Christ is here to redeem them. They are expected to open their inner eyes now to see that it is rather reasonable for one to die saving his own soul than dying for religions that offer no real spiritual benefit to the individual.

C. RELIGIOUS MANUALS: CRIMINAL IN INTENT AND CONTENT

The next formidable weapon of control and spiritual enslavement over humankind instituted by the principalities comes under **religious manuals**—the so-called **Holy Books** of the world. It is only natural that since the principalities instituted worldly religion to cut humanity off from the Father, they would also be the ones to provide their devotees with up-to-date manuals designed to bring out the deadliest effects they expect of their religious intrigues. As should be expected, these complex war manuals are criminal in intent and content.

For instance, though the Bible helps us to discern the perfect attributes of the Father, it overwhelmingly markets Jehovah/Allah as he, and that is a lie because Jehovah/Allah's deeds and utterances as documented in the verses starkly contradict the flawless qualities of the Father. Again, though prophecies about the coming of the heavenly Christ are well-documented in the Bible, as well as proofs that Jesus Christ of Nazareth is the expected Messiah, the Bible subtly misleads potential disciples of Jesus Christ by promoting false apostles like Paul of Tarsus who preach worldly prosperity in the name of Jehovah/Allah, the antichrist. The Quran, on its part, bluntly embraces religious violence in the name of Jehovah/Allah and has absolutely nothing positive to say about the heavenly Christ and his redemptive mission in the world.

These ungodly books are great propaganda machinery for the gods. They are very subtle spellbinders. They offer the principalities unprecedented opportunity to execute the battle against humanity right within peoples' gullible minds. First, they attack and disable peoples' innate reasoning faculties, replacing their natural yearning for knowledge with blind *beliefs*. Second, they smother peoples' common sense, conscience, and spiritual personalities, replacing them with blind faith. What emerges then, are unconscious followers of what the books say and not what is agreeable to good reason. That way the so-called holy books of the world have systematically transformed one-time loving and peaceable humanity into religious hypocrites, dogmatists, fanatics, zealots, bigots, terrorists, and suicide bombers. People should think deeply about this.

Books like the Holy Bible, Glorious Quran, Book of Mormon, Vedas, Puranas, Mazdean Scriptures, Kabala and the rest are evil in most subtle ways. They are undoubtedly, the greatest source of human disunity in our world today. Of course, they are not given to strengthen but rather to undermine human unity; to perpetually stifle our innate humanitarian instincts to forestall our collective spiritual evolution. Incentive for all kinds of social vices in our world today can be traced to the pages of these ungodly scriptures—religious antagonism, wars, ethnic cleansing, terrorism, suicide bombing, ritual killings, and various kinds of religious racketeering. Colossal damages are steadily done to human integrity and spirituality through interpretation of the sheer satanic verses, as intended by the clandestine authors. Never in the history of humanity has any evil been meted out on people that are not inspired by one or more of these books. That is exactly what Gabriel means in Quran 57:22 where he says, "Naught of disaster befalleth in the Earth or in yourselves but it is in a Book before we bring it into being."

Indeed, the Torah presented the Jewish religious head-hunters with nitty-gritty information on the expected Messiah; how they were to identify and crucify him, how two thirds of his apostles were to be persecuted and killed and the remaining one third forcibly transformed into Jehovah/Allah's devotees. Zech 13:7-9 reads, "Awake, O sword ... against the man who stands next [opposed] to me," says Jehovah/Allah of hosts. "Strike the shepherd, that the sheep may be scattered; I will turn my hand against the little ones. In the whole land, says Jehovah/Allah, two thirds shall be cut off and perish, and one third shall be left alive. And I will put this third into the fire, and refine them as one refines silver, and test them as gold is tested. [In the end] They will call on my name, and I will answer them. I will say, 'They are my people'; and they will say, 'Jehovah/Allah is my *God*.'"

When Jesus Christ spoke to his apostles about his final suffering and crucifixion, he confirmed that he was the Shepherd that Jehovah/Allah referred to as '*the man who stands [opposed] to me*'. "You will all fall away because of me this night;" he said to them, "for it is written [in Zech 13:7-9], 'I

[Jehovah/Allah] will strike the shepherd, and the sheep of the flock will be scattered.'" [Matt 26:31]

Finally, while the Bible empowers evil-minded clergies to rape minds of their numerous laities and defraud their souls, the Quran inspires casehardened suicide bombers to terrorize peace-loving humanity and massacre innocent people; all in strict accordance with Jehovah/Allah's dictates in the pages of the so-called Holy Books.

D. VIOLENCE, FEAR, AND BLIND FAITH

Closely connected with attacks through religion and the religious manuals are **violence, fear, and blind faith.** Jehovah/Allah relies heavily on fomenting violence among people and blowing his own trumpet to attract undue attention to himself. Whipping up violence in human communities creates social insecurity and that helps him to instill fear in the people, which in turn compels them to look up to him through his various devilish agents for protection. That has been a time-tested strategy for him and the other gods. Jehovah/Allah personally approves wars and fighting for his ignorant religious followers because that serves his purpose. He trains and loves regular soldiers, religious *shohids* and violent-minded individuals in the society who make up his visible fighting armies on Earth. David sang his praises saying, "He trains my hands for war and gives my fingers skill for battle." [Ps 144:1 (NLT)] Abraham, Moses, David, Solomon, Muhammad, and other known religious *holy men* inspired by Jehovah/Allah were sufficiently violent at heart to qualify as men after Jehovah/Allah's own heart. He used then to lay foundation for religious intolerance, religious terrorism, and senseless wars.

We read in the Quran how Jehovah/Allah transformed peace-seeking Muhammad of Arabia first into a highway robber and then into a rampaging religious warrior and expansionist. The Quran tells us that Jehovah/Allah only manages to retain religious worshippers by encouraging religious intolerance and wars; by setting people against each other.

- "Warfare is ordained for you," he decrees, "**though it is hateful unto you**; but it may happen that ye hate a thing which is good for you …
- Fight in the way of Allah against those who fight against you.…

- And fight them until persecution is no more, and religion is **all for Allah**. ...
- For had it not been for Allah's [way of] repelling some men by means of others, cloisters and churches and oratories and mosques, wherein the name of Allah is often mentioned, would assuredly have been pulled down.
- Verily Allah helpeth one who helpeth him [to fight his devilish cause on Earth]." [Qur'an 2:216, 190; 8:39; 22:40]

Ironically, what Jehovah/Allah says to the Muslims he had already said to the Jews and customary Christians. History shows clearly how the god of Abraham helped his Jewish religious salves to fight to establish his temples and synagogues and to extend influence and shores of Judaism at their own peril. The same way, he helped customary Christian crusaders to found, protect, and expand his churches, cloisters, and oratories all over the world. His method remains the same with Muslim terrorists and suicide bombers to whom he gives the impression that terrorizing fellow human beings is the best way to preach the love of Jehovah/Allah and cause entire human race to surrender unconditionally to his colonial will.

All the tearing up and casting down escapades of Jehovah/Allah in Egypt and elsewhere in the old world, as recorded in the Bible, were purely for that purpose. Exodus 14:31 and 20:1819 read,

- "And Israel saw the great work which Jehovah/Allah did against the Egyptians, and **the people feared Jehovah/Allah; and they believed in Jehovah/Allah** and in his servant Moses," and
- "when all the people perceived the thunderings and the lightnings and the sound of the trumpet and the mountain smoking, **the people were afraid and trembled**; and they stood afar off, and said to Moses, "You speak to us, and we will hear; but let not Jehovah/Allah speak to us, lest we die."

Jehovah/Allah's terrible epithets, like "the roaring lion of Judah," "devouring fire," "consuming one," "the god that answereth by fire," "he who makes destruction flash forth against the strong" and others are all intended to elicit fear and unconditional surrender to his will in people who blindly extol the evil deeds associated with such nicknames. Thus, Jehovah/Allah has become the chief dread of ignorant humans on Earth. Meanwhile, he is just an empty barrel that makes the most noise.

Both his prophets and the laypersons alike are in dread of his expected doomsday, of which he says in Zeph 3:8, "Wait for me, for the day when I arise as a witness. For my decision is to gather nations, to assemble kingdoms, to pour out upon them my indignation, all the heat of my anger; for in the fire of my jealous wrath all the Earth shall be consumed." Even Muhammad confessed that fear was the only reason he surrendered to Allah. "I am commanded to be the first of those who surrender (unto him)," he confessed, "Lo! If I disobey my Lord, **I fear the doom of a tremendous Day**." [Quran 39:12-13] No wonder the Jews concluded earlier that for them, "the fear of Jehovah/Allah is the beginning of wisdom." And ignorant customary Christians, feeling so afraid even to discourse their own fears and doubts about Jehovah/Allah, keyed in completely to Jewish religious foibles. But people who know the truth are not perturbed by Jehovah/Allah's doomsday. Every true Christ-follower knows that "he does not come into [any form of] judgment but has passed from death to life." [John 5:24]

Principalities' attacks on ignorant masses are not limited to religious intrigues. They have other subtle ways of inculcating in ignorant humans the spirit of violence, fear, and blind faith in worldly providence. These devils are all-around and well mobilized. They are gods of Earth's system of things; so, they literally rule our whole world. The Bible says, "The whole world is in the power of the evil one[s]." So, we should expect their attacks to be from every facet of our day-to-day existence on Earth.

Earth's complex system of government that the principalities invented is made up of three symbiotic departments, namely **religious**, **secular** and the **underworld**. They hold the reins in virtually all their agencies. Humanity is pelted from all these fronts through activities of our own kinsmen and kinswomen whom the principalities entice with material rewards to function as their viceroys and serve their ulterior interest on Earth. They put them in power not to uplift humanity but to control and subject the masses to perennial material worries to promote and sustain spiritual lethargy in people's minds, while promoting materialism. Of course, the most effective weapons against humans are humans themselves. In the final analysis, it is human beings that enslave human beings. The principalities only manipulate people's obsessions and selfish tendencies to get them to turn against their own suffering brethren. Therefore, greed, lustful desire for power, fame, worldly goods, material comfort and enjoyment render humans completely defenseless.

E. SCOURGE OF VIOLENCE IN BIBLE PROPHECIES

Jehovah/Allah's end-time promise in Joel 2:28-29 that talks about him indiscriminately pouring out his spirit of dreams, visions and spiritual hallucination on all flesh agrees completely with Dan 12:4, which states that knowledge—*of his full intentions*—shall increase in the time of the end. Religious believers take such prophecies for granted, presuming that they necessarily speak of spiritual upliftment of human beings on Earth and of general increase in spiritual awareness. They deliberately ignore the basic and consistent context of all prophetic pronouncements made by Jehovah/Allah in the Old Testament and therefore fail to see the clear pointers to the malicious intents of his end-time divine unction, as given in the book of Joel.

Immediately after verses 28-29 that promise global spiritual phantasm, verse 30 speaks of him giving "portents in the heavens and on the Earth [of] *blood and fire and columns of smoke*," making it clear that the prophecy is more about increase in violence and spiritual blindness than about increase in knowledge of the Father and fellowship with Jesus Christ. Joel 2:28-29 is direct sequel to Isaiah 29:9-10, which reads, "Stupefy yourselves and be in a stupor, blind yourselves and be blind! Be drunk, but not with wine; stagger, but not with strong drink! **For Jehovah/Allah has poured out upon you a spirit of deep sleep, and has closed your eyes, the prophets, and covered your heads, the seers**." It is clear therefore that Jehovah/Allah's proposed spirit of mass hysteria only refers to one of his many end-time battle strategies.

The general theme of Old Testament prophecies is Jehovah/Allah's indignation with human beings on Earth and his sworn determination to terrorize and slaughter defenseless multitudes to avenge his worsening loss of credibility and relevance in the spiritual affairs of enlightened humans. Isaiah 34:2 says, "Jehovah/Allah is enraged against all the nations, and furious against all their host, he has doomed them, has given them over for slaughter." And in Isaiah 47:3 he says, "**I will take vengeance, and I will spare no man.**" Complex nature of that programmed vengeance was to culminate in the dreaded great tribulations of the end-times that Jesus Christ alludes to in Matthew 24:21. "Alas for the day!" says Joel 1:15, "For the day of Jehovah/Allah is near, and as destruction from the Almighty it comes." And Amos 5:18-20, describing the manifold nature of so-called

Jehovah/Allah's days of vengeance, says, "It is darkness, and not light; as if a man fled from a lion, and a bear met him; or went into the house and leaned with his hand against the wall, and a serpent bit him." So, we can be sure that the last days will be very perilous, and not necessarily filled with genuine spirit of the Father; and that will be the direct result of attacks from Jehovah/Allah and the principalities.

"My decision," states Jehovah/Allah in Zephaniah 3:8 "is to gather nations, to assemble kingdoms, to pour out upon them my indignation, all the heat of my anger; for in the fire of my *jealous wrath* all the Earth shall be consumed." And in Jeremiah 23:20 he assures us that "The anger of Jehovah/Allah will not turn back until he has executed and accomplished the intents of his mind. **In the latter days you will understand it clearly**." No doubt, Jehovah/Allah and the principalities harbor bottled-up indignation—*jealous wrath*—which was orchestrated by the sudden appearance of the heavenly Christ and the steady rise of Christ-consciousness within their false Earthly dominion. And they are determined to fight with every weapon within their powers to reclaim and mislead as many unsuspecting human souls as possible before the final demise of their ungodly regime. Only by reading these so-called prophetic pronouncements in their proper context will we begin to make sense of the present-day paradox of worsening state of wickedness and ungodliness in the face of global increase in religious knowledge, activities, and Jehovah/Allah fellowship.

No doubt we are already living in the perilous days of the principalities' vengeance. Our present generation is teaming with all manners of *inspired* religious experts—*anointed* prophets, dreamers, visioners, preachers, TV evangelists, imams, religious scholars of various creeds and intellectual abilities. They all supposedly possess greater knowledge of *God* and preach religious goodness on global scale; yet the world is now full of wickedness, violence, crimes, and corruption in leadership more than at any other time in human history. Of course, Jesus Christ tells us in Matthew 24:11-12 that "many false prophets will appear and deceive many people" in the last days, and because there will also be "increase of wickedness, the love of most will grow cold."

That tells us clearly the integrity of the rush-hour prophets and dreamers that Jehovah/Allah promises in the book of Joel. They are all supposed to be 'men of *God*,' empowered to massively propagate and sustain Jehovah-consciousness on Earth and thereby distract humanity from knowledge of the Father and of his spiritual redemption plan for our fallen souls. Jehovah/Allah's end-time religious paratroopers are all messengers of doom—unmistakable antichrists, wearing false gabs of righteousness. They are paid religious mercenaries, employed to hunt down unsuspecting souls for the principalities. One can easily identify them by their fruits. According to 1 Cor 13:23, "if one has prophetic powers, and understands all mysteries and all knowledge, and if he has all faith, so as to remove mountains, but has not love, he is nothing. If he gives away all he has, and if he delivers his body to be burned, but has not love, he gains nothing." Present-day men of *God* are simply hypocrites and sycophants ignorantly basking in the caustic patronage of Jehovah/Allah.

Our generation is equally witnessing exponential advances in science, technological inventions, and information technology. We generally see these as gains, but they are serious spiritual distractions. Increase in knowledge of science and technology does not necessarily amount to increase in the knowledge of the Father and of spiritual realities. And certainly, being able to spend a lifetime in the heavens as humans—as proposed by *Mars One* project—cannot be an alternative to outright transition to perfect heavenly existence as redeemed spirits.

Talking about increase in information and knowledge in the last days; the World Wide Web now "brings the accumulated knowledge of the world to everyone's fingertips," as predicted by Arthur C. Clarke in the May 1970 issue of *Popular Science* magazine. In a very short time, the Web has really opened humankind to multiple exabytes of nitty-gritty information on nearly all known subjects as never ever imagined possible. However, practical evidence of all that increase in worldly knowledge is a greater increase in spiritual emptiness, obsessive worldliness, social insecurity, and general regression into *original ignorance*. It is evident that the internet today readily supplies adequate information to all kinds of social miscreants, including suicide bombers, which help them fine-tune their nefarious activities.

But abundance of knowledge is not bad in itself; in fact, knowledge of 'good and evil' as provided by the internet is very important for humankind in these last days. Adam and Eve fought for it, and we now have it in abundance. It now depends on individuals to use available knowledge either to the eternal glory of their souls or to their ultimate spiritual damnation. The choice is entirely personal. *Free will* has now become logical for humans on Earth.

F. FILM INDUSTRY AND THE MEDIA: VISUAL SCHOOLS OF VIOLENCE

Inspired end-time religious paratroopers are not the only messengers of doom deployed by the principalities in these last days to revolutionize ungodliness. Operators of our modern film industries and the news media in general stand out in their professions as mass communicators or educators. Most of them are equally inspired by the principalities; and in the name of creativity and acting, they persistently feed ignorant masses with nothing but lies dressed up as realities. They systematically set standards by their consistent choice of movie storylines and news materials that silently popularize misleading ideals, violence, crimes, immorality, and bad governance, which in turn inculcate in people the spirit of violence, fear, and blind faith in worldly providence. Human mind is very impressionable. People easily learn what they see or hear; and it becomes a deep part of them when the subject is recurrent. Effect of unguarded information and dramatizations on our young minds is even more devastating.

Young people look out for role models upon whom to fashion their own lives. The film industry and the media readily present them with bogus characters, dramatized as heroes and heroines of impossible situations, and the young ones believe in them completely. Constantly watching their fake role models dramatize violence, crimes, and sexual recklessness in movies exposes them to bad ideals and they inwardly accept these social vices as reputable. There is simply too much recklessness and bloodshed in modern movies and our news media equally seem to be irredeemably hooked on capturing violent scenes in their everyday reportage. These too, are very effective battle strategies of the wicked principalities.

Today, our world is really teetering on the brink of Armageddon. Large number of our youth easily take to violent crimes, militancy, gangsterism, cultism, drug abuse and all manners of fraudulent lifestyles because these are what they see and hear about every day. Now, considering that the youth are leaders of tomorrow, what kind of tomorrow can we possibly hope for when our young minds are ill-prepared today?

G. HOME BREAKUPS: CONTROLLED ATTACK ON ROOT OF HUMANITY

Human nature is community-based, and the family is the fundamental unit of structured community. The family is the root of humanity. Overall health and survival of any given society rests on collective integrity and strength of its families. Spiritual future of humankind equally hinges on virtuous family institutions. Although an imperfect institution of the world, the family stands out as closest ideal to true communism. It is the closest that life without the Father can get toward selfless love, welfare state and genuine transmittal of upright value system from generation to generation. Although basic in concept, the family is far more complex than the society itself, as it embodies the foundation of every aspect of existence upon which other institutions of the society are founded. The family is the center of emotions, religion, and government; it is the cradle of education, religious morality, law and order, industry, and business activities.

If the family dies, humanity dies with it; and so will the principalities and their foolish dreams. So, they are not fighting to obliterate formal family institution on Earth but rather to control and undermine its standard heritages in ways that guarantee them continued relevance in human societies. The principalities do that in so many subtle ways; in many cases, using the Bible, the Quran, and other religious books of Law to give backing to ungodly standards.

The Bible is full of inciting pronouncements by Jehovah/Allah that are aimed at creating serious psychological difficulties between husbands and their wives. Starting with the fictitious curse of Adam and Eve in Genesis 3:16-17, which blames Adam for listening to Eve, his wife, on such matter of ultimate spiritual importance to their family, it openly incites husbands to *rule* over their wives. Increased rate of family breakups today is deeply rooted on contradictions between impracticable biblical standards and the more enlightened ideas about true companionship between husbands and their wives. We now know that effective communication between husbands and wives is central to successful family life. Certainly, husbands should listen diligently to their wives on all matters of family interest. It is in no way helpful or godly for husbands to think of themselves as lords over their wives.

Apart from planting seed of discord between husbands and their wives, Jehovah/Allah equally lays stumbling block between parents and their children with his devious 5th Commandment. Exodus 20:12 reads, "Honor your father and your mother, that your days may be long in the land which Jehovah/Allah your *God* gives you." On the surface, this may sound like a holy injunction, but coming from the mind of the ultimate schemer and greatest enemy of enlightened humanity, it is a direct weapon of intimidation and control given to ignorant parents over their gullible children.

It was on the strength of this injunction that Abraham intimidated and virtually murdered his obedient son, Isaac, in cold blood in the name of trying to prove his love and faith in Jehovah/Allah. On the strength of the false authority bestowed on parents by the so-called 5th commandment most unenlightened parents see their children as investments and owned properties. Evidently, Abraham thought of Isaac as his personal ram and so had no qualms accepting to sacrifice—to butcher and burn him up for a *pleasing odor* to the bloodthirsty Jehovah/Allah. My mother once told me to drive away my wife and take away her two little children from her because Jehovah/Allah told her through his prophet that she was not my true wife. When I challenged the prophecy as devilish, she quickly invoked her ill-given authority of the 5th Commandment. But I knew Jehovah/Allah better than she thought she did, and so I did not allow them to destroy my young and innocent family.

The Bible is also full of express and unspoken support by Jehovah/Allah for immoral acts committed by ignorant patriarchs who were but his religious stooges. He made friends with dimwitted polygamists and showed no displeasure with their blatant involvement in immorality and family scandals. It was not mere coincidence that men portrayed as Jehovah/Allah's best friends in the Bible—Abraham, Jacob, David, Solomon—were all failures in their family lives. Solomon was the worst family desecrator in entire history of humankind, yet Jehovah surnamed him *Jedidiah*, meaning "beloved of Jehovah/Allah." Thus, with such mindless patriarchs Jehovah/Allah systematically laid false foundations and precedents for unsuspecting followers of biblical standards.

At this juncture, it should be stressed that *normal* family is one formed *formally* between one man and one woman, based on marital commitments that center on bearing and raising virtuous offspring for an upright society. In this regard, a man and a woman formally joined together in marriage represent the actual unit of society. Jesus Christ reiterates in Matthew 19:4-6 that people were strictly made male and female for the purpose of eventually matching the two in *righteous marriage* to produce a single couple—*one flesh*—for the great task of raising virtuous offspring for a happy society. According to him even "*he who made them from the beginning* made them male and female and said 'For this reason a man shall leave his father and mother and be joined to his wife, and the two shall become one flesh.' So, **they are no longer two but one flesh.**"

Polygamy, gay marriage, voluntary single parenting, and all weird modern-day sexual associations that people call marriage are *unnatural.* They represent unwarranted abuse of formal family institution, being some of the ways through which the principalities undermine true family heritage. Remarkably, Paul tells us in the book of Romans that these are some of the ways Jehovah/Allah fights back, as enlightened men and women are increasingly refusing to recognize him as the Father. "Since they did not see fit to acknowledge Jehovah/Allah [as the Father]," he writes, "Jehovah/Allah gave them up to a base mind and to improper conduct. ... "For this reason, Jehovah/Allah gave them up to dishonorable passions. Their women exchanged *natural* relations for *unnatural,* and the men likewise gave up natural relations with women and were consumed with passion for one another, men committing shameless acts with men and receiving in their own persons the due penalty for their error." [Romans 1:28, 26-27] Of course, these also agree with Isaiah 29:9, which states Jehovah/Allah's end-time agenda clearly. His aim has always been to stupefy and mislead enlightened humanity.

Other ways through which the principalities undermine family cohesion include direct religious encroachment, external pressures from extended family system, unwarranted financial strain from modern-day public school system, faulty societal value system as propagated by the film industry and the media and general economic hardship brought about by bad public governance. New age juvenile attitude that is largely dictated by false standards set by social media networks, as well as movie, music, sports, and fashion industries, equally put so much strain on family integrity. Bad children are a great source of bitterness for the family. Raising decent children that meet perfect family standards in modern-day societies has now become an uphill task for most upright parents. There are bad parents too, whom the principalities sponsor as infiltrators.

Finally, no one should doubt that the family is under serious attack in our present generation. Jesus Christ alerts us that the principalities will make the family central target of their end-time attacks because of increasing

Christ-consciousness on Earth. A man's greatest foes "will be those of his own household," he says. Luke 12:52-53 (NLT) reads, "From now on families will be split apart, three in favor of me, and two against—or two in favor and three against. 'Father will be divided against son and son against father; mother against daughter and daughter against mother; and mother-in-law against daughter-in-law and daughter-in-law against mother-in-law.'" This is already happening.

Notwithstanding the delicate nature of family ties therefore, people should look closely to identify and resist Jehovah/Allah's sponsored infiltrators within their own families. And talking about the 5th Commandment, Jesus Christ says, "Anyone who loves his father or mother more than me is not worthy of me; anyone who loves his son or daughter more than me is not worthy of me; and anyone who does not take his cross and follow me is not worthy of me." [Matt 10:37-38 (NIV)] Here, Jesus Christ authoritatively rewrites Jehovah/Allah's crafty 5th ordinance and directly calls on every one of us to stand for the truth and to do what is always right, regardless of contrary opinions of our mothers, fathers, daughters, or sons.

H. ANNIVERSARIES AND CELEBRATIONS; CARNIVALS AND CONTEMPORARY HAPPINESS

Human life is ephemeral and full of tribulations by design as well as by nature. Life without the Father cannot be otherwise. It is a passing phase of projected physical consciousness within milieu of spiritual death. So, man only lives once and dies forever. The Bible captures the true nature of man in Job 14:1-2, which reads, "Man that is born of a woman is of few days, and full of trouble. He comes forth like a flower, and withers; he flees like a shadow, and continues not."

Now, the question of ethics centers on how man should spend the *few days* that Mother Nature allocates to him on Earth. Naturally, the principalities legislate on matters of right and wrong as they concern man because they rule the system. And their legislations appear as verses of the various worldly scriptures or so-called Holy Books. Hence, the Bible, Quran, Vedas, Book of Mormon, Satanic Bible, Puranas, Mazdean Scriptures, Kabala and others are also known as Books of Law. These books together establish worldly standards, which are by no means perfect; and people perforce live by code of ethics documented in the verses. The hypnotic verses work in conjunction with programmed innate tendencies of human nature to elicit from people range of behavioral patterns that are in harmony with the system.

The books make it clear that human existence is just fleeting phase of soul fantasy—that ought to be full of imaginations that are unrestricted by reality. The Quran calls this life "comfort of illusion ... a pastime ... a sport." Regarding enjoyment therefore, the books favor hedonism as ideal for all humans. They make it clear that it is lawful for human beings to find the highest illusory enjoyment for themselves within the few days of their fantasia. Just like the flower before it withers away, man should so adorn himself and revel to the highest degree before he vanishes. After all no one expects a rose that blooms to look less than rosy before it withers away.

In fact, Quran 2:14 explains to us the kind of enjoyment designed and intended for man: "Beautified for mankind," it says, "is the love of the joys (that come) from women and offspring, and store-up heaps of gold and silver, and horses branded (with their mark), and cattle and land." Famous Wisdom of Solomon surmises that "There is nothing better for a man than that he should eat and drink and find enjoyment in his toil. This ... is from the hand of *God*." It also adds that "A feast is made for laughter, and wine makes life merry, but **money is the answer for everything**." [Eccl 2:24; 10:19(NIV)] So, the books are not concerned with any spiritual consideration for man or for man's soul. In fact, the principalities view such idea as highly inimical to the system and fight in any way they can to oppose it.

Solomon spoke the mind of the principalities and was prepared to be their exemplar on the matter. They counted it to him as wisdom. In his days, that wisdom was not surpassed by any other, and he was honest enough to live out the doctrine. He was exceedingly rich and flamboyant. He ate, drank, and enjoyed himself to the fullest in the company of a thousand likeminded women, like no other king before or after him. "Whatever my eyes desired I did not keep from them;" he said, "I kept my heart from no pleasure ... my heart found pleasure in all my toil." [Eccl 2:10]

At the end of all that experiment in merrymaking however, Solomon became completely disillusioned. The Bible tells us that he became very unhappy and that his heart was turned away from his god—the same god who approved and sponsored his jamboree lifestyle in the first place. In other words, Solomon tried and failed to prove to himself that his doctrine of hedonism was good enough for any man. To him *money was not really the answer for everything* after all; at least money could not buy him true happiness and inward contentment. In fact, he ultimately concluded that following the line of merrymaking and sensual pleasures in this life only leads to pains, vexation of heart and eternal loss; that people who occupy themselves pursuing the riches and pleasures of this life are but blind fools. "I hated life," he confessed, "because what is done under the sun was grievous to me; for all is vanity and a striving after wind." [Eccl 2:17]

Solomon ended up preaching someone else's *redemptive* gospel; one that is diametrically opposed to the system. Thus, he incurred anger of the principalities who were the system watchdogs. Jehovah/Allah turned against Solomon because he turned around to speak against the program that he was empowered to promote. 1 King 11:9, 14 say that "Jehovah/Allah was angry with Solomon, because his heart had turned away from Jehovah/Allah, the god of Israel, who had appeared to him twice [evidently, on the matter] … and Jehovah/Allah raised up an adversary against Solomon."

The question now is how does Solomon's failed experiment with love of money and contemporary happiness really affect average Bible believer? How is it affecting the whole humanity today? Do we see Solomon as a practical example of a bad role model, and his creed, a calculated stump of deception boldly planted into the Bible for hopeless souls who do not aspire beyond the life of man? Average Bible lovers still feel addicted to Solomon's original idea just because it is found in the Bible. To them *money is* still *the answer for everything* and reveling lifestyle remains ordained by *God* for all men. Aside from what the Books say or do not say about enjoyment, human nature craves for nothing else. Human beings just want to have fun, and the only reason they ever seek any reasonable occupation is to find the resources with which to do just that. The system is programmed that way.

That brings me to the position of shortsighted atheists. Just like Solomon, they believe that man should eat, drink, and enjoy himself today because tomorrow he dies. But unlike him, they do not see the hand of any real *God* in whatever is done under the sun. In their case, they pursue the pleasures of this life out of profound despair, because they are not able to see beyond the horizon of mundane human existence. Nevertheless, pursuing nihilistic view of this life still brings nothing but pains, vexation of heart and eternal loss as Solomon experienced it. What is needed in this age and time is balanced view of man's present realities vis-à-vis the ultimate spiritual needs of his soul.

Man is designed to have fun, but he must work for it. That is what he does—what he has always done. However, we know now that though man's body lives today and dies tomorrow, man's soul lives forever and in fact, has imperishable treasures to aspire for that are beyond human existence. All things may be lawful for man, but not all things are helpful for his soul. Pursuing the riches and pleasures of this passing life is a serious spiritual distraction and one sure form of painful self-enslavement for one's body and soul.

Eternal future of man's soul depends on his diligent disentanglement from worldly goods and on positive sacrifices in this life. Contrary to the wishes of the principalities, Jesus Christ asks, "What does it profit a man, to gain the whole world and forfeit his life?" He counsels, "Do not lay up for yourselves treasures on Earth, where moth and rust consume and where thieves break in and steal, but lay up for yourselves treasures in heaven, where neither moth nor rust consumes and where thieves do not break in and steal. **For where your treasure is, there will your heart be also.** [Mark 8:36; Matt 6:19-21]

True wisdom is giving up the whole of this vanity for an eternal value. This means choosing to die to human nature so that one might blossom spiritually. Jesus Christ explains that it is meaningless dressing up a grain of wheat that should simply be deposited into the ground to die so that it can yield much fruit. "Truly, truly, I say to you," he says, "unless a grain of wheat falls into the Earth and dies, it remains alone; but if it dies, it bears much fruit. [In any case,] he who loves his life [of the world] loses it, and he who hates his life in this world will keep it for eternal life." [John 12:24-25]

Indeed, this message does not sound clear enough. Is Jesus Christ telling human beings to hate themselves? Is he calling for outright suicide? Outright rejection of the joys that come from material prosperity is suicidal, and that is a greater unhappiness. Man is designed to survive on food, drink, sex, laughter, and other like activities; and all these things cost money. Is he telling people that they should stop seeking the universally accepted means of livelihood—money? Certainly not! What Jesus Christ is calling for is moderation, not self-destruct. He is asking man to spend more quality time on matters of spiritual benefit; to avoid unnecessary distractions associated with undue fixation on worldly treasures and pleasures. On the other extreme, desert hermits who practice extreme austerity in the name of religious methods are but misinformed. That is why Jesus Christ quickly adds, "Your heavenly Father knows that you need them all. ... Seek first his kingdom and his righteousness, and all these things shall be yours as well." [Matthew 6:32-33]

As we already know, it is official responsibility of the principalities to uphold human nature; to safeguard original blueprint of world system of things. But the last days of that *comfort of illusion* is at hand indeed. Christ's ultimate mission is to stall Mother Nature altogether; to redeem captive souls caught in the matrix of vanity and lifelessness. So, his ideals terminally endanger not just office of the principalities, but also the whole system. As should be expected therefore, the principalities are presently fighting hard to uphold the Law of human prosperity and pleasure as defined by original Solomonic doctrine. Their end-time program of attacks in this area involves casting stronger spell of hedonism on all flesh, aimed at reinvigorating peoples' obsessions with pursuit of pleasure and contemporary happiness via alcoholism, sex and drug additions, uncontrollable party spirit, unrestrained materialism, and through addictive, cyclic anniversaries, and festivities.

The psychology behind yearly or recurrent anniversary celebrations, whether religious or secular; national, familial, or personal, is that they gradually turn into unending rituals, developing in people a deep sense of belonging with Mother Nature. With enormous variety of festivals and holidays spread throughout every calendar year and craftily woven around ethnic cultures and peoples' natural tendencies, people only talk about spiritual salvation and going to heaven while inwardly looking forward to their next favorite festivals or holidays for the coming year. To a very large extent, it is the social jamborees and commercial incentives woven around these recurrent festivals and holidays that generally shape peoples' lifestyles around the world.

Take the Christmas period for example. Apart from being a period mostly characterized by large feasts, rowdy and ostentatious public behaviors, drunkenness, gluttony and even gambling, it is also a period of brisk commercial activities. All over the world, peoples' routines during this period are almost entirely dictated by the profit-oriented whimsies of merchants and advertisers. In fact, so many people live for this period, such that immediately one Christmas season ends, they begin to prepare for the next one. How can such people be serious about spiritual salvation that entails not only total secession from all worldly events but also outright exit from the world?

We should not lose sight of the religious origin and motive behind festivals and holidays. It is of extreme importance to Mother Nature that the people seem to be happy in the system. Fate of this existence depends entirely on that, as absolute state of unhappiness will spur genuine desire for outright spiritual redemption. It all started, like weekly days of freedom from routine toiling granted plantation slaves by the slave master on which to adorn themselves, sing and dance to entertain him. Such *free* days are days of another kind of toiling however, even though the slaves did not perceive that. "Remember the sabbath day, to keep it holy," says the Bible book of Law, "Six days you shall labor, and do all your work; but **the seventh day is a sabbath to Jehovah/Allah your *God*, ...**" [Ex 20:8-11] Thus, the so-called weekly '*holy days*' were born; set aside by the principalities as days to receive religious worship and thanksgiving from their human slaves.

These religious days of worship differ from religion to religion. While some traditional religions reckon their week by four-market-day cycle, the popular religions used the Gregorian weekdays, for example, *Friday* for Muslims, *Saturday* for Jews, and *Sunday* for Christians. Sunday also happens to be a common-law holiday in most countries of the world. In most cases, people toil more on these so-called rest days than on ordinary days of the week. Take a Sunday for instance; while the laity may psychologically feel less stressed out by unending religious activities lined up for the church service, the clergy really get fagged out carrying out their statutory obligations to both the laity and their gods on a day that everybody ought to be resting in his or her home.

Our modern festivals or '*holidays*,' derived from the so-called '*holy days*,' have since been transformed into days of extreme self-indulgence. Thus, beginning with the primitive weekly days of religious rituals, woven into peoples' religious traditions and cultures that commemorated the gods as well as natural events, such as the annual course of the sun or the phases of the moon, our present world is now teaming with inexhaustible list of annual festivities of secular as well as religious nature, commemorating historical events and peoples of interest in various nations, communities, and families of the world. There are also various merrymaking events peculiar to families and individuals that are associated with weddings, births, and deaths. The problem with all these is that people earnestly look forward to these festivities year after year to the detriment of their spiritual pursuits.

I. SEXUAL DEGENERACY: REGRESSION TO SHAMELESSNESS OF ANIMALS

Sexuality, which includes *all* forms of erotic sensations, experiences, responses, and actual sexual activities, is *natural* to all animals, humans, and the gods inclusive. This generally finds expressions through our animalistic thoughts, fantasies, desires, beliefs, attitudes, values, behaviors, practices, roles, and interpersonal relationships. Sexuality was absolutely a matter of instinctual drive in *all* animals, controlled entirely by biological and mental impulses to which pre-Edenic man had no compulsion to resist. Sexuality to man was like one being on the driving seat of a car, but with the steering and brake pedals controlled by someone else outside the vehicle. I call that nothing but carnal bondage of hapless souls. Nevertheless, everything about it was *natural* to worldly existence.

Sexuality is the hub of everything that is ungodly about Mother Nature. As we already know, the Father is the sole radiator of true life; and true life exists only within his perfect heavenly domain. Life of the world, as generated by Mother Nature is purely a life of unrestrained sexual expressions, invented by heavenly dropouts within the realm of darkness to serve as alternative to spontaneous divine activities within the heavenly domain of the Father. Life without the Father is outright sinful and false. Therefore, worldly existence is a sinful idea in its entirety. We are not just sinners because of our bizarre sexual inclinations as individuals; everything about our world is sinful from its foundation. The world was brought forth in iniquity, and our mothers conceive us through sinfulness. That is exactly what David is saying in Psalm 51:5, which reads, "Behold, I was brought forth in iniquity, and in sin did my mother conceive me."

Before the divine liberation of Adam and Eve in the Garden of Eden, humankind lived *naturally* like every other species of animals—without any conscious form of sexual restraint. Bestiality, homosexuality, lesbianism, rapes, incest, and other forms of unwholesome sexual practices were natural to all animals, humans, and the gods. No one legislated against sexual improprieties. Sexual immorality was not an issue at all. Jehovah/Allah and the gods did not legislate on sexual morality for animals, humans or for themselves because they were equally animals and lacked spiritual integrity. They rather legislated against knowledge of good and evil, which they feared would bring spiritual enlightenment to humankind. They knew that spiritual refinement and knowledge of divine mores among the humans would jeopardize their colonial interests and weaken their control over the people.

The so-called gods raped and impregnated daughters of men at will; the goddesses, likewise, seduced and frolicked with sons of men, and sons of men themselves openly had sex with lower animals. There was no moral ethics on sexuality of animals whatsoever. Genesis 2:18-24 tells the story of how Jehovah/Allah tried to find a suitable sex partner—*helper*—for man among the animals before the invention of wo-man. "It is not good for the man to be alone," he said, "I will make **a helper who is just right for him**." Then he started by presenting various wild animals and birds to man for courtship, "but still there was no helper just right for him [amongst the beasts]. ...Then Jehovah/Allah invented a woman and brought her to the man." "**At last!**" the man exclaimed. "**This one** is bone from my bone, and flesh from my flesh! She will be called 'woman,' because she was taken from 'man.'" [Gen 2:18-23 (NLT)] Even then, the Scripture still reports, "the man and his wife were both naked, but they felt no shame [about their uncensored sexual activities]." [Gen 2:25 (NLT)]

According to Zechariah Sitchin, in his book, *The 12th Planet*, "The clear implication is that the status of Man vis-à-vis the gods was not much different from that of domesticated animals. The gods had merely upgraded an existing animal to suit their needs. Did the lack of 'knowing,' then, mean that, naked as an animal, the newly fashioned being [man] also engaged in sex as, or with, the animals? Some early depictions indicate that this was indeed the case." [Zechariah Sitchin, *The 12th Planet*, page 366, fig. 156]

What Jehovah/Allah and the gods feared about the *new* man and the possibility of him acquiring knowledge of good and evil happened on the fateful day in Eden when Adam and Eve received the unique Light from Heaven. Convinced of eternal values of heavenly wisdom and expected spiritual refinement that that entailed, the couple accepted the gift of knowledge of good and evil from the heavenly Christ against the threat of death from the gods. And the Scriptures says, "At that moment their eyes were opened, **and they suddenly felt shame at their nakedness**. So, they sewed fig leaves together to cover themselves." [Gen 3:7 (NLT)] The heavenly Envoy miraculously imparted a measure of spiritual consciousness to human minds on that day, and thus inaugurated the start of humankind's spiritual evolution toward holiness and the Divine Tree of true Life. Today, the civilized world generally speaks of people's sexual habits and behaviors in terms of what is *natural* and or *unnatural*, *moral* and or *immoral*, *lawful* and or *unlawful*; and that is a great plus for the spiritual evolution of humankind. Some government and religious institutions have been compelled to evolve some reasonable definitions and social standards by which our civilized societies can *manage* sexuality.

Unfortunately, people have steadily mistaken the moderating effects of the imported goodness of the heavenly Redeemer in the world as proof that the Father created the world. Deluded religious believers, have continued to take for granted the gains of what was a clear Divine Intervention of the heavenly Christ in Eden through Adam and Eve, holding that it was the devil that opened their eyes to the shamelessness of sexuality. Therefore, I should state emphatically here that sexuality was indeed a *shameful* invention until the heavenly Christ imported sense of morality and spiritual integrity into the world through Adam and Eve. Whether we choose to recognize it or not, holiness and godliness are not fundamental aspects of worldly existence. As the Scripture shows, foundation of the world was primordial darkness; and man, himself, was born ignorant and with a depraved nature that pointed in opposite direction from the Father, the heavenly Christ, and righteousness. Therefore, the Father is not creator but redeemer of the world.

Someone once wrote in the "*Facebook*," "If I had been present at the Creation, I would have given some useful hints for a better arrangement of the universe." Whoever that person was, he had finally discovered the truth right within himself. Believing that he could have even done better as mere enlightened human was an honest way of asserting his deep-rooted conviction that the world was indeed a creation of some depraved minds and not of the perfect Father. Regrettably, this type of forthrightness is lacking in official thoughts and arguments put forward by some of our great religious philosophers and thinkers about human sexuality.

Because Thomas Aquinas (1225-1274) strongly believed that the Father created the world, his argument about human sexuality lacked vision. He argued that "If we suppose the corporeal nature to be created by the good Father, we cannot hold that those things which pertain to the preservation of the corporeal nature and to which nature inclines, are altogether evil; wherefore, since the inclination to beget an offspring whereby the specific nature is preserved is from nature, it is impossible to maintain that the act of begetting children is altogether unlawful." But sexuality is not all about begetting offspring. It is not really a question of whether sexual entanglements in the world are lawful or not, but whether they are helpful to our distressed souls. If we are genuinely seeking outright spiritual salvation and resurrection from the world, should we also be trying to preserve and perpetuate corporeal nature that enslaves our souls?

Pope John Paul II (1920-2005), on his part, portrayed human sexuality as "dignified and beautiful," and called it "a special gift of *God* that is preserved and respected by reserving it for marriage." Then, he argued, "Sex is sanctified by the rebirth of Christ." Well, the Pope himself embraced celibacy because he aspired to become a *holy Vicar* of the *God* in question. And *virgin birth* of Jesus, more than anything else, confirms that sex, even between husband and wife, and even for the purpose of procreation, is ungodly. It was for the same reason that Jesus Christ himself never married; and he explained that "There are different reasons why some men don't marry. Some were born without the ability to produce children. Others were made that way later in life. And others [like Pope John Paul II] **have given up marriage because of** the Father's **kingdom**." [Matt 19:12 (ERV)] Now, how can something that one really needs to give up to be in harmony with divine nature be '*a dignified, beautiful, and special gift of* the Father? I am sure the Pope could not have honestly said that to victims of gang rape and other sexual abuses; or to millions of sufferers of other forms of sex-related afflictions and maladies in the world. If we accept that celibacy and virginity are virtues, then, sexuality is a fundamental flaw of corporeal nature.

Well, Jesus Christ further says in Luke 20:34-36 (TLB) that "Marriage is for people here on Earth, but when those who are counted worthy of being raised from the dead get to heaven, they do not marry. And they never die again; in these respects, they are like angels, and are sons of the Father, for they are raised up in new life from the dead." He also added however, that not everyone would be able to muster the required willpower to completely overcome the strong *natural* sexual-drive in worldly beings; in which case he recommended strict one-man-one-woman marriage, and for-better-for-worse. Considering the strength of will required even to restrain oneself to one legitimate sex partner to meet Christ's stringent stand on marriage, his immediate disciples concluded that it was better to avoid marriage altogether. "If such is the case of a man with his wife," they said to him, "it is not expedient to marry." [Matt 19:10] An ancient Sumerian proverb conveys the same insight. It says, "Man: For his pleasure: Marriage; On his thinking it over: Divorce." [Zechariah Sitchin, *The 12th Planet*, page 45]

Paul reechoed the Messiah's position in his response to questions raised by the Corinthians concerning sex and marriage. "It is well for a man not to touch a woman," he said to them. "But because of the temptation to immorality, each man should have his own wife and each woman her own husband. ... I say this by way of concession, not of command. I wish that all were as I myself am. ... To the married I give charge, **not I but the Lord [Jesus Christ]**, that the wife should not separate from her husband (but if she does, let her remain single or else be reconciled to her husband) - and that the husband should not divorce his wife." [1 Cor 7:1-2, 6-7, 10-11]

Not surprisingly, official stand of the three major religions that profess Jehovah/Allah as *God* on Earth directly contradict the divine position of the heavenly Christ on human sexuality. The Catholic Church teaches that sexuality is "noble and worthy," even though it officially embraces celibacy and monasticism. Judaism on its part, considers celibacy—*one ***giving up marriage because of God's kingdom***—to be outright sinful. Islam equally opposes celibacy and monasticism, arguing that sexual desire is a natural urge that should not be suppressed. Hence, Islam approves for a man to have more than one wife. Thus, Jehovah/Allah successfully planted subtle stumps of deception in Judaism, customary Christianity and Islam concerning human sexuality that readily enable him to manipulate carnal weaknesses of followers of these religions to undermine their spiritual growth.

Jehovah/Allah never really disguised his thoughts for man right from the very beginning. He never intended the humans to outgrow animal nature so that he would continue to dominate and rule over them with ease; and certainly, he never wanted them to become aware of their spiritual potentials, hence he forbade the knowledge of good and evil for them. Facts on ground prove decisively that Jehovah/Allah has been anti-the Father, anti-Christ, anti-Adam and Eve, anti-human morality, and anti-spiritual redemption of fallen human spirits right from the genesis. And he has never stopped devising ways to return enlightened humanity to its primitive state of original ignorance, sexual indiscretion, shamelessness of animals and spiritual timidity. Manipulating human ignorance and carnal weaknesses became two of his deadliest weapons against humanity.

Before the second advent of the heavenly Christ on Earth in human form, ignorance and spiritual oblivion still characterized humans' general outlook in life. Jehovah/Allah posited himself as *God Almighty* and people extolled and worshiped him as such because they did not know the difference. People equally revered the rest of the principalities as Archangels of the Father. Two thousand years after Christ's divine ministry, crucifixion and ascension from the world, Jehovah/Allah and the principalities are now struggling to keep up with their many lies. But Jesus Christ has clearly revealed the Father to the world by his unique gospel of the Kingdom and by his exemplary lifestyle, thus, making it obvious that Jehovah/Allah is merely an impostor.

Divine mission of the heavenly Christ in human form indeed brought about positive increase in spiritual awareness of human beings. With more and more people increasingly realizing that Jehovah/Allah has been nothing but a false Almighty, he is becoming more and more enraged and obstinate. He felt he had no better option than to fight. "Your nakedness shall be [re]uncovered, and your shame shall be seen," he vows, "I will take vengeance, and I will spare no man. ... "Turn to me and be saved, all the ends of the Earth! For I am *God*, and there is no other. By myself I have sworn, from my mouth has gone forth in righteousness a word that shall not return: 'To me every knee shall bow, every tongue shall swear.' [Isa 47:3; 45:22-23]

Jehovah/Allah inspired Paul to present his trumped-up charges against enlightened humankind and to outline his ultimate battle moves, which anchor solely on him manipulating inherent vulnerabilities of human carnal nature to try to make nonsense our spiritual enlightenment and to thwart our steady progression toward holiness and true eternal life:

> "For although they knew Jehovah/Allah," he says, "they neither glorified him as *God* nor gave thanks to him, but their thinking became futile, and their foolish hearts were darkened. Although they claimed to be wise, they became fools and exchanged the glory of the immortal *God* for images made to look like mortal man and birds and animals and reptiles. Therefore, **Jehovah/Allah gave them over in the sinful desires of their hearts to sexual impurity** for the degrading of their bodies with one another. They exchanged the truth of Jehovah for a lie. ... Because of this, **Jehovah/Allah gave them over to shameful lusts**. Even their women exchanged natural

relations for unnatural ones. In the same way the men also abandoned natural relations with women and were inflamed with lust for one another. Men committed indecent acts with other men and received in themselves the due penalty for their perversion.

Furthermore, since they did not think it worthwhile **to retain** the knowledge of Jehovah/Allah [as *God*], **he gave them over to a depraved mind**, to do what ought not to be done. They have become filled with every kind of wickedness, evil, greed and depravity. They are full of envy, murder, strife, deceit, and malice. They are gossips, slanderers, *God*-haters, insolent, arrogant and boastful; they invent ways of doing evil; they disobey their parents; they are senseless, faithless, heartless, ruthless. Although they know *God's* righteous decree that those who do such things deserve death, they not only continue to do these very things but also approve of those who practice them." [Romans 1:21-32 (NIV)]

In the name of socio-economic civilization, civil rights, human liberty, sexual rights, battle for gender equality that culminated in sexual revolution and the rise of feminism, religious enlightenment and naturism, the human society has shamelessly thrown off the *aprons of morality* that Adam and Eve secured for humankind at great price and regressed into animal nature. Jehovah/Allah has indeed succeeded in no small measure with his express intent to "re-uncover the nakedness of civilized humankind and return us to state of shameless animals."

Nudists' culture is fast becoming a social ideal officially espoused by cultural, religious, and political movements that directly and indirectly advocate a return to spiritual primitivism of pre-Edenic eras. Nudism is equally becoming the major theme of our fashion, movie and music industries and the media in general. Homosexuality, lesbianism, bestiality, prostitution, pornography, sex trafficking and sex merchandizing in general; child pornography, clergy sexual abuses, ritual sex, rapes, incest, polygamy, adultery, and all manners of sexual perversions have become the order of the day. Today, there are over 500 identified paraphilias or bizarre sexual inclinations in people that can only be rightly attributed to concerted attacks by end-time evil spirits from Jehovah/Allah. Yet, people do not recognize the warning signs.

Resultant effects of widespread sexual depravity in the society are widespread breakdown of moral standards, law, and order; especially as powerful institutions and influential individuals in the society now widely condone, approve, and defend these vices. These naturally lead to all kinds of social ills—wickedness, cruelty, bitter conflicts, senseless wars, killings, religious fanaticism, racism, ethnic cleansing, and more. Widespread sexual depravity in the society is also a potent disease vector, with over 340 million sexually transmitted diseases a year worldwide. No doubt, our present world is indeed under the control of ruthless demonic forces whose sole agenda is to reduce humankind to *civilized* animals that Jehovah/Allah had always wanted us to be.

Finally, let me say that there is a varying degree of natural tendency in every one of us toward some forms of sexual indiscretions because basic human nature is sinful. No human being will ever become perfect in the world, but we can fight and become perfect spirits in heaven. Human souls will be able to overcome Jehovah/Allah and his evil spells if only we can endeavor to open our eyes and see how the forces of good and evil play out in our individual lives. We will also need disciplined mindset, and that can only come with knowledge of the truth and a genuine understanding of the true nature and mission of Jesus Christ in the world. "You are truly my disciples," the Messiah says, "if you remain faithful to my teachings. And you **will know the truth, and the truth will set you free**." [John 8:31-32 (NLT)] Genuinely holding on to Jesus Christ as Savior of our helpless souls will make us brave and invincible. Of course, he knows our limitations and assures us that for as long as we are in the world, "Temptations to sin are sure to come; but woe to him [Jehovah/Allah] by whom they come!" "I have said this to you," he reminds us, "that in me you may have peace. In the world you have tribulation; but be of good cheer, I have overcome the world [and its principalities]." [Luke 17:1; John 16:33]

Jesus Christ expects us to treat one another with genuine love and understanding irrespective of our sexual failings, bearing in mind that we are all victims of concerted principalities' attacks. That will help to lessen the burden of guilt that weighs sinners down and gives Jehovah/Allah the upper hand in the battle. "So, watch yourselves!" he counsels, "If another believer sins, rebuke that person; then if there is repentance, forgive. Even if that person wrongs you seven times a day and each time turns again and asks forgiveness, you must forgive." [Luke 17:3-4 (NLT)] Readily forgiving and encouraging one another for perseverance will once again begin to rebuild and unify humanity and help us to retain divine aura of the indwelling Holy Spirit in our lives, which is indispensable in this battle for true eternal life.

J. UNITED NATIONS: EPITAPH OF A ONCE UNITED HUMANITY

The principalities murdered human unity at the Tower of Babel. True communism died on the same day. United Nations is a capitalists' idea of universal communism, inspired by the principalities to make mockery of genuine love, equity, peace, unity, and mutual respect among the various peoples of the world.

Inspired through the horrors of World War 1 fought between August 1914 and November 1918, some of the most powerful nations of the world spearheaded formation of the League of Nations as a federation of international alliance for the preservation of peace. Based on the principle of collective security, its basic aim was to prevent another worldwide war. But the seed of violence, international rivalry and wars was already deeply sowed and fertilized on the very day that the principalities scattered the peoples and confused their common language "that they may not understand one another's speech," says Genesis 11:7.

In principle, movement for international cooperation was supposed to be a battle front against the principalities, but the League had serious drawbacks. While in principle every representative of its member states in *the General Assembly* had one vote, the real power to effect change lied with the few most powerful countries that held permanent seats in *the Council*. The League failed in part because it found it hard to secure required consensus among its *super* members to oppose aggression, as each of them sought only her individual interests. Thus, when Japan, Italy, and Germany started military aggression in the 1930s that ultimately led to World War II (1939-1945), the League could not secure the necessary consensus to act against them, because they would not agree to condemn their own actions.

Secondly, the League was not able to cater fully for the selfish interests of all the world's most powerful countries, and so could not secure their membership, most notably, the United States. Although U. S. president Woodrow Wilson's plan in 1918 for a general association of nations formed the basis for the Covenant of the League of Nations, United States never became a member because her Senate failed to approve Article X, which contained the requirement that all members preserve the territorial independence of all other members, even to joint action against aggression.

The United Nations officially came into existence on October 24, 1945, as a replacement international *peacekeeping* organization, with the renewed goal of preventing future wars on the scale of World War I and II. But it inherited the principal flaws as well as the organizational machinery of the failed League. Realizing that it could not function without the financial and military support of the world's most powerful nations, especially the United States, it gave them irrevocable *veto* authority over its most important actions as incentive, and they held permanent seats in its most powerful body, the Security Council. As the winning powers at the end of World War II, the United States, the United Kingdom, France, Russia (formerly the Soviet Union), and China became the veto powers. Today the fate of entire humankind is still in the hands the *super* five. They are literally the rulers of the world, as any Security Council resolution backed by five of them has the force of international law and is binding on all members of the UN. Thus, the United Nations represents colonialism on global scale.

Any one of the so-called superpowers can veto important decisions of the Council that are not in total agreement with her own national interest. Although the UN has a set of rules for use of force in today's world, the *super five* do not always follow the rules. In many cases, they take unilateral action when the UN fails to grant authority to their wishes. The United States in particular, notoriously uses the UN as a personal tool to intimidate and bully other nations, openly propagating the wishes of the principalities. During the Cold War, she used the UN as a forum to break the USSR. And in 2003 she went ahead and invaded Iraq even when the Security Council did not give explicit approval for a military action against the country. She is presently manipulating the UN to create opportunity to break out against Iran.

Nations cannot be united under a forum that holds few member nations as super members and the rest as inferior and inconsequential. And certainly, there cannot be peace in a world where colonialism exists; where the few powerful nations reserve for themselves the sole right to produce and stockpile weapons of mass destruction while breathing down on other nations, ransacking their homes at will and destroying their chances of peaceful pursuit of technological and economic development. Such a situation naturally spawns deep-rooted resentment and revolution, which, as we can see today, international terrorism is just one form. As John Fowles writes in *The Aristos*, "It is not poverty that spreads revolution, but the knowledge that poverty is not universal." Only genuine respect and balance of forces between the nations can create the kind of restraint necessary for a workable peace in a capitalist world.

The United Nations is a practical example of the ills of capitalism. Capitalism breeds selfishness, superiority complex and arrogance; it promotes ignorance, which serves interest of the principalities. The hub of that ignorance is with the so-called superpowers. Seeing themselves as super developed countries, they imagine that helping the underdeveloped nations to build their societies and attain real independence will make them less developed as they really are. But that will rather spur them to seek greater development. Free flow of progressive knowledge in the world can only lead to evolution of good and mutual appreciation. Potentials exist in the world for limitless development. But because the so-called developed nations are busy stamping down the undeveloped ones, they are not able to take giant steps toward attaining higher development. Hence, they are equally underdeveloped.

Real development is product of a great heart. Greatness is not a quotient of physical size of a person or a nation but a measure of how far and wide his positive influence extends beyond him. A truly developed person or nation develops his surroundings. A *great* nation thriving amid shanties, slums and ghettos is a shame to real development. The five super nations are super ignorant for believing that there is anything superlative about them. If they are truly developed, illiteracy, poverty and diseases will no longer exist anywhere in the inhabited world. The sickening state of the world today is a shame on the five superpowers as well as on all the other so-called developed nations of the world. They had great opportunities to have transformed the Earth into real paradise for the human family, but they squandered it all.

In my honest estimation, no great nation exists on Earth. The United States of America is big for nothing, the United Kingdom is underdeveloped in spirit, France is backward in mentality, Russia is a powerful scarecrow and China is petty-minded. No doubt, these nations perfectly qualify to hold veto rights in a United Nations that is founded and operated by the principalities to undermine human dignity; to thwart genuine love, peace, unity, and spiritual development of humans on Earth.

There cannot be any doubt that the UN silently serves the will of the principalities through its various programs, agencies, committees, and commissions. For instance, in November 1999, the general Conference of UN Educational, Scientific and Cultural Organization (UNESCO) proclaimed *International Mother Language Day*. And in May 2009, the UN General Assembly passed a resolution, calling upon all Member States "to promote the preservation and protection of all languages used by peoples of the world." The same resolution proclaimed 2008 as the *International Year of Languages*, stating that it is **to promote unity in diversity and international understanding, through multilingualism and multiculturalism.** This is absolute nonsense. Unity in diversity is a fallacy in this type of world. Here, the UN is openly giving official backing to the express will of the principalities.

Multilingualism and multiculturalism are the greatest setback to human unity and international understanding. The facts on ground are overwhelming. They were the ultimate weapons of war invented by the haughty ones at the Tower of Babel to permanently divide-and-rule humanity. The Bible speaks clearly on this, and people should stop reading the verses upside down. In Genesis 11:6-7 (NLT), Jehovah/Allah said to his partners in crime, "**The people are united**, and **they all speak the same language**. After this, nothing they set out to do will be impossible for them! Come, let's go down and **confuse the people with different languages**. Then **they won't be able to understand each other.**" Therefore, multilingualism and multiculturalism are curses on humanity; not uplifting values to be promoted and memorialized. They are the main reasons we hate, antagonize, and do not understand one another in the world. If the UN is not working for the principalities, it will be calling for total abolition of diverse languages and a return to the one common language that united the whole peoples of the world. It will be sincerely working to evolve a workable lingua franca for entire human race.

How about the crucial issue of human rights and human rights abuses all over the world? What evidence exists that the UN is genuinely committed toward promoting and encouraging respect for human rights and fundamental freedoms for all peoples, regardless of race, color, sex, language, or religion, as stipulated in its charter? The Universal Declaration of Human Rights adopted by the UN in December 1948 enumerates *inalienable* rights and freedoms belonging to every individual member of the human family. Among other things, its articles proclaim that:

- "all human beings are born free and equal in dignity and rights,"
- "no one shall be held in slavery or servitude; slavery and the slave trade shall be prohibited **in all their forms**,"
- "everyone has the right to freedom of movement and residence within the borders of each state,"
- "everyone has the right to freedom of thought, conscience and religion;"
- "everyone has the right to freedom of opinion and expression;"
- "everyone, without any discrimination, has the right to equal pay for equal work,"
- "everyone has the right to education. Education shall be free, at least in the elementary and fundamental stages. Elementary education shall be compulsory."

In the end however, the Universal Declaration of Human Rights remains merely an academic classic as the UN lacks the will and authority to enforce its fine tenets over its member nations.

Creation of the state of Israel by the UN partition plan of November 1947 is always cited as one of the major accomplishments of the UN, yet nothing is said about its partial handling of the resultant Arab-Israeli conflict, which is rife with human rights abuses. The US makes sure that Israel is untouchable in all circumstances, thereby confirming the assertion that she is essentially a satellite state of Israel, founded and empowered by Jehovah/Allah, god of Israel, to protect and propagate the Zionist New World Order. According to Rabbi Meir Kahane (1932-1990), an American-born Israeli political extremist, "There are not several messages in Judaism. There is only one. And this message is to do what *God* [Jehovah/Allah] wants. Sometimes *God* [Jehovah/Allah] wants us to go to war; sometimes he wants us to live in peace.... But there is only one message: *God* [Jehovah/Allah] wanted us to come to this country [the United States] to create a Jewish state." The United States is a giant puppet in the hands of the principalities; the United Nations is her magic wand. Therefore, the whole of United Nations is a forum for puppets.

Finally, what enlightened humanity needs is not "United Nations" but

"United Peoples." United Nations represents triumph of nationalism over true communism, over true egalitarian existence of the human family. In principle, the Universal Declaration of Human Rights advocates egalitarianism, while the UN stands for nationalism, which directly and indirectly fosters colonialism, racism, racial discrimination, ethnic cleansing, and inter-national conflicts. Enlightened humanity needs to demolish all known machinations of the principalities. We need to abolish contemporary nationalism and return to *Babelian* egalitarianism.

K. CAPITALISM

Man was destined to *prosper* on Earth; to have limitless opportunities for self-improvement and self-enjoyment, without interference from the principalities. This is implicitly stated in the nativity statement of empowerment pronounced over humankind by the custodians of the human experiment as documented in Genesis 1:28. It reads, "Be fruitful and increase in number; fill the Earth and **subdue it**." This may suggest communism or collectivism in a broad sense, but human nature is essentially individualistic. Another name for individualism is selfishness and that in its natural form is capitalism—pursuit of personal goals for personal gains. Capitalism is in perfect harmony with the rational nature of man and the principalities. It will be impossible for humankind to *subdue* the Earth without such a system that supports free enterprise.

In modern terms, capitalism is a socio-economic system that is based on the principles of individual's rights to own means of production and distribution of goods and services; and to seek personal profits through investment of capital and employment of labor. But capitalism is as ancient as human existence on Earth. Jehovah/Allah is the prototype of modern-day capitalist class. He was a self-seeking employer of labor. There is absolutely no doubt about that. He invested in a nature park in Eden and deployed Adam and Eve to *till and keep* it in return for their daily sustenance because he wanted to gain something of greater value from the overall venture. That was practical capitalism. Apart from Adam and Eve tending his nature park to earn their living, he expected to gain their unflinching loyalty; to have them worship him as god. That, too, was a natural aspect of capitalism.

By posing as god to Adam and Eve, Jehovah/Allah unequivocally introduced *godfatherism* and idol worship as an inevitable aspect of capitalism.

Thus, he proved that although in principle human nature offers every individual equal opportunity in the capitalist system, it gives no guarantee that every individual will become employer of labor or even self-sufficient. Some are bound to be rich and others poor, some masters and others bondmen. Some are bound to serve and worship others to earn their living in the system. In fact, Jehovah/Allah assured his Jewish bondmen in Deuteronomy 4:11 that poverty is an indelible aspect of human existence. "For the poor will never cease out of the land," he told them.

Thus, as the master of his Edenic enterprise, he decreed for Adam and Eve the dos and don'ts that suited his selfish interests and not necessarily ones that were godly. He owned the economic means and hence the power to decide their fate in the prevailing circumstance. The same is still the case with modern-day capitalist class—the bourgeoisie. Very few rich and powerful industry owners, as well as influential governing authorities of economic institutions—secular, religious and underworld—play gods over their numerous hapless laborers, because they are masters of the prevailing socio-economic situation. In principle, the government institution is positioned to regulate the capitalist stage to ensure controlled poverty level of the helpless masses. But in most cases the government is generally biased in favor of the rich and influential in the society.

Greed is another strong aspect of human nature that is perfectly in harmony with capitalism. In fact, without the strong and insatiable drive for more and more personal achievements or gains humanity would still be living in jungles. Capitalism generally brings about development; greed and hard work makes that possible, as individuals are free to explore personal ideas and economic possibilities to be the *best* they can be. In other words, economic freedom brings about economic prosperity, and people are free to accumulate more and more of whatever they strongly desire. There is no restriction on how much wealth an individual can accumulate or on how far he can progress in a capitalist economic system. In principle, capitalism eradicates poverty because it gives equal opportunities to every individual to create his own wealth; and full effort is equal to full success.

However, **capitalism** encourages building personal wealth *at all costs*. The *best* that people can be in a capitalist economy is always tied to money and accumulation of more and more money. It fuels unhealthy obsessions in people, fosters extreme selfish tendencies, greed and lustful desire for power, fame and material comfort and enjoyment. Resultant effect of that trend is widespread economic poverty, as the rich naturally get richer and the poor poorer. Capitalism brings about unhealthy spirit of competition by men and women trying to excel in vanity. That in turn promotes materialism, avarice, pride and arrogance, jealousy, inequity, injustice, opportunism, power mongering, desire to dominate and enslave others, corruption in governance, colonialism, class bias, racism, international discrimination, and worsening levels of economic poverty in all the nations on Earth. Most of all, capitalism seriously weakens peoples' resolve for spiritual pursuits.

Therefore, capitalism is a very deadly weapon in the hands of the principalities over ignorant human beings on Earth. It is responsible for virtually all the social ills bedeviling our society today. Our forms of public governance, societal value system and activities of our socioeconomic institutions are entirely capitalist in nature. They continually reenact principalities' deadly blow on true humanity in the battle of Babel. Thus, capitalism is a continual celebration of defeat of true communism and collapse of our collective spiritual thrust that the true Tower of Babel symbolized.

L. MONEY: ULTIMATE WEAPON OF SELF-DAMNATION

Money is the engine of capitalism. **The love of money** is perhaps the most overwhelming of all the weapons of control employed by the principalities. We read in 1 Tim 6:10 that "love of money is the root of all evils; it is through this craving that some have wandered away from the faith [from the Father] and pierced their hearts with many pangs." The newest craze in today's world concerns ignorant men and women competing to be named among *The world's Billionaires* in *Forbes Magazine*, without a single thought about the masses that they impoverish in pursuance of their selfish obsessions; without regards to the grave spiritual disadvantages associated with such vanity.

But **love of money** is not a unique obsession of the few; it is a universal bewitchment. Today's world is teaming with dupes; people who are determined to make money at all costs. It is very hard these days, to find people who can be completely trusted on money matters. And anybody who cannot be trusted on money matters cannot be trusted on anything else. Such a person is a potential murderer. Usually, people we trust and hold in great esteem—brothers, sisters, close relations, and friends—will dupe us the most. People even mortgage their own lives to make money that they may never be alive to enjoy. Mercenaries for instance, are professionals who sacrifice their lives for money to fight other people's wars. We have mercenaries in all fields of economic endeavors in today's world. So many people today knowingly sell their souls to the devil for money and the fame it brings, by becoming involved in all kinds of secret rituals that are usually associated with ritual killings. They knowingly choose to make money today and die tomorrow. Armed robbery, pen robbery, corruption in public offices, religious racketeering, kidnapping, drug trafficking, money laundering and all manners of money swindling are various means of making money at all costs. Such societal vices are on the increase in all the nations on Earth today.

According to John Fowles, author of *The Aristos*, "money is utility not a matter of faith." And as far as material needs of man are concerned, Solomon says in Eccl 10:19 that "money answers everything." Indeed, man cannot live without food; and without money, he cannot obtain the food that he needs in today's world. So, everyone *loves* to have enough money to spend on his daily sustenance. Thus, love of money becomes a necessary evil committed by every living human being on Earth. But the gap between the rich and the poor is steadily widening all over the world; the rich are increasingly getting richer and the poor poorer. As a result, many people are compelled by circumstances beyond their control to engage in all manners of legal and illegal, moral and immoral activities for money; just to make ends meet.

The records are very clear however, that Jesus Christ preached against materialism; he spoke firmly against pursuit of riches, prosperity, or worldly possessions. He taught that "a man's life does not consist in the abundance of his possessions." [Luke 12:15] In fact, he preached against *Money*, emphasizing that it was a weapon of damnation belonging to and manipulated by *Caesar* or the ruling principality, whom he personified as Money itself. In other words, Jehovah/Allah, as the chief principality over the Earth, is *Money* that rules our world today. This calls for wisdom!

According to Revelation 13:16-18 (NIV), "He [Money or Jehovah/Allah] also forced everyone, small and great, rich, and poor, free and slave, to receive a mark on his right hand or on his forehead, **so that no one could buy or sell unless he had the mark, which is the name of the beast** or the number of his name. ... His number is 666." To simplify the mystery, Jehovah/Allah is the Beast that rules our world; his nickname is Money, and the cryptic number of that name is 666. People who pursue worldly riches are naturally devoted to Money/Jehovah and not to the Father. Hence, Jesus Christ says in Matthew 6:24 (NIV), "No one can serve two masters. Either he will hate the one and love the other, or he will be devoted to the one and despise the other. **You cannot serve both** the Father **and Money.**" No one can serve the Father and Jehovah/Allah at the same time.

This presents serious dilemma to customary Christians who serve Jehovah/Allah, the god of material prosperity, while pretending to be followers of Jesus Christ. They know that all known friends of Jehovah/Allah in the Bible were very rich and famous. **Abraham** "was very rich in cattle, in silver, and in gold … he had sheep, oxen, he-asses, menservants, maidservants, she-asses, and camels." [Gen 13:2; 12:16] Jehovah/Allah made for **David** "a great name, like the name of the great ones of the Earth," as he promised him. [2 Samuel 7:9] And **Solomon** "excelled all the kings of the Earth in riches," … and he "made silver as common in Jerusalem as stone." [1King 10:23, 27] But customary Christians deliberately refuse to accept the natural conclusion, which is that these so-called men of *God* served god of material prosperity and not the Father.

Customary Christians argue that *money* is not the root of all evils but *the love of money*. Well, as we have seen, everyone who loves to be alive loves money to a certain degree. And since Christ equates Jehovah/Allah, the god of this world, to Money, it means that Jehovah/Allah and not just the love of Jehovah/Allah is the root of all evils on Earth. That agrees completely with Amos 3:6, which asks, "Does evil befall a city, unless Jehovah/Allah has done it?" and with 1 John 5:19, which says that "the whole world is under the control of the evil one." No one doubts that Money controls this world; indeed, "*no one can buy or sell unless he has the mark*." Therefore, customary Christians need stronger argument that can cancel out Christ's emphatic statements against the love and worship of Money, at least, in their own mentality. Paul of Tarsus provides them with the perfect alibi in 2 Cor 8:9, where he says, "For you know the grace of our Lord Jesus Christ, that though he was rich, yet for your sake **he became poor, so that by his poverty you might become rich**."

To hypocritical customary Christian believers, this single devious verse cancels out everything that Jesus Christ says against the worship of god of this world and the pursuit of worldly possessions. It provides them justification and the needed impetus to openly embrace Jehovah/Allah as god and master of their false faith in the Father. The truth remains however, that Jesus Christ was never poor in any way, physically or spiritually, if by poverty Paul means that he was ever in want for his daily needs and sustenance for the whole thirty-three years he lived as human on Earth. The word *poverty* simply does not apply to Jesus Christ. He was very rich spiritually; he had no consciousness of lack and he never experienced lack. If that amounted to being poor in the world, why would true followers of Jesus Christ not desire to be as *poor* as he was? Why should they aspire to become richer than he was? So, there is no way Paul and his followers can justifiably wish away Christ's actual position on worldly riches, which holds that "it is easier for a camel to go through the eye of a needle than for a rich man to enter the kingdom of the Father." [Matt 19:24]

Of course, Jesus Christ knows that people need money to buy bread of this life and he assures that people who seek the kingdom of the Father first—who serve the Father and not Money in their overall disposition—will never lack the very necessities of this life. "These things dominate the thoughts of unbelievers," he says, "but your heavenly Father already knows all your needs. Seek the Kingdom of the Father above all else, and live righteously, and he will give you everything you need." [Matt 6:32-33 (NLT)] But the Father giving us "everything we need" to get by in this life does not mean giving us the kind of riches and public éclat that distinguished Jehovah/Allah's staunch votaries in the Old Testament. Becoming "the richest person on Earth" comes with the risk of eternal self-damnation. No true Christ-follower would like to take that chance. No true Christ-follower would like to be named among *the world's Billionaires* in *Forbes Magazine*. I would not!

Ironically, although Paul of Tarsus presents Jesus Christ as *poor God* to give leeway to customary Christian followers of Jehovah/Allah, evangelical prosperity preachers publicly say that they are not serving the *poor God*. They say that it is the right, and therefore, should be the dream of every churchgoer to become exceedingly rich on Earth. To them it does not matter if one gains the whole world and forfeits his life. Pastor Chris Okotie wrote in his book, *The Last Outcast*, that "The Church of Jesus Christ has only one need now. That need is to enter into the financial blessings of Christ Jesus. We have everything else...." It is obvious that prosperity pastors like Okotie are deliberately confused about whose Church they minister for. The Church and financial blessings he referred to were certainly those of Jehovah/Allah the *Mammon*, and not of Jesus Christ, who according to 2 Cor 8:9 is the *poor God*. Needless to stress that desiring to excel in worldly riches is aspiration of fools. For, "He who loves money will not be satisfied with money; nor he who loves wealth, with gain: this also is vanity," says Eccl 5:10.

Sense of physical poverty is entirely pathology of the human mind. Lower animals have no consciousness of lack because they do not have minds. Neither does a madman who has lost his mind. Sense of poverty is affliction of unsound or unenlightened minds. It is unnatural to true sons of the Father. A sound or enlightened mind will have no consciousness of poverty because he is rich in spiritual values. Physical poverty is a mindset brought about by systematic hypnotic influence of the warring principalities, and it is made endemic by programmed capitalist world instinct. As we all know, money has gradually become universal benchmark for our societal value system. Right and wrong have also become a matter of cash. People who have money can buy justice, while those who do not have it go to jail. For people who have *the mark* of Jehovah/Allah's empowerment, money indeed, answereth all things of material nature. They are the movers and shakers of society. They can literally buy their way through any situation here on Earth, while people who do not have it seemingly pine away. Jehovah/Allah knew that not everyone will receive *the mark*; hence he assured the Jews that "the poor will never cease out of the land." [Deut 15:11]

In any case, real poverty has nothing to do with having or not having money. Some people have the mark of the Beast and yet are still physically very poor. Real poverty concerns spiritual Earth. Spiritual poverty cannot be assuaged by money. Money cannot buy anything that is of true value. It cannot buy true love, peace, happiness, and genuine fulfillment; it cannot even buy life of this world. Above all, money cannot buy spiritual salvation. Ultimate success in this life is not a quotient of financial prosperity; it is not having the mark of the beast written on one's forehead but having one's name written in Christ's book of true eternal life.

CHAPTER FIVE: THE ULTIMATE MAN

BEFORE AND AFTER MAN ENCOUNTERED THE HEAVENLY CHRIST IN EDEN

I was a big-time poultry farmer at one point in my life; rearing up to 1500 broilers, per batch, for table meat. I travelled great distance, from Lagos to Aderupoko Farms in Abeokuta, Ogun State, to obtain sound day-old chicks; and I fed and nurtured them day and night until they reached market weight in seven weeks. I spent sleepless nights heating their nursery cribs, cleaning, and disinfecting their environment to keep them safe and healthy; and I employed the services of qualified veterinary doctor that administered needed vaccines and medications. I personally nursed the sick ones in the sickbay and buried the ones that could not make it to the final weighing and slaughter. There was no doubt that I loved my birds; I provided for them everything that they needed to mature perfectly. In fact, I was their god.

Unfortunately, I was not their messiah. My love for them was entirely self-seeking, and it lasted for only seven weeks for every batch. I fattened them purely to fatten my proceeds at the end of every batch. Thus, my love never improved or changed their fate. At the end of seven weeks, collectors from Fasakin Foods came, weighed, and carted them all away to their factory for slaughter. And in matter of hours, they were turned into frozen chickens, ready to be supplied to meat shops and supermarkets for the stomachs of final consumers who cherished their white meat for protein and healthy living. So it was that everyone involved in the transient lives of my broilers loved them for all the wrong reasons. Such remains the life and fate of poultry and livestock reared for food by *dedicated* farmers all over the world. They are *loved* and cared for by the people who eventually sacrifice them for personal gains.

Lower animals are in serious bondage in the world, especially in the hands of ignorant humans. Most people do not feel or see anything abnormal about inhuman treatment of lower animals. Humans do not readily appreciate that lower animals possess both brains and redeemable souls as humans do. Yet, like the humans, they feel physical pains, joy, fear, and love; meaning that they equally feel inner grief in their souls over their hapless spiritual status in the world of matter. The only reason they are not fighting for spiritual salvation as humans do now is because they have not received divine enlightenment in their souls as humans did, and therefore, do not possess active minds to coordinate their emotions. They were not as privileged as humans to have a heavenly Messiah appear among them to inform and guide them through the divine process of spiritual rebirth. Despite increasing activities of numerous animal rights activists all over the world, fate of farm animals remains utterly hopeless, because activists are merely human sympathizers without unique authorities as our heavenly Redeemer.

Although man occupied a slightly higher level of consciousness within the hierarchy of organic animals than poultry and livestock, he was, by basic nature, equally reared to perish. His days are very "few and full of trouble," says the Bible, "He comes forth like a flower, and withers; he flees like a shadow, and continues not." [Job 14:1-2] The Bible might have portrayed Adam and Eve as royal gardeners, but they were indeed a class of livestock in Eden. They were bondservants to yet a higher species of organic animals; fed and kept temporarily alive for the pleasures and benefits of the masters of their situation. Although they possessed highly developed brains and redeemable souls as the principalities, they were kept in total darkness about the spiritual heritage of all souls and the possibility and need for spiritual refinement. Like the lower animals, "the man and his wife were both naked [before the gods], but they felt no shame." [Gen 2:25] They toiled and labored in Jehovah/Allah's nature park without any knowledge, hope or prospect of eternal spiritual freedom or possibility of ultimate transition to perfect spiritual existence. "The whole duty of man," according to the Bible, was to "fear [his] god, and keep his commandments." [Eccl 12:13] There was absolutely nothing in that for man.

Like other livestock, man's life was meaningless, hopeless, and short-lived by cosmic design. His overall fate was irrevocably doomed to death. All the entities involved with the making of man and his world were opportunists; they exploited his acute state of ignorance and played gods over him. Pretending to be divine and superlative, self-arrogated principalities who were but a more enlightened species of animals, simply partitioned ignorant humans into communities of religious animals and enthroned themselves as religious idols, lords, kings and gods over the various peoples. Thus, story of man and the so-called gods was purely a case of some animals being more equal than others within the cosmic animal world; a case of some half-blinded opportunists enthroning themselves over totally blinded ones. Man was in total blind subjection to Jehovah/Allah and the principalities, as the lower animals were to man. That was the grand cosmic situation before the revolutionary events that took place in Eden and the gods meant it to be everlasting.

Suddenly, a unique human rights activist—one with absolute redemptive authority—appeared for man in Eden and decisively altered the cosmic situation in his favor, giving meaning to fate of man's soul. The divine encounter brought sudden enlightenment to man's soul, activated a functional mind within his person and opened a vista of divine opportunities and possibilities before him; most importantly, giving him the hope of ultimate spiritual resurrection. The Scripture proclaims man's sudden divine experience in these words: "The people who walked in darkness have seen a Great Light; those who dwelt in a land of deep darkness, on them has light shined." [Isa 9:2] That **Great Light from Heaven** was none other than the Heavenly Christ, in his first appearance in the world as Spirit of Knowledge.

Adam and Eve lived in eternal blind subjection to Jehovah/Allah and the principalities who were the lords, kings, and gods of the cosmic stage, but timely intervention by the heavenly Luminary granted them immediate release from *divine* enslavement in Eden and inaugurated divine process for ultimate spiritual resurrection of their souls and those of their posterity. That process is presently running its due course and his solemn word of assurance to man's soul in the genesis remains in focus—"You will not surely die." [Gen 3:4 (NIV)] Jehovah/Allah and the principalities had threatened that man would surely die the very day he sought knowledge of, or learned the truth of, the secret cosmic equation that held him in eternal bondage to the system. "But you must not eat from the tree of the knowledge of good and evil," commanded Jehovah/Allah, "for when you eat of it you will surely die." [Gen 2:17 (NIV)]

That initial standoff between the Great Light from heaven and the lying principalities was decisively settled right there in Eden. Inspired by the heavenly Light, Adam and Eve ate of the *forbidden* fruit of knowledge and immediately "the eyes of both were opened, and they knew that they were naked [or spiritually blinded]." [Gen 3:7] And rather than drop dead as the gods had threatened, Adam and Eve came alive in their souls and automatically learnt how to rationalize their emotions. They "sewed fig leaves together and made themselves aprons" of moral rectitude, and thus, inaugurated the starting points of evolution of man's knowledge and mankind's slow but steady return journey to the Heavenly Tree of true Life.

Inaugurated on the same day by the Unique Light from heaven was foundation of abolitionist movements against all forms of human enslavement in the world, both physical and spiritual. The lying principalities on their part started the most complex propaganda battle of resistance against express will of the heavenly Father for man. Enlightened man had become a dangerous threat; a terminal enemy, cursed and literally embattled by his own gods. Genesis 3:17-19 captures dept of the principalities' resolve to make life unbearable for liberated humankind: "Cursed is the ground because of you; in toil you shall eat of it all the days of your life; thorns and thistles it shall bring forth to you; ... In the sweat of your face you shall eat bread till you return to the ground, for out of it you were taken; you are dust, and to dust you shall return." Thus, Jehovah/Allah suddenly turned from being the master and mentor to tormentor of mankind. The world was never to be the same again after that fateful day in Eden.

People who look closely at the tale of Eden will see the hidden triangle of contending forces, representing the unrepentant **captors**, their blinded **captives,** and the loving heavenly **Redeemer.** They will see that salvation of fallen human souls is a battle between Good and Evil; and they will not be in any doubt as to who is who behind the battle lines. Jehovah/Allah and the principalities are *evil* captors who would not let their slaves go; humans are *unconscious* captives who do not even know that they are in bondage, while the Great Light from heaven is Jesus Christ, the *good* Redeemer and Abolitionist with absolute divine authority.

However, the heavenly Christ did not come into the world to redeem man by force of arms, but rather to enlighten him enough to the point that he would willingly choose to work out his own divine redemption. And that was going to take some time, considering the deep-rooted nature of human ignorance. So, while the heavenly Light allowed ample time for light of truth to duly permeate utterly blinded minds of humans, the lying principalities settled down to conceive the most complex propaganda machinery unimaginable to unsuspecting humans, designed to discredit the heavenly Envoy, and ultimately to try to turn the captives against their own true

Redeemer.

Jesus Christ captures the ensuing battle scenario with one of his parables of the battle of the kingdom, given in Matt 13:24-25. It reads, "The kingdom of heaven may be compared to a man who sowed good seed in his field; but while men were sleeping, his enemy came and sowed weeds among the wheat, and went away." And he explains the wisdom of heaven in allowing ample time for the battle of true life. "Let both grow together until the harvest," he says, "lest in gathering the weeds you root up the wheat along with them; ... at harvest time I will tell the reapers, 'Gather the weeds first and bind them in bundles to be burned, but gather the wheat into my barn.'" [Matt 13:29-30] So the willful captors knew quite well that their time was indeed numbered.

THE HEAVENLY LIGHT IN HUMAN FORM

The crucial mystery for today's man to unravel concerns the true identity of the heavenly Luminary that appeared to Adam and Eve in Eden; that permanently altered not only the course of human history but also that of entire cosmic world order. Any man who resolves the puzzle correctly in his mind will live; the one who does not will die.

Who really was the *Great Light* from heaven whose sudden appearance in the world dispelled the perpetual darkness that enshrouded the inner eyes of man? Where did he come from? What was his express mission in the world? Has he lived up to his word of assurance to man in Eden? And does his express will agree completely with that of Jesus Christ whom the whole world acclaims as his divine Incarnation? The principalities dismissed the redeeming Great Light that appeared in Eden as serpent the devil. But today's man has had all the time that was needed and should be able to supply reasonable answers to these and other questions regarding the true nature of the heavenly Luminary. Modern man has heard the stories, seen the manifestations and experienced the difference for himself, so he has no excuse still pretending to be unable to differentiate between good and evil.

It was obvious that the *Great Light* from heaven that appeared in Eden was unique and revolutionary. His express will and activities directly undermined the cosmic interests and authority of the principalities right from the onset. The gods desired everlasting dominion over blinded, dead human souls, but the heavenly Light came to liberate the captives and give them life in abundance. "You will not die" was the central theme of his assurance to man. Therefore, his divine mission in the world was to give life to dead souls. Although the principalities arbitrarily branded him an inconsequential serpent to save their faces, their real immediate reaction, as the Bible captures in Genesis 3:22-24 and 11:5-8, starkly portray panic and great discomfiture at his sudden advent. Their immediate action and utterances gave them away not just as second fiddles but also as heavenly renegades and agents of darkness. The *Great Light* from heaven was, therefore, the legitimate authority. He was someone far superior in power and wisdom to Jehovah/Allah and all the cosmic ruling powers of the world.

It was also evident that advent of the heavenly Light took both man and the gods by surprise. The principalities did not have prior-knowledge or even the slightest premonition of his sudden appearance in the world, which proved the fact that they were completely cut off from the goings on within the heavenly domain of Divine Light. So, we know that the heaven that the Great Light came from was exclusive, and it transcended entire spheres of the cosmic world of organic animals ruled over by Jehovah/Allah and the lying principalities. And since the will of that heaven authoritatively outlawed the whims of entire cosmic world order, we know also that that was the true Heaven—the very domain of the Father of Lights.

Surely, the Great Light from heaven had remained faithful to his divine mission, and to his word of promise to mankind. He abolished the onset of divine enslavement of humans in Eden and obliterated the memory of Jehovah/Allah's so-called Garden of Eden forever. Suddenly, what Jehovah/Allah had called everlasting Paradise became an everlasting wasteland and a failed dream for him, even to this day.

The Great Light from heaven came that we may become educated, and today, intellectual accomplishments of the modern man speak volumes. Evolution of human knowledge has seen various tiers of schools built all over the world and education made the basic right of every human being. The modern man, having made astounding advances into various branches of knowledge—arts and literature, science and technology, astronomy, philosophy, metaphysics and so on, can today point to the *World Wide Web* and speak of *Information Superhighway* as some of the tangible legacies of the silent endowments of the heavenly Light on mankind.

The days of spiritual primitivism and social savagery that characterized

Edenic and ancient eras of absolute human bondage to the gods have almost entirely given way to global civilization and religious freethinking. Institutionalized ritual worship of the principalities with the associated horrors of open animal and human blood sacrifices that went on all over the world has become a thing of the past. Perpetrators and victims of ritual sacrifices suffered and died for want of knowledge. People know better today. Dirty and smelly shrines of the gods, even in the remotest corners of the civilized world, have been cleared out and the sites set aside for valuable social edifices like schools and recreation grounds for children. The gods on their parts have perforce gulped down the very potion for soul blindness that they prepared for mankind and have sunken deeper and deeper into obscurity, although they still have clever ways of infusing evil stimuli into every good idea of unsuspecting humans.

Today, Jehovah/Allah no longer foments public nuisance or disturbs people's peace openly in the name of being the mighty one of Israel. He no longer multiplies plagues over defenseless population of peace-loving people, nor does he pull down walls of Jericho over sleeping communities as he used to. He can no longer open the ground and swallow people who do not agree with his lopsided sense of justice and equity. He has gone totally clandestine. The Great Light of truth has ultimately banished him to the darkest part of his own dungeon forever, while for mankind, "The darkness is [progressively] passing away and the true light is already shining." [1 John 2:8-9] The inner beauty and dignity of man is increasingly becoming evident, as Jehovah/Allah steadily fades away from spiritual consciousness of truly enlightened humanity. However, it cannot be disputed that Jehovah/Allah still has dominion over great multitudes of unthinking religious men and women. While some of them are purely beguiled, great numbers are greedy followers who knowingly sell their souls to him in return for all kinds of worthless material gains—money, power, fame, protection, and the likes.

Given above are only brief summations of innumerable impacts of the heavenly Light in the life of humankind. Time has shown that he was not an inconsequential serpent and enemy of man, as the lying principalities had insinuated, but rather a true heavenly Redeemer beamed into the world by the Father of Lights to redeem fallen sons of Light trapped within eternal realm of darkness and spiritual death. As the whole world will agree, consistency and continuity has remained the hallmark of his unfolding influence, from the very day he appeared to man in Eden as Light of

Knowledge to this day. That is where the link with Jesus Christ, the Son of man, is made. Overwhelming evidence exist, which prove that Jesus of Nazareth was one and the same Redeeming Light that first appeared to man in Eden. At his own appointed time, and in accordance with his word of assurance to Adam and Eve, he manifested in human form to bear witness to the truth of what really transpired in Eden. He confirms that in John 18:37, saying, "For this I was born, and for this I have come into the world, **to bear witness to the truth.**"

Biblical account of the divine visitation of man as given in the book of Genesis is fraudulent. It deliberately presented only one-sided narration given by the disgraced Jehovah/Allah to save his face in a situation that caught him completely off guard. He made himself prosecutor, jury, and judge in a case where he was actually the defendant. His integrity was the one called into question by the events of Eden, so he had no right to be the only one to be heard or the one to declare himself winner. The Genesis account deliberately omitted the Redeemer's side of the story, as well as that of Adam and Eve. So, the issue was still open to discussion. Nevertheless, the Redeemer made a promise to Adam and Eve that he would reappear when the time was right in a form that humans would be able to relate with to personally restate his divine mission in the world.

Adam and his sons prophesied that "The True Light that enlightens every man was coming into the world" in human form. And at his own appointed time, he materialized amid Adam's descendants. Jesus, the Son of man became the divine Incarnation of the heavenly Light. The prophecies would have been meaningless if they were not implying that Jesus Christ had once been on the stage in a form that was not known to humans; and that even after relinquishing his mortal cloak he would continue to be who he has always been, and still be the sole Redeemer of mankind. The whole world does not seem to have any problem accepting that Jesus Christ is *Light from Light*; that he is the true Light of the world, the heavenly Redeemer of mankind, the Truth, and the only Way to true life eternal. Yet, even though people also agree that he is "the same yesterday and today and forever," they have deliberately refused to make the link between his days in human form among the Jews and his yesterday with Adam and Eve in Eden as Spirit of Knowledge.

It should be stressed at this juncture that the true prophets of the Old Testaments were sons of Adam and therefore, disciples of the heavenly Light and not of Jehovah/Allah. Jehovah/Allah, who did not have the slightest clue about the first coming of the heavenly Christ in Eden, did not also have details of his second coming. He shamelessly attached himself to sons of Adam to try to steal the stage, and he succeeded by enticing Abram with meaningless material rewards. Nevertheless, all Jehovah/Allah had to work with were disjointed information he gleaned from words of the true prophets. That was why, in most cases, he made fool of himself pretending to be the one sending the heavenly Christ, while at the same time making wrong predictions through his own false prophets concerning some aspects of his actual ministry.

Jehovah/Allah predicted that the heavenly Christ was coming to assume dominion over the world literally; that "to him was given dominion and glory and kingdom, **that all peoples, nations, and languages should serve him.'** [Dan 7:14] Therefore, when he tempted the Messiah at the start of his ministry and offered to grant him authority and dominion over the kingdoms of the world if he would worship him in return, he was still unsure what the Messiah had come into the world to do. Jesus Christ refuted that false prophecy, saying that "The Son of man came not to be served but to serve, and to give his life as a ransom for many." [Matt 20:28]

Jehovah/Allah had also predicted that the Messiah was coming to overthrow and rule as king in Jerusalem to bring peace to the whole world—"Rejoice greatly, O daughter of Zion! Shout aloud, O daughter of Jerusalem! **Lo, your king comes to you; triumphant and victorious is he**, humble and riding on an ass, on a colt the foal of an ass. I [Jehovah/Allah] will cut off the chariot from Ephraim and the war horse from Jerusalem; and the battle bow shall be cut off, and he [Jesus Christ] shall command peace to the nations; **his dominion shall be from sea to sea, and from the River to the ends of the Earth.**" [Zech 9:9-10] This false prophecy formed basis of the unfounded concerns of Jehovah/Allah's chief priests and agents of Roman Empire who accused Jesus Christ of trying to install himself as king of the Jews. Jesus Christ assured them that he had not come for their thrones of darkness, but rather to retrieve lost sons of heaven trapped within the kingdoms of darkness. "My kingship is not of this world … my kingship is not from the world," he told them. [John 18:36]

In other cases, Jehovah/Allah simply aimed at confusing the simple message of the true prophets of the heavenly Christ with interpolations of impossible dreams of his own for an indefinite future. The following prophecies given by Jehovah/Allah have absolutely nothing to do with coming of the heavenly Light in human form; and they certainly do not fit into Christ's divine mission plan. He deliberately used 'the Lord' in his *predictive* prophecies to make unsuspecting readers think he was referring to the Messiah, but they were all about himself:

> **ISAIAH 2:2-4:** "It shall come to pass in the latter days that the mountain of the house of the Lord [Jehovah/Allah] shall be established as the highest of the mountains, and shall be raised above the hills; and all the nations shall flow to it, and many peoples shall come, and say: 'Come, let us go up to the mountain of the Lord [Jehovah/Allah], to the house of the *God* of Jacob; that he may teach us his ways and that we may walk in his paths.' **For out of Zion shall go forth the law, and the word of the Lord [Jehovah/Allah] from Jerusalem**. He [Jehovah] shall judge between the nations, and shall decide for many peoples; and **they shall beat their swords into plowshares, and their spears into pruning hooks; nation shall not lift up sword against nation, neither shall they learn war anymore**."

> **ISAIAH 65:17-25:** "For behold, I [Jehovah/Allah] create new heavens and a new Earth; and the former things shall not be remembered or come into mind. ... The wolf and the lamb shall feed together; the lion shall eat straw like the ox, and dust shall be the serpent's food. They shall not hurt or destroy in all my holy mountain, says the Lord [Jehovah/Allah]."

Again, Jesus Christ counters all that, saying, "Do you think that I have come to give peace on Earth? No, I tell you, but rather division; ... I came to cast fire upon the Earth; and would that it were already kindled!" [Luke 12:51, 49]

ZECHARIAH 8:3-5; EZEKIEL 37:24-28; ZECHARIAH 14:9: "Thus says the Lord [Jehovah/Allah]: I will return to Zion, and will dwell in the midst of Jerusalem, and Jerusalem shall be called the faithful city, and the mountain of the Lord [Jehovah/Allah] of hosts, the holy mountain. ... Old men and old women shall again sit in the streets of Jerusalem, each with staff in hand for very age. And the streets of the city shall be full of boys and girls playing in its streets."

"**My servant David shall be king over them; and they shall all have one shepherd.** They shall follow my ordinances and be careful to observe my statutes. ... and **David my servant shall be their prince forever**. ... My dwelling place shall be with them; and I [Jehovah/Allah] will be their *God*, and they shall be my people. Then the nations will know that I the Lord [Jehovah/Allah] sanctify Israel, when my sanctuary is in the midst of them for evermore."

"**And the Lord [Jehovah/Allah] will become king over all the Earth**; on that day the Lord [Jehovah/Allah] will be one and his name one."

It was these kinds of deliberately jumbled information about the true identity and mission of the coming Messiah that warranted Jesus Christ to ask his disciples, "Who do men say that the Son of man is? [Matt 16:13] None in his audience was exactly sure. Some thought he was re-embodiment of king David, John the Baptist, Elijah, Jeremiah, or just another prophet. He told them that he was not another prophet, but Light of the prophets. He also assured them that he was not their David as Jehovah/Allah had predicted, and asked them to reason it out themselves: "How can the scribes say that the heavenly Christ is the son of David? David himself, inspired by the Holy Spirit, declared, 'The Lord said to my Lord, Sit at my right hand, till I put thy enemies under thy feet.' David himself calls him Lord; so how is he his son?" [Mark 12:35-37]

He further tried to make them understand that he had been the same patient Redeemer that appeared to Adam and Eve in Eden all along by trying to contrast his eternal nature with the fleeting lifetime of the mortal man, Abraham. [Abram was prophet of the heavenly Christ; Jehovah/Allah abducted him, altered his course, and renamed him Abraham, and then used him to establish the disoriented twelve tribes of Israel.] He said to them, "Your father Abraham rejoiced that he was to see my day [of physical manifestation on Earth]; he saw it and was glad. ... And "Truly, truly, I say to you, before Abraham was, I am." [John 8:56-59] But they did not understand. Yet, the Scripture tells us about the old man Simeon whom the heavenly Light had promised that he would not see death before he had seen him in his human form. Simeon's testimony at the dedication of baby Jesus proved that he was indeed Abraham of old. He took the child up in his arms **and blessed the Father** and said, "Lord [Jesus Christ], now lettest thou thy servant depart in peace, according to thy word; for mine eyes have seen thy salvation which thou hast prepared in the presence of all peoples, a light for revelation to the Gentiles, and for glory to thy people Israel." [Luke 2:29-32]

Testimony of John the Baptist who sealed off the true prophets of the heavenly Christ came next. John the Baptist came specifically to officially establish the link between the heavenly Light that appeared to Adam and Eve in Eden and his human form—to bear witness to the divine Incarnation, that all might believe through him. He described the expected Messiah as "one, the thong of whose sandal he was not worthy to untie," and said that he came baptizing with water, that he who baptizes with the Holy Light might be finally revealed to Israel. When he was convinced that all the signs converged fully on one unique man from Nazareth, he testified; "I have seen it ... and I tell you that he is the Son of the Father. ... "This is the one I was talking about when I said, 'He comes after me, but he is greater than I am, because **he existed before I was born** [just as he existed before Abraham was born].'" [John 1:34, 15]

Finally, Apostle Simon Peter saw the link in his soul and solved the mystery when he declared to the misled Israelites that Jesus was the expected Great Light from heaven. "You are the Christ, the Son of the living Father," Peter stated. The Messiah blessed him for that insight and said to him, "Blessed are you, Simon Bar-Jona! For, flesh and blood has not revealed this to you, but my Father who is in heaven. And I tell you, you are Peter [i.e., Courage of Rock], and on this rock I will build my church [ministry], and the powers of death shall not prevail against it." [Matt 16:17-18]

Perhaps the most comprehensive testimony of the link between Jesus of Nazareth and the heavenly Light that appeared to Adam and Eve in Eden is given in the first chapter of the Gospel book of John. The first five verses make it clear that the Father, the heavenly Christ, and the Father's eternal creation all existed to eternity, well ***before the world was invented***. It was obvious from the verses that neither the Father nor the Christ created the world that was characterized by darkness and death. Rather, the Father sent the heavenly Christ into the world to give true light and spiritual resurrection to captive souls trapped in it. And Christ, the Light, will shine in the world of darkness for as long as his mission lasts. Darkness will once again overtake entire world at the close of his ministry when he finally withdraws.

John 1:1-5 (TEV) reads, "**Before the world was created**, the Word [of Life] already existed; he was with the Father, and he was the same as the Father. From the very beginning the Word was with the Father. Through him the Father made all things; not one thing in all [spiritual] creation was made without him. The Word was the source of life, and **this life brought light to mankind**. The light shines in the darkness, and the darkness has never put it out." Here John tells the story of the heavenly Christ's involvement with human salvation not from the beginning of human world, but rather by beginning with proof of his eternal divine nature.

John 1:14-18 (TEV) adds, "The Word [of Life] became a human being and, full of grace and truth, lived among us. We saw his glory, the glory which he received as the Father's only Son. ... Out of the fullness of his grace he has blessed us all [humanity], **giving us one blessing after another**. ... No one [in the world] has ever seen the Father. The only Son, who is the same as the Father and is at the Father's side, he has made him known [in the world]." There is no doubt that Jesus of Nazareth was the perfect exemplar of divine glory. His deeds and utterances set him completely apart from every other entity that ever walked the surface of the Earth in human form. Jesus Christ is unique in every way. In entire history of organic existence, no entity, physical or metaphysical, has ever touched lives of humankind positively as he has. Everything good that ever happened to humankind is attributable to the light of spiritual refinement, represented by Jesus Christ. If not for him, humankind would have remained blinded livestock in the jungle of Eden, naked and shameless like the lower animals.

Now, how did Jesus Christ make the link between himself and the heavenly Light that appeared in Eden? How did he prove that he was one and the same personage? Well, he purposely tailored his ministry to fulfill selected signs he inspired in his true prophets, and he quoted parts of their prophecies that correctly capture his true mission in the world. The Great Light in Eden was a revolutionary; he promised liberation of captive human souls from eternal bondage to Jehovah/Allah and the lying principalities and assured that man will not surely die because he imbibed the fruit of knowledge. Jesus Christ ratified the promises and exemplified them in practical human terms.

On one Sabbath day in Nazareth, he entered the synagogue and read from the book of prophet Isaiah what proved to be his mission statement, and that tallied exactly with the express mission of the heavenly Light in Eden. Luke 4:18-19 reads: "The Spirit of the Father is upon me, because he has anointed me **to preach good news to the poor. He has sent me to proclaim release to the captives and recovering of sight to the blind, to set at liberty those who are oppressed, to proclaim the acceptable year of the Father.**" His express mission, like that of the heavenly Light in Eden, remained directly opposed to the cosmic whims of Jehovah/Allah and the principalities who rule the world, which was why they plotted his crucifixion.

Jesus Christ says emphatically that he is the Light that promises life to the world. "I am the light of the world; he who follows me will not walk in darkness, but will have the light of life, he says, "As long as I am in the world, I am the light of the world;" meaning that the world had no light before his first appearance and will eventually revert to total darkness when he finally departs at the end of his divine mission. [John 9:5] Then, he assures us that he is here only "for a little longer." [John 12:35] Neither Jehovah/Allah nor any of the so-called ruling gods of the world could contest Christ's testimony of himself, because they know that they all are indeed full of darkness. They are the notorious powers of darkness that rule the world of darkness. 2 Esdras 14:20 confirms that "This world is a dark place, and its people have no light" before the arrival of Jesus Christ on the stage. Surely, the world will not be an overwhelming *dark place* if Jehovah/Allah or any of the ruling principalities has light in himself. Eph 6:12 refers to them as "world rulers of this present darkness," and "spiritual hosts of wickedness in the heavenly places." And no wonder 1 John 5:19

says that "the whole world is in the power of the evil one[s]."

Jesus Christ did not just claim to be the Great Light that appeared in Eden, he proved it by reenacting the events of Eden in the street of Jerusalem with one of his practical parables. Like the lower animals, man was created without knowledge of the difference between good and evil. In fact, such knowledge was forbidden for humankind, and that was tantamount to forced spiritual blindness. In that state, Adam and Eve were literally *born blind*, but divine encounter with the Great Light from heaven restored their sight. Jesus Christ restored the sight of a man *born blind* in the street of Jerusalem, the present Eden, to correlate opening of inner eyes of Adam and Eve who were literally born blind in the old Eden. As usual he chose to perform that good work on a Sabbath day to undermine authority of Jehovah/Allah who was god of the Sabbath.

He purposely sent the blind man far away to Silo'am to wash off the clay plaster he had placed over his eyelids to make sure that when he regained his sight he did not immediately see or know who had done it for him. It was also intended to portray the strength of faith Adam and Eve had in the words of a total stranger to their situation. When the blind man believed, obeyed, and had received his miracle, his neighbors and regular benefactors doubted if he was indeed the same blind beggar that always sat by the roadside. He assured them that he was the one. "Then how were your eyes opened?" they asked him. He answered, "The man called Jesus made clay and anointed my eyes and said to me, 'Go to Silo'am and wash'; **so, I went and washed and received my sight**." "Where is he?" they asked. He answered, "I do not know." [John 9:10-12]

The Messiah allowed the simple man who had never seen before his divine visitation to testify openly in his own words when directly confronted by tough supporters of Jehovah/Allah—the Pharisees. Not even his parents would interfere in his special testimony. "**He is of age**, he will speak for himself," they said to the inquisitors. They meant that like humanity, their son was grown enough and, in a position, to differentiate between what is good and what is evil.

It seemed most reasonable for me to reproduce exact dialogue between the Pharisees, the man, and the Messiah because the very words make direct link between Jesus Christ and the heavenly Light in Eden. Besides, this part of the Scripture is one of my favorites:

The Pharisees: "How did you receive your sight?"

The man born blind: "He put clay on my eyes, and I washed, and I see."

Some Pharisees: "This man [Jesus Christ] is not from *God* [Jehovah/Allah], for he does not keep the sabbath."

Other Pharisees: "How can a man who is a sinner do such signs?"

The Pharisees: "What do you say about him, since he has opened your eyes?"

The man born blind: "He is a prophet [he is a good man]."

The Pharisees: "Give *God* [Jehovah/Allah] the praise; we know that this man is a sinner."

The man born blind: "Whether he is a sinner, I do not know; one thing I know, that though I was blind, now I see."

The Pharisees: "What did he do to you? How did he open your eyes?"

The man born blind: "I have told you already, and you would not listen. Why do you want to hear it again? Do you too want to become his disciples?"

The Pharisees: "You are his disciple, but we are disciples of Moses. We know that [Jehovah/Allah] has spoken to Moses, but as for this man, we do not know where he comes from."

The man born blind: "Why, this is a marvel! You do not know where he comes from, and yet he opened my eyes. We know that *'God'* does not listen to sinners, but if anyone is a worshiper of *'God'* and does his will, *'God'* listens to him. **Never since the world began has it been heard that anyone opened the eyes of a man born blind. If this man were not from *'God,'* he could do nothing.**"

The Pharisees: "You were born in utter sin, and would you teach us?"

They branded the man a sinner and cast him out of their presence, exactly as Jehovah/Allah did to Adam and Eve in Eden. The Messiah heard all about it and then went to reassure him. It should be noted that the Pharisees believed that Jehovah/Allah was *God*, while the man born blind was attributing the work of Jesus Christ to the Father.

> **Jesus Christ:** "Do you believe in the Son of man?"
> **The man born blind:** "And who is he, sir, that I may believe in him?"
> **Jesus Christ:** "You have seen him, and it is he who speaks to you."
> **The man born blind:** "Lord, I believe."
> **Jesus Christ:** "For judgment I came into this world, that those who do not see
> may see, and that those who see may become blind."
> **Some Pharisees:** "Are we also blind?"
> **Jesus Christ:** "If you were blind, you would have no guilt; but now that you say,
> 'We see,' your guilt remains."
> [John 9:13-41]

Kernel of the man's testimony is this: "Never since the world began has it been heard that anyone opened the eyes of a man born blind. If this man were not from the Father, he could do nothing." It was never heard in the world before the heavenly Light did it for Adam and Eve in Eden, and it was never heard again till Jesus the Son of man did it for the blind beggar in the street of Jerusalem.

Jesus Christ expects the world to see that the man's natural testimony perfectly mirrored what would have been Adam and Eve's testimony at the time they experience the same miracle of receiving their sight in Eden. Human beings have indeed come of age since Eden when Jehovah/Allah, like the Pharisees in the man's case, branded the heavenly Messiah serpent and sinner. The question for enlightened humans today is "Was the unique Sight Restorer in Eden really an inconsequential serpent and enemy of the Father and mankind as Jehovah/Allah had alleged?" Or "Was Jehovah/Allah not simply a venomous liar, like the Pharisees in the man's case?"

We should all be able to answer these questions for ourselves in this age, knowing, like the blind beggar did, that though we were all born blind, now we see. We should be able to firmly assert that if the entity encountered by Adam and Eve in Eden were not from the Father, he could not have restored the sight of inner mind to humankind. And as for Jehovah/Allah; the heavenly Envoy called him a liar in Eden for telling man that knowledge of good and evil would kill him instantly, even though he knew that it would rather open his inner eyes and give him opportunity to be like the Father, knowing good and evil. We all want to be like Jesus Christ, and therefore, like the Father; it is sinful not to. So, Jehovah/Allah lied indeed. Jesus Christ equally affirmed in Jerusalem that Jehovah/Allah was a chronic liar and murderer. "Jehovah/Allah was a murderer from the beginning, and has nothing to do with the truth, because there is no truth in him," he said. "When he lies, he speaks according to his own nature, for he is a liar and the father of lies." [John 8:44]

Meanwhile, the Messiah restates the mission of the heavenly Light in the world, assuring us that he is the one; and that he has not come to condemn but to redeem lost sons of Light in the world. "I have come as light into the world, that whoever believes in me may not remain in darkness. ... "The light is with you for a little longer. Walk while you have the light, lest the darkness overtake you; he who walks in the darkness does not know where he goes. While you have the light, believe in the light, that you may become sons of light.' [John 12:46, 35-36]

Crux of the issues at stake in Eden concerned the choice between eternal Life and eternal Death. The heavenly Father is Divine Light and Divine Light is eternal Life. But as we already know, "This world is a dark place, and its people have no light," meaning also that its peoples have no life. The only reason the Father beamed his heavenly Light into the world was to give life; to resurrect and grant true eternal life to fallen sons of light lost in it. "For the Father so loved the world [his lost sons in the world]," says the Scripture, "that he gave [sent] his only Son, that whoever believes in him should not perish but have eternal life. ... the Father sent the Son into the world, not to condemn the world, but that the world might be saved through him." [John 3:1617]

The question is, are sons of the world willing to regain their perfect divine nature as sons of light?

Ordinarily, all fallen, dead sons of heaven would have gladly embraced the Father's magnanimous gesture with utmost penitence, humility, and gratitude, as in the case of the proverbial prodigal son. But the world was a far more complex situation. Majority of the dead here are not even aware that they are dead, and the few that know the facts prefer eternal death because they feel that they have already carved out jealously guarded niches for themselves in the system as lords, kings, and gods over the totally blinded ones. Organic existence represents a second degree of spiritual degeneration or death—a cyclic process of programmed artificial consciousness of physical life and death. It completely blinds transmigrating souls to the basic reality of the first degree of spiritual death that matters. Lords of the system manipulate reflexive fear of dying that is firmly impressed upon the blinded souls to hold them in eternal subjection to the system. That thick layer of illusion promotes what we call survival instinct, which defines life of the various species of animals.

Now, the heavenly Light did not necessarily come into the world to abolish physical life and death; they are mere illusions. But he must first help souls that had completely lost touch with reality to get through that programmed mass of darkness to the point they can appreciate their true status as fallen dead souls. To want to live, a living organism must first be helped to see that he is in fact, dead. The heavenly Light needed first to open the eyes of blinded human souls to appreciate that they were dead entities. The best way to make a blind man see that he is standing at the edge of a precipice is to help him regain his sight. That was why the heavenly Messiah started his redemptive mission for humankind with the miracle of sight restoration in Eden, before dealing with the main issue concerning resurrection from the first degree of spiritual death, which matters.

As Son of man, the heavenly Messiah would live the life of humans and die their death too to destroy that illusion of reflexive fear of death that holds the souls in bondage to this lifeless existence. When he lives our life, dies our death, and then continues to live for evermore, we will see clearly that our present life and death are mere illusions, and that what we need is his kind of uninterruptible life. Heb 2:14-15 explains it this way: "Since therefore the [fallen] children [of the Father now] share in flesh and blood, he himself likewise partook of the same nature, that through death he might destroy him who has the power of death, that is, [Jehovah/Allah] the devil, and deliver all those who through fear of death were subject to lifelong bondage."

It was an important aspect of Christ's mission in the world that he must endure the worst type of human death to show his followers that even though physical death might be painful to bear; that it is inevitable and in fact important to get over with it once and for all for our final transition to true eternal life. At the right time, "Jesus began to tell his disciples plainly that it was necessary for him to go to Jerusalem, and that he would suffer many terrible things at the hands of the elders, the leading priests, and the teachers of religious law. He would be killed, but on the third day he would be raised from the dead." That sounded suicidal to his disciples and Peter tried to forbid such evil happening to their good Master. "This will never happen to you!" he said to him. But Jesus Christ rebuked that familiar voice of reflexive fear of death in him, saying to him, "Get away from me, Satan! You are a dangerous trap to me. You are seeing things merely from a human point of view, not from the Father's." [Matt 16:21-23 (NLT)]

He told them that "unless a grain of wheat falls into the Earth and dies, it remains alone; but if it dies, it bears much fruit." [John 12:24] He assured them that they too must overcome the reflexive fear of physical death, as a pre-requisite to becoming his true disciples. "If any of you wants to be my follower," he said to them, "you must turn from your selfish ways, take up your cross, and follow me [and die as I die]. If you try to hang on to your life, you will lose it. But if you give up your life for my sake, you will save it." [Matt 16:24-25(NLT)] All his apostles eventually proved worthy followers and willingly gave up their life of the world for the love of Christ. Therefore, we are sure today that they live because their Redeemer lives.

No one who truly understands how important it was to Jesus Christ that he suffered and died the worst type of humans' death will ever argue that his death was unlike all human deaths. His physical death was absolute and conclusive otherwise he would not have been able to regain his full divine nature. And if he had failed to fully resurrect himself, how then can anyone expect that he will be able to resurrect anyone else? It is a dishonor to imply that there was any shortcut to his physical death or that there was a carryover from his physical outing into his divine nature. Any religion that preaches resurrection of his dead physical body and or ascension into heaven in his physical form is antichrist. Such doctrines clearly contradict express tenets of Christ's divine mission.

The heavenly Light came into the world to help us discard human nature completely so that we can put on our full heavenly nature. So why would he ascend into heaven with the same encumbrance himself? What would the heavenly Light need human body for after his exit from the mud house; after it had fully served its purpose? Beyond the cross, the heavenly

Christ had nothing more to do with the mud body. As he said before his actual exit from the body, "It is finished." Without question, the mortal body, Jesus, was made from dust, and to dust it returned, as is the case with every dead human body. "What I am saying, dear brothers and sisters," reads 1 Cor 15:50 (NLT), "is that our physical bodies cannot inherit the Kingdom of the Father. These dying bodies cannot inherit what will last forever."

Nevertheless, this does not in any way justify or absolve Jehovah/Allah and any of the individuals involved with the conspiracy, betrayal and gruesome murder of Jesus, the Son of man. He made it clear that they were all evil men. "The Son of man goes as it is written of him," he said, "but woe to that man by whom the Son of man is betrayed! It would have been better for that man if he had not been born." [Matt 26:24] Jehovah/Allah, entire principalities, top Jewish religious authorities, officiating agents of Roman Empire, Judas Iscariot, ignorant centurions, and the irate masses that planned and carried out his public humiliation and crucifixion were all murderers. Yet, the Messiah forgave and prayed for them all: "Father, forgive them; for they know not what they do." [Luke 23:34]

Next, Jesus Christ raised Lazarus from physical death, a man who had died for a whole four days, to correlate the promise the heavenly Light made to mankind in Eden that he will not surely die because he received heavenly wisdom. Knowledge is life; people rather perish for lack of it. He wanted mankind to see that the promise was not arbitrary; that the Son of the Father is indeed capable of restoring dead human souls to true eternal life. But raising Lazarus from physical death was only a practical parable designed to help mankind visualize spiritual resurrection that the heavenly Light promises.

He purposely delayed going to Mary and Martha when he heard that Lazarus their brother was ill, and then that he had died. He needed to stress the fact that he was not there when he died and that by natural logic he was not supposed to live again. "Lazarus is dead," he finally told his disciples, "and for your sake I am glad that I was not there, so that you may believe." [John 11:14-15] It was important to him that people understand that the heavenly Christ was not involved with the invention and running of the world of organic existence that sustains spiritual death of fallen human spirits. If he were, he would not be able to give life to anyone because he would not have life himself. The world was product of fallen dead spirits. Everyone involved with the sinful world is spiritually dead, which is why no one involved with it can be able to give life to anyone else. Jesus Christ explains this better in John 8:34-36, saying, "Truly, truly, I say to you, everyone who commits sin is a slave to sin. The slave does not continue in the house for ever; the son continues for ever. So, if the Son makes you free, you will be free indeed."

The short dialogue between Jesus Christ and Martha who went to meet him on his way to their house is another important portion of the Bible that makes direct link between the heavenly Light in Eden and Jesus Christ. It is also one of my favorites, and it is self-explanatory:

> **Martha:** "Lord, if you had been here, my brother would not have died. And even now I know that whatever you ask from the Father, the Father will give you."
>
> **Jesus Christ:** "Your brother will rise again."
>
> **Martha:** "I know that he will rise again in the resurrection at the last day."
>
> **Jesus Christ:** "I am the resurrection and the life; he who believes in me, though he die, yet shall he live, and whoever lives and believes in me shall never die. Do you believe this?"
>
> **Martha:** "Yes, Lord; **I believe that you are the Christ, the Son of** the Father, **he who is coming into the world**." [John 11:20-27]

Mary, Martha and their brother, Lazarus, were not apostles of Jesus Christ, but they had exceptional insight and faith in him. They had no iota of doubt that he was the expected Glorious Light that first appeared to their forebears, Adam, and Eve, in Eden. No wonder they were so close to the Messiah's heart and enjoyed the honor of being called his special friends. And so, when he arrived and saw the sisters weeping at their brother's death, he wept with them, like a friend indeed. "**Jesus wept**"; not because he was hopeless and helpless like the weeping humankind, but because his love for his vulnerable friends was overwhelming. It literally broke his heart to see human beings completely shaken and helpless before mere false death, without the slightest knowledge of the real death that confronts their souls. The Jews at the funeral could almost touch the kind of love that melted away the heart of the wonder-working Messiah, and they exclaimed, "See how he loved him!" But some of them also wondered if he was overpowered by the situation. "Could not he who opened the eyes of the blind man have kept this man from dying?" they said. [John 11:36-37]

Well, Jesus Christ did not come into the world to stop physical blindness and death; he did not come into the world to keep anyone from dying, but rather to redeem humankind from spiritual blindness and death. Nevertheless, he wanted to use the death of Lazarus to prove that he had authority over entire worldly processes of Mother Nature. Raising Lazarus from physical death was in direct contravention of the irreversible cosmic process of life and death and therefore, a direct confrontation and triumph over Jehovah/Allah who holds the power of death over the humans. He ordered the dead man out of the tomb—**"Lazarus, come out!"** And he obeyed. Then he literally commanded Jehovah/Allah who holds the power of death to **"Unbind him, and let him go!"**

Thus, Jesus Christ gave physical expression to spiritual resurrection, which he promises everyone who believes in him. And he says, "Truly, truly, I say to you, the hour is coming, and now is, when the [spiritually] dead will hear the voice of the Son of the Father, and those who hear will live. ... he who hears my word and believes him who sent me, has eternal life; he does not come into judgment, but has passed from death to life." [John 5:25-25]

ISRAEL AS LIGHT BEARER TO REST OF MANKIND

It is important, at this juncture, to restate the uniqueness and irrevocable status of Adam's family as Legatee of Divine Light in the world. Descendants of Adam and Eve were the prophets, apostles and first disciples of the heavenly Christ in the world. They are, therefore, Light Bearers and a blessing to the rest of human families. Indeed, "salvation comes through the Jews." [John 4:22 (NLT)] Nothing can alter that divine election, not even their present unconscious romance with Jehovah/Allah, the impostor. But the notion of Israelites as the "Chosen Ones" and the "Sons of the Promise" needs to be explained and understood in its correct perspective, especially by present day Jewish people.

Incongruous history of their involvement with Jehovah/Allah, the ravaging fire and pillar of darkness, can only make sense to both the Jews and the Gentiles when viewed in the light of truth, as ministered by Jesus Christ. When the light bearers to the world abandoned the genuine *beacon of light and good hope* for the *pillar of fire and darkness,* they became a stumbling block instead of a blessing to the rest of human families. Jesus Christ called the Jews "the salt of the Earth," and then asked, "But what good is salt if it has lost its flavor?" [Matt 5:13 (NLT)] He told them, "You are truly my disciples [only] if you remain faithful to my teachings. And you will know the truth, and the truth will set you free." "But we are descendants of Abraham," the Jews argued. "We have never been slaves to anyone. What do you mean, 'You will be set free'?" [John 8:31-33]

Evidently, the Jews did not even know that they were in bondage, and that was the worst kind of bondage. They did not know the difference between being *descendants of Abraham* and being *descendants of Adam*. So, the facts need to be set straight for the good of all. The Jews need to be set free in mentality from their *temporary* bondage to the pillar of fire and darkness so that spiritual evolution of humankind will gain final momentum in the right direction.

Of course, we all know now that Adam and Eve were not the only couple on Earth at the time of the divine visitation. Many other families existed in the old world, but the Great Light from heaven chose to contact Adam and Eve. His promises of spiritual emancipation and resurrection were made to humankind through Adam's family. His mandate to prophesy his eventual return in human form was also given to Adam and his descendants. Thus, Adam became the first prophet of the heavenly Light in the world. His descendants became the "Chosen" of the heavenly Christ and "Sons of his divine Promises." Descendants of Adam were not Chosen of Jehovah/Allah and he promised them nothing but persecution.

As we all know, Jehovah/Allah, the god of Eden, was terminally opposed to Adam's divine visitation right from the very beginning. The records are very clear even from his one-sided account of the events of Eden. First, he stigmatized Adam and Eve as sinners, poured scorn on their divine Guiding Light, calling him a serpent and deceiver; and then he swore to permanently create enmity between him and their descendants. "I will put enmity between you and the woman, and between your offspring and hers." [Gen 3:15 (NIV)] Secondly, he placed eternal curse on Adam's family, as well as on their source of livelihood. And thirdly, he officially severed relationship with Adam's family, drove them out of his jurisdictional presence and placed all kinds of obstacles, both seen and unseen, in their way to the Father who is the divine Tree of Life.

Next, he joined forces with the other colonizing principalities to make good his threats; his principal aim being to permanently prevent Adam's descendants and entire humankind from regaining true eternal life that the divine Guiding Light had promised. He said to his partners in crime, "Now these human beings have become like one of us and have knowledge of what is good and what is bad. **They must not be allowed to take fruit from the tree that gives life, eat it, and live forever.**" So, Jehovah/Allah sent them out of the Garden of Eden … Then at the east side of the garden he put living creatures and a flaming sword which turned in all directions. **This was to keep anyone from coming near the tree that gives life.**" [Gen 3:22-24 (GNT)]

We already know today that Jesus Christ represents the heavenly Light as well as the Tree that gives true eternal life to mankind. So, Jehovah/Allah and the principalities are antichrists; and they do not want us to reach the Messiah to be saved. Thus, Jehovah/Allah's position as chief enemy of the heavenly Christ, of Adam's descendants and of mankind is without a shred of doubt.

As we can see from Jehovah/Allah's one-sided lies about the events of Eden, he had been a fraudster from the very beginning, pretending to be the Father when he was but a dead lowlife. For obvious reasons, he did not want mankind to acquire heavenly wisdom, which would have made us aware of our spiritual death and of the need to seek the Father's divine grace with genuine penitence, humility, and urgency. Knowledge of good and evil would have also prepared our minds well in advance for the redemptive mission of the heavenly Christ. But when Jehovah/Allah could not stop us from receiving the fruit of knowledge from the Father, he did his utmost to confuse our understanding of the true nature of our heavenly Messiah, and even successfully manipulated us to persecute and put him to death with our own hands, as he swore in the beginning.

We should now open our inner eyes to see how Jehovah/Allah shamelessly manipulated his way back into the lives of Adam's descendants and turned the table of honor upside down in his own favor, allowing him to reap where he had not sowed. A sound-minded person stands by his own words at all costs. Perhaps, only lower animals return to lick up their own vomits. For someone who called himself almighty god, Jehovah/Allah did far worse than that. Not long after he had stigmatized Adam's family as unpardonable sinners, cast them away from his jurisdictional presence, cursed them and their sources of livelihood and solemnly swore eternal enmity with them and with their heavenly Redeemer, he started sneaking around the family like bereft desert mischief-maker, which he was, seeking to bribe his way back into the heart of any of the sons of the prophet.

But Adam's family remained faithful to their divine calling, holding firm to the name of the Father, and looking forward to the promises made to them by the heavenly Christ—promises of his second coming in human form, of spiritual emancipation from the world and of ultimate resurrection to true eternal life. Generations after generations of Adam's descendants were named after the Father and the heavenly Light; they had absolutely nothing to do with Jehovah/Allah. But he persistently sought opportunity to breach the strong family tradition, knowing that he was absolutely nobody without the chosen sons of Adam. Abram became the unfortunate sellout. For some mysterious reasons Terah, Abram's father, had decided to migrate from his natural homeland in Ur of the Chaldeans to Canaan, which was Jehovah/Allah's territory of defunct Garden of Eden, taking with him Abram and his wife, Sarah, and Lot his grandson who was an orphan. They however got up to Haran and settle there.

Abram's father died in Haran, and immediately after that Jehovah/Allah waylaid him and made his dubious move. It should be noted that Abram was, at the time, dealing with some serious emotional pressures. His father's death, life in a foreign environment, his responsibility toward Lot, his dead brother's son and especially his wife's barrenness; all these left him vulnerable to Jehovah/Allah's insincere endearment. Deuteronomy 32:10 says, "He [Jehovah] found him in a desert land, and in the howling waste of the wilderness; he encircled him, he cared for him, he kept him as the apple of his eye." Jehovah/Allah encircled Abram as a hawk encircles the chick for lunch, not as the hen encircles her brood for protection. This fact should be strongly stated. It should also be mentioned that going by the biblical book of generations of Adam down to Abram, it took Jehovah/Allah well over eleven millenniums to finally find the breach in Adam's family that his entire miserable life as a deity depended upon. So, sneaking his way back into Adam's family did not come easy for him at all, and he succeeded only by coming through the back door and wearing a false mien of friendship.

In the manner of a seasoned swindler that he was, he approached Abram, pretending, as much as he could, to be just a benevolent, wonder-working pundit and a selfless friend. He began by showering him with unsolicited promises without immediately asking for anything in return. His only demand was that Abram should abandon everyone and everything about his family heritage and move into Canaan proper. "Go from your country and your kindred and your father's house to the land that I will show you," he told him. "And I will make of you a great nation, and I will bless you, and make your name great, so that you will be a blessing. I will bless those who bless you, and him who curses you I will curse; and by you all the families of the Earth shall bless themselves." [Gen 12:1-3]

Abram did not realize that his mystery friend was the same con man that enslaved his forebears, Adam and Eve, in Eden; that swore everlasting enmity with them and with their heavenly Redeemer. He could not see that he was tactically luring him and his wife back into his present Eden for his final revenge on the family and on their expected Messiah. Indeed, Genesis 13:10 calls the land of Canaan where Abram re-settled "the Garden of Jehovah/Allah," so people who do not read their Bible upside down can understand that Jehovah/Allah indeed, lured Abram back into Eden. Thus, while Adam and Eve's encounter with the heavenly Christ represented victorious departure from Eden, Abram's encounter with Jehovah/Allah represented a return to Eden, which was a spiritual regression.

Jehovah/Allah's promises centered entirely on giving Abram other people's **land, multitudes of descendants, fame, and material possessions** on Earth. Even though the Canaanites officially inhabited the land at that time, he assured Abram, saying, "Lift up your eyes from where you are and look north and south, east, and west. All **the land** that you see I will give to you and your offspring forever. I will make **your offspring** like the dust of the Earth, so that if anyone could count the dust, then your offspring could be counted. Go, walk through the length and breadth of the land, for I am giving it to you." ... "And I will bless you, and **make your name great**, so that you will be a blessing. [Gen 13:14-17; 12:2]

Thus, Jehovah/Allah's promises directly contradicted the promises of spiritual liberation from materialism and resurrection to true eternal life made to Adam's descendants by the heavenly Christ. Abram accepted the empty promises, signed a pact with the devil himself, and thereby betrayed Adam's family legacy to the archenemy of the Father, the Christ, and humankind. Jehovah/Allah celebrated his triumph by changing the name that distinguished Abram as prophet of the heavenly Christ to a name that made him mere disciple of Mammon; from "Abram"—*the Father is Exalted* to "Abraham"—*father of materialism*. What a terrible setback!

A. JEHOVAH/ALLAH AND HIS EMPTY PROMISES TO ABRAHAM

Jehovah/Allah's promises to Abram were not just materialistic; they were also deliberately mocking. Firstly, Abram was seventy-five and Sarah sixty-five when Jehovah/Allah began promising to make him father of multitudes, yet he watched them go through full-scale emotional agonies and humiliations over childlessness. For Sarah, it was particularly a whole lifetime of emotional anguish. It was not until Abram was a hundred and Sarah ninety that Isaac was born to them. People blinded by religious passion regard that as a miracle but that was calculated mockery on Jehovah/Allah's part; at least, Sarah felt it so. "Jehovah/Allah has made laughter for me;" she said, **"everyone who hears will laugh over me."** [Gen 21:6] Jehovah/Allah later continued to taunt the family with the same issue of childlessness by asking Abram to kill the child for him. Again, religious believers call that a trial of Abram's faith. But that clearly portrays the height of Jehovah/Allah's disdain and insensitivity to emotional pains of his followers.

In any case, promising to make a man have many descendants is meaningless. It is like promising to make a tree grow to have branches. Generational progression is a natural process of organic existence, not a matter of religious faith. It is natural for every family tree to progressively multiply in branches till it grows into a gigantic tree. My great grandfather did not enter any covenant with Jehovah/Allah, yet in less than four generations, his descendants are already a great multitude. Even then, having or not having descendants does not really mean anything to man that lives once and dies forever. Promising Abram multitudes of imaginary descendants without giving him physical sons and daughters that he could hold, feel, and call his own was utter wickedness. It was, to all intents and purposes, an empty promise.

Again, Jehovah/Allah promised to give to Abram's descendants a specific stretch of land "from the river of Egypt to the great river, the river Euphrates," which was at the time occupied by "the Ken'ites, the Ken'izzites, the Kad'monites, the Hittites, the Per'izzites, the Reph'aim, the Amorites, the Canaanites, the Gir'gashites and the Jeb'usites." Yet, despite all the stage-managed, monstrous fanfares surrounding the ill-fated Jewish Exodus from Egypt to the so-called Promised Land of Rest, to this day, Abram's descendants have not been able to occupy the full extent of that promised territory. And they will never be able to do so for as long as they continue to rely on Jehovah/Allah's violent methods, and the *intifada* continues. Neither will they ever experience genuine peace and national security until they renounce Jehovah/Allah in all his ways and begin to appreciate and really love their neighbors as they love themselves.

Even the most tyrannical human ruler will first think of rehabilitating present occupants of any stretch of land within his jurisdiction before ordering new occupants into it. Jehovah/Allah who called himself *God*, and therefore was supposed to be epitome of uprightness, justice, and equity, did not think it necessary to first relocate original inhabitants of the territories of the so-called Promised Land of Rest. He did not also care to tell Abram that his descendants would have to fight endless wars and shed their own blood in the process of trying to kill off the original occupants to claim the land.

The truth is that Jehovah/Allah is a fraudster; but the Jews have not recognized it yet. He never really intended to give them any Land of Rest, because such a place does not exist anywhere in entire universe. His real motive was to torture and massacre them endlessly to avenge his humiliating defeat in Eden in the hands of their forebears, Adam and Eve. It should be noted that the tiny territory called Israel today was not given to the Jews by Jehovah/Allah but by the United Nations as late as November 1947. Present state of Israel was indeed created by the UN partition plan of 1947 out of humanitarian considerations for the protracted homelessness and extreme afflictions of international Jewry. The small strip of land upon which the "Wailing Wall" stands in Jerusalem is the only portion of the so-called Promised Land that Jehovah/Allah specifically reserved for the battered sons of Abraham, representing everlasting memorial of his bitter blows on the proxy sons of his greatest enemies, Adam, and Eve. The Jews weep at the foot of the wall year in, year out. Surely, that does not symbolize a people enjoying the peace and tranquility of a true Promised Land of Rest.

But while Abram could be forgiven for not seeing that Jehovah/Allah was the same con man of the defunct Eden, present-day Jews have no excuse whatsoever continuing in bondage to the archenemy of their divinely chosen family. Accordingly, Jesus Christ says of the lost sons of Adam, "If I had not come and spoken to them, they would not have sin; but now they have no excuse for their sin. He who hates me hates my Father also. If I had not done among them the works which no one else did, they would not have sin; but now they have seen and hated both me and my Father." [John 15:22-24] That is very sad indeed!

Finally, Jehovah/Allah promised Abram material riches. And the Bible confirms that "Abram was very rich in cattle, in silver, and in gold ... and he had sheep, oxen, he-asses, menservants, maidservants, she-asses, and camels." [Gen 13:2; 12:16] Yet, Abram lived like a mindless pauper. Of his so-called great wealth, all he could give to his first-born son, Ishmael, and his mother, Hagar, as family inheritance the day he sent them away into the harsh wilderness of Beer-sheba was a day's ration of bread and a skin of water. Genesis 21:14 reads, "So Abraham rose early in the morning, and took **bread and a skin of water**, and gave it to Hagar, putting it on her shoulder, along with the child, and sent her away. And she departed, and wandered in the wilderness of Beer-sheba." The young boy and his mother nearly starved to death in the wilderness, all because Jehovah/Allah told Abram that it was okay not to use his ill-gotten riches to do what was right.

Like Abram, many infamous people in our world today who sell their souls to Jehovah/Allah, the devil, for great material possessions are not allowed to use their ill-gotten wealth to help even their own parents, siblings, and less privileged relations. Good blessing is when one is blessed, and he becomes a blessing to others. Abraham's kind of blessing was a curse even to himself, because the Bible tells us that "the thing was very displeasing to Abraham on account of his son." [Gen 21:11]

B. THEN JEHOVAH/ALLAH REDUCED ABRAM TO ABRAHAM

Jehovah/Allah took his time to remold Abram into Abraham. He tried him for spontaneity in responding to violence; and gave him pass mark after his return from stage-managed defeat of Chedorlaomer and his allies. A fake king of Salem [king of peace] named Melchizedek met him with bread and wine, congratulated and blessed him for his willingness to shed blood in the name of Jehovah/Allah at little or no provocation.

Then he tested him for total blind surrender to his will by asking him to kill and sacrifice Sarah's child of agony, Isaac, to him. Abraham obeyed. He traveled the long distance with the innocent child and there, "Abraham built an altar ... laid the wood in order ... bound Isaac his son, and laid him on the altar, upon the wood. Then Abraham put forth his hand and took the knife to slay his son." Then Jehovah/Allah stopped him and gave him a pass mark on that one too—"Do not lay your hand on the lad or do anything to him; **for now I know that you fear *God*,** seeing you have not withheld your son, your only son, from me." [Gen 22:9-12] But Abraham literally murdered Isaac on that very day. Isaac never really got over the trauma of his father's betrayal. Jewish history shows that Isaac simply faded away till his son Jacob appeared on the scene. It should be noted that Abraham did it because he **feared** Jehovah/Allah; not because he loved or had faith in him.

Through Abraham Jehovah/Allah systematically raised for himself a tribe of hardened apostates of the heavenly way, bound by oath to fight on his side against their expected heavenly Messiah. He told Abraham in advance the plans he had for his much talked about uncountable descendants. He told him, "Know of a surety that your descendants will be sojourners in a land that is not theirs, and **will be slaves there, and they will be oppressed for four hundred years**; but I will bring judgment on the nation which they serve, and afterward they shall come out with great possessions. As for yourself, you shall go to your fathers in peace; you shall be buried in a good old age. And they shall come back here in the fourth generation." [Gen 15:13-16]

Abraham did not wonder why Jehovah/Allah would subject his *blessed* descendants through such endless torment and humiliation; or how a people hardened through forced slavery could eventually become a blessing to anyone. But with hindsight we know today what Jehovah/Allah planned to do to Abraham's descendants. He planned to grill them in hardship, to destroy remaining traces of Adam's family legacies in them; to break them, to turn them into adamant religious mercenaries. He needed to be sure that they would not suddenly realize who they really were, like their father Adam did in Eden, and then turn against him. He voiced his deep-rooted fears through Moses when, even after subjecting them to protracted bondage in Egypt, he continued to torment, horrify, and massacre them in the wilderness for forty years during their ill-fated Exodus. Moses explained to them, saying, "Jehovah/Allah your *God* has led you these forty years in the wilderness, that he might humble you, testing you **to know what was in your heart, whether you would keep his commandments, or not.**" [Deut 8:2]

Most importantly, he wanted to create artificial bondage situation from which to *save* Abraham's descendants to impress upon their psyche the idea that he was the true Savior. He needed strong psychological sales point to weigh down their conscience forever, so that in the future he would be able to say to them continually, "I am Jehovah/Allah your *God*, who rescued you from the land of Egypt, the place of your slavery. You must not have any other god but me." ... You are my servant "whom I have *chosen*, the offspring of Abraham, my friend ... **You are my witnesses** ... and my servant whom I have *chosen*, that you may know and believe me and understand that I am He. Before me no god was formed, nor shall there be any after me. I, I am Jehovah/Allah, and besides me there is no Savior. ... I am Jehovah/Allah your Savior, and your Redeemer, the Mighty One of Jacob." [Ex 20:2-3(NLT); Isa 43:41:8; 10-11; 49:26] But the issue at stake in Eden was not necessarily about salvation from physical slavery but outright redemption from spiritual bondage. Evidently, Jehovah/Allah has no answer for that.

So, while descendants of Adam are **the Chosen of the heavenly Christ**, brainwashed descendants of Abraham became **Jehovah/Allah's chosen slaves**. Adam's descendants have never been in bondage to anyone, whereas Abraham's descendants have never been free. History shows clearly that they have always been slaves in other people's lands, slaves to materialism and worst of all, covenanted slaves of Jehovah/Allah, the Antichrist. He used them as handy religious mercenaries to fight his ungodly wars, which included crucifying their true heavenly Redeemer. Jesus Christ referred to descendants of Abraham as sons of the devil because that is what Jehovah/Allah is. "You are of your father the devil," he told them, "and your will is to do your father's desires. He was a murderer from the beginning, and has nothing to do with the truth, because there is no truth in him. When he lies, he speaks according to his own nature, for he is a liar and the father of lies." [John 8:44] He also called them "the lost sheep of Israel," and made retrieving them an important priority of his early ministry on Earth. His first commission to his twelve apostles was, "Go nowhere among the Gentiles, and enter no town of the Samaritans, but go rather to the lost sheep of the house of Israel. And preach as you go, saying, 'The kingdom of heaven is at hand [i.e., the true heavenly Redeemer is finally here].'" [Matt 10:5-7]

Predictably, Jehovah/Allah used Abraham and his false chosen people to truncate true history of mankind's spiritual salvation of which Adam is the inalienable foundation. It seemed foolproof to his petty criminal mind that cutting out over eleven millenniums of history of spiritual evolution of mankind from its actual roots in Adam and Eve and starting his own customized version from Abraham would make the truth of his past crimes against mankind go away forever. But as Jesus Christ assures us all, "nothing is covered that will not be revealed, or hidden that will not be known." [Matt 10:26] Abraham was a hybrid; he was a false Abram. He was a modified descendant of Adam and a sellout to the blessed family legacies. Adam was the Chosen House; Abraham was one vandalized room within the house. Such a room could not be bigger or more important than the house that contained and gave it meaning.

Adam was pioneer extraordinary in all matters pertaining to spiritual salvation of mankind. He was the true father of faith because he believed, against threat of losing his own life, in unknown spiritual qualities—in divine light, eternal life and possibility of incarnation of divine light into the world in human form—which were yet unimaginable to any other human mind at the time of Eden. To this day, world's greatest minds are still grappling with the true nature of Divine Light, eternal Life, death and resurrection of Incarnate Christ and spiritual resurrection of dead human souls. Adam confidently moved out of Eden and never looked back because he had absolute faith in ability of the heavenly Light to fulfill his promises to him, to his descendants and to entire humankind.

C. ABRAHAM: FALSE FATHER OF FAITH

Abraham's faith, like his vote of righteousness, was merely awarded to him by Jehovah/Allah as part of his propaganda strategies of dressing him up in false personality that mimicked Adam's. Of a truth, Abraham was one of the most faithless patriarchs that ever lived. Where was his great faith in Jehovah/Allah's ability to protect and provide for him and his wife the couple of times he pimped Sarah out pretending she was his sister for fear that the people might kill him if they knew she was his wife, and for the ultimate material gain he derived from so doing? Much of the material blessings Jehovah/Allah promised Abraham were realized through such dishonorable means. The Bible says that "for her sake [Pharaoh of Egypt] dealt well with Abram; and he had sheep, oxen, he-asses, menservants, maidservants, she-asses, and camels. ... And Abim'elech, king of Gerar "took sheep and oxen, and male and female slaves, and gave them to Abraham, and restored Sarah his wife to him. ... To Sarah he said, 'Behold, I have given your brother a thousand pieces of silver; it is your vindication in the eyes of all who are with you; and before everyone you are righted.'" [Gen 12:16; 20:14-16] But was Sarah really righted? Which woman could justify actions of a husband who repeatedly pimped her for selfish material riches?

Furthermore, Abraham and Sarah never really took Jehovah/Allah's promise of a biological child seriously. He fell on his face and laughed at Jehovah/Allah on one occasion when he mentioned his sardonic promise. "Shall a child be born to a man who is a hundred years old? Shall Sarah, who is ninety years old, bear a child?" he said to himself. [Gen 17:17] Was it faith that made Abraham complain repeatedly of childlessness, suggesting at one time that Eliezer of Damascus, a slave born in his house, was set to be his heir? If Abraham really believed Jehovah/Allah, he would not have accepted to try for a child with Sarah's maid, and afterward to plead that Jehovah/Allah should just allow Ishmael to be. Under this backdrop it was sheer religious propaganda to have purported that Abraham willingly accepted to kill his child of agony to prove his faith in Jehovah/Allah. He would have been under intense hypnotic influence to even allow Jehovah/Allah voice such cruelty. Anyway, the Scripture showed clearly that Abraham did it out of fear of Jehovah/Allah and not because he had faith in him. Jehovah/Allah's exact words were, "**for now I know that you fear *God*.**"

D. DOWNSIDE OF ABRAHAM AND HIS FALSE CHOSEN DESCENDANTS

Jehovah/Allah also used Abraham and his false chosen people to mimic important aspect of Christ's ministry to complicate and confuse mankind on the true nature and mission of the heavenly Redeemer. The heavenly Christ appeared as *Divine Light* to Adam and Eve; Jehovah/Allah appeared to Abraham as a wonder-working man of the desert and later to Moses as a *Burning Bush*. The heavenly Christ rescued Adam and Eve from divine bondage in Eden and sacked the Garden of Eden forever and he promised them he would appear in human form later. He also promised them and entire humankind spiritual emancipation from the world and resurrection to true eternal life. Jehovah/Allah promised to give Abraham other peoples' land here on Earth with all the bloodshed that was to be associated with that, multitude of offspring in perennial bondage and lots of material blessing. He freed Abraham's descendants from stage-managed slavery in Egypt, amidst lawless fanfares designed to promote him as a savior of sort, only to torment and massacre them in the wilderness for forty years. Even to this day, he still subjects them to perennial bondage in Jerusalem, the so-called Promised Land of Rest.

The heavenly Christ promised spiritual *resurrection of souls* to descendants of Adam as well as to all his true disciples in the world; he promised them perfect existence as sons of Light in the spiritual kingdom of the Father. "In my Father's house are many rooms;" he said, "if it were not so, would I have told you that I go to prepare a place for you? And when I go and prepare a place for you, **I will come again and will take you to myself, that where I am you may be also.**" [John 14:2-3] Jehovah/Allah, on his part, promised *resurrection of dead bones*, exclusively to descendants of Abraham. "Prophesy to these bones," Jehovah/Allah said to Ezekiel, "Behold, I will cause breath to enter you, and you shall live. And I will lay sinews upon you, and will cause flesh to come upon you, and cover you with skin, and put breath in you, and you shall live; and you shall know that I am Jehovah/Allah. ... **these bones are the whole house of Israel.** Behold, they say, 'Our bones are dried up, and our hope is lost; we are clean cut off.' Therefore prophesy, and say to them, Thus says Jehovah/Allah *God.* Behold, I will open your graves, and raise you from your graves, O my people; and **I will bring you home into the land of Israel.**" [Ezek 37:4-12]

He also promised to recreate the world, i.e., Jerusalem, for them. "For behold, I create new heavens and a new Earth; and the former things shall not be remembered or come into mind. But be glad and rejoice forever in that which I create; for behold, I create Jerusalem a rejoicing, and her people a joy. I will rejoice in Jerusalem and be glad in my people; **no more shall be heard in it the sound of weeping and the cry of distress.** ... The wolf and the lamb shall feed together; the lion shall eat straw like the ox; and dust shall be the serpent's food. They shall not hurt or destroy in all my holy mountain, says Jehovah/Allah." [Isa 65:17-25] Predictably, Jehovah/Allah promises nothing beyond this physical world of darkness; and needless to add that *the sound of weeping and the cry of distress* will forever be heard in Jerusalem.

The heavenly Christ worked with specific number of prophets and apostles for very good reasons, and today he has only disciples in the world. Because he was a true Spirit being and not of the world, he needed to announce his visit and prepare the minds of worldly beings before his physical manifestation. Accordingly, he chose and inspired prophets of good hope, of Adam's lineage, to foretell his physical manifestation and proclaim his mission in the world. The prophets prophesied, beginning from Adam to John the Baptist who finally ushered the Messiah unto the worldly stage with definite words of introduction that marked official termination of the prophets and prophecy era.

John the Baptist went about proclaiming, "After me comes he who is mightier than I, the thong of whose sandals I am not worthy to stoop down and untie. I have baptized you with water; but he will baptize you with the Holy Spirit." [Mark 1:7-8] And after baptizing and watching him start his ministry, John the Baptist formally signed off, saying to his own followers, "No one can receive anything except what is given him from heaven. You yourselves bear me witness, that I said, I am not the Christ, but I have been sent before him. He who has the bride is the bridegroom; the friend of the bridegroom, who stands and hears him, rejoices greatly at the bridegroom's voice; **therefore, this joy of mine is now full. He must increase, but I must decrease.**" [John 3:27-30] Indeed, the prophets were inspired to say that the Messiah was coming. When he eventually came, there was nothing more to prophesy about and therefore, no need for prophets anymore. Any other person who claimed or claims to be a prophet after John the Baptist is most certainly false. All present-day prophets of customary Christianity are not of Jesus Christ but of Jehovah/Allah, the impostor.

While in the world in human form, the heavenly Christ chose specific number of apostles to preach his arrival and to serve as symbolic custodians of his Earthly ministry. He chose *only* twelve apostles for very important reason; to symbolize the twelve tribes of the lost sheep of Israel. That was his way of saying that no matter how violated and fragmented Jehovah/Allah would have rendered descendants of Abram, they were still latent sons of Adam and therefore essentially still his inalienable disciples. Even in falling into the hands of the enemy and seemly failing as light bearers to the world, they were still able to fulfill their divine calling to very large extent. Israel will ultimately be the downfall of Jehovah/Allah. And I am sure that worries him greatly.

The heavenly Christ knew that Jehovah/Allah was criminal-minded and would try to play smart with his Abrahamic gimmick. He knew also that he would not be wise enough to see far into the future to know how it would all play out in the end. No matter how hard a foster parent tries, the child will always grow up to seek out his true parents. And anyone who holds what belongs to a child and raises his hand will assuredly lower his hand and relinquish it when his hand begins to pain. Despite what Jehovah/Allah may have considered his gains with the abduction of Abram, Christ's mission remains on course; his prophets prophesied his coming, his twelve apostles preached his presence, and today his disciples fill the whole world.

Jehovah/Allah, on his part, makes mockery of the office of prophets. A man who is at home does not send messengers to members of his own household; he tells them whatever he needs to tell them personally. He does not prophesy what he will do tomorrow; he does it when tomorrow comes. Jehovah/Allah is a man on the ground; he can personally deliver his message to anyone at any time anywhere on the surface of the Earth. He says himself, "I am a *God* who is everywhere and not in one place only. No one can hide where I cannot see them. Do you not know that I am everywhere in heaven[s] and on Earth?" [Jer 23:23-24 (GNT)]

Indeed, before the sudden demise of his Edenic dream he walked around the nature park in person and had everyday conversations with Adam and Eve. When he first waylaid Abram, he approached and discussed with him as a man. When he needed to tell him that his wife would conceive, he went to his house, sat down to a meal, and delivered his prediction personally. Again, when he wanted to invade Sodom and Gomorrah he went to Abraham's house and dialogued with him as a close friend. Also, the Bible confirms that "Jehovah/Allah used to speak to Moses face to face, as a man speaks to his friend." [Ex 33:11] He did not need prophets, apostles, priests, or disciples because he had no personal mission or definite project set in the future. Everything about his life on Earth was done on a day-to-day basis. However, when he had fully found his feet among his false chosen people and settled down to his serious business of being the Antichrist, he gradually began to metamorphose himself into a false transcendent spirit and a superior partner of Jesus Christ in the matter of mankind's spiritual salvation. He began to inspire false prophets to confuse words of Christ's true prophets, false apostles to preach a false Christ to mankind and all manners of bogus religious officials inspired to propagate him as *God Almighty* in the world.

Micaiah narrates in 1 Kings 22:18-23 (GNT) how Jehovah/Allah inspired four hundred false prophets that deceived Ahab into battle against Syria in Ramoth-gilead. "I saw Jehovah/Allah sitting on his throne in heaven," reports Micaiah, "with all his angels standing beside him. Jehovah/Allah asked, 'Who will deceive Ahab so that he will go and be killed at Ramoth?' Some of the angels said one thing, and others said something else, until a spirit stepped forward, approached Jehovah/Allah, and said, 'I will deceive him.' 'How?' Jehovah/Allah asked. The spirit replied, 'I will go and make all of Ahab's prophets tell lies.' Jehovah/Allah said, 'Go and deceive him. You will succeed.' ... "This is what has happened. Jehovah/Allah has made these prophets of yours lie to you. But he himself has decreed that you will meet with disaster!"

Yet, that was not an isolated case at all; sending evil spirits to confuse and torment people was a business Jehovah/Allah was so accustomed to. We read in certain verses of the Bible that "an evil spirit from Jehovah/Allah tormented Saul"; that he once said of prophets of Jerusalem, "Stupefy yourselves and be in a stupor, blind yourselves and be blind! Be drunk, but not with wine; stagger, but not with strong drink! **For Jehovah/Allah has poured out upon you a spirit of deep sleep**, and has closed your eyes, the prophets, and covered your heads, the seers." And he also confessed that he gave the Jews, obviously, through his false prophets, "statutes that were not good and ordinances by which they could not have life." [1 Sam 16:14; Isa 29:9-10; Ezekiel 20:25]

The same Jehovah/Allah promises indiscriminate outpouring of his lying spirits upon all flesh in Joel 2:28-29—"And it shall come to pass afterward, that I will pour out my spirit on all flesh; your sons and your daughters shall prophesy, your old men shall dream dreams, and your young men shall see visions. Even upon the menservants and maidservants in those days, I will pour out my spirit." People do not have to think too hard to understand that Jehovah/Allah pouring out his spirit of mass hysteria on mankind will be his last-ditch battle strategy to bastardize the true gospel of Jesus Christ on the religious platform. We are already witnessing frantic and blasphemous activities of Jehovah/Allah's end-time false prophets in all religious of the world. When all that fails, as it will, Jehovah/Allah will ultimately resort to final rounds of raw violence as the prophesy goes: "And I will give portents in the heavens and on the Earth, **blood and fire and columns of smoke**. The sun shall be turned to darkness, and the moon to blood, before the great and terrible day of Jehovah/Allah comes. And it shall come to pass that all who call upon the name of Jehovah/Allah shall be delivered; for in Mount Zion and in Jerusalem there shall be those who escape, as Jehovah/Allah has said, and among the survivors shall be those whom Jehovah/Allah calls." [Joel 2:30-32]

E. RIDICULOUS GAMBIT WITH ONE HOMELESS MELCHIZEDEK

The most stupid and overambitious aspect of Jehovah/Allah's overall ruse with Abraham concerns him claiming to be God Most High with Jesus Christ being his son and subordinate. In Genesis 14:17-24 (TEV) we read about Abraham's encounter with one desert marauder named Melchizedek who came out from nowhere to meet him alongside the king of Sodom to share war loots after his stage-managed victory in the war against Chedorlaomer and his allies. It reads:

> When Abram came back from his victory over Chedorlaomer and the other kings, the king of Sodom went out to meet him in Shaveh Valley (also called King's Valley). And Melchizedek, who was king of Salem and also a priest of the Most High *God*, brought bread and wine to Abram, blessed him, and said, "May the Most High *God*, who made heaven and Earth, bless Abram! May the Most High *God*, who gave you victory over your enemies, be praised!" **And Abram gave Melchizedek a tenth of all the loot he had recovered.**
>
> The king of Sodom said to Abram, "Keep the loot, but give me back all my people." Abram answered, "I solemnly swear before **Jehovah, the Most High *God*, Maker of heaven and Earth**, that I will not keep anything of yours, not even a thread or a sandal strap. Then you can never say, 'I am the one who made Abram rich.' I will take nothing for myself. I will accept only what my men have used. But let my allies, Aner, Eshcol, and Mamre, take their share."

The cheap stunt was intended to insinuate that Jesus Christ was Melchizedek while Jehovah/Allah was the Father. Paul was inspired to present the argument that narrowed things down to the desired points and most Bible scholars today simply key into the sheer blasphemy. Paul presented Melchizedek not just as King of Peace but also as "King of Righteousness, without father or mother," in attempt to prove that he could have been none other than Jesus Christ himself. But the facts on ground did not quite tally. In the first instance, the desert marauder who received a tenth of all the war loots recovered by Abram, obviously, because he was personally instrumental to Abram's victory, was a kind of king of peace that supported violence and human slaughter in wars. In any case, Melchizedek was called a *King* of Peace, while Jesus Christ is *Prince* of Peace, meaning that Melchizedek contradicted the Father who is the true King of Peace. However, since he was only a priest to Jehovah/Allah who was erroneously presented as the Most High *God*, it meant he was a nobody. He must have been one of Jehovah/Allah's lowlife accomplices, archangel Michael perhaps, who roamed about the wilderness in those days starting and winning wars for people and sharing in the booties. He is the archangel habitually associated with war matters. Surely, he was someone Abram knew well enough in person.

Of course, Jehovah/Allah is the ceremonial possessor of the highest rank among the principalities. He is the *most high* among the *gods*. Quran 40:15 calls him "possessor of the highest rank." So, being presented as occulted Most High *God* did not make him the Father of Jesus Christ. And certainly, it did not prove that he had any part in Christ's mission in the world. In any case, the heavenly Christ had never been a man, and he had never appeared to anyone on Earth as man before his official Incarnation into the world as Jesus Christ. And he has remained the *only* heavenly being involved with the spiritual salvation of mankind. The Father too, has never been a man and he has never had any physical contact with the world. He sent the heavenly Christ into the world but has been entirely removed from the direct aspects of his mission in the world. As the Scripture says, "No one has ever seen the Father; the only Son, who is in the bosom of the Father, he has made him known." [John 1:18] Certainly, Jesus Christ did not make Jehovah/Allah known in the world; he has been the notorious blower of his own trumpet right from his miserable days in Eden.

Another awful insinuation propagated by ignorant Bible scholars is that Jehovah/Allah asking Abraham to kill his only son for him prefigured how the Father planned to kill his only Son for the world. Jehovah/Allah makes spiritual salvation of mankind seem like mere divine game of satire.

Religious believers who succumb to the senseless insinuation accept such written stunt as good enough justification for the gruesome murder of Jesus the Son of man by Jehovah/Allah and his bloodthirsty accomplices. Nevertheless, it was wicked for Jehovah/Allah to even contemplate the thought of asking Abraham to kill Sarah's child of agony. Abraham had no right to kill someone else to prove that he had faith in Jehovah/Allah. Isaac was not his ram or personal property, but an autonomous soul that needed to work out his own personal salvation. Abraham was not faithful; he was suffering from original ignorance.

Certainly, the Father did not send his Son into the world to be molested and killed by the same people he had come to give life to. Killing Jesus, the Son of man in cold blood was a heinous crime, for the natural law of the Father says that we should not kill. John 3:16-17 reads, "For the Father so loved the world that he gave his only Son, that whoever believes in him should not perish but have eternal life. For the Father sent the Son into the world, not to condemn the world, but that the world might be saved through him." Nothing in the Father's magnanimity suggests that he sent the Son into the world to be condemned and killed by the world. Nothing in the Father's divine will speaks about ultimate blood sacrifice or about him demanding the gruesome murder of his Son as official ransom to fulfill his everlasting love and redemption of his fallen sons in the world. The Father did not say that whoever kills his Son will have eternal life, but rather that "whoever believes in him [in his words and guidance] should not perish but have eternal life."

Finally, what Jehovah/Allah has placed upon himself is an overweight crown that will eventually weigh him down to the ground. As Jesus Christ says, heaven humbles everyone who exalts himself. Jehovah/Allah is an impostor; he is *"the thief that comes only to steal and kill and destroy [our souls]."* [John 10:10] His deeds and utterances in human history, his overall influence on unsuspecting descendants of Abraham, as well as on entire humanity, prove beyond doubt that he is the actual culprit in the Edenic saga. All we have learnt from him are violence, both in thought and action, arrogance, intolerance, vengeance, and war. But the time has finally come for Jehovah/Allah to be reduced to what he really is, animal in the cloak of god. We must strip him of all false titles he has arrogated to himself. It must be said in clear words that Jehovah/Allah is not the Father. He is not the true Father of Israel and certainly, not the Lord and Savior of humankind. He is false Father, false Christ, and archenemy of humankind.

THE HEAVENLY CHRIST VS THE LYING PRINCIPALITIES

A. DIVINE LIGHT VS INNER DARKNESS

As we can all see from the biblical account of events of Eden, divine process for the spiritual redemption of humankind commenced with the sudden appearance of the Great Light from Heaven and with the call of Adam and Eve in Eden. Beyond that point in time, the world existed in the Outer Darkness, outside the Father's Heaven—outside the realm of Divine Light. Organic existence, the cosmic world order and hierarchy of species functioned as autonomous artificial reality. There was no war, battle, or any form of interference from the heavenly Father or the heavenly Christ. Also, beyond that point in time, man was, like every other lower animal, mindless by design. He lived in harmony with the natural processes of Mother Nature; he did not sin against anyone or fall from any previous glory because he had none. And certainly, the world had absolutely no need or future intention of relieving or redeeming man from his designed nature.

The sudden appearance of the heavenly Light in Eden was the first of such incident in entire history of worldly existence. His divine presence and express mission directly threatened cosmic world order—its principles, ideals, and perpetuity. Most importantly, his divine will overruled the basic interests and authorities of the cosmic ruling powers, which explained why they were terminally *opposed* to his divine mission in the world. But speaking of opposition; darkness cannot really oppose the will of light. The basic scenario in Eden was straightforward; darkness ruled in Eden, but when Divine Light appeared, darkness disappeared. A simple darkroom experiment can help people understand that better. No matter how enduring the darkness in a closed room may be, once the light source comes on it vanishes completely. Thus, superiority of light over darkness is incontestable.

Battle for the spiritual redemption of dead human souls between the heavenly Redeemer and the lying principalities is a fight between Good and Evil. But just as we cannot imagine darkness standing face-to-face to fight with light, we cannot really speak of a *fight* between good and evil. Divine goodness necessarily drives away evilness. A fight between good and evil can be likened to socking dirty linings in good detergent solution; when the linings are lifted and rinsed, they are made as clean as new. What we call war in the case of good and evil is but the process of evil fleeing in the face of goodness. In the case of darkness before light, the fleeing is instantaneous. But with dirt, as with evil, we can literally observe the fleeing taking place. But no matter how tough the dirt may seem; it must give way in the presence of ultimate detergent. The principalities are the dirt, i.e., the corrupting influence; mankind is the dirtied linings, while Jesus Christ is the ultimate detergent. Only he can wash clean dirtied human souls and rekindle their original glory. The principalities cannot fight him.

A proverbial folktale in my village goes like this: Once upon a time, the tortoise, always cunning and mischievous, was wanted by the king to answer for one of his many misdemeanors. The king sent his toughest palace guard to arrest and bring tortoise to the palace. The guard went to his house and effortlessly picked him up in the air and started walking back to the palace. Then tortoise whispered softly in his ears; "please my good brother, kindly put me down and give me just two minutes to pick up something very important from my house." The guard accepted and put him down on his feet. The tortoise walked back into his house and started scattering his property as if in frantic search of something very important indeed. After thoroughly scattering his belongings, the tortoise said to the guard, "now you can take me to the king." The guard wondered why he had gone through all that trouble for nothing, as he did not see him take anything from the house. He could, in fact, see that he was looking for nothing in particular. Indeed, the tortoise was not trying to take anything from his house but rather to leave something—a strong false impression. Anyone who would come to his house and hear that he had been taken by the mighty palace guard should conclude that he did put up formidable resistance, as a great warrior should. That was his message. But it was all a lie.

Like the cunning tortoise, the principalities are merely scattering their domain, pretending to be acting tough in the face of divine summons. They are busy scattering things on Earth and making the world unbearable for ignorant humankind, so that they might appear as formidable opponents of the heavenly Messiah. But they know that they cannot contest the sovereign will of the Father. And so, because the principalities, as agents of darkness, were not able to oppose the will of the heavenly Light directly, they directed all their frustration and rage on mankind who was the principal beneficiary of his redemptive mission. "I will take vengeance," says

Jehovah/Allah, "and I will spare no man." [Isaiah 47:3] But Jehovah/Allah was not acting alone; he spoke on behalf of the disgruntled council of ruling principalities. By intensifying their corrupting influence on humankind, they hope to ensure that people are permanently distracted from spiritual pursuits. That is tantamount to piling more and more dirt on people's souls; thus, making it harder for them to reach the Messiah for their ultimate cleansing. That way the principalities hope to remain in contention for longer time. It is against this backdrop that we can properly understand the true nature of the war between Jesus Christ and the principalities.

That brings me to Rev 12:7-9, which reads, "Now war arose *in heaven, Michael and his angels* fighting against the dragon; and the dragon and his angels fought, but they were defeated and there was no longer any place for them *in heaven*. And the great dragon was thrown down, that ancient serpent, who is called the Devil and Satan, the deceiver of the whole world - he was thrown *down to the Earth*, and his angels were thrown down with him." Evidently, these verses refer to the first advent of the heavenly Light in the world, which marked commencement of the war for the salvation of human souls. Without mincing words, verses like these are deliberately misleading. Some of the metaphors are simply blasphemous. As we have seen, it is impossible for any kind of war to arise between light and darkness in the true Heaven, within eternal domain of Divine Light. The incident did not take place in heaven but here on Earth, and the heavenly Christ never had angelic assistance of any sort. No archangel or angel was ever involved in any of the three stages of the war for mankind's spiritual salvation but the heavenly Christ alone.

First, the heavenly Christ appeared in Eden as **Spirit of Knowledge**, activated functional minds in ignorant human beings and granted them initial spiritual awareness. Then he commissioned his chosen prophets from among captive human souls to further create awareness by prophesying his expected Incarnation. Secondly, he materialized on Earth as **Son of Man** as prophesied, elected twelve apostles and preached resurrection of dead human souls to human minds. And at the close of his Earthly ministry, he promised to return as **the Comforter** and to remain with his disciples till the end. "No, I will not abandon you as orphans—" he said, "**I will come to you**. Soon the world will no longer see me, **but you will see me**. Since I live, you also will live. When I am raised to life again, you will know that I am in my Father, and you are in me, and I am in you." ... "And be sure of this: **I am with you always**, even to the end of the age." [John 14:18-20;

Matt 28:20 (NLT)] Adam and Eve saw and experienced the heavenly Christ in Eden as **Spirit of Knowledge**; his Apostle saw and experienced him as **Son of Man** in Israel. Today, his true disciples all over the world see and experience him as **Holy Spirit of Truth**.

So, the heavenly Christ presently oversees his own ministry as the Holy Spirit of Truth, clarifying matters in human minds. He is more than sufficient for his divine mission in the world. He is not in league with any archangel or angel. On the contrary, Michael, Gabriel and all the other so-called archangels belong to the world ruling council of unrepentant principalities, presided over by Jehovah/Allah. Revelation 12:3 refers to this inglorious gang as "great red dragon, with seven heads and ten horns, and seven diadems upon his heads."

B. GOSPEL TRUTH VS RELIGIOUS PROPAGANDA

The principalities responded to the first stage of the battle in Eden with slander and sheer religious propaganda. They dismissed the heavenly Redeemer as inconsequential snake and as enemy of the Father and mankind. Yet, their immediate actions showed clearly that they were confounded and overpowered. Indeed, the victory scoreboard showed clearly that the Messiah decisively routed them from their original comfort zone; he authoritatively sacked their Edenic slave camp forever and set Adam and Eve free permanently. Nevertheless, the principalities embarked on massive religious propaganda campaign to re-colonize the people's minds and to sustain their lies. And they have succeeded for very long time with that. Even to this day, multitudes of religious believers are still heavily deluded about the straightforward events of Eden. Multitudes still worship Jehovah/Allah, the principal loser, as *God Almighty* and venerate the so-called archangels as his powerful messengers. But their days are really numbered.

For the second phase of the battle against Christ's mission on Earth, the principalities eschewed their chronic personal differences and jointly projected Jehovah/Allah to the status of false Most High to use him to impersonate the Father. According to Rev 17:13-14, "These are of one mind and give over their power and authority to the beast; [so that] they will make war on the Lamb [as a united front], and the Lamb will conquer them [anyway]." Thus, they invented from among themselves false Father, false Christ, false Holy Spirit, false angels, false prophets, and false apostles; and with such blasphemy, they have succeeded in attracting to themselves multitudes of false believers in the Father, as well as false followers of Jesus Christ. Jehovah/Allah became the false Father; Michael [i.e., Melchizedek] became the false king of peace and false Christ, while Gabriel became the false Holy Spirit [in Pentecostal evangelism, he is called Holy *Ghost*, for he is indeed, a dead spirit].

The Quran refers to Gabriel as *the holy Spirit* in his capacity as minister of information in Jehovah/Allah's cabinet. In Quran 2:87 the lying principalities say, "We gave unto Jesus, son of Mary, clear proofs (of Allah's sovereignty), and **we supported him with the holy Spirit**." Then, footnote to that verse explains, "'*The holy Spirit is a term for the angel of Revelation, Gabriel (on whom be peace).*'" Surely, Allah and his partners are blasphemers. In any case, Gabriel is called '*holy Spirit*' or '*holy ghost*' and that is quite different from 'Holy Spirit of Truth' that belongs with the Father and with Jesus Christ.

Together, Jehovah/Allah and his gang of liars promote all kinds of false ideals for ignorant humans to emulate. Michael instigates *holy* wars, as well as secular conflicts and gives credence to keeping and making peace by means of wars and human slaughter. Gabriel, working in his capacity as minister of information, promotes religious goodness, designed to fool the deeply religious people into think that they are already in heaven. Then, Jehovah/Allah, working closely with Gabriel, the *holy ghost*, manipulates multitudes of false men of *God* to preach false gospel of Jesus Christ as well as his own doomsday gospel of wrath and vengeance. Jehovah/Allah also inspires puppet scribes and bible scholars who interpolate and extrapolate verses in the Bible to alter contextual meanings of the Scriptures to suit central cosmic agenda of the principalities.

The principalities used their own apostle Paul to whisk off the true gospel of Jesus Christ from its true custodians, the sons of Adam, buried it in the catacombs of Roman Catholic Church of Jehovah/Allah in Rome and then floated Antichrist's version of false gospel of Jesus Christ for unsuspecting customary Christians. Subtle gospel according to Paul ensures that people worship Jehovah/Allah as *God Almighty in the name of Jesus Christ*. It also lays stumps that enable indoctrinated religious intellectuals to advance blasphemous ideas that hold Jehovah/Allah to be both the Father of Jesus Christ and the Messiah himself. Meanwhile, modern-day bible scholars work tirelessly on laundering incriminating Bible texts and trying in vain to explain away unexplainable contradictions and false ideals of

Yahwistic Christianity.

The principalities sponsored massive worldwide customary Christian evangelism, with the principal aim of reducing Jesus Christ to merely one of many founders of religious movements on Earth. That way, belief in Jesus Christ was reduced to a matter of religious affinity. They also hoped that being at the forefront with their own version of falsified gospel of Jesus Christ would ensure that the truth, if and even when it finally resurfaces, would be hardly acceptable to already indoctrinated religious minds. They seem to be winning now; but without knowing it, they work for the Messiah instead. They have done more in spreading Christ-consciousness than fighting against it that today, Christ's influence and authority are already felt all over the world. Of course, they are not wise enough to see how it will all play out. When the time is right, a twinkle of an eye is enough for the heavenly Christ to overcome the best of Jehovah/Allah's artifices to re-enlighten and reclaim all true sons of heaven that he might have misled. Jesus Christ makes that assurance where he says, "All that the Father gives me will come to me; ... and I give them eternal life, and they shall never perish, and no one shall snatch them out of my hand. My Father, who has given them to me, is greater than all, and no one is able to snatch them out of the Father's hand. I and the Father are one." [John 6:37; 10:28-30]

In the present Holy Spirit phase of Christ's ministry on Earth, the principalities prosecute the war directly in people's minds, inculcating in them contemporary mindsets that are very hard to eradicate. In a world already supercharged with violence and antisocial and immoral ideals, they use various methods of mind control to dictate tendencies that amount to people willingly soaking themselves in more and more dirt. Today, people have so much addiction to keep them permanently occupied with things of the world—religious rigmaroles, the internet and social networking, cable television dragnet, movie magic, computer and electronic thingamajigs, sports and gambling, tourism, carnivals, trendy megastores and shopping frenzy, fashion mongering, lavish lifestyle, sex merchandizing and more.

But all these addictions require plenty of money to sustain. As the Bible says, "money answers all things." Therefore, love of money has become the root of all human additions in today's world. Today, deep-rooted love of money, material possessions, power and fame has become a righteous obsession in people, and many religiously pursue dubious avenues of get-rich-quick. While religious agents of the principalities authoritatively preach worldly prosperity in the name of *God*, the media and movie industries showcase lavish lifestyles of people who have become *blessed* with lots and lots of money. So, more and more people willingly sell their souls to the devil to belong to the world of moneybags—people who have *made it* in this life.

Conclusion of people who have *made it* in the world is usually that "this life is good." They instinctively say to themselves, "what a wonderful world." But most often than not, people who say that this life is good only refer to the bittersweet joys derived from luxury inventions of man that seem to embellish the miserable lives of the few that can afford it, not to raw human nature that weighs down souls of millions of the underprivileged. With that kind of mindset, it is indeed difficult for such people to desire another life and another world, no matter how perfect and glorious they may be. As Jesus Christ says, "no one after drinking old wine desires new; for he says, 'The old is good.'" [Luke 5:39] Their preoccupation is to extract as much sensual pleasures out of this life now, rather than bothering about some unknown heavenly bliss tomorrow. And what they call enjoyment is usually only derived from partying, foods, hard drugs, alcohol, and sex. But these do not only offer transient pleasures; they almost always lead to greater unhappiness.

Take sexual gratification for instance; many people suffer untold bitterness that are directly and indirectly related to brief moments of sexual ecstasy. Indeed, sexual climax may be regarded as the highest form of sensual happiness possible in this life, but it only lasts for very brief seconds and comes with lots of pains. Anyone who feels sexual climax continuously for one whole hour will fall sick; for one whole day, the person will go mad, and for a whole month, he or she will simply drop dead. So, what kind of happiness is that? Male antechinus, mouse-like marsupials, are a bizarre example. They exhibit extreme suicidal sexual habit and actually mate themselves to death in the last stage of their lives. "These species experience extreme sexual behavior. Mating can go for 12 or 14 hours at a time, and they have lots of partners. They use up all possible energy and body tissues on competitive mating, which causes synchronized death after mating in males," says Dr. Diana Fisher. [http://www.scienceworldreport.com/articles/10167/20131012/male-antechinus-die-excessivemating.html]

Human nature is a spiritual complication; Jesus Christ is the ultimate resolution. But man must play his own part in the battle for his own personal salvation. People must make definite choices on how to lead this life. Jesus Christ represents perfect ideals. He shows us the light with which to see our way out of the dark world, and he holds the door open for us to walk through and into perfect existence. He says, "I am the door; **if anyone enters** by me, he will be saved, and will go in and out and find pasture." [John 10:9] We are the ones to do the walking out of vanity and walking into spiritual reality. The choice is absolutely ours to make. And we should always bear in mind that "no weapon fashioned against us by the principalities shall prosper, but the ones we fashion against ourselves *must* prosper." The Son of man overcame the world so that we might be able to overcome ourselves. He became the Ultimate Man for us to emulate him to perfection. It is perfectly within our power to shun materialism and say no to devils' flashy allures, just as the Son of man did.

JESUS CHRIST: THE ULTIMATE MAN

A. THE GOLD SEEN BY ADAM AND EVE

The gold seen by one man can easily be deemed rusted by his adversaries, even though common sense tells us that rusted gold does not exist. Jehovah/Allah and the principalities maligned and dismissed the Great Light from heaven that Adam and Eve received in Eden as serpent, even though his precepts proved otherwise. They also ridiculed and libeled Adam and Eve as irredeemable sinners, even when facts on ground proved they were the noblest and bravest human beings that ever lived. For thousands of years, the whole mankind joined the lying principalities in making jest of the noble legatees of Divine Light in the world. But Adam and his descendants never wavered in their faith in ability of the heavenly Light to fulfill all his promises—to liberate mankind and give life to fallen dead souls in the world. For thousands of years, they faithfully prophesied his eventual manifestation on Earth in human form as he promised.

"Now faith is the assurance of things hoped for, the conviction of things not seen," reads Heb 11:1-2, "For by it the men of old received divine approval." Adam and Eve stand out as epitomes of true faith, and for that they gained the Father's irrevocable approval as first disciples of the heavenly Christ in the world. Even when the rest of mankind was still totally in the dark about spiritual matters, they believed, among other things, in the fact that Light is Life and in possible incarnation of Divine Light on Earth.

Their unparalleled faith came to fruition about two thousand years ago.

Behold, "the true Light that enlightens every man" eventually manifested, as they prophesied, in the person of Jesus of Nazareth. "**The Word of Life**" that was spoken about for past thousands of years finally "became flesh and dwelt among us, full of grace and truth; we have beheld his glory, glory as of the only Son from the Father. ... And from his fullness have we all [whole of mankind] received, grace upon grace." [John 1:14-17] The heavenly Redeemer was no longer Light that was seen only by Adam and Eve; the whole world has now seen "and testifies that the Father has sent his Son as the Savior of the world." [1 John 4:14]

Spiritual salvation of mankind is no longer mere hypothetical formulation by Adam's family. The power behind the divine election of mankind in Eden has finally showed himself in a way that entire mankind can relate to. Thus, Incarnation of the heavenly Light on Earth became the greatest miracle in the chronicle of divine ascent of mankind. It decisively settled millennia long controversy of Eden and vindicated Adam and Eve for imbibing his *forbidden* fruit of knowledge and believing in his ability to redeem and resurrect our souls. Apostle John's testimony sums up the miracle of his Divine Incarnation:

> "That which was from the beginning, which we have heard, which we have seen with our eyes, which we have looked upon and touched with our hands, concerning **the Word of Life** - the life was made manifest, and we saw it, and testify to it, and proclaim to you the eternal life which was with the Father and was made manifest to us - that which we have seen and heard we proclaim also to you, so that you may have fellowship with us; and our fellowship is with the Father and with his Son Jesus Christ. And we are writing this that our joy may be complete. ... And **we know that the Son of the Father has come** and has given us understanding, to know him who is true; and we are in him who is true, in his Son Jesus Christ. This is **the true Father and eternal life**." [1 John 1:1-4; 5:20]

That Jesus Christ of Nazareth is the unique human rights activist with absolute divine authority that appeared for mankind in Eden has been duly established for all times. That he was the most peaceable, the most benevolent and the most dependable person to ever walk this Earth is also without doubt. Great men and women had walked the Earth since the invention of mankind on it, but Jesus Christ stands out as the **Ultimate Man**. There is no possible basis for comparison between him and any other. "And there is salvation in no one else," says the Scripture, "for there is no other name under heaven given among men by which we must be saved." ... "Therefore, the Father has highly exalted him and bestowed on him the name which is above every name, that at the name of Jesus every knee should bow, **in heaven and on Earth and under the Earth**, and every tongue confess that Jesus Christ is Lord, to the glory of the Father." [Acts 4:12; Phil 2:9-11]

How we receive him as individuals determines eternal fate of our individual souls. According to John 3:18-20 (NIV), "Whoever believes in him is not condemned, but whoever does not believe stands condemned already because he has not believed in the name of the Father's one and only Son. This is the verdict: Light has come into the world, but men loved darkness instead of light because their deeds were evil. ... "But to all who believed him and accepted him, he gave the right to become children of the Father [again]. They are reborn—not with a physical birth resulting from human passion or plan, but a birth that comes from the Father." [John 1:12-13 (NLT)]

It is shocking therefore, how people respond on the internet to the question "who was the greatest man that ever walked the Earth?" Depending on their religious and other flimsy affiliations, some people mentioned founders of religious movements, like Abraham, Moses, Muhammad of Arabia, Gautama the Buddha, Confucius, Paul and the like. Others mentioned names of past political leaders, like Alexander the Great, Julius Caesar, Mahatma Gandhi, Nelson Mandela, and so on. Some still mentioned names of known scientists, inventors, musicians, footballers, film actors and so on. Remarkably, no one mentioned Adam or Eve. None mentioned Jehovah/Allah, Michael, Gabriel, or any of the known archangels that walked and still walk the Earth. The answers simply prove that most people take entire spiritual ascent of man for granted; evidently, because they are still living in original ignorance. And that is a very sad index in the present stage of evolution of man's knowledge.

Jesus Christ was not a founder of religious movement. He did not write any religious book. Certainly, he neither founded, nor inspired anyone to found customary Christianity that worships Jehovah/Allah as the Father. Jesus Christ was not a sectarian religious leader but Redeemer of the whole world. He came for salvation of all fallen souls in the world—for salvation of entire humankind. He says himself: "I have other sheep that are not of this [Jewish] fold; I must bring them also, and they will heed my voice. So, there shall be one flock, one shepherd." [John 10:16] Anyone who does the will of the Father is a disciple of Jesus Christ, irrespective of species, race, creed, class, or gender. And the will of the Father is that we should love one another as we love ourselves.

Jesus Christ did not mandate his apostles to set up the Church that will segregate itself along religious line, but rather to go into the world and preach salvation of the Father to all mankind. His true apostles did just that. They preached the good news of the Kingdom to all flesh as the Messiah directed. They founded no sectarian religious movement. Customary Christianity was entirely the brainchild of Jehovah/Allah, founded by Paul of Tarsus, under the false influence of the *blinding light* of Damascus. Paul was a staunch apostle Jehovah/Allah from beginning to the end; he was, therefore, a false apostle of Jesus Christ. Accordingly, customary Christianity that he founded worship Jehovah/Allah as *God Almighty*, while pretending to be followers of Jesus Christ. Hence, the Messiah specifically says to followers of Paul, "Not everyone who says to me, 'Lord, Lord,' shall enter the kingdom of heaven, but he who does the will of my Father who is in heaven. On that day many [customary Christians] will say to me, 'Lord, Lord, did we not prophesy in your name, and cast out demons in your name, and do many mighty works in your name?' And then will I declare to them, '**I never knew you**; depart from me, you evildoers.'" [Matt 7:21-23]

B. HE MADE US HUMANS; HE WILL MAKE US LIVING SPIRITS

Before the glorious advent of the heavenly Christ in Eden we were all blinded, dumb animals. Then, he made us human beings, and he is working still to transfigure us into living spirits. We were all in eternal bondage to the selfish principalities; he redeemed and started us on the slow but steady evolution to spiritual perfection. We were all hopeless dead souls, he gave us hope of true eternal life, and he works still to accomplish our spiritual resurrection. How can any right-thinking human being take for granted everything that Jesus Christ has done, and continues to do for humankind? How can any enlightened mind compare greatness of caged animals with that of the one who liberates them? Or on what basis can redeemed captives be compared in greatness with their own Redeemer? Abraham, Moses, Muhammad, the Buddha, Confucius, Gandhi, and the rest were all 'favored slaves' of Jehovah/Allah and the principalities, who were themselves wayward lowlifes, bound for eternal perdition.

I expected people to be comparing Jesus Christ with Jehovah/Allah, Michael, Gabriel, or any of the so-called archangels who have roamed about on Earth since the invention of mankind. Most people deliberately overlook the fact that the principalities are raw men that have physically played active parts in human history. The Bible shows clearly that Jehovah/Allah and the so-called archangels are men that dwell here on Earth. It documents various incidents of their personal interactions with men and women of old. They had walked the Earth ever before the arrival of Jesus Christ on the stage, and they continue to walk the Earth to this day, because they have no other place to go. But what real value can anyone honestly say that Jehovah/Allah or any of the wandering deities that colonize us ever added to the life of mankind? What can they possibly offer since they are fallen dead souls like every one of us? They are self-seeking opportunists, and their only interest has always been to enslave and play gods over us.

To this day, they still hold mankind in bondage through complex machinery of worldly processes—through enslaving activities of worldly religious movements, secular government agencies and underworld operatives. They are agents of darkness and all we have learnt from them are evil deeds that perpetuate our bondage to sinful nature—"sexual immorality, impurity, lustful pleasures, idolatry, sorcery, hostility, quarreling, jealousy, outbursts of anger, selfish ambitions, dissension, division, envy, drunkenness, wild parties, and other sins like these." [Gal 5:19-21(NLT)] In contrast, Jesus Christ has imbued in us divine awareness and desire for spiritual refinement. He brought into our lives genuine spirit of "love, joy, peace, patience, kindness, goodness, faithfulness, gentleness, and self-control." And "Those who belong to Christ Jesus have nailed the passions and desires of their sinful nature to his cross and crucified them there." [Gal 5:22-24 (NLT)]

In all our long years of religious servitude to Jehovah/Allah and the gods of the world, they never talked about giving anyone any spiritual blessing. We never knew that spiritual freedom was a possibility; we never knew about perfect spiritual existence or that ultimate redemption from this life was possible. We never knew about the Father and about our spiritual heritage in Divine Light. The principalities made sure we were kept in total darkness about our spiritual rights, forbade for us knowledge of good and evil, which would have given us necessary spiritual insight. With the help of Jesus Christ, we now know that we are savable souls and that we need spiritual salvation as a matter of urgency. It was also with his help that we now know for sure that true life does not exist anywhere in the material universe; that **true life** is external to entire universal nature. We know now that mankind is not the only thing that dies; the whole universe is dying too.

Looking up to Jehovah/Allah or any of the lowlife principalities to assist us to find true life in the world is doomed, because they are dead entities themselves. Jesus Christ is the only entity that ever convincingly demonstrated existence of perfect heavenly life and gives assurance of helping human souls through the transition process. "I am the resurrection and the life;" he says, "he who believes in me, though he die, yet shall he live, and whoever lives and believes in me shall never die." [John 11:25-26] Indeed, his precepts are life giving in themselves; and his practical examples prove beyond doubt that he truly has access to eternal fountain of true life.

Love is the greatest attribute of the Father; without love, the Father will not exist. In fact, the Father is Love. While Jehovah/Allah busied himself breaking people's necks to force them to accept that he is *God Almighty*, Jesus Christ came into the world and did for human beings things that only the Father could do for them, without asking for anything in return. He preached good news of eternal salvation to the oppressed masses and identified fully with the downtrodden. He fed the hungry, healed the sick, raised the dead, comforted the broken-hearted and forgave our sins. More especially, even while we were yet sinners, he called us his friends and laid down his life that we may find true life. "Greater love has no man than this," he says, "that a man lay down his life for his friends." [John 15:13]

Even though he was one with the Father, Jesus Christ humbled himself to the point of taking on our lowly nature to exemplify love and godly ideals that we should emulate to gain the Father's great reward of eternal life. He became our divine Exemplar; just like when a perfect dance instructor demonstrates a complex dance move for trainee dancers to imitate in the process of learning to become seasoned dancers. Acting that role for our sakes did not diminish his divinity in any way, any more than does acting the role of a big child reduce the respect and true status of a responsive kindergarten teacher. With great humility, and yet with absolute authority, Jesus Christ redefined love away from Jehovah/Allah's misleading ideals by which we could never have found life. Jehovah/Allah admits that he "gave us statutes that were not good and ordinances by which we could not have life." [Ezek 20:25] Hence, Jesus Christ says, "You have heard that it was said [by Jehovah], 'You shall love your neighbor and hate your enemy.' But I say to you, **Love your enemies and pray for those who persecute you, so that you may be sons of your Father who is in heaven;** ... For if you love those who love you, what reward have you? Do not even the tax collectors do the same? ... **You, therefore, must be perfect, as your heavenly Father is perfect**." [Matt 5:43-48]

Thus, Jesus Christ encourages us to rise above unprofitable human nature. But he knows that it could be very difficult for a human being to forgive one who afflicts him; and that to love and pray for such a person could even be harder. So, he did not just enjoin us to "love and pray for our enemies"; he laid down personal example for us to emulate. As he hung on the cross in great physical pains, he looked with greater compassion on the very people who afflicted him and prayed, "Father, forgive them; for they know not what they do." [Luke 23:34] Only the ultimate man can love like that in human situation. Accordingly, he could say to us, "A new commandment I give to you, that you love one another; **even as I have loved you,** that you also love one another. By this all men will know that you are my disciples, if you have love for one another." [John 13:34-35] His ultimate guideline for true love is, "Do to others as you would like them to do to you." [Luke 6:31(NLT)] Unlike Jehovah/Allah's law of compulsory retaliation—*the tit for tat*—Christ's guideline is honest, infallible, and timeless.

Let me quickly say that Jesus Christ is not preaching sensual love; love that is based on human sentiments and societal norms, that one can only show to selected individuals in his life. For instance, a man who loves his wife is not expected to love any other woman and vice versa. I guess Hollywood, Bollywood, Nollywood and all the other movie–woods of the world preach worldly love better. What Jesus Christ preaches is **selflessness**—agape love—which is unconditional and knows no barrier. Christ's type of love is one that a husband can freely show to his wife as well as to every other man or woman that he comes across in his daily existence, anywhere and at any time.

The closest definition of selflessness is found in 1 Cor 13:4-8 (NIV), which reads, "Love is patient, love is kind. It does not envy, it does not boast, it is not proud. It is not rude, it is not self-seeking, it is not easily angered, it keeps no record of wrongs. Love does not delight in evil but rejoices with the truth. It always protects, always trusts, always hopes, always perseveres. **Love never fails**." There is no better way to describe the Ultimate Man, Jesus Christ, than to say that he is Absolutely Selfless. In entire history of human existence on Earth no other entity fits into that perfect mold. Jehovah/Allah is particularly widely off the mark.

C. INCOMPARABLE FRIEND AND MESSIAH

Man's days on Earth are not just *few* but are also *full of trouble*. This applies equally to the lower animals as well as to Jehovah/Allah and the gods. But ephemerality is not the worst blight of worldly existence; it is the lack of peace—the limitations, the struggle for resources, the worries, the stress, the suffering, and the unhappiness. Life without the Father is full of trouble, for peace cannot exist in the absence of true love. Life in the heavenly domain of the Father is eternal, serene, and blissful because the Father is Love. The Father is King of Peace, while his official Envoy to the world, Jesus Christ, is Prince of Peace. Jehovah/Allah, on the other hand, is man of war, and that title alone tells us the extent of *the troubles* that bedevil his personal life. He says himself that he is jealous, wrathful, and vengeful; therefore, *'man of war'* is a perfect epithet for him.

That brings me to the issue of transferred aggression. The world is wholly an unhappy place because the rulers lack inner peace and have no room for true love in their lives. "When the righteous are in authority, the people rejoice;" says Prov 29:2, "but when the wicked rule, the people groan." Thus, Jehovah/Allah's statutes and ordinances directly reflect his personal inadequacies and frustrations. His circumstances demand that he fights for everything that he gets. For him, it takes war to achieve peace. But peace of the world, as we all know, is always fragile because it is not based on genuine love.

Jesus Christ did not come into the world to give that kind of peace to mankind. He came to give us peace of mind, which comes with knowledge, and is grounded in our souls. Borne out of true love; peace of Christ is not affected by the worsening state of worldly existence. "Peace, I leave with you;" he says, "my peace I give to you; **not as the world gives** do I give to you. Let not your hearts be troubled, neither let them be afraid." [John 14:27] He authoritatively abolishes Jehovah/Allah's jungle penal code of *tit-for-tat* and encourages us to put his divine principle of total non-violence into practice. "You have heard that it was said [by Jehovah], 'An eye for an eye and a tooth for a tooth.' But I say to you, Do not resist one who is evil. But if anyone strikes you on the right cheek, turn to him the other also; and if anyone would sue you and take your coat, let him have your cloak as well; and if anyone forces you to go one mile, go with him two miles." [Matt 5:38-41] No doubt, any peace arising from total non-violence will be genuine and enduring.

Jesus Christ says to the Jews who were the experimental models of Jehovah/Allah's peacemaking skill, "Would that even today you knew the things that make for [genuine] peace! But now they are hid from your eyes [by Jehovah]." [Luke 19:42] Genuine peace is the byproduct of true love. The wicked can never have or radiate peace. The Jews and their Muslim brothers will never have peace for as long as they hold on to Jehovah/Allah's violent ordinances that incite them to despise and war against their neighbors.

Jesus Christ is the ultimate humanitarian and teacher of moral and spiritual ethics. His deeds and teachings stand out in terms of originality, genuineness, and authority. They prove beyond doubt that his goodwill is far-reaching for mankind. No one else ever showed genuine concern for the quality of human lives. No one else ever addressed issues of spiritual salvation of human souls. Jesus Christ is not just concerned with the quality of transient human lives on Earth; his teachings are particularly intended to prepare human souls for eternal glory in the heavenly kingdom of the Father.

There is no doubt that Jesus Christ had the power to eradicate sickness and poverty on Earth completely, and to reform worldly existence. He had the power to bring about permanent state of genuine love and peaceful coexistence of peoples of the world. But he did not do that because the world itself is irredeemable. He healed terminal illnesses that the world had no answers for, fed hungry multitudes with foods that were inexhaustible and raised a couple of confirmed dead people only to show his divine authority and as a sample of what heavenly existence entails. So, while he wants us to love and live in peace with one another on Earth in the interim, he does not want us to lose sight of the fact that we ought to be aspiring for a total getaway and outright secession from worldly existence.

In contrast, Jehovah/Allah is a false humanitarian; his goodness toward mankind is only skin-deed and insincere. In fact, permanent state of human suffering and death serves ultimate interest of his wicked cosmic regime. In his name, worldly religions preach paltry *almsgiving* in response to worsening state of poverty and inequity in the world, while the *serpent on pole* represents his best possible answer to recurrent and incurable nature of worldly diseases and death. The serpent on pole is a symbol of universal pharmacology; people literally look up to it to fine cure for their recurrent minor ailments. It is entirely useless as a cure for terminal illnesses and death. Comparing Jehovah/Allah's impermanent solutions to Christ's eternal liberation from entire worldly ills, the Scripture says, "As Moses lifted up the bronze snake on a pole in the wilderness [as Jehovah's symbol of synthetic remedy for physical ailments], so the Son of Man must be lifted up, so that everyone who believes in him will have [perfect] eternal life." [John 3:14-15 (NLT)]

Jesus Christ presents himself as divine ideal for us to emulate unto perfection. To become like him is the goal for mankind—the climax of evolution of man's knowledge. However, no man will ever become exactly like Jesus Christ in the world. No one can ever love as he did. As the sole redeemer of the world, he is unique and absolute in his nature and divine purpose. Nevertheless, we can successfully become his good disciples, by genuinely applying ourselves to selflessness in our everyday dealings with others. "By this," he says, "all men will know that you are my disciples, if you love one another." ... "I have set you an example that you should do as I have done for you. I tell you the truth, no servant is greater than his master, nor is a messenger greater than the one who sent him." [John 13:35; 15-16]

Finally, the Ultimate Man was one with the Father even in the cloak of man. Jesus Christ was both Son of the Father and *Son of man* at the same time. The heavenly Light that appeared to Adam and Eve in Eden was Light from Divine Light; meaning he was bona fide aspect of Divine Light. And since Divine Light is the Father, Incarnation of the heavenly Light was literally Son of the Father. Remarkably, part of the Nicene Creed correctly recognizes Jesus Christ as *"the only Son of the Father, eternally begotten of the Father, Father from Father, Light from Light, true Father from true Father, begotten, not made, of one Being with the Father."*

Putting it in different ways, the Scripture says, "He is the image of the invisible Father, ... For the Father was pleased to have all his fullness dwell in him, and through him to reconcile to himself all things, whether things on Earth or things in heaven, by making peace through his blood, shed on the cross." ... "The Father has life in himself, and he has granted that same lifegiving power to his Son. And he has given him authority to judge everyone because he is the Son of Man." [Col 1:15, 19-20 (NIV); John 5:26-27 (NLT)] In John 10:30 NLT), Jesus Christ simply tells us; "The Father and I are one." So, we can be sure that we are looking up to the true Source of eternal Life.

The following *Essays on Christ* are from the article *"Was Jesus The Greatest Person to Ever Walk This Earth?"* – Copyright 2005-2014 Voice in the Wilderness Ministry. [Retrieved from the web site April 10, 2014]:

THE LIFE OF CHRIST

"This Jesus of Nazareth, without money and arms, conquered more millions than Alexander, Caesar, Mohammed, and Napoleon; without science and learning, He shed more light on things human and divine than all philosophers and scholars combined; without the eloquence of schools, He spoke such words of life as were never spoken before or since and produced effects which lie beyond the reach of orator or poet; without writing a single line, He set more pens in motion, and furnished themes for more sermons, orations, discussions, learned volumes, works of art, and songs of praise, than the whole army of great men of ancient and modern times." - Philip Schaff

THE FAMOUS ESSAY, ONE SOLITARY LIFE

"Here is a man who was born in an obscure village, the child of a peasant woman. He grew up in another village. He worked in a carpenter shop until He was thirty, and then for three years He was an itinerant preacher. He never owned a home. He never wrote a book. He never held an office. He never had a family. He never went to college. He never put his foot inside a big city. He never traveled two hundred miles from the place where He was born. He never did one of the things that usually accompany greatness. He had no credentials but Himself. While still a young man, the tide of

popular opinion turned against Him. His friends ran away. One of them denied Him. He was turned over to His enemies. He went through the mockery of a trial. He was nailed upon a cross between two thieves. While He was dying His executors gambled for the only piece of property He had on Earth—His coat. When He was dead, He was taken down and laid in a borrowed grave through the pity of a friend."

"Nineteen long centuries have come and gone, and today He is the centerpiece of the human race and the leader of the column of progress. I am far within the mark when I say that all the armies that ever marched, all the navies that ever were built, all the parliaments that ever sat and all the kings that ever reigned, put together, have not affected the life of man on this Earth as powerfully as has that one solitary life."

THE INCOMPARABLE CHRIST

"More than nineteen hundred years ago there was a Man born contrary to the laws of life. This Man lived in poverty and was reared in obscurity. He did not travel extensively. Only once did He cross the boundary of the country in which He lived; that was during His exile in childhood."

"He possessed neither wealth nor influence. His relatives were inconspicuous and had neither training nor formal education. In infancy He startled a king; in childhood He puzzled doctors; in manhood He ruled the course of nature, walked upon the billows as if pavements, and hushed the sea to sleep. He healed the multitudes without medicine and made no charge for His service."

"He never wrote a book, and yet all the libraries of the country could not hold the books that have been written about Him. He never wrote a song, and yet He has furnished the theme for more songs than all the song writers combined."

"He never founded a college, but all the schools put together cannot boast of having as many students. He never marshaled an army, nor drafted a soldier, nor fired a gun; and yet no leader ever had more volunteers who have, under His orders,

made more rebels stack arms and surrender without a shot fired."

"He never practiced psychiatry, and yet He healed more broken hearts than all the doctors far and near. Once each week the wheels of commerce cease their turning and multitudes wend their way to worshipping assemblies to pay homage and respect to Him."

"The names of the past proud statesmen of Greece and Rome have come and gone. The names of the past scientists, philosophers, and theologians have come and gone; but the name of this Man abounds more and more. Though time has spread nineteen hundred years between the people of this generation and the scene of His crucifixion, yet He still lives. Herod could not destroy Him, and the grave could not hold Him."

"He stands forth upon the highest pinnacle of heavenly glory, proclaimed of God, acknowledged by angels, adored by saints, and feared by devils, as the living, personal Christ, our Lord and Savior."

NAPOLEON

"Christ alone has succeeded in so raising the mind of man towards the unseen that it becomes insensible to the barriers of time and space. Across the chasm of eighteen hundred years Jesus Christ makes a demand which is beyond all others difficult to satisfy. He asks for that which a philosopher may often seek in vain at the hands of his friends, or a father of his children, or a bride of her spouse, or a man of his brother. He asks for the human heart; He will have it entirely to Himself; He demands it unconditionally, and forthwith His demand is granted. Its powers and faculties become an annexation to the empire of Christ. All who sincerely believe in Him experience that supernatural love towards Him. This phenomenon is unaccountable; it is altogether beyond the scope of man's creative powers. Time, the great destroyer can neither exhaust its strength nor put a limit to its range.

BUT NOT UNTIL WE REALIZE AND ACCEPT THAT JEHOVAH/ALLAH IS THE ANTICHRIST

Ignorance is bondage and death; knowledge is salvation and life but only when it is applied. Climax of evolution of man's knowledge guarantees eternal life in perfect bliss. But that will not be possible until enlightened human beings realize and confront concerted opposition to that glorious possibility. Life of the world is unavoidably characterized by misery and death. The situation is becoming more gruesome by the day because human beings live in greater ignorance today than ever before. And people do not wonder why this should be so, considering the seeming level of enlightenment in the modern world.

We need to be constantly reminded of the life and death battle situation between us and the wicked principalities that rule the world. "For we are not contending against flesh and blood, but against the principalities, against the powers, against the world rulers of this present darkness, against the spiritual hosts of wickedness in the heavenly places," says the Scripture in Eph 6:12. It is imperative therefore, that we keenly examine every step we take in our everyday lives, whether as individuals or as groups, to be sure we are not playing into the hands of our archenemies; that we are not caught in the pervading snare of falsehood spawn by the sneaky principalities. The situation demands that we should keenly seek knowledge and genuine enlightenment, while being weary of all religious belief systems that negate the common sense.

The Scripture further states that "The whole world is in the power of the evil one[s]," and it unequivocally presents Jehovah/Allah as the principal authority, presiding over the ruling council of wicked principalities. "Jehovah presides in the great assembly; he gives judgment among the 'gods,'" says Psalms 82:1 (NIV). Facts on ground agree completely with those assertions. It is foolish therefore for enlightened humanity to continue to worship and sing praises of Jehovah/Allah and his partners merely on the strength of blind religious faith, without keenly considering how his rule is practically affecting the physical and spiritual wellbeing of true humanity.

Jehovah/Allah has never disguised his utter disapproval of mankind's divine election. He has remained terminally opposed to spiritual ascent of humankind right from the genesis. His deeds and utterances have remained consistently opposed to the Father's redemptive mission for the spiritual salvation of human souls. The Scripture sets the records clear that he spearheaded the crucifixion of mankind's Messiah in Jerusalem, hoping that that would put a full stop to his divine mission in the world. But since things did not seem to work out as planned, he resorted to religious vandalism. Climax of evolution of man's knowledge will not yield true life until enlightened humankind realizes and accepts that Jehovah/Allah, the chief god of the world, is indeed, the Antichrist. He is the brain behind the worsening state of social anarchy that threatens the very existence of our present so-called civilized generation. Jehovah/Allah is the instigator of all forms of man's inhumanity to man—Islamic terrorism, tribal hostilities, and senseless bloodshed in every region of our world.

Wars, barbarism, cannibalism, and religious primitivism used to be exclusive characteristics of primitive existence. But today's civilized peoples speak and act more primitive and thoughtless than prehistoric bush men. From present crop of adamant and corrupt world leaders to religious-minded intelligentsia and from very greedy industrialists to dishonest working class, humanity seems to be completely wired for utter self-destruction. In the name of the lawless gods and senseless religious belief systems, even highly educated people condescend to thinking and behaving like wild animals. There are escalating cases of religious terrorism, mob action, gangsterism, suicide bombing, kidnapping, ritual rapes, ritual murders, organized religious racketeering and impudent noise polluting in the name of religious worships. All these amount to modern-day barbarism.

Every day we tune to our radios and television sets we are confronted with unprecedented social calamities being perpetrated by ignorant men and women in the names of the gods and religions, highlighting man's inhumanity to man. We see wickedness in diverse forms. We see violence, willful destructions, bloodshed, deaths, and people weeping all over the world. We see *"blood, fire and columns of smoke,"* which Jehovah/Allah threatened would mark his last days of vengeance on enlightened mankind. Yet, people deliberately refuse to see that he is the brain behind the endless wave of violence and societal decadence that ridicule our modern-day civilization.

In the name of Allah and sheer barbaric religious faith, even well-educated Muslim scholars support and co-plan suicide bombings and human massacres that target defenseless masses in our towns and villages.

They argue that people who do not believe in Allah are infidels, and that killing them is not wickedness but a meritorious service to Allah. They also hold that dying for the cause of Allah attracts eternal reward in some implausible paradise. Yet, they mostly recruit only children of less privileged Muslims—the *alamajiris*—as suicide bombers, while shielding themselves, their relatives, and their own children from personally dying for the cause of Allah. There is no doubt that Allah is a very bad influence on such Muslims. Belief in Allah negates their humanity completely. Thus, their high levels of education and supposed enlightenment turn out to be curse rather than blessing to true humanity.

Of course, Allah boasts in Quran 58:22, saying, "Thou wilt not find folk who believe in Allah and the Last Day loving those who oppose Allah and his messenger, even though they be their fathers or their sons or their brethren or their clan. As for such, he hath written *faith* upon their hearts and hath strengthened them with a *spirit* from him, and he will bring them into Gardens underneath which rivers flow, wherein they will abide. Allah is well pleased with them, and they are well pleased with him. **They are Allah's Party**."

There is no doubt that Muslim fanatics are possessed by evil *spirit* from Allah. He infuses in them his end-time spirit of religious fanaticism, adamancy, and self-damnation, while giving them false promise of a rosy future in limbo. They are also crippled by irrational fear of some imaginary Day of Judgment by Allah. "They have an awning of fire above them and below them a dais (of fire), says Quran 39:16. "With this doth Allah appall his bondmen. O my bondmen, therefore, **fear** me!" he says.

Indeed, Muslim fanatics are slaves of Allah. They deserve sympathy of truly enlightened minds, and they earnestly need the salvation of Jesus Christ. They need to know that there is no judgment or condemnation whatsoever for anyone who belongs to **Party of Jesus Christ**. "Truly, truly, he does not come into judgment," says the Messiah, "but has passed from death to life." [John 5:24] But belonging to **Party of Jesus Christ** does not in any way mean being a churchgoer. Many churchgoers belong to **Allah's Party** without knowing it. As the Messiah says, "Not everyone who says to me, 'Lord, Lord,' shall enter the kingdom of heaven, but he who does the will of my Father who is in heaven." [Matt 7:21] A true Christ-follower is a normal human being who loves, or at least genuinely tries to love, his neighbor as he loves the Father and as he loves himself, while a real Muslim is one who is totally consumed by his "love" for Allah that he sees it as his duty to kill his neighbor to please him. That is sheer travesty of love.

Fanatic Muslims are not the only ones possessed by Jehovah/Allah's end-time evil spirit of violence, adamancy, and self-destruct. Followers of all other religion of the world—Judaism, customary Christianity, Hinduism, Buddhism, and all other traditional religious faiths—are equally very much blinded to Jehovah's true intentions for mankind. All worldly rulers are possessed; all countries of the world and their people are possessed. In the name of other forms of religion—nationalism, racism, tribalism, and social caste systems—normal-looking human beings readily transform themselves into wild beasts and freely commit pogroms, genocides, brutal massacres, and unimaginable crimes against one another without mercy or any remorse. Indeed, Jehovah/Allah's prophesied outpouring of evil spirit of *religious* madness was meant to be indiscriminate—"*on all kinds of people,*" the Bible says. "After this," says Joel 2:28-30 (ERV), "I will pour out my Spirit **on all kinds of people**. Your sons and daughters will prophesy, your old men will have dreams, and your young men will see visions. In those days I will pour out my Spirit even on servants, both men and women. I will work wonders in the sky and on the Earth. **There will be blood, fire, and thick smoke**." The attack is already activated.

Nothing in that prophecy even slightly suggests that Jehovah/Allah intended the later-day outpouring of his spirit as goodwill to mankind. Rather, he made it clear that his attacks on mankind in the later days of his bottled-up indignation will be from all fronts. He says in Amos 5:19-20 (NLT):

- "In that day you will be like a man who runs from a lion—only to meet a bear. Escaping from the bear, he leans his hand against a wall in his house—and he's bitten by a snake. Yes, the day of Jehovah will be dark and hopeless, without a ray of joy or hope." He buttressed that in Isa 24:17-18 and 34:2, saying,
- "Terror, and the pit, and the snare are upon you, O inhabitant of the Earth! He who flees at the sound of the terror shall fall into the pit; and he who climbs out of the pit shall be caught in the snare. ...
- "For Jehovah is enraged against all the nations, and furious against their entire host, he has doomed them, has given them over for slaughter."

Now, religious believers may continue to assume that Jehovah/Allah is merely singing lullabies of mercy and endearment to humanity. But history and unfolding events in the world today strongly prove that the principalities are not joking at all. Only a tree hears that it would be cut down and continues to stand and dance the waltz on the same spot. Mankind should do something meaningful to regain unity of its peoples and to overcome Jehovah/Allah's spell of mutual destruct. Modern human beings have enough information at their disposal to understand the way the world is going. We have enough information to squarely confront Jehovah/Allah and his wicked gang of accomplices. But the first enemy to overcome is religion in all its forms. Something is cynical about religion that renders the believers mentally blind, deaf, and dumb. Religion eats away people's common sense. The more religious people become the more senseless things they do in the name of mere beliefs. In that regard, it must be concluded that religion is the ultimate folly of our modern generation.

CHAPTER SIX: WHO INVENTED THE UNIVERSE?

Usually, the question people ask is "Did *God* create the universe?" or "Do you believe that *God* created the universe?" No allowance is made for people who do not even know who or what *God* is. That way, *God* is tactically posited as the only possible candidate, and so the general assumption is always that he did. Einstein was in that same predictable frame of mind when he said, "I want to know how *God* created this world." He took for granted the basic need to know who or what *God* is first, and to ascertain that he created the universe, before going further to examine how he did it. One must first define *God* before asking if he created the universe or not. If one knows who or what *God* is, he will know what he can or cannot do; he will know the things that are compatible or incompatible with his agreed nature. If we endeavor to know and define the *God* we have in mind first, then it will become very easy for us to know if he created the universe or not.

Anyway, evolution of man's knowledge has reached decisive stage in our present generation when we should be able to proffer right answers to critical questions about our world that defied older generations. "There is a time for everything, a season for every activity under heaven," says the Scripture, "A time to be quiet and a time to speak up." [Eccl 3:1, 7] In the past, people who knew some of the answers "kept quiet, for it was an evil time." [Amos 5:13] Even the heavenly Christ had to wait for the right time to reveal the Father *plainly* to human beings. "I have spoken of these matters in parables," he said, "but the time will come when this will not be necessary, and I will tell you plainly all about the Father. . . . "Oh, there is so much more I want to tell you, but you can't understand it now. When the Holy Spirit, who is truth, comes, he shall guide you into all truth" [John 16:25, 12-13 (TLB)] Well, many of us will agree that the Spirit of Truth is already here with us on Earth. Therefore, now is the time to know and speak out about the Father in plain words.

Understanding and accepting the origin and authorship of our makeshift universal habitat is among the greatest hurdles to cross in our homeward journey toward our **heavenly home**. For, a person who does not know where he is, cannot know where he wants to go. Ordinarily, this is simple. Normal people do not talk about *going home* unless they are sure they are not at home. The most basic thing anyone who is lost knows is that he is not at home. The question is do human beings know that they are *lost* spirit beings? Do we know that we are not at home? For some complicated reasons, we do not know anything for sure. We cannot even tell whether we are mortal Earthlings or fallen spirits. And so, believing that we are at home in the universe makes it impossible for most of us to genuinely consider *going home* a spiritual exercise that should take us away from entire spheres of the physical universe as we know it now.

For us to make genuine progress toward the climax of evolution of man's knowledge, we must crack the puzzle surrounding creation of the universe in which we have all been cocooned in mortal Earthen bodies and reduced to mere humans. In this regard, noisy debates between evolutionists and creationists have been aimless indeed—a sheer public display of intellectual ignorance. Firstly, 'Evolution' is a very simple word, meaning growth. Everything grows from simple to complexity in Mother Nature; and after growth death follows. Secondly, in the context of our present consciousness, 'Creation' is a word that simply refers to any intelligent invention. Every invention that has a defined route to an end is a creation, irrespective of whether it serves good or evil purpose; irrespective of whether it is perfect or imperfect. For instance, computer viruses are 'intelligent inventions,' programmed and set in operation in peoples' personal computers by computer geniuses with evil intentions. In the context of the universe, nothing about 'natural evolution' or 'natural creation' portrays perfection that we can honestly attribute to the Father and his actual spiritual creation. In determining universal craftsmanship, the central point of consideration should not be whether the universe is an intelligent invention, because it is. It should be whether it is a perfect creation. Not every intelligent invention is a creation of the Father, but every creation of the Father is perfect, intelligent invention.

Did our heavenly Father create for us the world that holds our spirits captive, and he is also trying to save us from it? Did he turn us into helpless mortal humans, and for what purpose? Did he, could he, have possibly created a universe that turns out to be 'completely meaningless?' The Scripture gives simple answer to all the above. It says, "**All** that is in the world ... is not of the Father but *is of the world*." [1 John 2:16] Straightaway, we know that the universe is an intelligent invention by *the world*. What we need to determine here then is what or who ***the world*** is.

THE UNIVERSE: A TEMPORARY DISORDER IN THE FATHER'S ETERNAL SPIRITUAL CREATION

A. STRAW SHACK ON SERENE LANDSCAPE OF DIVINE RESERVE

The Bible tells story of creation of our world. It is story of a beautiful, serene nature reserve and a temporary straw shack. A homeless drifter strays into the perfect, dark, serene landscape of the divine reserve. And groping his way around, he arbitrarily picks materials that are within his reach and makes for himself a ramshackle home. Now, the question is not about who owns the divine reserve, or the resources found therein, but about who erected the shambles on it.

When we refer to the universe as *cosmos* or an ordered system, we blatantly deny the erratic nature of the forces that confront us every day of our existence here, and thereby make mockery of perfect divine order and existence that the Father represents. Natural disasters, such as, Earthquakes, volcanic eruptions, avalanches, uncontrollable tsunamis caused by underwater Earthquakes, violent weather conditions we experience as blizzards, squalls, hurricanes, cyclones, tornados, and typhoons that ravage our cities; all these are symptoms of a chaotic system. Uncontrollable nature of universal forces translates directly into unpredictable nature of human lives and deaths on Earth. We live endlessly with natural tragedies of the flawed invention and yet we refuse to acknowledge the bizarreness of attributing it all to the perfect Father. Not only in large scale natural disasters can we see the chaotic nature of universal experiment; all forms of human indiscretions or improper dispositions—outburst of anger, greed, deceitfulness, sexual immorality, unwanted pregnancies—are all manifestations of uncontrollable nature of universal forces. All manners of diseases and human ailments that culminate in death, even obesity that is caused by eating disorder; these and more are all traces of imperfection brought about by imbalance of forces in universal craftsmanship.

Human beings do not doubt the *meaninglessness* of universal craftsmanship; they do not deny the clumsiness of Mother Nature—the whole sinful process of sexual duplication of false life on Earth. What they find difficult to overcome is the awe-inspiring quasi magnificence and wonders that human senses perceive in it. That is even the lesser of the difficulties confronting ignorant humans. Religious dramatization of Jewish version of an inconclusive ancient Akkadian fable on creation has stuck to peoples' psyche as if with indelible glue. Bible account of the Genesis barely talks about how a group of alien human-gods with advanced knowledge of science cloned *Homo sapiens*—in their own image and likeness—by mingling their own blood with that of primitive *ape-man* aborigines on planet Earth about 10,000 years ago. It says absolutely nothing positive about creation of the great expanding universe that has been in existence for over 13 billion years.

The whole fable opens with Genesis 1:1 that simply says, "In the beginning Elohim [*gods*] created the heavens and the Earth;" *heavens and Earth* strictly referring to our isolated, tiny, and young solar system. The rest of the story merely describes observable features that were strictly peculiar to planet Earth, which were cleverly formulated with the benefit of hindsight. Yet, religious believers completely assume that invoking into place a *second-generation* sun over the dark planet Earth on the first day of a six-day creation, as the tale postulates, was the genesis of the universe, and that the groping entity that emerged out of primordial pitch darkness screaming 'let there be light' was the perfect Father himself. But Jesus Christ tells us that the Father is *Eternal* Light *in whom there is no darkness at all*, meaning he could not have emerged out of any kind of darkness at any given point in time. He could not have been the stranded entity invoking artificial lights of burning solar gasses to light up his Earthly world.

This is just a sample of the devastating effect of religious brainwashing. Religion turns truths upside-down and compels believers to see them as upright. Hence, even when they read truths as truths, they still understand them upside-down. The Scripture says explicitly that **"all that is in the world ... is not of the Father** *but is of the world*." Religious believers read this as incontrovertible truth but understand it as saying the direct opposite. Although the universe seems magnificent and wonderful to human senses, the Scripture calls it "completely meaningless." Religious believers sing songs with that; and though they call the Father 'the Perfect Creator,' they still find it difficult to accept that he could not have been the creator of such irredeemable vanity. Surely, something is wrong with religious believers—a powerful spell places thick veil of ignorance over their eyes and minds. Indeed, Romans 11:8 (NLT) says, "Jehovah has put them into a deep sleep. To this very day he has shut their eyes so they do not see, and closed their ears so they do not hear."

Our seasoned philosophers and scientists have not fared better in this regard. They equally show symptoms of thwarted reasoning. They have not even been able to detect the confidence trick played on human minds by *inspired* fabricators of the Bible creation fable. The so-called creation story says absolutely nothing about the universe but solely about features pertaining to our tiny planet Earth. Hence, in place of seeking to prove that universal craftsmanship is, to all intents and purposes, flawed and therefore cannot be a product of the flawless Father, our respected philosophers and scientists spend valuable time debating about the meaning of English words and phrases such as 'creation,' 'evolution,' 'believe in *God*,' 'atheism,' and so on. If they had concentrated on the search for perfection within universal framework, they would have seen for sure that the universe is indeed heavily flawed; and they would have been led directly to the Father within his perfect eternal beyond. Then, they would have had no time for the kind of intellectual squabbles that have kept them from being positively involved in useful research and real intellectual pursuits that promote spiritual enlightenment of human minds.

What difference does it make that creationists 'believe in the Father,' while evolutionists 'do not.'? That people believe or do not believe in the Father only portrays humankind's helplessness with the fact that the Father cannot be seen or felt in the universe. If people who 'believe' in the Father see or feel his presence in the system, they will stop believing, because then, they would have known him. Therefore, 'I believe in the Father and 'I don't believe in the Father are two meaningless declarations. Since the person who says, 'I believe in the Father cannot at the same time honestly say, 'I know the Father,' he is no different from the person who honestly says 'I don't believe in the Father' because he does not know the Father. The common denominators here are ignorance or lack of knowledge of the Father and the deep-rooted inner yearning to know the Father. Without these denominators the polarity will not exist in the first instance.

Nevertheless, we all know deep in us that perfection does exist beyond universal framework, otherwise human mind will not contemplate it. Wisdom demands therefore, that we drop the short-cut approach of 'believing' for the more profitable pursuit of divine knowledge, which will lead us directly to the perfect Father and to his true heavenly creation. Jesus Christ assures us that we can indeed, know the Father. Why then do we continue to dwell on blind beliefs rather than making effort to acquire true knowledge?

Anyway, spells do not last forever. Jehovah/Allah's spell of spiritual blindness cannot be an exception. Now is the time for human beings to show genuine resolve; to shake off the dark veil of spiritual primitivism and reflect spiritual enlightenment. Now is the time for them to think and understand things the way they are, to prove that *"the true light that enlightens every man"* has indeed come into the world. The way we think and see our world now should reflect the fact that, indeed, "the darkness is disappearing and the true light is already shining." [1 John 2:8] To that effect, Eph 5:14, 8 exhort us all, saying, "Awake, O sleeper, rise up from the dead, and Christ will give you light [of spiritual insight]. ... For though your hearts were once full of darkness, now you are full of light from [Jesus Christ], and your behavior should show it!"

For those of us who read the Bible and can discern between truths and falsehoods within the texts, all that is required is a little bit of purposeful reasoning in matters of crucial importance, such as this one. To be able to see greater picture of reality, we should free our minds from parochial and fabricated image of creation portrayed by the Bible's account. *Creation*, or rather description of the natural features pertaining to planet Earth cannot mean the same thing as creation of the universe, which captures the true origin of everything that is wrong with our present existence. With the right mental image of *original sin*, Jehovah/Allah's childish argument that pins meaninglessness of entire universal craftsmanship on Adam and Eve for eating *a* certain fruit of knowledge on tiny planet Earth will simply become laughable. The ills of the universe transcend whatever took place or takes place on planet Earth. Of course, Jesus Christ assures us that our present understanding of *sin, righteousness* and *judgment* is widely off the mark.

The heavenly Christ came into the universe as heavenly envoy of Divine Light to enlighten us about our world and our present status as fallen sons of Light. He tells us plainly that we are presently estranged in a *nether* world that is not of the Father. "You are from *below*, I am from above; you are of this world, I am not of this world." [John 8:23] But he equally made it clear that we belong to the Father's heavenly Kingdom—*above*, and not to our present world of darkness—*below*. His words to us at close of his Earthly ministry, before his departure from the world, were explicit; "I am ascending to my Father and your Father, to my God and your God." [John 20:17] We are supposed to deduce from his words that our world is not in harmony with perfect Divine Design; that the Father is not the author of it, and that we are simply heavenly renegades.

B. THE UNIVERSE IS NOT A CREATION OF THE FATHER

The universe is not a creation of the Father! This needs to be stated clearly and emphatically. It is rather a *temporary* disorder within the Father's perfect, *eternal*, spiritual creation. Where the Scripture says that '**the universe is not of the Father**,' it clearly says that '**the universe is of *the world*.**' It makes it explicit that everything about the universe and its operating system that is powered by Mother Nature—*"the lust of the flesh and the lust of the eyes and the pride of life"*—is not in harmony with Divine Thought. Of course, we know that all resources in existence belong to the Father. What the Scripture is telling us is that although the resources exploded to generate the expanding universe and the finite region of the perfect, infinite realm of darkness in which the explosion took place belong to the Father, the Father did not perform or endorse the craftsmanship. The question we should be asking therefore is "Who is, or are, *the world* that stands contrary to the Father's Divine Ideal; that exploded the universe within the perfect infinite realm of darkness? This question is not difficult to answer at all. Clues abound all around us in our present generation.

As we already know, the Father is Spirit; his actual creations are spiritual and eternal. the Father's eternal spiritual manifestations include *only* two infinite realms of *absolute* light and *absolute* darkness, which are eternally demarcated. A universe of undifferentiated darkness and light was not a divine idea. It was not ordained within Ultimate Reality. The finite universal eruption within the realm of absolute darkness, representing an unwarranted blend of darkness and artificial light, is an aberration—a rebellious contradiction to the Father's perfect eternal design.

Besides the fact that universal craftsmanship falls well below Divine Ideal, we already know that the Father did not designate the realm of *absolute* darkness for any creative activity. We know also that the Father does not personally create finite worlds or universes. He is rather the infinite resources and the eternal arena within which his sons create, in accordance with inviolable divine norm of perfection. All perfect worlds within his eternally designated realm of heavenly homes are creations of his perfect sons. There is no doubt that our material universe was an invention of certain sons of the Father. However, because the universe was invented outside the designated realm of heavenly homes, in direct contravention of divine norm of perfection, the sons of the Father in question could only be fallen, dead ones.

As inconclusive as Bible's creation account is, however, we can reasonably discern the whole history of our world of darkness from the very first five verses of the book of Genesis. The so-called Earthly creation account gives us clear idea of where universal creation was taking place and who the creators were. The Hebrew word that is translated as *God* in modern Bible translations of the Genesis account is *Elohim*. This word stands for plural deities and therefore means "gods." Jehovah's religious votaries shamelessly switch words in the Bible, with questionable translations, to alter meaning of texts to save him embarrassments for his many lies. To get the true meaning of the texts therefore, the verses should rightly read:

> In the beginning Elohim [*gods*] created the heavens and the Earth.
> 2 The Earth was without form and void, and darkness was upon the face of the deep; and the spirits of Elohim [*the gods*] were moving over the face of the waters.
> 3 And Elohim [*the gods*] said, "Let there be light"; and there was light.
> 4 And Elohim [*the gods*] saw that the light was good; and Elohim [*the gods*] separated the light from the darkness.
> 5 Elohim [*the gods*] called the light Day, and the darkness they called Night. And there was evening and there was morning, one day.

According to verse two, the story is about a group of dislocated spirit beings stranded in a region of absolute darkness. "Let there be light" is the first reaction of people who once had light and then were *suddenly* confronted with total light outage. People in my country, Nigeria, will not have any difficulty understanding reaction of the gods, as they are confronted daily with that kind of situation due to very poor national electricity power regime. As we already know, true sons of Divine Light reflect his divine nature within the realm of lights in accordance with inviolable heavenly norm that sustains eternal exclusion of darkness from heavenly arena. They can never have occasion to start screaming for light within the domain of Divine Light. Only sons of light that violate the heavenly norm will *instantaneously* forfeit their divine nature and become totally engulfed in absolute darkness; only such corrupted sons can be clamoring for some forms of artificial light. Therefore, it is not difficult at all to know who the groping spirits in the Genesis account were. They were sons of Light who violated the heavenly norm of perfection and were automatically spewed out of perfect heavenly existence and into the outer darkness.

The fact that the groping spirits immediately recognized the need to separate Day light from Night darkness showed that the *heavenly dropouts* were fully aware of the divine norm that meticulously established eternal divide between light and darkness. However, they could only rely on artificial cyclic divide created by orbital interactions between the sun, the Earth, and the moon. Meanwhile, the whole world remains an irredeemable 'dark place.' Eternal norm of the Father's true creation strictly disallows that light and darkness should exist in the same place at the same time. If the universe was formed within the bounds of the heavenly norm of perfect existence, we would not be here struggling to rise above limitations or seeking redemption from darkness, ignorance, poverty, insecurity, sickness, and physical death.

Universal creation is not spiritually ideal; therefore, it represents gross unreality. It might seem real to human senses, but it really is a very bad dream of dead spirits. Denying this fact makes ineffective our most earnest desire to transit to ideal heavenly existence. Maintaining that all is well with our world is deliberate ignorance and that is the height of continuing spiritual backsliding. Everything is not good, beautiful, and wholesome with the universe, as suggested by the Bible account. If it were, the heavenly Christ would not have come to us, and we would not be yearning for ultimate redemption. Hence, enlightened minds earnestly seek total emancipation of their souls from all kinds of involvement with it.

Who then were the heavenly dropouts that brought disorder to the peaceful realm of perfect darkness? In the first place, that the universe is of *the world* means that it is not the work of a single individual. No single fallen entity outside the Father's heavenly household possesses enough energy to orchestrate the kind of great explosion—what scientists call the *big bang*—that gave birth to what we now call the expanding universe. It is laughable that ignorant religious believers attribute creation of the whole universe to Jehovah/Allah alone—such a powerless dead soul that relies entirely on gangsterism, mob action and mass following of hypnotized religious agents and devotes for his daily survival.

Secondly, the only group of individualized creative energies that presently do not conform to heavenly ideal is the family of fallen dead spirits entrapped in the outer darkness—*below*, to which we all belong. Referring to all of us as inglorious heavenly defectors, Jude 6 calls us "the angels that did not keep their own position but left their proper dwelling." We are the inglorious family of overambitious spirits spewed out of the Father's presence as we violated the heavenly norm of perfect existence. Every individual spirit found anywhere within the vast expanding universe, whether known by man or not; whether called Lucifer, Satan, Jehovah/Allah, principality, god, archangel, angel, devil, demon, human, animal, or what have you, is a fallen spirit and a bona fide member of the inglorious heavenly dropouts. We all contributed in our various capacities to the making of our universe.

Exploding of the expanding universe was the joint venture of the entire heavenly dropouts; and jointly we have continued to create and recreate the world. It is much like when a group of individuals are *compelled* to pull their *meager* resources together in a grand joint enterprise; like when diverse individuals came together to found the great USA. United States of America is not the creation of one hard working individual. No such single individual exists in the whole universe that could have possibly accomplish such a feat. In fact, we are so dead to our natural creative potentials as fallen sons of Light that we cannot accomplish anything meaningful outside the Father's designated realm of self-sufficiency without banding efforts of many individuals together.

From sexual duplication of false life on Earth to founding and managing families, towns, cities, and countries; from interpreting basic principles of nature to inventing and perfecting processes and inventions, Mother Nature is all about togetherness in conflict. Popular proverbs rightly hold that 'no one is an island in the world,' and that 'majority is power.' In whichever mortal forms our spirits hibernate in all over the universe, we are still jointly creating, recreating, and doing our best to uphold our failed universal experiment. We are all various categories of creators—spiders are creators; also, insects, birds, human beings, gods, demons, witches, and what have you. Collectively, **we are *the world*** that invented the universe, and collectively we work ceaselessly to maintain it. However, it will eventually pass away, as every bad dream does, because it is finite, transient and at variance with Divine Ideal. But all sons of Light in it stand called to be resurrected and returned to their proper, heavenly home, in accordance with the Father's gracious will. For, "it is not the will of my Father who is in heaven," says Jesus Christ, "that one of these little ones should perish." [Matt 18:14]

ULTIMATE FATE OF THE UNIVERSE

There is a paradox that religious believers must resolve for themselves before they can truly key into Christ's gospel of 'home-going'—that of vague dual citizenship. On the one hand, they believe that the heavenly Christ will come back to take them to his perfect heavenly paradise where life is eternal and blissful. Indeed, Jesus Christ makes solemn promise to that effect. "Don't let your hearts be troubled. Trust in the Father, and trust also in me," he says, "There is more than enough room in my Father's home. If this were not so, would I have told you that I am going to prepare a place for you? When everything is ready, **I will come and get you, so that you will always be with me where I am**." [John 14:1-3]

On the other hand, however, they are equally waiting for a kind of *New Jerusalem* with golden streets that Jehovah/Allah promises to lower down from heavens to Earth for them when present heavens and Earth have passed away. In the *New Jerusalem*, according to Jehovah/Allah's own solemn promise, "No longer will babies die when only a few days old. No longer will **adults die** before they have **lived a full life**. No longer will people be considered old at one hundred! Only **the cursed will die** that young! [Isaiah 65:20]

Thus, these believers are torn between outright ***spiritual rapture*** that promises to transform believers into resurrected spirit beings and transport them back into the realm of lights where they belonged and ***the new paradise-on-Earth*** where they will continue to be mortal human beings;

and where, according to Jehovah/Allah's promise, "the wolf and the lamb will live together; the leopard and the goat will be at peace. Calves and yearlings will be safe among lions, and a little child will lead them all;" where "the cattle will graze among bears. Cubs and calves will lie down together. And lions will eat grass as the livestock do. Babies will crawl safely among poisonous snakes," and "a little child will put its hand in a nest of deadly snakes and pull it out unharmed." [Isaiah 11:6-8(TLB)]

Surely, a future that promises refurbished city of Jerusalem for mortal human beings cannot be the same as heavenly Paradise that promises spiritual resurrection and outright liberation from entire universal experience for fallen dead human spirits. Offering to save a man drowning in deep muddy sea cannot be the same as turning the muddy sea into clear, clean water for him to continue his drowning. Evidently, one cannot be in heaven with Christ enjoying blissful life as perfect spirit and at the same time be in the new paradise-on-Earth as human being, chewing grass with lions and livestock. Such dual citizenship is impracticable. Religious believers must make the choice between the promise of Jesus Christ and that of Jehovah/Allah. They must choose between becoming full citizens of Christ's heavenly Paradise and continuing as mortal human beings in Jehovah/Allah's New Jerusalem zoo on Earth; between spiritual eternal life and long human life span that still ends in death. The difference is clear.

People who choose Jesus Christ will have to reject Jehovah/Allah and all his false promises and vice versa. Unfortunately, religious believers do not yet recognize that Jesus Christ and Jehovah/Allah are on the opposite sides of our salvation tug of war, which was why the heavenly Christ talked about drawing all men from Earth to himself. "I, when I am lifted up from the Earth," he said, "will draw all men to myself;" for "my kingship **is not of this world.**" [John 12:32; 18:36] Jehovah/Allah, on his part, states his defiant position clearly, saying, "Jehovah will become king **over all the Earth**; on that day Jehovah will be one and his name one." [Zechariah 14:9]

One needs not be a prophet or superhuman to recognize that Jehovah/Allah's manifesto is the false one here. We already know that heavens and Earth will pass away, and that will include the so-called New Jerusalem in the heavens. One will be dim-witted to imagine that Jehovah/Allah, who was not able to revamp his first paradise-on-Earth or repair his present ailing world, will eventually perform super magic, and generate a workable second paradise-on-Earth when the whole world would have melted away. In any case, who would knowingly trade perfect eternal life as true son of Light in the Father's realm of perfect existence with a repeat of human life experiences in Jehovah/Allah's improbable Earthly empire?

Evolution of man's knowledge has always been geared toward spiritual salvation—toward spiritual rebirth, regeneration, or resurrection. It has always been all about *returning* to our eternal heavenly home to reunite with our true Father. How then can any right-thinking person even think twice about Jehovah/Allah's false manifesto? How can any enlightened mind allow Jehovah/Allah to fool him into settling for spiritual retrogression? Indeed, if all our labor for spiritual salvation is just for mere remodeled version of Earthly existence, then we have labored in vain. "If for this life only we have hoped in Christ," says 1 Cor 15:19, "we are of all men most to be pitied." If Jehovah/Allah is all that we expect the Father to be, we are doomed forever. And if the imperfect fleeting universe represents everything we expect from the Father as the perfect Creator, then the concept of the Father and creation are vanity forever.

What people need to have, is concrete information on the fate of the universe. The Scripture says in plain words that "**heavens and Earth** *will pass away*." What really does the Bible mean by *'passing away'*? Is it saying that heavens and Earth will completely cease to exist or simply that they will literally put on a new look? For human beings whose experience and scope of imagination is limited to Earth and its continual seasonal rejuvenations, heavens and Earth passing away—i.e., ceasing to exist—can be very difficult to imagine. It can be hard for average human being on Earth to envisage the universe ceasing to exist one day. In fact, religious believers prefer to think of the statement as mere allegory. Most of them strongly believe that the Bible is figuratively talking about universal renewal, which is why they do not find it difficult to believe that Jehovah/Allah will indeed substitute present wicked Jerusalem-on-Earth with a brand new one from the heavens in a process of *planned* universal rebranding.

Indeed, Jehovah/Allah tells his followers in plain words that the world will not cease to exist; that he will rather be refurbishing existing situation. He says in Isaiah 65:17 "Look! I am creating new heavens and a new Earth—so wonderful that no one will even think about the old ones anymore." He makes it clearer in Quran 14:48 that he talks about general renewal rather than outright passing away. "On that day," the verse reads, "… the Earth will be *changed* to other than the Earth, and the heavens (also will be *changed*)." And so, most religious sects on Earth instinctively understand heavens and Earth passing away exactly the way Jehovah/Allah wants them to.

Jehovah's Witnesses are, perhaps, the most outstanding advocates of Jehovah/Allah's new world order. To them, end of the world simply means end of present Earthly system of things, especially of Earthly system of government. Apart from the mysterious 144,000 elects who, according to them, are destined to rule with their own Christ in heaven, the entire sect earnestly wait for Jehovah/Allah's *second* paradise-on-Earth. This happens to be the subconscious position of all the people who choose Jehovah/Allah's end-time manifesto over that of Jesus Christ. And according to Jehovah/Allah, religious believers submit to his religious dictates '*willingly or unwillingly.*' "Seek they other than the religion of Allah," asks Quran 3:83, "when unto him submitteth whosoever is in the heavens and Earth, willingly or unwillingly?"

Ironically, even reputed *pillars* of Christ's gospel of heavenly exodus could not demonstrate clear understanding of the status quo. Because customary Christians allowed themselves to be fully engulfed in Jewish religious idiosyncrasies, they equally think and understand like Jehovah's Jewish votaries. Even Paul, with all his acclaimed spiritual insight, never managed to prove he understood that Jesus Christ and Jehovah are on opposite sides of our salvation battle line. For him, Jehovah's promise of new heavens and Earth simply "means that anyone who belongs to Jesus Christ has become a new person. The old life is gone; a new life has begun!" [2 Cor 5:17]

How about Apostle Peter? Did he demonstrate clearer understanding of Christ's position on universal meltdown? He writes in 2 Peter 3:10, "But the day of the Lord will come as unexpectedly as a thief. Then the heavens will pass away with a terrible noise, and the very elements themselves will disappear in fire, and the Earth and everything on it will be burned up." Then he concludes in verse 13, "But we are looking forward to the new heavens and new Earth he has promised, a world filled with God's righteousness." The question is, did Jesus Christ ever promise Peter or anyone else that he would create a new heavens and Earth for human beings? What he promised was that he would prepare a place in heaven and take resurrected spirits of all his followers there before universal meltdown. Evidently, Peter got it all mixed up. He was right about the universe practically passing away, but wrong about a replacement world. That bit belongs entirely to Jehovah's defiant manifesto.

What then does Christ's own end-time manifesto say about the passing away of the universe? Was he telling us that the entire universe will completely disappear or that he will come back to revamp world's imperfect systems? Well, Jesus Christ never spoke in parable about the fate of our imperfect universe. It will surely cease to exist because it is only a temporary disorder on the flipside of the Father. The heavenly Christ would draw **all** resurrected spirits to his heavenly paradise; and there is more than enough room there for all the present inhabitants of the perishing world. It is only natural that when he has drawn all men to his heavenly paradise, end of the empty and ill-fated universe will follow. Drawing all men to himself means that Jehovah/Allah's dream of ruling over people in his fictitious new Earth will come to naught. That is why Jehovah/Allah vows to fight; to retain both his world and his human slaves.

But that is not really in his power. So, because he cannot fight the heavenly Christ or avert the Father's divine verdict on the universe, he vows to take out his anger and frustration on uninformed human beings whose position in the battle line is not well defined. "I will take vengeance, and I will spare no man" he says, "For the day of Jehovah is great and very terrible; who can endure it? ... For my decision is to gather nations, to assemble kingdoms, to pour out upon them my indignation, all the heat of my anger [and frustration]; for in the fire of my jealous wrath all the Earth shall be consumed." [Isaiah 47:3, Joel 2:11, Zephaniah 3:8] Now, how can any clear-thinking person decide to set his hope on promise of a new world order made by this kind of character?

Jehovah/Allah will go on rampage as the end of the world draws nearer, and we now know why. Jesus Christ calls it the period of great tribulation for humans on Earth. He says in Matthew 24:21-22, "For there will be greater anguish than at any time since the world began. And it will never be so great again. In fact, unless that time of calamity is shortened, not a single person will survive. But it will be shortened for the sake of the Father's chosen ones." Then he tells us in definite terms in verse 29 that the physical universe will indeed disappear. "Immediately after the anguish of those days," he says, "**the sun will be darkened, the moon will give no light**, the stars will fall from the sky, and the powers in the heavens will be shaken." [Isaiah 34:4 deployed all the right words to hammer home the definite message—"The heavens above will *melt away* and *disappear* like a rolled-up scroll. The stars will fall from the sky like *withered* leaves from a grapevine, or *shriveled* figs from a fig tree."]

Needless to stress that with all the stars in the universe darkened and shaken off, the world literally comes to an end. Without a single dot of artificial light left within the universe, it will simply revert to its primordial state of absolute darkness and inactivity, as originally designated by the Father, while redeemed sons of Light are returned to the Father's heavenly home where they belong eternally. "For it is my Father's will," says Jesus Christ, "that all who see his Son and believe in him should have eternal life. **I will raise them up [to heaven] at the last day.**" [John 6:40] Therefore there is absolutely no place for a new Jerusalem-on-Earth in Christ's divine mission.

For people who prefer scientific assurances, ultimate effect of the second law of thermodynamics is real. It guarantees that entire universe will gradually, but assuredly, waste away in time—i.e., return to original state of thermodynamic equilibrium. The realm of absolute darkness or the primordial situation, as created by the Father, was an isolated system that represented a state of perfect order. The cosmic explosion, orchestrated by the fallen spirits, that triggered massive expansion of particles of matter, which we now call the expanding universe, temporarily disturbed that state of eternal order. All the things that make up the universe—galaxies, stars, planets, organic life, human inventions, and so on—evolve out of these floating debris of matter, that will eventually settle down again. Fallen spirits are only struggling in vain to create semblance of order within the universal mushroom, which cannot possibly be sustained forever. It is like someone struggling to maintain or repair his rickety old car indefinitely. The question is how long can he do that? The moment he stops trying or even while he continues to try, the car will eventually reach its final state of irreparability and must be scrapped.

Our observable universe can also be likened to the mushroom of an atomic bomb; and its fate, to that of atomic bomb radioactive fallout. All debris and dust displaced by the violent detonation and drawn into atomic bomb mushroom, obeying the greater law of Earth's gravity, eventually *fallback* to Earth surface. In the same way, universal debris and dust will ultimately succumb to the greater gravitational pull of the primordial arena. It may seem now that the universe will expand forever, but all the particles flung into the universal mushroom by the big bang at the beginning of time will surely return to primordial state of equilibrium to bring about the end of time.

Our chaotic universe rose from a serene, ordered arena, and it goes back to serene, ordered arena! The little stock of order imparted into the universal mushroom by remnants of divine light will eventually become fully expended. Of course, we are all conversant with some of the inviolable laws that govern the natural world. Whatever goes up must come down; whatever has a beginning must have an end, and anything that wears out bit-by-bit will eventually wear out completely. I am sure that most people have also heard about the heat death of the universe. Encarta Encyclopedia explains, "The entropy of an isolated system, and of the universe as a whole, can only increase, and when equilibrium is eventually reached, no more internal change of any form is possible. Applied to the universe as a whole, this principle suggests that eventually all temperature in space becomes uniform, resulting in the so-called heat death of the universe." ["Physics." Microsoft® Encarta® 2009 [DVD]. Redmond, WA: Microsoft Corporation, 2008.]

The nearest evidence of universal melt down to human beings is the imminent death of our own sun. As we all know, our sun is a second-generation star, meaning it was formed from heavier elements ejected from first-generation stars that lived and died before she was born. The sun itself is only a nuclear fusion reactor, burning its limited reserve of hydrogen fuel to give off the light and heat energies that create and sustain organic life on our planet Earth. It will eventually use up its fuel reserve and die, of which about 37 percent is already spent. Now, the older the sun gets, the hotter it will become—the more hydrogen is burned, the more helium, the by-product, accumulates in its core and the hotter the sun becomes. It is reckoned that in the next three billion years, the sun will be hot enough to boil off the oceans on Earth surface. The Earth as we now know it will cease to exist, and needless to stress that all living things on it, including human beings, would have long died off before that. The question then is, at which point in time is Jehovah/Allah's replacement *new* Jerusalem-on-Earth expected to spring into existent—before the death of all living things on Earth, before the death of the sun itself, or after the death of all the stars in the universe?

Death of the universe may take time by human reckoning, but it will surely happen. People should not be mixed up about this. All traces of imparted order will vanish from universal setting, but serene, ordered nature will continue to exist in eternal realm of darkness the way the Father made it. Apart from the forces of thermodynamic equilibrium working faithfully to return everything to eternal status quo, there are other physical and spiritual forces at play in the universe that are yet undiscovered by scientists and enlightened minds on Earth, which may even be working at faster pace to the same end. Since we know for sure that the universe is both finite and transient, should we really be wasting our time, doubting, or arguing whether it will last forever?

CHAPTER SEVEN: THE FATHER'S ETERNAL, *UNCREATED* MANIFESTATIONS AND THE HEAVENLY NORM

THE FATHER IS ETERNAL, INFINITE ORDERED EXISTENCE

I made fundamental assertions concerning the true nature of the Father in the first chapter. Although divine truths strike a chord in every man's subconscious, some people resist them vehemently because they firmly disconfirm their long-held *religious beliefs* about what the Father is. Further breaking down some of these truths, will however, enable us to gain clearer knowledge of the Father, and of his eternal, *uncreated* manifestations. The fact that the Father is not one specific dignitary enthroned on one gigantic cathedra in one remote corner of the cosmos was clearly stated. The Father is the whole of eternal, infinite, *ordered* Existence; meaning, he is boundless, infinite-dimensional, *uncreated*, perfect Manifestation that has no beginning or end. He is Ultimate Reality that comprises positive and negative aspects, representing the two extreme realms of perfect light and perfect darkness that are eternally demarcated. Nothing exists outside the Father, as nothing can exist outside infinity.

Sons of the Father can be likened to innumerable molecules that make up Great Ocean of waters. They are individualized emanations of Absolute Spirit, endowed with creative prerogatives and divine *freewill* to function as *creative energies* within the Father. They are eternal beings within the Ultimate One. In Psalms 82:6, Jehovah acknowledges the true status of our immortal spirits, saying, "You are gods, sons of the Most High, all of you." Innumerable creative expressions of the Father's limitless potentials through his *sons* ultimately form what we call worlds or universes at limitless levels of consciousness within the realm of light or realm of divine activities.

The Father is Creativity; every aspect of him is a creator. The Father is not *creator* of finite worlds; rather he is limitless resources and the infinite arena within which his sons create, in accordance with divine norm. Attempting to refer to the Father as *a* creator reduces him to a mere unit of himself. That is utterly disrespectful.

In this regard, we can liken the Father to great New York that comprises the natural resources, the grand arena and the people who build skyscrapers within it. New York is not a specific person; it does not build its skyscrapers, the people that make up New York do. Jesus Christ does make this clear in John 14:2-4 where he says, "There is more than enough room in my Father's home. ... *I am going to prepare a place for you* ... **When everything is ready**, I will come and get you, so that you will always be with me where I am." Jesus Christ promises to create a *new world* for his followers within the positive side of the Father, which is the designated realm of divine homes. The Father is not creating the new paradise for us, his Son, the heavenly Christ is. There is a great difference between the Father and New York however; the Father is Infinite Living Arena with Infinite Intelligence and Ultimate Mind, while New York is unconscious piece of space within imperfect nature.

The way we see our *invented* universe, as uninformed human beings, greatly hinders our knowledge of the Father. We take lightly the fact that the universe is called imperfect, and accept Jewish religious prejudices as documented in the Bible as absolute truths. The Jews introduced two false *Gods* to humankind; one is Jehovah, the other is the Bible. We must put the two in their proper places to be able to reach sound understanding of what the Father is. By posing as *God Almighty* to human beings on Earth, Jehovah reduced our scope of imagination of the Father's infinite nature to this mundane world, while the Bible paints picture of perfect, eternal, infinite Father as creator of an imperfect world that has a beginning and therefore an expected end. With knowledge of the truth freely delivered by Jesus Christ, we know now that the Father is far more encompassing than mundane nature, and that no entity in entire existence can narrate story of the Father's *eternal* creation, or rather, his eternal infinite manifestations as he has no beginning or end.

Mystery writers of the Bible misfired when they imagined that narrating the fabricated story of how Jehovah transformed desolate Earth's environment for human habitation in six days would fool ignorant human beings forever. We know better now. Our imperfect universe is a makeshift invention of *fallen* sons of the Father. Its beginning is known, and its end is certain. It is an *unrighteous* world because it exists outside the designated realm of divine homes. Universal arena and all the resources contained in it belong to the Father, quite all right, but universal craftsmanship is neither of him nor is it in accordance with Divine Ideal. The Father is originator of every element or substance in existence, but he is not creator or inventor of systems, especially imperfect and sub-divine systems such as our universe. The Father is everything that exists, but not everything that exists is of the Father. Although all substances on Earth are part of the Father for instance, he is not inventor of human machinery, electronic gadgets, and fancy products; motor cars, airplanes, computers, ornaments of gold and so on, that we use here on Earth. As 1 John 2:16 says, "All that is in the world, the lust of the flesh and the lust of the eyes and the pride of life, **is not of the Father** but is of the world."

That, not withstanding, aestheticians, poets, psalmists, religious eulogists and *holy men* of all creeds and classes still see the universe as wonderful masterpiece, possible only by the very fingers of the Father. Renowned philosophers of old, most of whom were also theologians, generally adored material nature and identified the universe with the Father, the being with supreme intelligence. Even our scientists; they too see the beauty and godliness of corporeal nature in the intricacies of their mathematical methods that seem to meticulously piece together the hidden jigsaws of divine laws of the universal contraption. "A lot of [Nobel] prices have been awarded for showing that the universe is not as simple as we might have thought," wrote Stephen Hawking in his book, *A Brief History of Time*. Therefore, just because the universe has seemed very complicated by human standards, many religious-minded scientists concluded that it must have been the work of an all-knowing, all-seeing, all-mighty and all-perfect Creator. But so also will some primitive bush people think of the wonderfully made Abraham Lincoln Aircraft Carrier, for instance, as the Father's own creation. Yet, all that we see in the universe are but components of the flying rubbles of matter that we had stirred up within the perfect primordial arena as fallen sons of the Father.

THE UNIVERSE IS VANITY FOREVER

No normal human being disputes the fact that the natural world is complicated, and even wonderful. Neither does any normal human being dispute the fact that it is an imperfect creation. The problem then centers on how to reconcile an imperfect creation with the perfect Father. That is practically impossible to do. Thus, although positive atheists do not deny apparent wonders in mundane nature, they rightly deny existence of the Father in the universe. They cannot sincerely reconcile obvious flaws in the natural world with the flawless nature of the Father. And they are not afraid to be true to their conscience.

That is the crux of the matter. While one might mistakenly credit the creation of a *perfect* finite world to the Father, attributing this *imperfect* universe to him simply does not agree with common sense. What the true atheists are saying is not necessarily that the Father does not exist, but that he does not *exist* here in the universe; or rather, that the universe does not exist in its proper place in the Father. They find it extremely illogical that the all-loving Father can be present in a universe that is dominated by evil. For, as the Scripture says, "The whole world is in the power of the evil one." [1 John 5:19]

Positive atheists are very honest people that are maliciously libeled by popular opinion for refusing to share the romanticized view of the universe. Theologians, philosophers, as well as big-time scientists; all grapple with the same inner conflict as do the positive atheists and every one of us, regarding *the problem of evil*—the question of how to reconcile existence of evil in the world with the Father who is omnipotent, omniscient, and omnibenevolent. They also reach the right conclusions in their good conscience as do the positive atheists but choose to *believe* as religious believers do; obviously, because believing is easier, and believers are in the majority.

For a moment, believers in the aptness of the natural world forget that the human mind is also an integral part of the so-called wonderful creation and yet it is so defective, as a tool, to fathom both self and its environment. Thus, we all live with indelible stigma of universal imperfection. An all-knowing, all-seeing, all-mighty and all-perfect Father will fashion offspring that mirror his eternal qualities. Human nature is a disgrace to godliness by nature and by design. Human activities manifest imperfection. There cannot be a place for such imperfect idea in the perfect mind of the Father. An all-knowing Father will not emanate self-ignorant beings that contradict his eternal nature. If, as religious believers think, human beings are indeed formed in the *image and likeness* of an all-knowing Father, then ignorance will not have a place in our general disposition. And believing that an entire *perfect* universe suddenly became ruined beyond redemption because Adam and Eve *sinned* on Earth, is like saying that Adam and Eve recreated the Father. Such a belief is sheer sacrilege. In any case, Adam and Eve did not sin against the Father; they were rather blessed legatees of the redeeming goodness of the Father in the world.

The Bible states with strong emphasis in the book of Ecclesiastes that the universe is **"vanity upon vanity,"** and none of us seems to disagree with that truth. New Life Translation of the Bible puts it this way: "Everything [in the universe] is meaningless … **completely meaningless!"** The question is, how can any honest-minded person credit such a creation to the perfect Father? The Quran, on its part, says in *Al-Imran*, 3:185 that **"the life of this world is but comfort of illusion."** This is another way of saying that our present existence is manifest unreality. In other words, everything that defines human life in the world—our birth, growth, thought patterns, educational pursuits, religious beliefs, and conventional ideas of the Father; our deeds, hallmark of accomplishments, passions, joys, sufferings, sorrows, and death—are all illusion. How can any right-thinking person fail to conclude that the universe is the work of some overambitious illusionists? Or who on Earth truly imagines the Father as author of meaninglessness and illusion?

In his summation, one Elder Efubom Effiong Ukpong Aye of Calabar, at 92, said that "whoever made the universe and whoever invented the life of this world is only making an experiment." He talked from long years of personal experiences, and he "chose to believe in Jesus Christ" as the way out of what has clearly become a failed experiment. At 65, I also, have seen my share of the meaninglessness of universal existence, and I say that now is the time for human beings to come to terms with the hard realities about the Father and our true selves to escape the futility of sheer *unrighteous* existence. What is important now is how the rest of human beings see the world. Universal experiment is not just meaningless; it is also hopeless. It is "like chasing the wind," says the Bible, "What is wrong cannot be righted. What is missing cannot be recovered." [Eccl 1:14-15] What this means is that we must look beyond the meaningless universe—beyond its bungling, petty-minded deities—for the Father, his true eternal creation, and for heavenly life of perfection.

The cosmic ruling authorities, principalities, gods, rulers, and leaders of the world—both spiritual and temporal—are merely in business trying to transform primordial emptiness into a place of perfect comfort and happiness. Self-deluded cosmic alchemists create the master illusion; religious leaders preach hope in possibility of such an outcome, while political leaders of the world make a mockery of providing social salvation to its godless inmates. It will never work. From time to time, some deluded politicians and so-called *holy men* arise, believing that they have the Father's divine mandate to end human sufferings on Earth. But looking back to the history of such *heavenly mandates* one sees that they had all been false hopes.

Jesus Christ promises to relocate our redeemed spirits to a *righteous* world that he is preparing for us in the Father's designated realm of heavenly homes. **The universe is vanity forever!** Transforming arid deserts in the Middle East into flowering gardens *underneath which rivers flow* is misleading. Pretending to transform garbage-ridden towns and cities, like Lagos in Nigeria, into mega-cities without first reducing the poverty level of the inhabitants of such cities is a full-time exercise in futility—a *chasing after wind*! Cities that were more grandiose had been built in the past where, today, we have nothing but waste mounds and archeological sites.

The truth about the universe is simple and clear! "*What is wrong cannot be made right. What is missing cannot be recovered.*" This is despite religious gospel of hope in a perfect future to be generated by some colonizing infidel posing as *God Almighty* to less informed fellow inmates of the meaningless world. Believing that the universe can be made perfect by anyone is utter ignorance. The Father will not do that because it will mean upholding the present disorder within his eternal manifestation. Jesus Christ has not come to perfect the universe, but rather to abolish it, and to restore perfection to eternal realm of absolute darkness. Therefore, expecting or hoping that human life will become blissful in a distant *New* Jerusalem is religious hallucination, and investing in human government for that purpose is futility and more spiritual bondage. In the words of the Quran, since "The life of this world is but comfort of illusion ... a pastime and a sport," those who settle for that are clearly "beguiled by false hope." [Quran 3:185; 6:32; 15:3]

Now that we have known the true origin, authorship, and fate of our transient world of vanity; now that it has become obvious to many of us that the universe, in all its quasi magnificence and wonders, is not the creation of the Father, what then is the true, eternal creation of the Father? What is the heavenly norm of the Father's true Creation? Can the human mind possibly comprehend the Father and his actual creation? How are we a part of the Father and of his true creation? And where can his heavenly kingdom be found, or rather, experienced?

WHAT ARE THE *ETERNAL* MANIFESTATIONS OF THE FATHER?

A. UNKNOWABLE BEGINNING

Let me start by stating clearly once more that the Father is eternal and infinite, and so are his actual creations or manifestations. As a child cannot describe where and how his parent was born, no entity in existence, no son of the Father can narrate story of how he evolved—what and how he created or the sequence of his creations. All that we can know and describe about the Father and his eternal manifestations is the status quo because we are all members of his household. For example, a man's offspring will never be able to narrate in sequence how their father built the family house in which they were born and brought up, but they can describe the general layout. What I am describing here therefore, is the eternal layout of the Father, which we all ought to know deep in our souls, as sons of the Father.

Jesus Christ says in Matt 5:45 that the Father "makes his sun rise on the evil and on the good and sends rain on the just and on the unjust." Religious believers quickly cite that as a proof that the Father is the creator and operator of the universe. But Jesus Christ only made that statement to help us appreciate greatness of the Father's love for us, even in our present status as little *denigrators* of the Father's impeccable nature. The full meaning of his words is made obvious when we read in full verses 43-45, which says, "You have heard that it was said [by Jehovah], 'You shall love your neighbor and hate your enemy.' But I say to you, **Love your enemies and pray for those who persecute you, so that you may be sons of *your Father who is in heaven*;** for he makes his sun rise on the evil and on the good, and sends rain on the just and on the unjust."

Jesus Christ is saying that our Father *who is in heaven* is infinite nature that sustains entire existence; and that he loves both his good sons and the fallen ones equally. Artificial light of the sun and all other luminaries in the universe belong to him, and they shine on the just and unjust only because he allows them to. We can all imagine what the situation will be if a character like Jehovah/Allah has absolute control over the sun and the rain. He will surely, use them as weapons of control on his enemies, as well as on his friends.

Besides, Jesus Christ also says in John 14:2-3 "In my Father's house are many rooms." In very plain words, he is telling us in this place that *the Father's house* is not here in the universe, and the universe is not in the Father's house, even though all resources in existence belong to him. Neither the Father nor the Son, Jesus Christ, dwells here in the universe. These are clearer proofs that the Father did not create the universe. The Father's house is the *Heaven*, which is the infinite arena divinely designated by him for innumerable perfect worlds to be created by his perfect sons. *Heavens* of this world, which merely refer to random clusters of flying rubbles of matter in space are counterfeit. Although the universe seems to have more than enough room for its wayward inhabitants, it is an *unrighteous* world because it is created by heavenly dropouts outside the Father's heavenly house. The Father sent his perfect Son, Jesus Christ, to *redeem* us from our ill-fated experimental world. But he first goes to create a perfect world for us within *the Father's house*. Then he will come back to *relocate* redeemed spirits there; and our false universe will finally roll away like the scroll of a very bad dream.

Deuteronomy 22:5, 10 and 11 record three remarkable ordinances that Jehovah gave to his Jewish religious slaves. They read, "A woman must not put on men's clothing, and a man must not wear women's clothing. **Anyone who does this is detestable in the sight of Jehovah your *God*.** ... You must not plow with an ox and a donkey harnessed together. ... You must not wear clothing made of wool and linen woven together."

In the context of the Jewish situation, the wordings of these decrees do not really mean much, but they, at least, do paint the picture of a lawgiver who has the idea that it is godly to put meticulous demarcation between incompatible features. The irony of it all, however, is that Jehovah/Allah, *the one who kills and makes alive and arbitrarily metes out both blessing and disaster on whoever he wishes*, is not bound by the same standards in his own dealings. He is a *lawless* lawgiver who reserves a separate, open-ended standard of goodness for himself and another for his bondmen. His reason is always that he is almighty and therefore, accountable to no one. "For who is like me, and who can challenge me? What ruler can oppose my will?" he asks. ... "For Who is he that can stand before me? Who has given to me, that I should repay him? Whatever is under the whole heaven is mine." [Jer 50:44; Job 41:10-11] With such an attitude, it can be clearly seen that Jehovah/Allah is not like Jesus Christ who enjoins his followers to love one another just as he loves them—just as the Father loves everyone.

When we relate the three ordinances to Jehovah's original injunction in the Genesis, forbidding all human beings on Earth from ever acquiring or even desiring to acquire the ability to differentiate between what is good and what is evil, we appreciate the height of the hypocrisy in his Deuteronomic ordinances to the Jews. He knew that it was godly to differentiate what is good from what is evil; yet he vehemently prevented his Edenic human slaves from having that knowledge. Yet again, he saw nothing contradictory in basing his later ordinances upon people's ability to make that distinction.

Evidently, Jehovah/Allah never wanted humans on Earth to know what the Father is like, lest we should have the opportunity to discover that he is indeed an impostor. Amazingly, the being he dismissed as serpent and devil in the biblical account helped humankind to understand that **having the ability to differentiate good from evil is a prerequisite for becoming like** the Father. Of course, some of us know now that the so-called serpent in Eden was none other than the heavenly Christ, who inspired in mankind the very rudiments of spiritual enlightenment. He exposed Jehovah/Allah as a liar then and proved that he had dubious intentions. "Jehovah knows that **your eyes will be opened** as soon as you eat it," he assured the Edenic inmates, "**and you will be like** the Father, **knowing both good and evil.**" [Gen 3:5]

Adam and Eve believed him on behalf of entire humankind and today, we all know better. Today, we all know that the Father is perfect; not because he does not know evil, but because he puts eternal demarcation between good and bad in his overall manifestations. More especially, we also know now that the Father wants us to be like him, in being able to separate out all ungodly accretion upon our true spiritual personalities. Jesus Christ confirms that in Matthew 5:48, where he says to us, "You, therefore, must be perfect, as your heavenly Father is perfect." The emphasis here is that the Father is perfect. Therefore, we are to expect his eternal creation to be perfect too.

When the born-again customary Christians recite 2 Cor. 6:14—"Do not be mismated with unbelievers. For what partnership has righteousness and iniquity? Or **what fellowship has light with darkness**"—it is usually to intimidate or to prove that they are godlier than their opponents or rival sects. Beyond that sarcastic display of sectarian superiority complex, nothing shows that so-called born-again Christians understand the full implications of what the verse entails. That light and darkness has no fellowship does not apply to any person or situation in our universe whose lifeline is mutual co-existence of *light and darkness*. The universe represents an imperfect blend of *righteousness and iniquity*. No one can possibly separate the two here. Here in the universe, the believer cannot help being *mismated* with the unbeliever; righteousness always has partnership with iniquity, and light cannot do without darkness. What then is the message in the text that these people do not yet understand? Well, that light and darkness do not co-exist strictly describes the Father, his spiritual creation, and its eternal norm. Light and darkness are eternally separated in the Father.

On the contrary, good and evil are not separated in Jehovah/Allah's overall character. He is both god and devil in his illusory Earthly empire. Throughout the scriptures that he largely inspired, he never tried to pretend to be all-good, all-loving, or all-forgiving. His laws and ordinances to his various religious sects ratify his overall character and convincingly prove that he is a very unprincipled character. In fact, he proudly says that he controls the dreadful *treasures of darkness,* and that no evil befalls anyone on Earth unless he has done it. As the self-acclaimed *alpha and omega* of man's world, as well as the heartbeat of *yin and yang* or good and evil, his best possible character can only be good and evil mangled together. He says so plainly in various verses of the Bible, but his blinded religious devotees simply do not get it— "I kill and I make alive; I wound and I heal ... I form light and create darkness, I bring prosperity and create disaster; I Jehovah, do all these things." These are some dramatic ways of saying, "I Jehovah, 'am imperfect." He blows hot and blows cold, and that is simply not in the character of perfection.

B. ABSOLUTE DIVIDE BETWEEN LIGHT AND DARKNESS

In 1 John 1:5 (NLT), Apostle John reported the *new* insight the apostles gained from the heavenly Messiah, regarding the true nature of the Father — "This is the message we heard from Jesus and now declare to you: The Father **is light, and there is no darkness in him at all.**" There was need for Jesus Christ to divulge that special information to his apostles. In the days of the apostles, it was generally believed that the Father could turn himself into a *pillar of darkness* and or a *pillar of fire* as circumstances demanded. Before the second coming of the heavenly Christ in human form, Jehovah had deceived the whole world into believing that he is the Father and that the Father can choose to dwell in thick darkness, in fire, or in some other mundane phenomena of the natural world. The Jews witnessed the gimmicks firsthand during their ill-fated Exodus from Egypt. Exodus 13:21 says, "And Jehovah went before them by day in a *pillar of cloud* [darkness] to lead them along the way, and by night in a *pillar of fire* to give them light, that they might travel by day and by night." Apostle John relayed that vital information both to give us a hint on the true nature of the Father's creation, and to help us understand with certainty that Jehovah who can be enveloped in thick darkness is indeed an impostor.

James 1:13, 16-17 equally highlight distinctive nature of the Father that we should expect to reflect in his eternal creation or manifestations: "Let no one say when he is tempted, 'I am tempted by the Father; for the Father **cannot be tempted with evil** and he himself tempts no one … Every good endowment and every perfect gift are from above, coming down from the Father of lights with whom there is **no variation or shadow due to change**." The Father is all-goodness; evilness does not exist in him or in his eternal creation. With the vital information above, we also know now with certainty that Jehovah, the tempter, who incited Abraham to murder his innocent son, Isaac, is not the Father.

By extension, we equally know with certainty that the cryptic tempter who tried to entice Jesus Christ with the rulership of the godless world at the beginning of his Earthly ministry was none other than Jehovah, the god-com-devil of man's world. The very words of the tempter in Luke 4:5-7 were unmistakable. They capture Jehovah's chronic obsession with worldly dominion and worship. The text reports that he showed Jesus Christ the pseudo glory of Earthly kingdoms, or rather principalities, and then said to him, "To you I will give all these authorities and their glory; for it has been delivered to me [evidently, by the cosmic council of world rulers], and I give it to whom I will. If you, then, will **worship me**, it shall be yours."

Furthermore, we know now that the Father does not *kill and make alive*, he does not *mete out both blessing and disaster* on whomever he wills, and most certainly, he does not love only his friends while *visiting the iniquity of the fathers upon the children to the third and the fourth generation of those who hate him*.

The Father is Sovereign Perfectionist. Perfection means completeness in a flawless way. Although the Father is the totality of existence, his eternal potentials are explicitly ordered and demarcated so that his positive side does not contradict his negative side, and vice versa. Light and darkness are two principal eternal manifestations of the Father, representing the positive and negative aspects of him, but they do not co-exist in him. They are eternally separated from each other, manifesting separately as the two extreme realms of perfect light and perfect darkness. The realm of light represents sphere of absolute purity—of life and divine activities, while the realm of darkness stands at the other extreme as sphere of divine inactivity—a sort of divine quarantine for all the negative aspects of the Father. That is the basis of perfection of the Father's eternal creation, as well as the basis of his eternal character. Hence, we can rightly say that there are things the Father can do and things he cannot do. That is why we can say that the Father is light, not darkness; that he is good and not evil, even though darkness and evilness are all parts of the overall reality represented by the Father. That is also, why we can know for sure that the Father did not create our undifferentiated universe.

The Father is not a very pure and holy person, but the living essence called purity and holiness. Now, that cannot be possible if he had not quarantined all impurities and obscenities from the realm of his divine activities. To establish absolute light, life, purity, goodness, and all other unsullied qualities that make up his positive manifestation, he had to quarantine direct opposites of those divine qualities as his negative manifestation. Then he erected eternal demarcation between the two aspects of himself so that light remains absolute forever, and darkness remains absolute forever.

The Father's actual creation, therefore, is that miraculous feat of originating eternal order and decorum in himself that gives purpose and proper place to every facet of existence. The almightiness of the Father is firmly reflected in this divine feat, which no one else in existence can possibly replicate outside him. He is not almighty because he can do whatever he likes and can bully whoever he chooses to bully in the world. Perfect order and decorum can never exist in our imperfect universe and life here can never be harmonious and divine because it is located on the eternally negative side of the Father. Perfect life can only be experienced on the positive side of the Father where he designated as proper for it. No type of Jerusalem, promised by Jehovah/Allah, the impostor, can override the need for our fallen spirits to return to the *proper* sphere of eternal life in the Father if we genuinely desire perfect existence.

Thus, the human mind can indeed, comprehend the mystery of the true nature of the Father and of his actual spiritual creation. To be like the Father means to have every trace of darkness or spiritual impurity edited out of one's overall character. But since anyone that becomes like the Father cannot possibly exist in our undifferentiated world of darkness and light, every truly perfected spirit will ultimately transit to his heavenly domain where pure and perfect existence is possible. The heavenly Christ could not remain in the world longer than the little time necessary for him to personally deliver the Father's divine will to us. After all, who would like to spend a single minute extra in hell when he can easily return to the realm of perfect existence? He explained the details to us this way: "I came from the Father and have come into the world; again, I am leaving the world and going to the Father … For this reason, the Father loves me, because **I lay down my life, that I may take it again** [at completion of my mission in the realm of death.]" [John 16:28; 10:17]

For him to come into our world of dead spirits, the heavenly Christ literally died temporarily to his true nature for our sakes. His willingness to step out of the realm of true life and into the realm of spiritual death was the supreme sacrifice he made on our behalf. That was the actual *death* of Jesus Christ that saves our fallen spirits. Nailing him on the cross in Jerusalem, by Jehovah/Allah's connivance was a gruesome murder and an unjustifiable crime on our parts by every reasonable standard. Contrary to the barbaric doctrine of sacrificial Lamb, the Father did not send his Son into the world to be molested and killed by us. He sent him to redeem and resurrect our fallen, dead spirits. Thus, echoes John 3:16-17, which reads, "For the Father so loved the world that he gave his only Son, that whoever believes in him **should not perish but have eternal life**. For the Father sent the Son into the world, not to condemn the world, but **that the world might be saved through him**." Nothing in the express will of the Father implies that he sent his Son into the world for us to kill him. That we killed our own Redeemer was a proof that we are utterly evil in our present nature.

As we can see from my schematic impression of the Father's eternal spiritual creation, there are two extremes of eternal realities in the Father, delineated by Divine Rubicon. The realm of *absolute* light defines his unsullied eternal qualities—these include pure light, life, love, and spirituality. On the flipside of the Father is the realm of *absolute* darkness and it is eternally characterized by darkness, lifelessness, lovelessness, and materialism. Hence, when we say that *the Father is light, and there is no darkness in him at all*, we simply mean that there is no darkness in the positive side of the Father whatsoever. Furthermore, when we say that the Father is spirit, love, life, holiness, flawlessness, and so on, we are merely enumerating unsullied eternal qualities that define the Father's overall nature. It should be easier now for many of us to begin to understand *what* the Father is and *who* he is not.

C. THE FATHER IS SOVEREIGN PERFECTIONIST

When we think of the Father as perfection, we refer to the overall perfect state of his entire creation that embodies the two extreme realms of *perfect light* and *perfect darkness*. What that means is that in the true creation of the Father, perfect light is eternally separated from perfect darkness. However, when we talk of the realm of eternal life, we refer to the entire sphere of his positive influence, which he designated as proper for life and divine activities. He did not designate the realm of darkness to support life, as darkness naturally means absence of divine light and therefore, of divine activities.

The positive side of the Father is the heavenly Kingdom that we subconsciously yearn to return to, for we are all heavenly dropouts. Every living being in the world is a fallen spirit. And contrary to Jehovah's spurious claims in the Genesis, it is not his breathe that makes man a living being. He may have cloned *Homo* sapiens on Earth from already existing ape men, but he certainly did not create the human spirits that animate the human mortal bodies. Also, he did not create universal substances, or the planetary arena called the world. Our present makeshift universe is a rebellious contraption within the flipside of the Father, being the joint crash-landing exertion of all the fallen specks from the realm of light. Jehovah/Allah is merely an opportunistic colonialist, manipulating his slightly higher level of knowledge to dominate the less informed humans on planet Earth.

Now, we can refer to the realms of light and darkness as superstructures of the Father's eternal manifestations. Surely, human minds are familiar with light and darkness and can at least, imagine infinite expanses of absolute light and or absolute darkness. Finer eternal manifestations of the Father are contained within the two realms; especially within the realm of light that he designated for divine activities. Infinite resources in entire existence are also eternal manifestations of the Father. Eternal resources contained within infinite realm of perfect darkness sustain even our false existence. We call them natural resources; and as we can see, every aspect of our false lives depends on them. If the realm of darkness were not teaming with valuable material substances, and if primordial nature were not eternally imbued with potential energies, the great outburst of the fallen specks at the *big bang* would have yielded nothing.

The most important manifestations of the Father are his innumerable sons—individualized emanations or radiations of creative energies from himself that populate and activate the realm of light. Heaven teems with these perfect creative energies.

To help people understand this better, I would like to return to my analogy of the Father as the great New York. Imagine the vast expanse of space with tremendous natural resources called New York but without the individual New Yorkers that beautify and build skyscrapers in it. Without the relentless and innovative activities of the numerous New Yorkers, New York, as a creative arena, will lie dormant and will most definitely be unknown. The same is true about the Father. Even with infinite resources in entire existence, the Father will be dormant and unknown without divine activities within him. But we already know that the Father is light, and light is life and life is activities. Therefore, he radiated innumerable individualized specks of light or life to create divine activities within the realm of light. We can rightly say that the Father is known in heaven by glorious activities of his innumerable sons; and he is unknown in the world of darkness because the place is devoid of his radiated light energies. Corrupted activities of fallen dead sons of the Father in the universe denigrate the Father because they are borne out of rebellious abandonment of the heavenly norm.

Finally, the universe is not a creation of the Father but a temporary disorder within his eternal spiritual creation. It is a finite upset within infinite and eternal realm of perfect darkness—a tiny eruption of jumbled existence that will resolve itself with time. Most of us seek spiritual redemption from the world but without understanding the technicalities of it. We seek redemption because subconsciously we know that our present existence is corrupted and that our world is unrighteous. Jesus Christ tells us in plain words that our world is not anywhere within the proper domain of the Father's positive influence. He makes clear the fact that the positive side of the Father is spacious enough for every living son of the Father in existence; and that the Father did not have any reason to disrupt perfect state of eternal order in the realm of darkness only to create the imperfect universe for some imperfect beings.

Let me make it clear here too that the Devil is not a *creation* of the Father as some people postulate. The concept of the Devil as a "person" that is directly opposed to the Father is equally a blatant fallacy. Such a notion has no place in the Father's *ordered* spiritual creation whatsoever. Devil is not a person but a measure of level of spiritual degeneration characterizing fallen sons of the Father in the world. Even among human beings are found various categories of devils. The Father is the only Being in entire existence. All perfect ideas, essences or substances that make up the positive and negative aspects of realities are emanations of the Father. But heavenly sons of the Father who abused their divine freewill and violated the heavenly norm of perfection were spewed into the realm of nonbeing. They eventually degenerated into devils due to avoidable retributions and utter frustration.

We can understand the Father's creation as eternal process of *self-configuration*. The Father simply organized or ordered his potentials the way he deemed perfect, convenient, and proper. He erected eternal frontier between his ethereal, living essence and the corporeal bodies—between the spiritual and the physical, between light and darkness. This is a bit like a person who decided to partition his own apartment, locking away in one section all his undesirables while living in the other section with all his desirables. There is no other person in the entire apartment but him. Although he resides only in one section of the apartment, he alone holds the key to the other section too. No other person or enemy of his resides in the sealed-off section. In the same way, the Father is the only living being in entire existence. Everything else, including every one of us, emanated from him. While the realm of light represents his positive abode, no Devil or direct Opposer of his divine will dwells in the realm of his negative influence. Besides, the realm of absolute darkness is lifeless; any such Devil will be a dead one and therefore, nonexistent.

In the context of our transient Earthly existence however, the Antichrist as a person is a reality. He is the corrupted heavenly dropout, whom, being blinded by his inordinate desire to dominate and play god over his less informed brethren, tries to contradict the gracious mission of the heavenly Christ in the world. But he is just a shadow boxer. He knows very well that no one exists that can oppose the will of the Father, whether in the realm of light or in the realm of darkness, for the Father owns and holds the keys to the two sections of his one great home.

The Antichrist is a person having exact image and likeness of human beings. He is the celebrated superman-god of the Genesis creation fable. Majority of us know him only by his notorious appearances, deeds, and utterances as documented in human history here on Earth, while few of us know him intimately and in person. He is the superman mortal, cryptically referred to in Isaiah 14:12 as a *"fallen day star"* with unattainable dreams; and in Ezekiel 28:12 as being formally a *"signet of perfection, full of wisdom and perfect in beauty."* Lamentation over his blinded ambition goes like this: "How are you fallen down from heaven, O Day Star, son of Dawn! How are you cut down to the ground, you who laid the nations low! You said in your heart, 'I will ascend to heaven; above the stars of the Father, I will set my throne on high; I will sit on the mount of assembly in the far north; I will ascend above the heights of the clouds, **I will make myself like the Most High.**'" [Isaiah 14:12-14]

Jehovah/Allah's dream of becoming *God Almighty* over ignorant human beings on Earth is not a hidden one. It has been his terminal obsession and his myth too. It came to abrupt flop in the first Eden with the very first, glorious advent of the heavenly Christ into the world. Since then, he wallows in desperation, still hoping to succeed, even though his ultimate end is already known. Jehovah/Allah is only the spur of a vanishing dream. The Bible already declares of him, "But you are brought down to Sheol, to the depths of the Pit. Those who see you will stare at you, and ponder over you: 'Is this *the man* who made the Earth tremble, who shook kingdoms, who made the world like a desert and overthrew its cities, **who did not let his prisoners go home**?'" [Isaiah 14:15-17]

Jehovah/Allah is the Antichrist. He is the mighty man of war who has successfully arrogated to himself the undisputed title of *god, king,* and *lord* over ignorant humankind on Earth. Yet, he remains full of grief, wrath, and frustration for not being able to forestall humankind's steady spiritual advancement toward the Father who is the true eternal life. Strangely, people who believe that Jehovah/Allah is *God Almighty* never wonder why he is also living with so much frustration, jealous rage, wrath, and unfulfilled dreams. Jehovah/Allah is a peculiar character indeed. He is well known for dreaming impossible dreams. Once, he dreamed of turning the parched lands of old Eden into a Garden of Paradise here on Earth. When that failed, he nursed the idea of making Jerusalem a Promised Land of Rest— *a land flowing with milk and honey*—for a handful of his unconscious Jewish devotees. That dream fizzled out too, and Jerusalem, as we all can agree today, remains *a land that devours its inhabitants*, with the *intifada* and other regional crises in the area showing no sign of ever abating.

Jehovah/Allah's newest dream is the hope of calling down from the heavens a *New* Jerusalem that will be made of pure gold, where there will be no more night; and where, according to Zech 14:9, he hopes to finally become king over the whole Earth. It reads, "And Jehovah will become king over all the Earth; on that day Jehovah will be one and his name one." What a great dream that is; but a mere dream all the same! A New Jerusalem within the realm of darkness that will not have night and day is one that should hope to have very efficient, incorruptible electricity corporation. I must say that only the less informed will think of such an unstable character as a direct *Opposer* of the Father.

ETERNAL NORM OF THE FATHER'S SPIRITUAL CREATION

The realm of Divine Light, as the realm of eternal life, is the proper abode of sons of Light. It is the designated arena for all creative activities of sons of the Father, where perfect worlds or universes are meant to be created. All creative activities within this realm are perfect because they are wrought in Light and therefore, in accordance with perfect heavenly standards.

Absence of Divine Light in the realm of darkness, on the other hand, means that it is not designated for eternal life or for creative activities of divine specks. Any divine speck that ventures into the realm of darkness will die to his true nature. He will become extinguished because he will be completely disconnected from his Divine Source. All his creative efforts will naturally yield imperfection. It is imperative therefore, that sons of the Father eternally function or curtail their divine activities within their *proper* bounds in the Kingdom, in order not to destabilize eternal status quo.

Usually, when people build houses, they set doors and windows at appropriate locations to serve the rooms, hallways, and various other compartments within the structures. People go in and out of the houses and rooms through doors and not through the windows even though there are no laws or formal directives to that effect. Evidently, besides the natural design intentions of house designers, doors do appear more convenient as thoroughfares than do windows. We can say that it is normal or proper to walk into peoples' houses through the doors and abnormal or improper to get in through the windows. That standard pattern of generally acceptable behavior in the society is called a *norm*, and it is binding on everyone who goes in or out of the houses or rooms, including the designers, house owners, their household, and their visitors.

A norm is a natural imperative. Going against it is not only considered disorderly, but it usually also carries inevitable consequences. A person seen climbing into someone's house through the window is naturally termed a thief. People can easily attack, wound, or even kill such a person as a result.

In the same way, people sometimes erect surrounding walls around their homes and set access gates into the properties. Again, people naturally go in and out of the walled homes through the gates and not over the walls. That standard behavior is also a norm, binding on both the owners and strangers who go in and out of the compounds. Anyone seen climbing into someone's compound through the walls is naturally treated as an intruder, and he stands to suffer grave consequences.

Again, every ordered state or municipality usually has specific areas designated for specific projects or activities, such as residential, industrial, and or recreational. Sometimes these are entirely determined by natural topography of the environments involved, in which case it becomes a norm for people to live by nature's unwritten directives. Generally, it is a norm that inhabitants of cities do not build their houses on established roads or try to drive their cars on waterways. People who go against such norms will suffer both natural and legal consequences.

We can draw another analogy from the story of the man who decided to partition his own apartment locking away in one section all his undesirables while living in the other section with all his desirables. If for instance, the man lives in the secure section with his household and every member knows that the insecure section has been segregated because it is heavily saturated with deadly gases from poisonous chemicals stored there, making sure that the place remains permanently locked up becomes a norm to the entire family members. Any member who violates the unwritten rule knows that he will personally pay the grave price. Evidently, there will not be a special outcome for the head of the family and a different one for other family members who violate the norm. A norm is no respecter of persons. What the toxic gases will do to the least important person in the family, it will also do to the head of the family if he violates the norm.

Now, purely for the purpose of this explanation, the Father's entire spiritual creation can be likened to the ship floating upon a deep dark ocean. Aboard the ship represents the positive aspect of reality and the domain of the Father and his living emanations, where life and divine activities exist and thrive. The deep dark sea below represents the negative aspect of reality—a no-go place—where no one can have life and no divine activity will prosper. For the Father and his heavenly crew to permanently sustain the perfect status quo and enjoy blissful existence on board eternally, there must be some guiding principles based on ethical responsibilities. There must be a *norm*, which is not like a *law* made by some lawless master for his slaves that is not binding on him too. The norm is rather a *principle* of right or proper action binding on every member of the heavenly yacht that defines the model lifestyle onboard. The unwritten norm stipulates that all normal creative activities should only be carried out on board. No member of the heavenly yacht should stray into the region of the deadly deep dark sea, as it would not support life or any normal creative activity. The same norm applies to the Father as well as to his living emanations within the heavenly yacht. He does not have a separate mode of righteousness for himself and another for his crew. This is what makes the Father the supreme model of justice and equity.

Evidently, justice and equity do not apply to our world; they cannot exist outside perfection. They do not apply to the cosmic oligarchy that rules our godless world. They do not apply to Jehovah/Allah, their principal agent on Earth, who notoriously operates above his own laws. He is the principal character for whom the adage was coined that says, *"follow my words and not my actions."* As one would expect, all Jehovah/Allah's votaries, both secular leaders and *holy men* of all religious creeds on Earth live by his personal example. Jesus Christ was referring to both Jehovah and his religious operatives when he advised his followers, saying, "The teachers of religious law and the Pharisees are the official interpreters of the law of Moses. So, practice and obey whatever [good deed] they tell you, but don't follow their example. For they don't practice what they teach." [Matt 23:2-3 (NLT)]

Furthermore, the Father loves every member of the heavenly yacht equally. He does not have a *chosen race*, or a Gentile race—a very thoughtless bias that is bound to rock any boat. Jesus Christ preached and lived the Father on Earth. He told us about the justice and equity in the Father's love, and he proved that to us by personal examples. He made us understand that he was himself living the Father's personal examples as he observed in his heavenly place. "I tell you the truth, the Son can do nothing by himself. He does only what he sees the Father doing. Whatever the Father does, the Son also does," he says in John 5:19. And because Jesus Christ lived what he preached, just as the Father does, he felt morally justified to say to his own disciples, "love one another; even as I have loved you. ... By this all men will know that you are my disciples, if you have love for one another." [John 13:34-35]

In view of the state of perfect equity and justice on the heavenly yacht, it is obvious that the norm had been established for the collective good of all members of the Father's household. Any behavior or action that deviates from the established norm will adversely affect the entire family members and undermine the general state of perfect equilibrium, both aboard and overboard, and between the heavenly yacht and the deep dark sea. To preclude that possibility, any such improper action will need to be restricted and checkmated automatically and the consequences borne directly by the negligent individual or individuals to avoid jeopardizing entire family members and upsetting eternal status quo.

For a start, any individual who fails to adhere to the established norm cannot continue in the family. He will be automatically spewed from the heavenly yacht to avoid contamination and desecration. A defaulter spewed out of the heavenly yacht plunges directly into the deep dark ocean. And since life is not possible in that realm of negative reality, the defaulter dies a natural death. In order that every member of the heavenly yacht understands the eternal consequences of improper conduct, the norm clearly stipulates that "any member that falls short of the norm will die." And in the spirit of perfect justice and equity, every member of the Father's household is fully endowed with *freewill* to deal with the situation, as a matter of eternal heritage. It is obvious here that neither the Father nor any other crew on board will kill the defaulter. His death will be purely because of *willful* negligence, resulting in him falling off from the region of life and into the asphyxiating deep dark ocean. But the defaulter does not just fall into the deep dark sea and expire once and for all; not at all, his struggles and agony continue forever.

We can now visualize the state of eternal death and see how it applies to our present universal situation. We are just like the heavenly defaulter who continues to struggle without end within the region of death trying to stabilize or save himself, or to invent a kind of false life for himself. For the heavenly defaulter, eternal death means dying continuously forever. The same is the situation with fallen human souls in the universal deep dark ocean. Indeed, anyone that attempts to destroy eternal state of order and decorum that sustains any aspect of spiritual status quo pays a grave price. We are all paying that price in the deadly universe. However, the Father, desiring none of us to languish in death forever, made divine arrangement for our redemption, of which Jesus Christ is the program officer.

The Bible captures the righteousness of the Father in Ezekiel 18:20, where Jehovah/Allah merely quoted the perfect heavenly norm, which he does not apply in his Earthly empire. "The soul that sins shall die. The son shall not suffer for the iniquity of the father, nor the father suffer for the iniquity of the son; the righteousness of the righteous shall be upon him, and the wickedness of the wicked shall be upon him." This is a description of the tenets of the divine norm of the Father's spiritual creation. As we all can see, the Father is as indebted to upholding the norm of perfection, as the least person in his heavenly domain, who is but a direct emanation of him. In fact, while some of his sons may be tempted to default on the strength of their personal freewill; the heavenly Christ was tempted by Satan in Jerusalem, for instance, but the Father just cannot fail, because he is infallibility himself. That is why the Bible says that "the Father cannot be tempted to do anything evil." [James 1:13]

As we all can agree too, the heavenly norm of perfection does not and cannot apply to our universe where *struggling*, selfish, opportunistic beings relentlessly lord it over the less privileged ones. In our world of darkness and imperfection, anything goes. There is always a separate standard of righteousness for the mighty and a separate one for the downtrodden. Jehovah/Allah, *who rules the kingdoms of men and sets self-centered rulers over them*, makes that explicit in his deeds and utterances on Earth. No doubt, he is the role model of worldly rulers in all cultures of our society. The wicked ones prosper in the world, and we see injustice and inequity in every facet of worldly governance. That should help reasoning minds to understand that the Father is not the author and ruler of our present situation. There is no practical justification for the popular religious opinion that credits heavily flawed universal craftsmanship to our flawless Father.

It is very easy to know the Father and to identify his true works. It is enough to bear in mind always that the Father is eternally flawless. No creation that has a flaw, even to a very negligible measure, is of him. 99.999% goodness is not perfection and therefore, cannot be attributed to the Father. Not minding how wonderful the universe seems to us as humans, since inherent flaws exist here, it is not the work of the Father. It is as simple as that. To that effect, Jesus Christ says to us, "Either make the tree good, and its fruit good; or make the tree bad, and its fruit bad; for the tree is known by its fruit. ... For figs are not gathered from thorns, nor are grapes picked from a bramble bush." [Matthew 12:33; Luke 6:44] The Father is perfect Grape Vine, while the universe is a bramble bush. The universe is an *unrighteous* invention because it is created in direct contravention of the heavenly norm that designates the realm of light as proper for all worlds or universes and the realm of darkness as eternally without divine activities.

CAN HUMAN MIND UNDERSTAND THE FATHER AND HIS PERFECT ETERNAL CREATION?

A. CAN THE HUMAN MIND DIFFERENTIATE BETWEEN GOOD AND EVIL?

Can the human mind understand the Father and his perfect eternal creation? We might as well ask, "Can the human mind possibly differentiate between what is good and what is evil?" The answer is a categorical yes! Thanks to Blessed Eve through whom the heavenly Christ activated functional minds in humans on Earth, thereby differentiating us permanently from senseless animals. Today, every human being on Earth knows what is good and what is evil, and that is the basis for understanding perfection. The human mind knows that our present situation is imperfect because it represents an unwarranted blend of good and evil. It knows that we will be in paradise if we can totally eradicate evil out of worldly existence. Human beings try relentlessly in their imperfect ways to do just that. Unfortunately, that cannot happen because evil is at home in the universe. It is the little amount of strayed goodness that can and should be extricated out of worldly situation. Therefore, the human mind can indeed, imagine a situation that is without an iota of evil.

However, that is not an easy thing to do at all for majority of human beings on Earth, especially the religious ones. Many of us can easily make long lists of things that are good and things that are evil but cannot put them in the proper perspective that makes the Father and his eternal creation stand out. The Father is absolute goodness; his eternal creation involved absolute separation of good and evil. Sadly, most of us find it so hard to apply this standard knowledge to our overall understanding of the Father. Evidently, our Edenic upbringing plays a major part in our chronic state of absentmindedness. By cloning away cognitive capacities of our primitive ancestors, Jehovah/Allah and his accomplices had schemed to prevent us from ever knowing and therefore, desiring to return to the Father. The first appearance of the heavenly Christ in Eden brought that entire evil plot to naught. Today, knowledge of good and evil has become commonplace to all of us, although we are yet to find the courage to coordinate and apply that knowledge to our full spiritual advantage.

The truth is that we all know the Father deep in our souls because we are all a part of him. The problem with us is that we are presently muddled up in meaninglessness, having wandered away beyond eternal bound designated by the Father for perfect existence. Every human being on Earth today possesses the knowledge of good and evil, which is our heritage from the brave achievement of Adam and Eve in the Garden of Eden. There is no human being on Earth today, who does not say that the Father is good and not evil. But not many of us appreciate absolute nature of that fact. Where Apostle John reported in his first epistle that *"The Father is Light,"* he added absolute emphasis, *"and there is no darkness in him **at all**,"* which was intended to convey the impeccable nature of the Father. Sadly enough, customary Christians' understanding of the Father never takes into consideration that special emphasis on the fact that *"there is no darkness in him **at all**."* That is why it has been practically impossible for many of them to rediscover or know the Father.

Beginning with the customary Christian creed; because that stringent distinction was not adhered to in the definition of its *God*, customary Christianity missed the first-hand opportunity to embrace the Father *in whom there is no darkness at all*. As a result, it played into the waiting hands of god of Genesis and completely veered off into the worship of a fallen creature rather than the true Creator of perfect spiritual ideas. The Necene Creed, also called **Nicen Constantinopolitan Creed,** is an ecumenical Christian statement of faith accepted as authoritative by the Roman Catholic, Eastern Orthodox, Anglican, and major Protestant churches. The very first verse of that creed reads, "We believe in one *God*, the Father, the Almighty, **maker of heaven and Earth, of all that is seen and unseen.**"

That statement might sound accurate in the ears of multitudes of unenlightened customary Christian believers, but it is predicated on the erroneous assumption that the Father was author of the universe.

Allowing themselves to *believe* that the heavily flawed universal craftsmanship is of the flawless Father was the greatest mistake of the so-called fathers of customary Christian faith, as the Scripture states clearly that "all that is in the world ... is not of the Father." Dogmatizing that grievous error puts a permanent ceiling over the spiritual development of the gullible believers. Today, customary Christian believers see nothing sacrilegious equating the Sovereign Father to Jehovah/Allah, a mere tribal deity and *archangel* who runs errands for the actual cosmic entities that rule the world of organic beings. They see no difference between Divine Light and *the Consuming Fire*.

The same creed also professes belief in Jesus Christ as *"God from God, Light from Light, true God from true God."* If this means that the believers accept Jesus Christ as the physical expression of the Unseen Father in the world, then one would have expected them to also take whatever Jesus Christ says about the world and about himself as direct declarations of the Father. The scripture says, "This world is a dark place, and its people have no light." [2 Esdras 14:20] The world continued to be an awesome *dark place* and Jehovah/Allah remained caught up in it until the heavenly Christ appeared into it—true Light from Light indeed. Against this backdrop, Jesus Christ declared to his listeners, "I am not of this world," and "As long as I am in the world, I am the light of the world." [John 8:23; 9:5] But do these texts really mean what they should to customary Christians?

Jesus Christ made open declarations in those important verses. Customary Christian believers would have easily grasped them if they had not truncated their spiritual horizon with the wry wonder of a magical Burning Bush. Jesus Christ wanted us to know that since he is not of this world that the world is not of the Father either. He also expected us to see that Jehovah/Allah who feels so at home in thick darkness cannot be anything else but a dubious character. "For everyone who does evil hates the light, and does not come to the light, lest his deeds should be exposed," says Jesus Christ. "But he who does what is true comes to the light, that it may be clearly seen that his deeds have been wrought in the Father." [John 3:20-21] It is evident that Jesus Christ is *Light from Light*. He wrought his goodness in the light, and today, the whole world attests that he is indeed *"Light from Light,"* and truly *"one with the Father."* The same cannot be said of

Jehovah/Allah who continues to meander about in dark niches in the world. It is a terrible sacrilege therefore, for anyone to mistake him for the Father.

I tried for many years without luck to impress upon one of my cousins and childhood friends the right mental image of the Father as *all-good and no evil at all*. He was an Anglican Church minister and that made the situation worse. He avoided reading my books because they seemed to shake the very foundation of his religious beliefs and profession. Like most church ministers I tried to reason with on this issue, my cousin felt so scared of my *"new gospel of God,"* as some of them called it. He believed that if Jehovah/Allah stopped being *God Almighty* today, the whole Church would collapse, and the world would come to an end. Indeed, this truth will eventually bring the world to an end. Jesus Christ makes it explicit that "this [*new*] gospel of [true Kingdom of the Father] will be preached throughout the whole world, as a testimony to all nations; **and then the end will come.**" [Matt 24:14] Professional religionists, deeply conscious of their economic advantages, are not prepared to imagine the terrifying implications of that truth.

Anyway, once, I had the following dialogue with my priestly cousin:

> I asked him, "When you stand on the pulpit, what do you teach your congregation; that evil is bad and unacceptable to the Father, or that some evils are godly and acceptable to him?"
>
> "I teach them that evil is bad and unacceptable to the Father," he responded.
>
> "Fine," I said, "when you see these evils that you preach to people about are you able to recognize them?"
>
> "Why not? I am an ordained priest," he answered.
>
> "Ok! If a friend of yours comes to your house one night armed, for instance; overpowers you, kills your first-born son and makes away with some of your valuables, would you say that his action is evil or good?"
>
> "Of course, such a person is evil and destined for the hell fire unless he repents."

"What if he has very good reason to do what he did?"

"There can be no good reason for such a heinous crime," he asserted.

"I agree with you completely on that. What then do you say in the case of Prophet Moses of Israel who was loved and nurtured from infancy into a prince of Egypt by the Egyptians; when he invaded Egypt at midnight hours, slaughtered all the first-born sons of the Egyptians and encouraged Israelite women to dispossess their Egyptian counterparts of their valuable ornaments of gold and silver? Was his action evil or good?"

"You see, it was not Moses that did it. It was *God Almighty* that sent the angel of death to seal the Jewish Passover and Exodus, which he promised his friend Abraham many years before."

"You have not answered the question. Was that grievous act good or evil, irrespective of the person that did it?"

"You see, Uche, Pharaoh sinned against *God Almighty* and had to pay for it. *God Almighty* had to teach him and his people a hard lesson, so that the whole world will know that he is the Almighty *God*."

"Exodus 12:30 says that 'there was a great cry in Egypt, for there was not a house where one was not dead.' Don't you see that as a human tragedy—a willful massacre of defenseless people by a bloodthirsty deity that should be sternly condemned?" I asked.

"You see, no one can judge or condemn *God Almighty*, for he says, 'I kill and I make alive; I wound and I heal; and there is none that can deliver out of my hand ... [and] I will be gracious to whom I will be gracious, and will show mercy on whom I will show mercy.'" [Deut 32:39; Exd 33:19]

It is clear from the above dialogue that although my cousin saw himself as an ordained *man of God* and preached to people that evil is not of the Father, his knowledge of the difference between what is good and what is evil was not properly aligned as it relates to the true nature of the Father. The fact that the Father is *all-good and no evil at all* meant nothing special to him. Hence, he was unable to assert with certainty and without fear that Jehovah's heartless deeds in Egypt were not godly but evil; and since his deeds were evil, that he was not the Father, who cannot be tempted to do anything evil.

We can see now that the human mind can indeed comprehend the Father and his *perfect* eternal creation, but religious-minded people deliberately sear their consciences to accommodate unfitting deeds and utterances of their various religious idols. For the so-called ordained *men of God*, consideration for their transient material advantages and rewards from the gods always takes precedence over the need to accept divine truths. They find it more *profitable* to protect long-established religious traditions, even when they contradict common sense, than risk reasoning themselves out of favor with their petty-minded deities. Hence, they deliberately refuse to notice divine truths, and make no effort to accept them when someone points them out.

B. TURNING BLIND EYE TO EVIL WHEN DONE BY JEHOVAH/ALLAH

On other occasions, when I discussed with a small group of church elders from a Roman Catholic mission in my neighborhood, I encountered the same standard attitude of religious believers deliberately refusing to condemn evil when Jehovah/Allah does it, just because their traditional religious belief holds that he is *God Almighty*. "Let *God* be true though every man be false," they always quote. [Rom 3:4] A member of the group had been a family friend for many years and had read one of my books and listened to my *new gospel of the Father* for a long time. He convened the meetings, according to him, because he believed that I was saying the truth and he wanted his friends to hear me too.

In my opening words during one of the meetings, I had stated that the Father is not here in the world, and made mention of the fact that we were all searching for the Father:

"Point of correction," interjected one of the elders, "you are the only one here searching for *God*; we have all found *God*. In fact, nobody in the Roman Catholic Church is still searching for *God*."

"Why then do we go to church every Sunday," asked my family friend; "is it not to seek *God*?"

"We go to church, not to search for *God* but to seek his favor?" the elder replied. "I do not doubt the fact that most people actually go to church not to seek the Father but to seek superhuman help for their worldly problems and needs," I tried to continue. "However, I am happy that you have all found *God*, so we can go straight to the definition of the *God* you have found."

"That's right," the elder responded sternly.

I asked each of them to give his personal definition of *God*, while I wrote them down on a jotter on the table before me. They confidently recited all the best qualities known to them and to me to be attributes of the perfect Father. Among other things, they all stated that *God* is Spirit, Light, Love, Life, and Truth; that he is perfect Creator, Omnipotent, Omniscient, and Omnipresent. They also stated that *God* is Benevolent, Peaceable, Forgiving, Patient; that his laws are flawless and his judgment just. One of the elders particularly added that *God* can neither deceive nor be deceived, and I loved that. No mention was made whatsoever about *God* being both good and evil as situations demand. None of them mentioned the famous refrains about *God* being the *consuming fire*, the *god of armies*, or the *god that answereth by fire*.

"Your definitions of *God* completely agree with my own idea of the Father," I continued. "Nevertheless, I would like to explore the fact that *God's* laws are flawless."

"Go ahead, make your point, we are listening," one of them said.

"Jehovah's law of compulsory retaliation—the *tit for tat* or an eye for an eye—is it flawless or flawed?" I asked.

"You see, *God's* laws are always perfect, it all depends on how people look at them,"
one of the elders answered automatically.

"How should someone look at Jehovah's laws and ordinances to the Jews, especially the law of compulsory retaliation or the *tit for tat* to make them flawless? I asked.

"You said yourself that *God* is forgiving, but Jehovah's law of compulsory retaliation hardens people's hearts and commands them not to forgive their offenders. I hope you know that Muslims inherited and practice that same Mosaic Law as Islamic Shari'ah, which today, still poses great challenge to the dignity of our civilized generation. I am also sure you know that Jesus Christ publicly condemned and revoked the *tit for tat* as inhuman right there in Jehovah's own city of Jerusalem. And today, human rights activists all over the world are working relentlessly to eradicate traces of it completely from our secular law codes in all human communities. Are you saying then, that the loving and forgiving *God* gave us laws that totally contradict his own nature, or perhaps, that Moses invented the laws of his own imagination?"

"You see, Mr. Chuku," the one they introduced to me as chairman of their charismatic group began to explain; he had been listening attentively as that was his first time of joining us at the meetings, "I know that the Ten Commandments that Moses received on mount Sinai that contain the 'thou shall nots' is flawless. I am sure they are from the perfect *God*. The six hundred and thirteen or so ordinances served the Jewish situation at the time. That is what I can say."

"The questions here are whether or not the *inhuman* Mosaic ordinances that Jesus Christ publicly invalidated were flawless or flawed, and whether or not Jehovah who gave them to Moses is indeed the flawless Father that we have all defined?" At that moment, I could sense that the chairman was becoming very uncomfortable and he immediately confirmed it.

"In fact, I am becoming very uncomfortable with this discussion," he said angrily, "I cannot sit here listening to blasphemy. And what authority does Mr. Chuku have to make him believe that he can judge the Lord *God Almighty*?"

He immediately left our table, went to sit on a separate table, and ordered a chilled bottle of beer for himself, for our meeting was taking place in a public recreation hall. The remaining elders continued to dialogue with me, but none of them was courageous enough to condemn whoever it was that conceived the inhuman ideas contained in the penal code of *tit for tat*— Moses or Jehovah. None of them could assert with certainty and without fear that the perfect Father could not have given Moses the laws that Jesus Christ publicly invalidated on Earth. The law of the Father ought to be eternally valid. The laws that Jesus Christ gave us— "love your neighbor as yourself," and "do unto others as you would have them do unto you"—are eternally valid. The truth is that the Mosaic *tit for tat* was inhuman and ungodly; therefore, Jehovah who conceived it is more of a devil than the Father. True Christ-followers will not find this too heavy to pronounce whenever and anywhere the situation calls for their personal opinions on such matters.

Religious believers have a unique problem. They show chronic symptoms of religious indoctrination. Indoctrination is a thorough and systematic brainwashing of someone with a set of doctored sectarian points of view that are especially designed to discourage independent thought or acceptance of other opinions. Canonized scriptures, creeds, doctrines, various sacraments, ordinances, and ordinations are some of the deadliest weapons of religious indoctrination. Over the years, religion has groomed multitudes of absent-minded believers who reason in preset patterns. Various sects keep their own members cocooned in their biased points of view about the Father, the world, and themselves, to the extent that they no longer see or feel the pulse of reality. History shows that not even scholarly minds—scientists, philosophers, intellectuals, theologians, lawyers—are immune to enslaving power of religious indoctrination. And that is very troubling.

Indoctrinated religious adherents are victims of a masterful battle strategy that Jehovah/Allah had long worked out and even prophesied in his scriptures. Jesus Christ talks about such people in Matthew 13:13, saying, "seeing they do not see, and hearing they do not hear, nor do they understand." Jehovah made Isaiah prophesy in advance, what he would do to supposedly enlightened minds in the later days to counteract the divine mission of the coming Messiah. His evil spell reads, "Stupefy yourselves and be in a stupor, blind yourselves and be blind! Be drunk, but not with wine; stagger, but not with strong drink! **For Jehovah has poured out upon you a spirit of deep sleep, and has closed your eyes**, the prophets, and covered your heads, the seers. ... 'Hear and hear, but do not understand; see and see, but do not perceive.' Make the heart of this people fat, and their ears heavy, and shut their eyes; lest they see with their eyes, and hear with their ears, and understand with their hearts, and turn [to their heavenly Messiah] and be healed." [Isaiah 29:9-10; 6:9-10]

He also planned a follow up for the later days, when he would literally drive the already indoctrinated religious zealots insane by indiscriminately pouring upon them his corrupted spirit of false prophecy, false dreams, and false visions. "And it shall come to pass afterwards," he revealed to Prophet Joel, "that I will pour out my spirit upon all flesh; and your sons and daughters shall prophesy, your old men shall dream dreams, and your young men shall see visions. Even upon the menservants and maidservants in those days, I will pour out my spirit." [Joel 2:28-29]

I must say that Jehovah/Allah's *later days* of intellectual sleepwalking and religious mass hysteria are already here with us. There are no real intellectuals in the world anymore; no independent-minded scientists whose ethical preoccupation is pursuit of knowledge rather than beliefs. The world is now full of religious believers. It is a common fact that there are more believers in the world today than scientists or thinkers. All kinds of *men and women of god*— apostles, pastors, bishops, evangelists, prophets, prophets of prophets, imams, gurus, monks, diviners, dreamers, and visioners—abound all over the Earth, preaching prosperity in the name of Jehovah/Allah and prophesying his expected dooms day for unbelievers. Even though most of these doomsday preachers pretend to speak in the name of Jesus Christ and the Father, they are completely enthralled to Jehovah/Allah, the impostor.

In direct reaction to this prevailing situation, Jesus Christ says, "And no one knows the Son except the Father, and no one knows the Father except the Son and any one to whom the Son chooses to reveal him." And "Not everyone who says to me, 'Lord, Lord,' shall enter the kingdom of heaven, but he who does the will of my Father who is in heaven. On that day many will say to me, 'Lord, Lord, did we not prophesy in your name, and cast out demons in your name, and do many mighty works in your name? And then will I declare to them, **'I never knew you**; depart from me, **you evildoers**." [Matthew 11:27; 7:21-23] I say emphatically that all the people who worship Jehovah/Allah *in the name of Jesus Christ* are friends of the Antichrist and therefore, evildoers.

The fact that Jehovah/Allah is a master schemer is beyond doubt. That makes him a machinator, not the Father. In fact, he says in Quran 68:45, "Lo! My scheme is firm." His strategy is to keep the believers mentally saturated with so much of regimented religious activities, thus making them feel that they are indeed working hard in the way of the Father. They see total involvement in meaningless religious activities as righteousness, while they hardly have time for quality inner reflections. How to revive minds of a whole world of Jehovah/Allah's indoctrinated victims and set them on purposive way of thinking about the Father, our irredeemable world, and the uniqueness of Jesus Christ as *"Light from Light"* is the colossal task for truly enlightened minds today. According to **Don Marquis** (1878-1937), a U.S. journalist and writer, "If you make people think they're thinking, they'll love you: but if you really make them think, they'll hate you." I must say that until this paradox is effectively reversed, the world will continue to be filled with multitudes upon multitudes of unconscious *believers* and less thinkers. This is a sad truth.

HOW ARE WE A PART OF THE FATHER AND OF HIS ETERNAL SPIRITUAL CREATION?

A. WHY ARE WE CALLED SONS OF THE FATHER?

To be able to answer this question, we need first to understand why we are called ***sons of*** God and then, why Jesus Christ calls God ***the Father***. Jehovah/Allah confesses in Psalms 82:6 that every one of us is god, being a part of the true omnipresent Father Almighty, even though we presently languish as humans in the nether world. He taunts us that he shall make us fall like every one of his gang of unrepentant *princes* or principalities of the world— "I say, 'You are gods, sons of the Most High, *all of you*; nevertheless, you shall die like men, and fall like any prince.'" Jesus Christ confirms in John 10:34-36 that we are indeed sons of the Father. There he tried to make his Jewish assailants understand that he was not just Son of the Father, but also the only conformable, *consecrated* Son of the Father in entire universe. "Is it not written in your law [in your scripture]," he asked them, "'I said, you are gods'? If he [Jehovah] called them gods to whom the word of the Father came (and [*that*] scripture cannot be broken), do you say to him whom the Father consecrated and sent into the world, 'You are blaspheming,' because I said, 'I am Son of the Father.'"?

Again, when he had completed his Earthly ministry, Jesus Christ specifically referred to his disciples as his own brethren, making it clear that his Father is also our Father. He said to Mary Magdalene, "Go to my *brethren* and say to them, I am ascending to *my Father and your Father*, to *my* God *and your* God." [John 20:17] It was for the same reason that he says to us in Matthew 11:9, "But you are not to be called rabbi, for you have one teacher, and **you are all brethren**. And call no man your father on Earth, **for you have one Father**, who is in heaven." All living beings in the whole world have one Father or Supreme Source who is not *here* in the universe but in *heaven*. This is important information at our disposal.

The Jews had great difficulty understanding how Jesus Christ could call *God* his Father or how he could be the Son of *God* since *God* is not known to have a wife. Muslims inherited the same religious narrow-mindedness; obviously because Islam and Judaism share the same deliberately confused foundation. They were both conceived by Jehovah/Allah, the impostor, and established upon falsehood and ignorance. In fact, the whole essence of Islam, as captured in Quran 112, is centered on the ignorant assumption that Jehovah/Allah is *God Almighty*, and that he must have a wife as human beings do to be able to beget sons. Gabriel compelled Muhammad to recite Allah's misleading position on that— "Say: He is Allah, the One! Allah, the eternally besought of all! **He begetteth not nor was begotten**. And there is none comparable unto him." [Quran 112:1-4]

Remarkably, Gabriel did not tell Muhammad that Allah is the Father; he told him that Allah is *the One*. What *One*? *The One* that did what? Well, Gabriel expected Muhammad and his uninformed religious followers to make the drastic conclusion. And they did; holding fast to the naive Quranic line of argument that simply holds the Father a barren island— "And they say: The Beneficent hath taken unto himself a son. Be he glorified! Nay, but **(those whom they call sons) are honored slaves**. ... And one of them who should say: Lo! I am a *God* beside him, that one we should repay with hell. Thus, we repay wrongdoers. ... **The Messiah**, son of Mary, was no other than a messenger, messengers (the like of whom) had passed away before him. And his mother was a saintly woman. And they both used to eat (Earthly) food." [Quran 21:26-29; 5:75] What a childish argument! Thus, the Quran helps Jehovah/Allah to completely bastardize our divine heritage as sons or rather, emanations of Divine Spirit.

Now, a man and a woman contribute just one gamete [cell] each to reproduce another human being and we call such a person their son. And today, after so many years of human reproduction on Earth, we do not find it absurd to believe that entire humankind is begotten by Jehovah/Allah infusing his breath into a single clay sculpture named Adam in the Genesis. Yet, Jews and Muslims find it so hard to imagine that the Father, who is infinite, absolute Spirit, can spiritually emanate innumerable replicas of himself. One wonders what the Muslims make of Allah's word in Quran 4:17, which says, "The Messiah, Jesus son of Mary, was ... His [Allah's] word which he conveyed unto Mary, and *a spirit from him*." If by contributing just a single tiny germ cell a man or woman can justifiably call another a son or daughter, one wonders what Muslims would say of Allah contributing a whole spirit from himself to create Jesus in the womb of Mary. Should that not have qualified Jesus to be called Allah's son?

Anyway, that is merely for the sake of argument because **Allah has no sons**, just as the Quran rightly asserts, being himself a fallen son of the Father. The heavenly Christ is the Son of the *Living* Father, not a spirit from Allah, who is but a corrupted, *dead* spirit stranded here in the realm of darkness. Apostle Simon Peter bravely declared the Sonship of Jesus Christ amid the Jews. "You are the Christ," he declared, "the Son of the Living God." [Matthew 16:16] In any case, the assertion that Allah ***begetteth not nor was begotten*** should have helped the Muslims and their Jewish brethren to understand that **we are not sons of Allah**, which explains why he calls and treats us as his slaves. According to him, even his prophets were merely favored slave prefects chosen from among us. Allah is a slave master, and a slave master naturally enslaves other people's sons and never his own. We are definitely someone else's sons, a fact that Jehovah/Allah concedes himself—"I say, '**You are gods, sons of the Most High, *all of you*.**'" We are strayed sons of the Living Father, held captive by godless entities in a godless world.

Evidently, Jews' and Muslims' understanding of the Father is limited to the root Zionist propaganda that ambiguously posits Jehovah/Allah as *the One*. Hence, they limit Sovereign Spirit and his infinite power of self-replication to humans' experience of sinful sexual reproduction. By portraying Jehovah/Allah as clumsy sculptor of man's dross body and expecting people to accept that he is the Father, even the Bible fails to capture the right image of the Father of human spirits. So-called archangel Gabriel deliberately played on the intelligence of uninformed religious slaves of Allah, for he surely knew the truth. The Father is the grand *begetter* or Father of every spirit being in existence and he does not need a female consort to do that. He is Sovereign Spirit and Divine Light that radiates in all directions. His true *sons* or radiated energies are also spirits and lights; they are not *mortal* human bodies, which are but disposable cloaks worn by the fallen spirits.

The man, *Jesus*, may have been the *Son of man*, but the heavenly Christ that incarnated in him, whom the Father sanctified and sent into the world, is of the Supreme, Omniscient Father, which is what Quran 3:46 means when it says of the Christ, "and he is of the Righteous." Nevertheless, the difficulties that the Jews and Muslims have concerning the Sonship of Jesus Christ still highlight the question about how we can be called sons of the Father, seeing that we are but imperfect, corporeal human beings.

Once again, the answer to that question lies in our clearer understanding of the true nature of the Father. As we already know, the Father **is everything that exists, but not everything that exists is of** the Father. This is the mystery of the Father's spiritual creation within which our true status as sons of the Father is clearly defined. For true spiritual realignment, in our journey toward our proper place in the Father, we are to understand "Kingdom of the Father" as the *positive sphere* of Ultimate Reality. This positive aspect of Ultimate Reality, the Father, represents unsullied purity and goodness, as opposed to the eternally separated negative aspect, which is the full embodiment of *perfect* darkness and serenity.

In this regard, when we talk of the Father, we are referring to the set of impeccable spiritual qualities that belong only to the positive aspect of existence. Therefore, when we refer to fallible human beings as sons of the Father, we are only referring to that part of us that belongs to the family of unsullied spiritual qualities. For instance, a good man is son of the Father because the Father is goodness. A kind, loving, peaceable person is son of the Father because the Father is kindness, love, and peace. Viewed in this simplified way, it becomes obvious that every human being on Earth is a son of the Father because no human being exists that is completely evil. In fact, no entity exists in the world that is completely evil. Nevertheless, human beings are not bona fide sons of the Father. They are not sons of the Father's Kingdom. By their direct involvement in the contrary realm of darkness and disorder, human spirits are presently *corrupted* sons of the Father. They ultimately need to be divinely extricated or redeemed.

B. OUR INNER GOODNESS IS PART OF ULTIMATE GOODNESS

True sons of the Father are unsullied emanations of him. Their attributes are far more profound than what applies to us as fallible human beings. In the first instance, the Father is Pure Spirit, Divine Light, and Eternal Life; his true sons share his exact likeness. They are individualized perfect spirits; specks of Divine Light and they have eternal life. Mortal man is not son of the Father—he was not *sculptured* by the Father but by the world. He can never become son of the Father because there is no place for flesh and blood in the heavenly household of the Father. When a man is called *son of the Father*, the appellation refers only to the spirit in the man, not to the man's mortal, physical body. Secondly, the Father is unsullied purity, absolute goodness, love, and the like; true sons of the Father are equally flawless. They are one with the Father in their overall nature. As a molecule of water within the vast ocean, so is the true son of the Father one with the Father in kind. Anything short of pure spirit and absolute goodness is not oneness with the Father and therefore cannot possibly exist within the hallowed sphere of the Father's positive influence.

Jehovah/Allah is a jumbled character. Good and evil are firmly intertwined in him. One does not have to be a prophet to know that he is not the Father, and that he exists outside the hallowed sphere of the Father's eternal domain of light. The Gospel of Phillip verse 10 contrasts Jehovah/Allah's undifferentiated world order with true heavenly existence, saying, "Light and darkness, life and death, right and left—are brothers of one another; they are inseparable (in worldly people). Because of this, among them—the good are not good, the bad are not bad, and their life is not life, and their death is not death. **So, one should begin with**

separating all these in oneself. Those who have detached themselves from the worldly become whole, eternal." Detaching oneself from worldly situation means separating out the godly part of oneself from worldly entanglements and returning to one's proper dwelling place within the spiritual status quo that firmly separates the two eternal polarities of light and darkness.

Our imperfect material universe represents diametric unreality—a temporary contradiction in the Father's eternal spiritual creation. It will eventually *waste* away because it is not within the hallowed domain of Divine Providence. Thus, we can be sure that the fate of our meaningless universe is *death*, while that of every corrupted, dead son of the Father within it is spiritual redemption and ultimate *resurrection*. But fallen sons of the Father must willingly choose divine resurrection by Jesus Christ over eternal death with the dying universe. The proper place of every son of the Father is in the eternal sphere of the Father's positive influence, the only place where true eternal life is possible. Many people refer to this place as the heavenly paradise, a state of absolute self-consciousness, or simply as the realm of light, which signifies a realm of absolute purity, holiness, life, love, and beauty of the Father's spiritual creation. Jesus Christ calls it the Father's house. And I call it the proper place to be.

In the man, Jesus, dwelt the heavenly Christ, *whom the Father consecrated and sent into the world* for the specific purpose of helping us to find our way back to our proper places in the Father's eternal spiritual creation. He became the ***only*** true Son of the Father ever to descend into the realm of spiritual death of his own volition, spurred entirely by the great love of the Father that he represents. In a very limited way, one can likened his mission in the world to that of the loving parole officer; a freeman who intervenes on behalf of the jailed prisoner, determined to secure total freedom for him. He became the ***Ultimate Man*** and the only true model for our spiritual evolution. As history testifies, the heavenly Messiah proved beyond every doubt, through his deeds and utterances, that he is indeed one with the loving Father and King of Peace, rather than with Jehovah/Allah, the disgruntled man of war. He implored his Jewish antagonists to apply common sense to resolving their unwarranted difficulties about his divine status. "If I am not doing the works of my Father," he told them, "then do not believe me; but if I do them, even though you do not believe me, believe the works **that you may know and understand that the Father is in me and I am in the Father.**" [John 10:37-38]

Here again, Jesus Christ gives us another rule of the thumb on how to appreciate our *lost* oneness with the Father. The limited good works that we radiate freely as human beings are good proofs that we are indeed *sons* of Ultimate Goodness. Perfect sons of the Father in his heavenly domain completely mirror his eternal qualities, but here, in the imperfect universe, none of us still possesses that mirror image of perfection, having fallen from our proper places in the Father's eternal creation. As human beings, we now possess the corrupted image and likeness of Jehovah/Allah, the man of war, which rather widens the distance between us and our true origin. Fallen human spirits ought to have no other business in the world other than trying to get away from it. Jesus Christ is the perfect model for us to emulate, and he tenderly beckons on us to return to our true selves—to reclaim our spiritual heritage, as perfect spirit beings, in the positive sphere of Ultimate Reality.

C. THE FATHER IS SOURCE OF ETERNAL, INFINITE EXISTENCE

Now, to understand why Jesus Christ consistently referred to **the Father** as such on Earth, we need to hold in mind the fact that the Father is indeed the Source of everything that truly exists, and then appreciate that he was speaking to *lost sons* of the Father who were no longer in tune with divine reality. He wanted to create a lasting impression in the minds of people who needed very much to be reminded where and who their true Origin is. "And call no man your father on Earth," he stressed, "for you have one Father, **who is in heaven**," [Matthew 23:9] Human lives and traditions on Earth reflect false images of reality. As we have seen, the universe is a temporary disorder within the Father's eternal creation—a manifest unreality—and as the Quran 3:185 asserts, a grand "illusion." Before the coming of Jesus Christ into the world, human beings had no knowledge of the Father as their Origin and certainly, never imagined that they belonged to some perfect heavenly household. The only father known to human beings is the one in animal cloak, which is a mere digression in the DNA sex matrix that represents the life of the world.

Even to this day, there are people still grappling with the fact that they are indeed *fallen spirit beings* or *heavenly dropouts* and not necessarily mortal human beings. Every *living being* in the universe is a *fallen spirit* or *fallen speck* originally kindled from Divine Light. Therefore, people we traditionally refer to as fathers and mothers on Earth are simply our brethren—fellow fallen sons of the Father. As the Source of entire existence, the Father is originator of everything that truly exists. Jesus Christ wanted to erase from our psyche that wrong tradition of referring to fellow heavenly dropouts as fathers in our present false existence to help us focus attention on our real Father and Source of true life that is not of our present world. Evidently, looking up to mere metazoan body—sheer gang of bacteria—as father on Earth is a sign of extreme spiritual degeneration. Once the body dies, illusion of fatherhood dies with it.

But why did Jesus Christ refer to the Source as 'Father' and not 'Mother'; and to his individualized emanated energies as 'sons' instead of 'sons and daughters?' Well, Mother Nature is purely a worldly invention; it has no place in the Father's eternal manifestations. Made up of male and female components, it represents proliferation of artificial life, powered exclusively by sex. Sex is the central process of artificial reproduction and continual regeneration of ephemeral worldly existence. Without the process of sexual bio-mechanics, worldly existence will not be possible. This is opposed to Father Nature, which pertains to self-proliferation by direct emanation or radiation. Just as the sun radiates its rays, the Father as Divine Light, radiates his own sons. Sons of the Father are simply Divine rays.

Male and female mortal bodies merely represent disposable garbs worn by fallen dead spirits in a hopeless attempt to overcome spiritual death. Men and women are nothing, but expendable sex machines employed by Mother Nature; they are mere implements of sensual pleasures for the animating souls. Mother Nature enslaves our fallen dead spirits in the sheer *sex game* that we call life on Earth. None of these will survive spiritual resurrection of our redeemed spirits, for there is no sexual or matrimonial consorting in heaven. Jesus Christ explains: "The *sons of this age* marry and are given in marriage; but those who are accounted worthy to attain to that age and to the resurrection from the dead neither marry nor are given in marriage, for they cannot die anymore, because they are equal to angels and are sons of the Father, being sons of the resurrection." [Luke 20:34-36]

In the context of this world, Jesus Christ refers to man and woman jointly as *sons of this age*. Strictly speaking, none of them is a heavenly idea. This should help people to understand that man and woman are equal and indispensable half components of this false existence. Like the two complementing principles of *yin* and *yang* upon which Mother Nature depends, they serve two unique purposes that achieve a single goal. One cannot say that man is more important than woman and vice versa, just as air cannot be said to be more important than water in the life of man. Contrary to patriarchal culture that purports superiority of masculinity over femininity and holds man to be the direct image of the Father, practical human experiences rather show spiritual preeminence of woman over man.

The truth is that over the years men have grown to be more involved with worldly dominion, holding adamantly to the false role that arrogates to them authority over all living things on Earth. Jehovah/Allah tactically introduced masculine stereotyping into inter-human relationships with the mock curse of man and woman in Eden, purely to divide and rule humanity on Earth, giving the false impression that manliness is closer to godliness. Men grabbed and held on tightly to that false advantage to their own spiritual detriment. Men who live by that unfortunate notion usually show symptoms of spiritual depravation, and they generally display acute character imbalance in their overall outlook in life. In contrast, Adam and Eve were true companions. They loved and respected each other and valued each other's contributions to the general wellbeing of their matrimony.

Jesus Christ made unmistakable statements, both in deeds and in words, in recognition of prevailing spiritual preeminence of woman over man. **EVE** was the first to receive the heavenly Christ as Spirit of Knowledge during his first advent into the world in Eden. He inspired her on the spiritual importance of knowledge of good and evil and she reflected diligently over it. And the Bible says, "So **when the woman saw** that the tree [of knowledge] was good for food, and that it was a delight to the eyes, and that the tree was to be desired to make one wise, she took of its fruit and ate; *and she also gave some to her husband, and he ate.*" [Gen 3:6] Eve was not inhibited to use her initiative. Thus, she became the very first disciple of the heavenly Christ on Earth. She also made Adam the first male apostle of Jesus Christ in the world. Today, entire humanity basks in the glory of her spiritual accomplishment, following her pioneer role in the spiritual evolution of man's knowledge.

The Blessed Mother, MARY was the first to receive the heavenly Christ into the world during his second advent into the world, in human form. She nourished the fetus in her womb for nine months, gave birth to baby Jesus, breast-fed, protected, and raised him up to be a man. She cherished and believed in him more than any other person in the world; and she ministered to him to the very end of his divine ministry on Earth.

No doubt, her motherly love and faith in Jesus Christ contributed in no small measure to the overall success of Christ's ministry on Earth. Accordingly, Mary, the mother of Jesus Christ, is called *Second Eve*, being the second most intimate disciple of the heavenly Christ in the whole world.

It is also on record that women were the most faithful and insightful disciples or followers of Jesus Christ during his Earthly ministry. While he spent all his time ministering to adamant men—trying in vain to make them understand simple truths about the Father and about our present unrighteous existence—women silently ministered to all his personal needs; and they understood spiritual matters even before he explained them. Even his very apostles deserted him during his trials and gruesome murder in Jerusalem, but the women stood by him all the way through. They personally shared all his grieves and followed to the final burial place of his battered body. They continued to minister even to the needs of his dead body, applying ointments to his wounds. Meanwhile, none of the male apostles even knew exactly where the dead body of their Messiah was finally laid, as they all scrammed and huddled up in one inner room, shivering with fear. Mary and Martha were known as special friends of Jesus Christ. Once, speaking about Mary, as she sat at his feet listening to his teaching, Jesus Christ said that she—woman—chose the most needful in this life, "**which shall not be taken away from her**." [Luke 10:41-42]

The third most significant disciple of Jesus Christ in the world is still a woman, **MARY MAGDALENE**. She was the first and the *last* person brave and faithful enough to perceive the resurrected Christ, because, as the Bible says, "Mary Magdalene came to the tomb early, *while it was still dark...*" [John 20:1] Jesus Christ actually handed over prime leadership role in his ministry to her before departing the world and not to Peter, James or any of the male apostles, as interpolated verses of the gospels insinuate. As Mary Magdalene tried to hug apparition of Christ's resurrection body, he said to her, "Do not hold me, for I have not yet ascended to the Father; **but go to my brethren and say to them**, I am ascending to my Father and your Father, to my God and your God." [John 20:17] This statement did not imply in any way that the resurrected Christ was going to meet with the apostles later or that he would appear to any other person on Earth after Mary Magdalene. He mandated her to inform the apostles that he was "ascending to the Father" purely because he did not plan to appear to them before his ascension. Other stories of appearances of Jesus Christ to people before his spiritual departure from the world were all false, being deliberately made up by so-called Church fathers to help them whisk away Mary Magdalene's divine right of spiritual headship over Christ's ministry on Earth.

D. HUMAN SOULS ARE FALLEN RAYS OF DIVINE LIGHT

Anyway, as Divine Light, the Father proliferates by self-radiation. He does not need any medium or female consort to fill the heavenly realm with his divine rays or specks. Quran 24:35 cryptically refers to the Father as self-glowing *Blessed Olive Tree of Light* that is not of the world and states implicitly that Allah is a fallen ray of light "originally kindled from him." The verse clearly pictures Allah as **a shining star in a dark niche**, and that vividly depicts the present status of every living being in the universe. It agrees perfectly with 2 Esdras 14:20, which says that "This world is a dark place, and its people [i.e., the fallen spirit beings in it] have no light." We are all fallen rays of light originally kindled from the Father who is the self-glowing Tree of perfect Light. This should not be difficult for human minds to grasp at all.

The Scripture refers to the heavenly Christ as "the true light that enlightens every man in the world" and adds, "**the light shines in the darkness, and the darkness has not overcome it.**" This is the simple attribute of true light, and a proof that Jesus Christ is indeed the only true Son of Light in the universe. The light of Jehovah/Allah, as we have seen, is not only constrained by physical darkness within the dark niches of the world, but his overall character, as displayed in human history, is also badly tainted by inner darkness.

The good news, however, is that the Father has already willed that the flickering lights of all fallen spirits in the world should be restored to perfect eternal glory; from the cosmic council of ruling entities to Jehovah/Allah and to the least of the various life forms in the universe. The Father does not desire that any of us should perish forever in the realm of darkness, but he wants us to allow the true light of the heavenly Christ to guide us out of our present dark pit of hell. As the only true light from the *self-glowing Blessed Olive Tree of Light,* Jesus Christ says, "I have come as [true] light into the world, that **whoever believes in me may not remain in darkness.** ... I am the light of the world; **he who follows me will not walk in darkness** but will have the light of life." [John 12:46; 8:12]

As Divine Light, the Father is the sole radiator of true life, which literally makes him both Divine *Tree of Light* and Divine *Tree of Life*. True life is spiritual, not organic. Therefore, to appreciate fully the difference between 'Father Nature' and 'Mother Nature,' let us liken the Father to the sun at the center of our solar system. Even as far away as 93 million miles from Earth, the sun is not just the principal illuminator and energizer of our planet, it is also the source of all the teaming organic life forms here. Without the light energies radiating from the distant sun, there will be no organic life on Earth whatsoever. In other words, the sun is the *begetter* of all organic life on Earth; meaning that mortal human beings are indeed *sons and daughters of the distant sun*. According to Nigel Calder, (1931-), British Science Writer and Broadcaster, "In a sense human flesh is made of stardust. Every atom in the human body, excluding only the primordial hydrogen atoms, was fashioned in stars that formed, grew old and exploded most violently before the Sun and Earth came into being." [Science: Quotation, *Encarta Premium 2009*]

No wonder, our ancient ancestors worshiped the sun as god and father of Earthly existence. Jews and Muslims should wonder how the sun is able to *beget* all of us without a female consort. Yet, the sun is but a mere nuclear reactor, steadily combusting its limited store of hydrogen fuel to generate and sustain false life on Earth. The sun will eventually use up its fuel reserve and die. When it does, all its numerous sons and daughters on Earth will die too.

In a very mundane way, the enormity of the light energies possessed and radiated by our *tiny* solar furnace and its ability to create and sustain life, howbeit organic, in very distant regions of empty space should help us to appreciate the fact that light is life. It should also help us to appreciate infinite nature of the Father's ability to radiate true life, being the divine tree of true light. Our sun is merely a source of artificial light that it mechanically generates by nuclear fusion. The life it produces of organic matter is false and ephemeral. There are about 100-400 billion stars in our galaxy, the Milky Way, of which our sun is one of the smallest; and there are about 2 trillion galaxies in the observable universe. Yet, the world remains "a dark place and its people have no light," and therefore, no life. People should think deeply about this.

The universe is lifeless because true light does not exist in it. That, my beloved brethren, is yet another proof that the universe is not the work of the Father. It is obvious that the Father is not the light of the universe. If he were, there will be no need for the billions of dim stars that only give birth to false, gloomy life on blighted planets; his perfect glory will fill entire universal space and its people will be a glowing population.

Now, we are all aware that Jehovah/Allah parades himself as the *light of the universe*. No one challenges him on that. But the universe is "a dark place and no one in it has light," meaning that Jehovah/Allah is *darkness of the universe* rather than its light. Despite his clumsy gimmick of hiding behind different names in different religions and cultures on Earth, Jehovah/Allah is, according to Quran 112:1, "the One" at the core of worldly darkness. Quran 114:1-3 refers to him as "the lord of mankind, the king of mankind, the god of mankind." Our ancient ancestors worshiped him as *the sun god*. Most religions and cultures on Earth still do so to this day. Jews and Muslims, for instance, compulsorily face the cardinal direction, east, when they pray as that symbolizes the rising place of the sun. Today, people all over the world customarily celebrate the New Year Day with bonfires and elaborate fireworks, as disguised, ritualistic tributes to the sun god.

The Bible, on its part, refers to Jehovah/Allah as *the sun of righteousness* in Malachi 4:2, an epithet that belonged to the Iranian mystery god, Mithra, whose birthday was celebrated every December 25 with ritualistic bonfires. The date was later, superficially switched to birthday of Jesus Christ by fraudulent fathers of customary Christian faith, but the secret fire rituals remained focused on the mysterious sun god. It is correct to say that Jehovah/Allah, the sun of the world, is synonymous with bonfire. He is more of fire than light. No wonder, the Bible calls him *Devouring Fire* and the *Consuming Fire*, and the Quran refers to him as *Raging Fire* and the *Consuming One*. [Deut 24:24; Heb 12:29; Quran 101:11; 104:4]

What we can all agree as human beings is that Jehovah/Allah's light is indeed a corrupted one since it has neither eradicated the physical and inner darkness that overwhelms our world nor guaranteed true eternal life to any inhabitant of the world. If he is true light, the world will not be a dark place and certainly, life here will not be hopeless and characterized by violence, injustice, suffering, and death. The Quran rightly portrays Jehovah/Allah as **a shining star in a dark niche.** That agrees perfectly with his character and with his actual status as fallen light that was originally kindled from the divine tree of true light. He is certainly not "the One" any right-thinking person should be looking up to for true eternal life. Jehovah/Allah's light was put to test at the Jewish Exodus and the whole world knows the outcome. Jewish forefathers made the mistake of trusting the *pillar of fire and darkness* to lead them to a *Land of Promise*. They lost their way in the wilderness for 40 years, till they all perished. Today, the *Wailing Wall of Jerusalem* remains an indelible reminder and the only proof the Jews have of the redemptive nature of Jehovah/Allah's corrupted light.

Jesus Christ is, without any doubt, the right One. According to the *Niceno Constantinopolitan Creed*, he is "*Light from Light*." The whole world saw, tried, and found him a worthy envoy of the Divine Tree of true Light indeed. Apostle John summed up the gospel truth in these words: "And we have seen and testify that the Father has sent his Son as the savior of the world. ... And this is the testimony, that the Father gave us eternal life, and this life is in [the light of] his Son." [1 John 4:14; 5:11] Accordingly, the scripture says, regarding his temporary presence in the world, "The people who walked in darkness have seen a great light; those who dwelt in a land of deep darkness, on them has [true] light shined." [Isaiah 9:2] The words that Jesus Christ spoke to us were spirit and eternal life; and because of his coming, many in the world have experienced, and many more are experiencing, spiritual rebirth every day.

WHERE CAN THE FATHER'S HEAVENLY KINGDOM BE FOUND, OR RATHER, EXPERIENCED?

This is where we must put our understanding of the Father's true nature to work. We know that the Father is Ultimate Reality that comprises the two extreme realms of absolute Light and absolute Darkness. We know also that the Father is infinite and omnipresent; that he fills entire existence. Therefore, his heavenly domain cannot be as far away from us, as custodians of worldly religions make people imagine. But the Father is Light in whom there is no darkness at all; meaning that an *inviolable* divide exists between his positive and negative domains. The Father's heavenly domain is the realm of absolute lights and the sphere of positive existence, reflecting a *state* of absolute purity, holiness, eternal life, love, beauty, and all perfect ideas. True sons of the Father are the lights that populate the Father's heavenly Kingdom. They possess absolute self-consciousness and epitomize the perfect norm of positive existence.

The realm of absolute lights is infinite; so also, is the realm of absolute darkness, meaning that although inviolable demarcation exists between them, they are not very far-away from each other. They are just a twinkle-of-an-eye apart—like a sudden jolt between dreaming and waking up. A simple darkroom experiment can help us to appreciate this. Simply flicking on and off the light switch brings about instantaneous disappearance of darkness and or light within a dark room. What this means is that the light source must be permanently sustained to hold off ever-present darkness and vice versa. With our experience in a world where electricity costs a fortune, we can all agree that this is not an easy feat at all. Hence, we can all appreciate the miraculous nature of the Father's actual creation that sustains *eternal* demarcation between absolute light and absolute darkness within his infinite nature.

As we already know, light is life; and the quality of life depends on the quality of light. The Father is Life eternal because Divine Light is eternal. True sons of Divine Light live by inviolable heavenly norm that sustains eternal exclusion of darkness from heavenly existence. Thus, heavenly life is eternally blissful, delightful, and serene. Violating the heavenly norm means allowing one's divine light to be overshadowed by darkness. Such a son *instantaneously* ceases to belong to the heavenly household of pure lights and becomes trapped within the realm of darkness. He automatically dies to his perfect divine nature, and that literally means spiritual death. He forfeits absolute self-consciousness and perfect life eternal for life of ignorance and imperfection.

This explains our present spiritual status as fallen dead sons of Light in the world of darkness. So, the question can be rephrased to read, where does the state of absolute lights exist, relative to our present false existence and who can make it across the inviolable divide?

Well, relative to our world of false lights, Kingdom of the Father is just a dream lifetime away, but the only souls that will experience that are the ones rekindled enough to banish away all traces of darkness that presently overshadow our true divine nature. Going to heaven is not necessarily about a very long trek, as with the Jewish Exodus, or about high-speed astral travel to a very distant paradise. It is rather all about the great difficulty involved in shaking off all traces of darkness from one's overall character—of crossing the *inviolable* divide between darkness and light.

In this regard, heavenly assistance becomes inevitable. Just as a drowning man cannot be able to lift himself clear of the asphyxiating satiety, fallen dead sons of Light in the world of darkness cannot rekindle their own lights. Someone that transcends their situation must flick on their light switches for them. In fact, they need a heavenly redeemer to rekindle their divine nature. That is where the heavenly Christ comes in. The Father sent him as heavenly envoy into our world to rekindle our lights, for only the Father can recreate dead lights. Accordingly, Jesus Christ says, "I have come as light into the world, that whoever believes in me **may not remain in darkness**." [John 12:46] For the little while he remains in our world, he represents the heavenly ideal for us to emulate. We must willingly shake off all traces of darkness with his divine guidance to qualify to experience perfect heavenly existence once again.

Jesus Christ tells us all what we must do to regain our spiritual heritage in the heavenly Kingdom. First, he says, "**You must be born anew.**" "Unless one is born anew," he says, "he cannot *see* the Kingdom of the Father." He means that we must be divinely rekindled; not in the way of the world— "not of blood nor of the will of the flesh nor of the will of man, but of the Father. [John 3:3; 1:13] Secondly, he says, "**You must love one another.**" "This is my commandment," he says, "that you love one another as *I have loved you.*" [John 15:12] As our heavenly exemplar, he says, "I have given you an example, that you also should do as I have done to you." [John 13:15] Finally, he says, "**You, therefore, must be perfect**, as your heavenly Father is perfect." [Matt 5:48]

Thus, true life after death means light after all traces of darkness has been edited out of it. Being born anew has absolutely nothing to do with religious reformation or with mode of religious worship. It is rather all about genuine self-reform and doing good works—putting the love of the Father in action in a world that is badly plagued by lack of love. As Jesus Christ has taught us, our daily prayer should be that *the will of the Father be done here on Earth the way it is done in heaven.* And we must reflect that through our daily activities in a world that is utterly broken by all manners of wickedness and vices.

I must say here that religious doctrine of *"new heavens and new Earth,"* as promised by Jehovah/Allah, is deliberately misleading. In fact, it is absolute nonsense. Lowering a regenerated *New Jerusalem* to Earth that its streets would be made of pure gold is not the same as raising resurrected human spirits to the Father's eternal sphere of positive influence. Spiritual salvation is not about regeneration of the world but about resurrection of individual fallen dead sons of the Father trapped in it. Jesus Christ did not promise to bring to Earth a salvaged heaven for redeemed human spirits but rather to take them from their present station to their natural dwelling place in the Father's eternal domain. Our present heavens and Earth and all their processes are products of spiritual fall. They were never divine ideas; and they can never be transformed into reality. It is all but dream of fallen dead sons of heaven, which must roll away as the sons are fully rekindled.

When all the false lights of stars and constellations give way for the divine, all false life in the universe will wither away forever. When the sons are fully rekindled, all vestiges of darkness in them will disappear completely. At least we can understand that when our sun dies, the Earth will become a barren wasteland—no gods, humans, animals, vegetations or man-made machines will remain alive in it. All products of Mother Nature that represent false existence on Earth will wither away forever. Therefore, heaven cannot be of this world as we know it.

Jehovah/Allah's promise to the Jews that "their bones shall rise again" is equally a misleading notion, aimed at contradicting spiritual resurrection of fallen dead human spirits promised by the heavenly Christ. It also forms basis of the false gospel of bodily resurrection of Jesus that customary Christianity blindly propagates to suit its erroneous notion of rapture or heaven-going. Spiritual salvation is strictly about *resurrection* of dead human spirits. It is not something that human eyes can observe. And it has absolutely nothing to do with *resuscitation* of dead human bones or bodies. Jesus did not rise bodily from physical death on Earth. That was irrelevant to his temporary spiritual death and resurrection that guarantee spiritual resurrection of our own dead spirits. Jesus, *the Son of man*, was born human; and he suffered and died as human, in accordance with the laws of our natural world. The Scripture says, "Since therefore the children [fallen sons of Light on Earth] share in flesh and blood, **he himself likewise partook of the same nature.**" [Heb 2:14]

Just as dreamers do not wake with their dream bodies and personalities, no resurrected son of Divine Light will retain any aspect of this false life and consciousness. Strangely, Jehovah/Allah equally says that all former things "shall not be remembered or come into mind" in the so-called New Jerusalem that he intends to invent. How then does he talk about bringing dead human bones to life if he is not deliberately trying to mislead the people? Besides, we all know that the process of reincarnation, as contained in Mother Nature, implies that every transmigrating soul would have accumulated several sets of bones from several lifetimes on Earth. Therefore, the question is raised regarding which body of bones would be reconstituted for a particular soul in Jehovah/Allah's so-called New World.

CONCLUSION

Our world is literally boiling over, threatened by all kinds of armed conflicts, deadly diseases, corrupt leadership, overpopulation, unemployment, organized crimes, and extreme poverty levels. Sadly, instead of uniting our forces in battle against the principalities who are the self-confessed architects of human adversities on Earth, we are busy oppressing, suppressing, and brutalizing one another in the name of religion, nationalism, political ideologies, and economic advantages.

Well, I have said what needs to be said, hoping that twenty-first century humankind will wake up and be courageous enough to do what needs to be done. If this life is a war, I fought it in good faith; if it is a game, I played it strictly as my spirit directed and if it is a joke, it is most certainly not on me.

Any authority, institution or ideology that instigates distrust and violence between peoples is enemy of true humanity. Any god that we must displease fellow human beings to please is an enemy. Such god should be firmly condemned and mutually resisted. Jehovah/Allah is a very bad influence on human communality. Religion is his major weapon of divide-and-rule against humankind. They should both be firmly condemned and mutually rejected by enlightened humanity.

SELECTED BIBLIOGRAPHY

The Holy Bible:
Revised Standard Version (RSV).
New Revised Standard Version (NRSV).
New International Version (NIV).
New Life Translation (NLT).
Good News Bible – With Deuterocanonical Books/Apocrypha (GNB).
Good News Translation (GNT).
The Living Bible (TLB).
Today's English Version (TEV).
The Meaning of The Glorious Qur'an, Text and Explanatory Translation by Marmaduke Pickthall, Taj Company Ltd.
"*A Brief History of Time – From the Big Bang to Black Holes*" by Stephen Hawking, Bantam Books, London 1988.
"*Einstein's Universe – The Layperson's Guide*" by Nigel Calder, Penguin Books, London 2005.
"*A History of God – The 4,000-Year Quest of Judaism, Christianity and Islam*" by Karen Armstrong, Ballantine Books, New York 1994.
"*The End of Marriage – Why Monogamy Isn't Working*" by Dr. Julian Hafner, Century, London 1993.
"*As A Man Thinketh*" by James Allen, Copyright 2001. <AsAManthinketh.net> As A Man Thinketh.net PO Box 2087 St. Augustine, FL 32085 USA.
"*Albert Einstein – God and Religion*"; Retrieved from www.zionism-israel.com.
"*The Aristos*" by John Fowles, Jonathan Cape, London 1965.

"*The 12th Planet – Book 1 of the Earth Chronicles*" by Zachariah Sitchin, Harper, New York 1976.

"*The Last Outcast*" by Chris Okotie, Marskeel Publishing Company Ltd., Lagos 2001.

"*Encarta Premium 2009*"

www.ingramcontent.com/pod-product-compliance
Lightning Source LLC
LaVergne TN
LVHW041748060526
838201LV00046B/948